SUMMARY

On the way back from a convenience store, high school student Subaru Natsuki was suddenly summoned to another world. The one ability the powerless boy gains is Return by Death, rewinding time upon his demise.
He strives to use this power for the happiness of those close to him.

Emilia went to take the Trial to break the stalemate in the Sanctuary.

Subaru, also granted qualifications by Echidna, the Witch of Greed, becomes unexpectedly involved in the Trial as well.

Facing his past, he hardens his resolve to walk forward, welling emotions in tow.
Subaru, successfully overcoming the Trial, finds Echidna waiting for him once more——

Returning after the Trial, Subaru worries for the frustrated Emilia, but takes up the chance to confront Roswaal with all the questions he harbors——

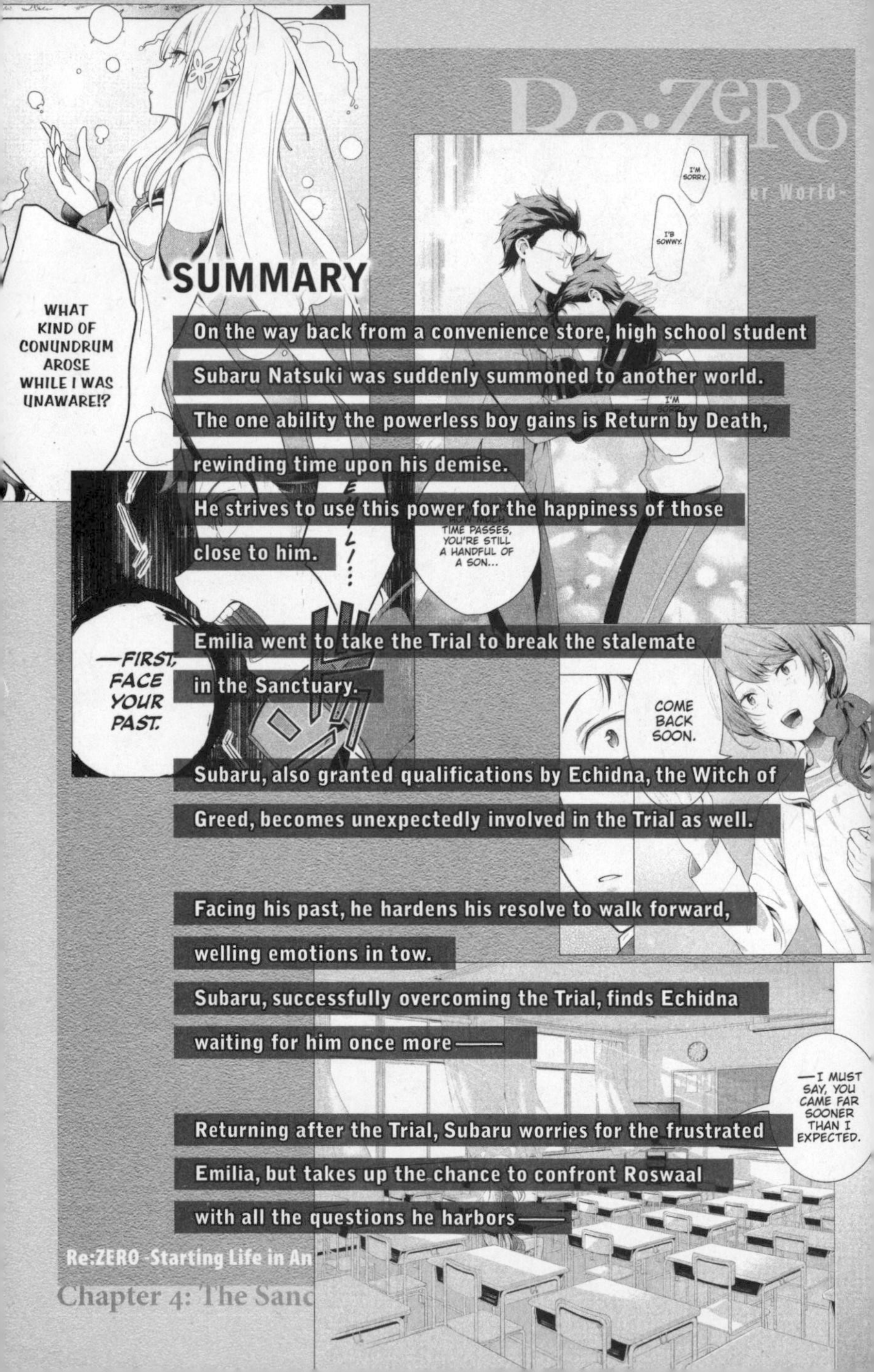
Re:ZeRo
er World-
I'M SORRY.
I'B SOWWY.
TIME PASSES, YOU'RE STILL A HANDFUL OF A SON...
WHAT KIND OF CONUNDRUM AROSE WHILE I WAS UNAWARE!?
COME BACK SOON.
—FIRST, FACE YOUR PAST.
—I MUST SAY, YOU CAME FAR SOONER THAN I EXPECTED.

Re:ZERO -Starting Life in An

Chapter 4: The Sanc

CHARACTERS

Re:ZERO −Starting Life in Another World−

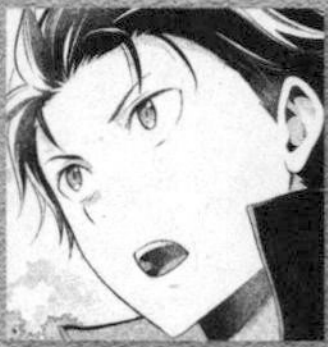

Subaru Natsuki

Modern Japanese boy transported to another world. Strives to use his only power, Return by Death, for the sake of those close to him.

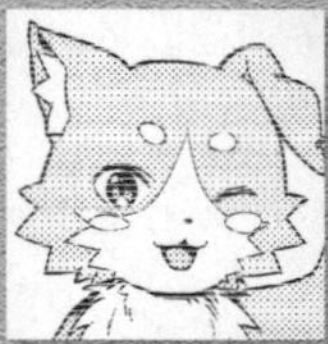

Puck

Spirit in cat form acting in concert with Emilia, who watches over her like a parent. In contrast to his appearance, he wields very powerful magic.

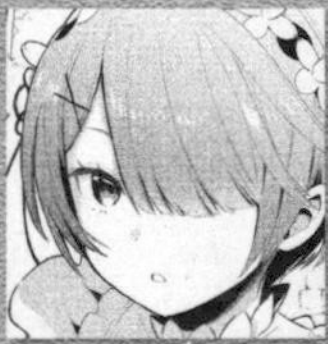

Ram

As a maid of Roswaal Manor, she runs the mansion alongside her twin sister, Rem. She is arrogant and foul-mouthed, but her gentle disposition runs deep.

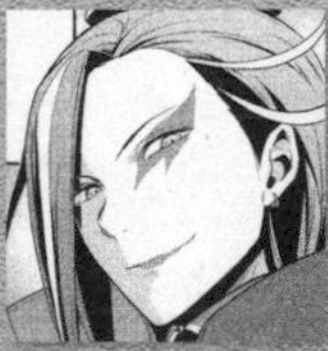

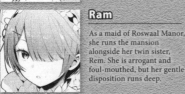

Roswaal L. Mathers

Holds the title of Marquis. Upper-ranking noble of the Kingdom of Lugunica. Sponsor of Emilia in the royal selection. A famous eccentric, he wears clown-like makeup and bizarre outfits.

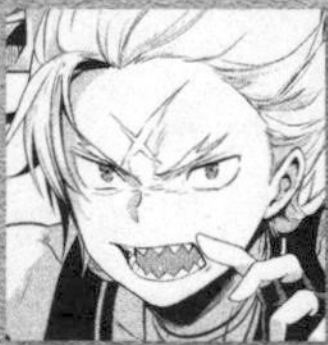

Garfiel Tinzel

A young man with a foul look, sharp fangs, a short temper, and barbaric personality to match. The limit of his combat ability is unknown, but he can easily hurl a land dragon weighing hundreds of kilograms.

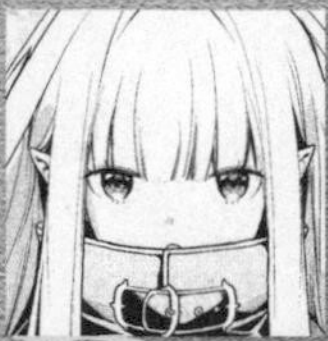

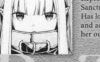

Ryuzu Bilma

Representative of the Sanctuary of Cremaldi. Has long known Garfiel and acts far older than her outward appearance.

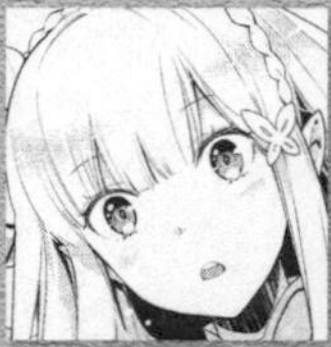

Emilia

Beautiful half-elf girl. Spirit mage served by the cat-form spirit Puck, one of those seeking to become the next Queen of Lugunica.

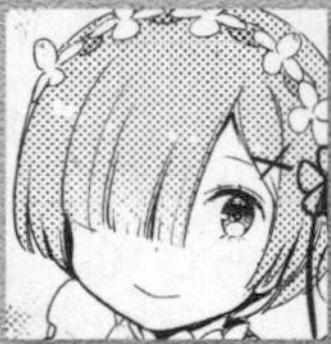

Rem

Demon girl working as a maid at Roswaal Manor where Emilia resides. After the battle with the Witch Cult's Archbishop, she vanished from the memories of others and became a so-called Sleeping Princess.

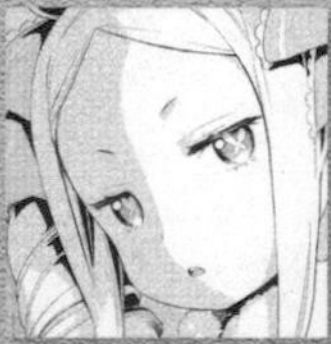

Beatrice

Calls herself the Librarian of the Archive of Forbidden Books at Roswaal Manor. A girl wearing an extravagant dress, she is an exceptionally high-end user of Dark Magic, allowing her to move freely throughout the mansion.

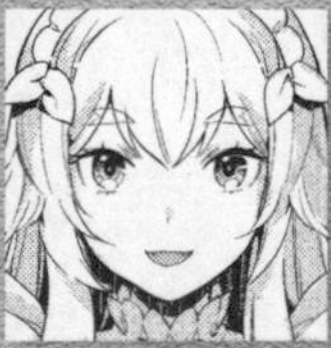

Frederica Baumann

Eldest maid of Roswaal Manor. Formerly on leave for personal reasons, she was summoned back by Ram.

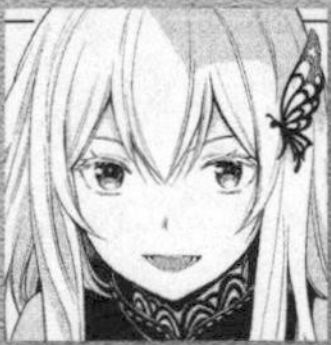

Echidna

One of the seven Witches, dubbed the Witch of Greed for craving all of the knowledge of the world. Destroyed by the Witch of Jealousy, her soul is presently captive in the Sanctuary's tomb.

Re:ZeRo

-Starting Life in Another World-

Chapter 4: The Sanctuary and the Witch of Greed

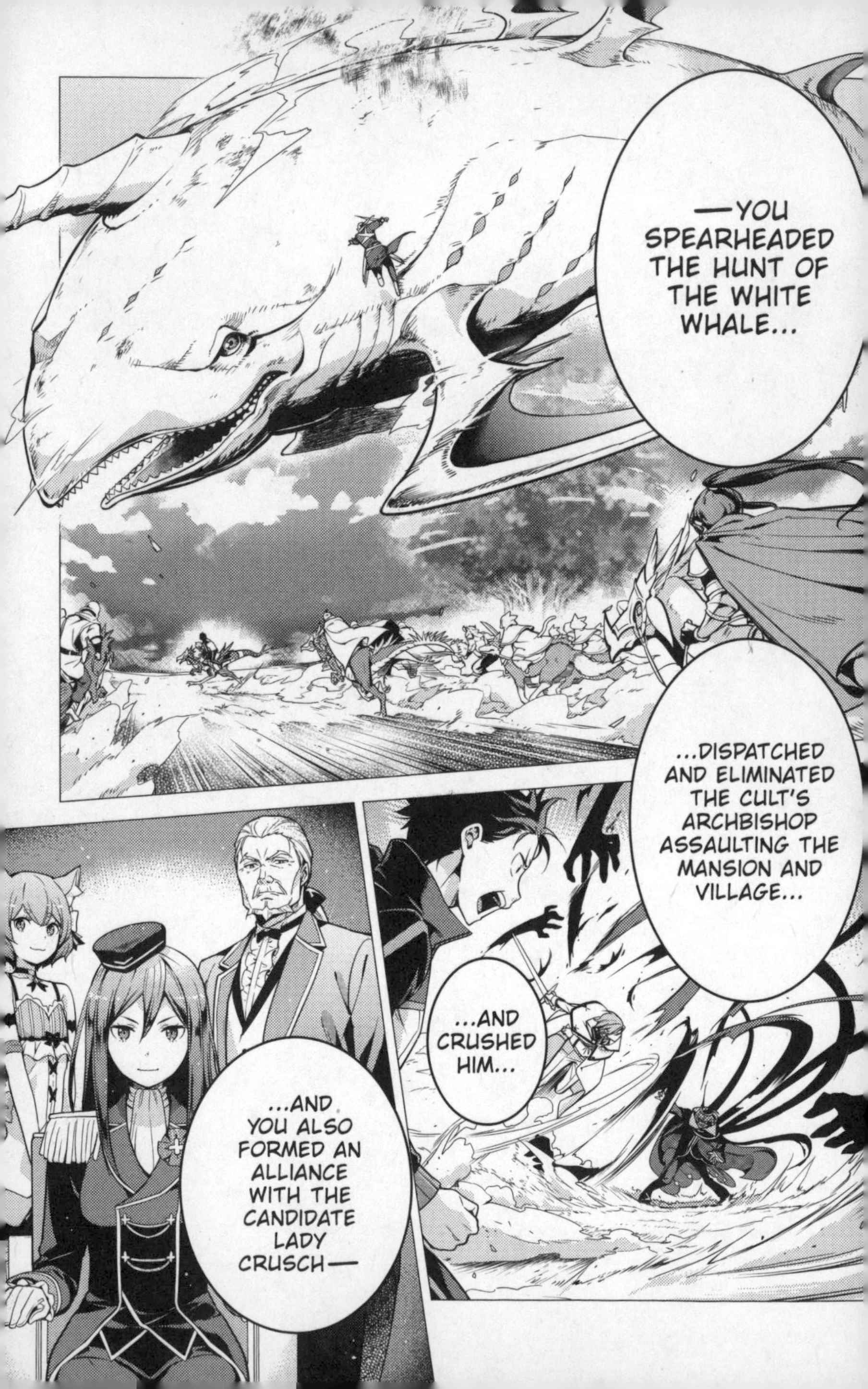
—YOU SPEARHEADED THE HUNT OF THE WHITE WHALE...
...DISPATCHED AND ELIMINATED THE CULT'S ARCHBISHOP ASSAULTING THE MANSION AND VILLAGE...
...AND CRUSHED HIM...
...AND YOU ALSO FORMED AN ALLIANCE WITH THE CANDIDATE LADY CRUSCH—

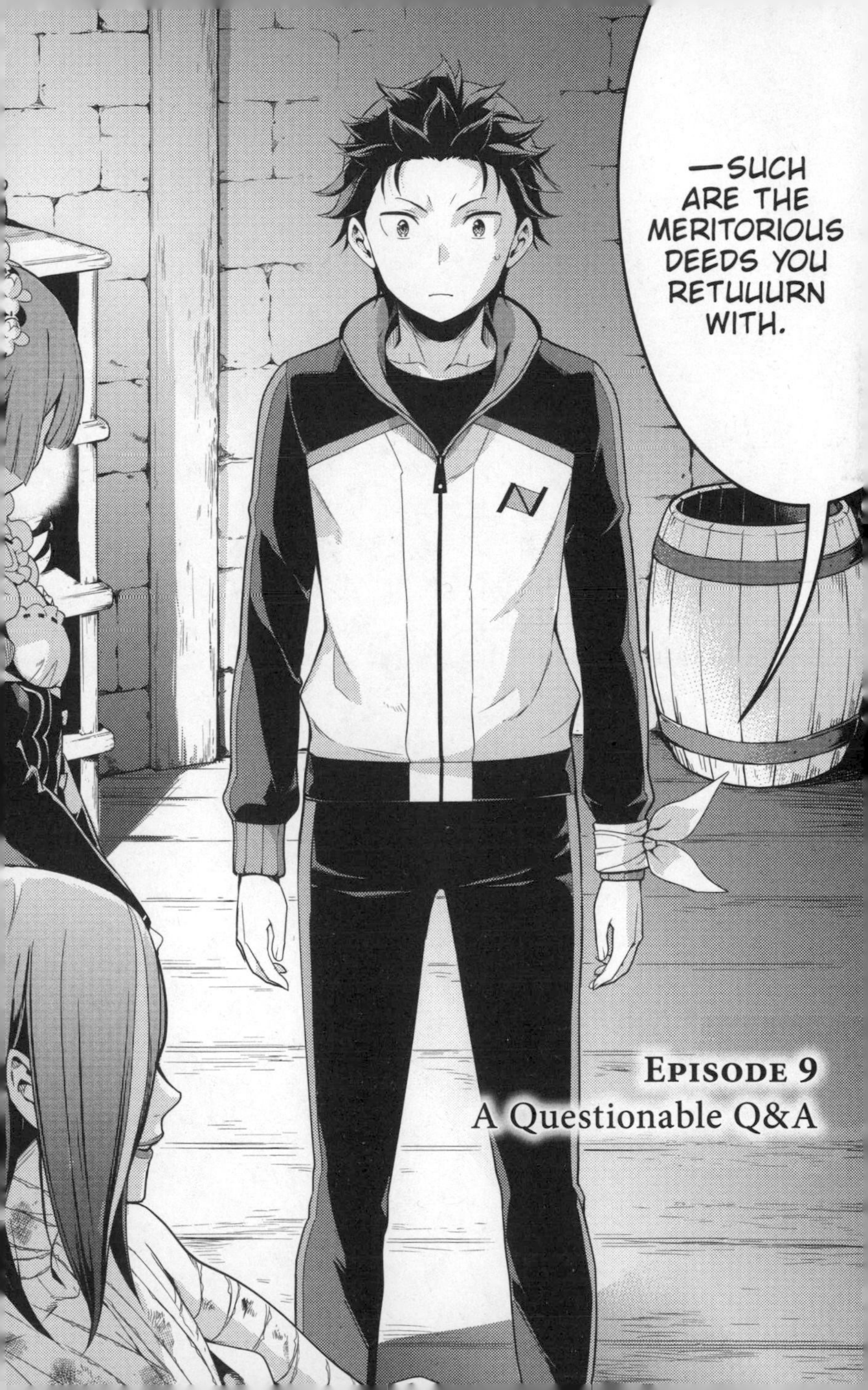
—SUCH ARE THE MERITORIOUS DEEDS YOU RETUUURN WITH.
EPISODE 9
A Questionable Q&A

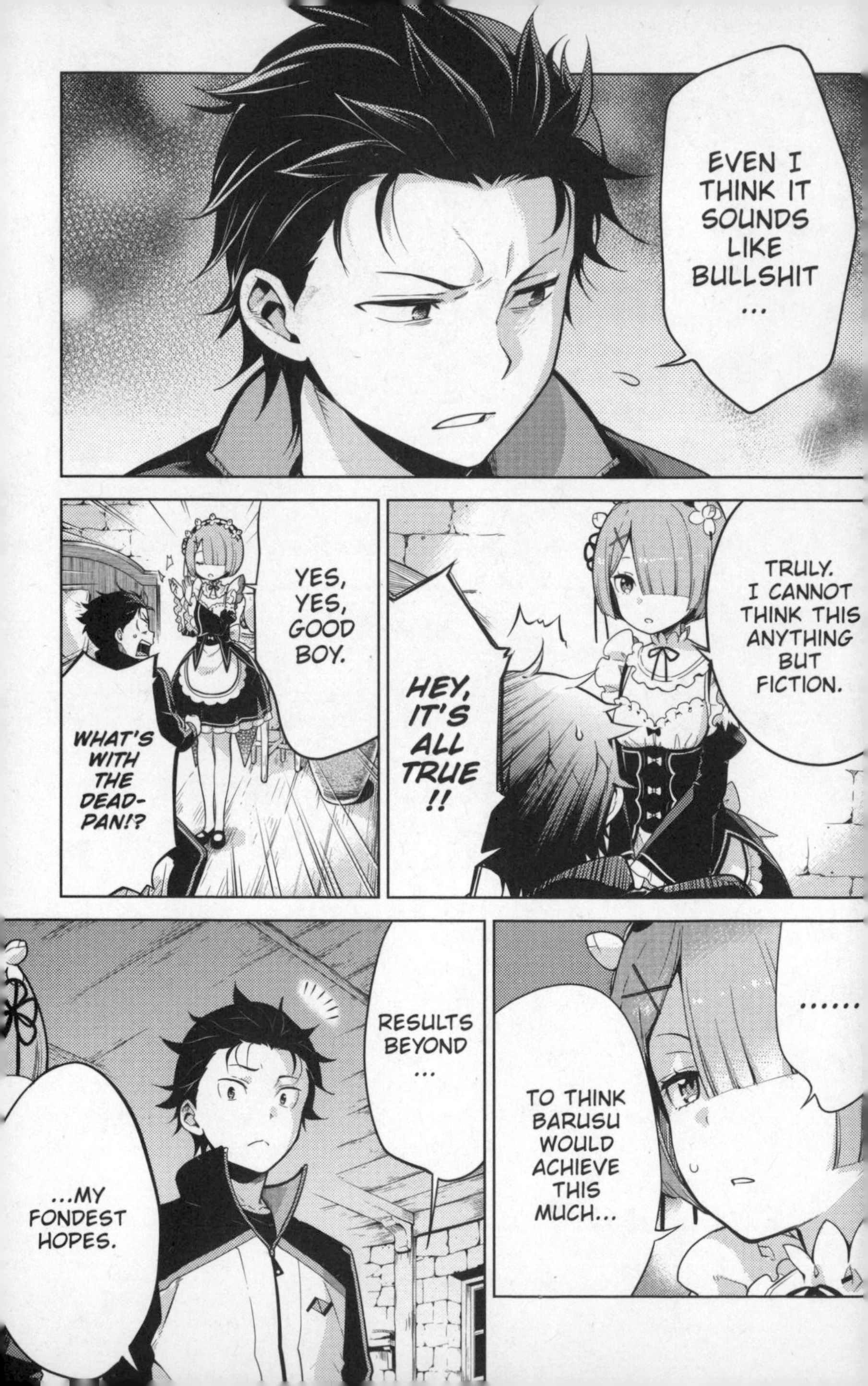
EVEN I THINK IT SOUNDS LIKE BULLSHIT ...
TRULY. I CANNOT THINK THIS ANYTHING BUT FICTION.
HEY, IT'S ALL TRUE !!
YES, YES, GOOD BOY.
WHAT'S WITH THE DEAD-PAN!?
......
TO THINK BARUSU WOULD ACHIEVE THIS MUCH...
RESULTS BEYOND ...
...MY FONDEST HOPES.

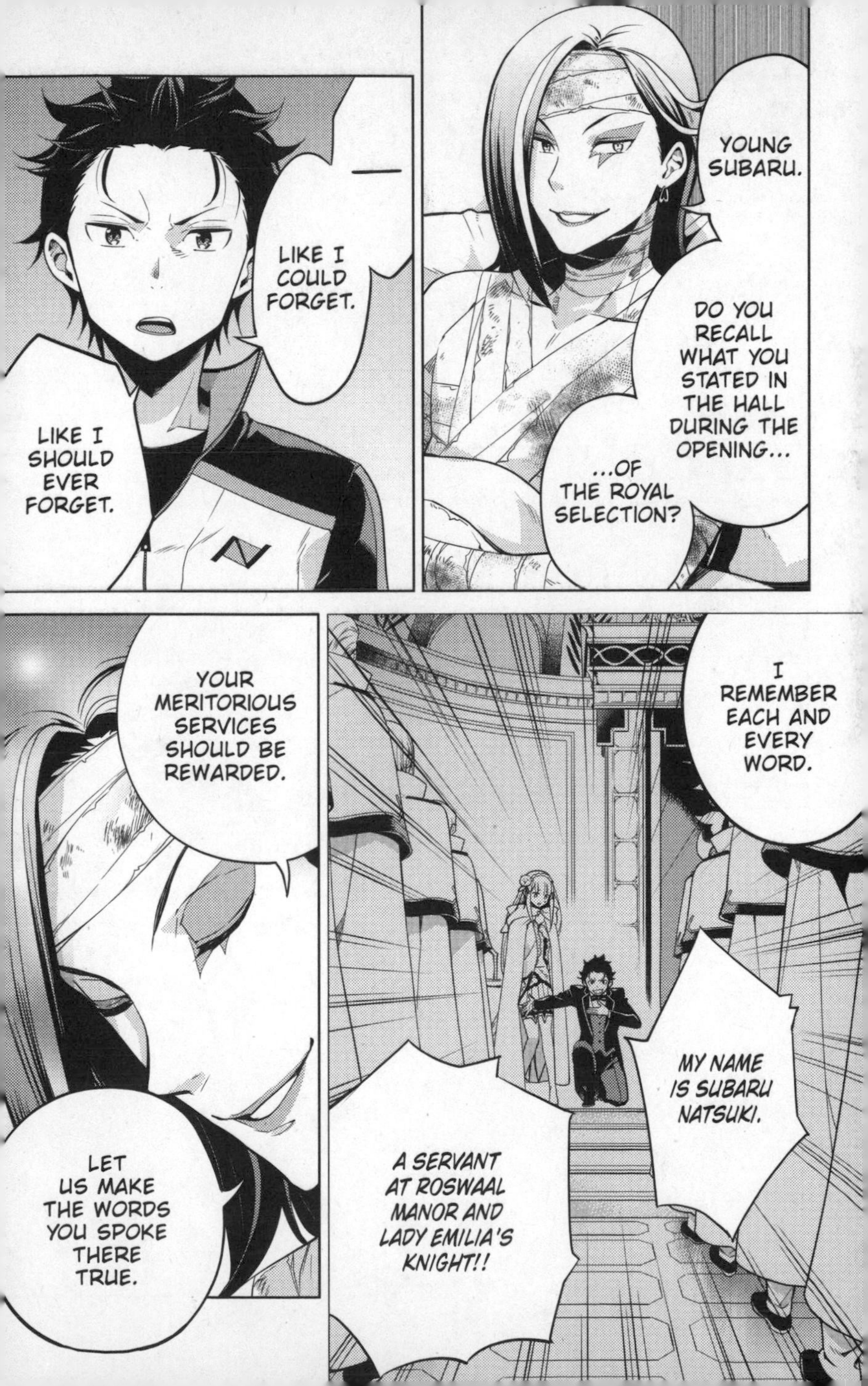
YOUNG SUBARU.
DO YOU RECALL WHAT YOU STATED IN THE HALL DURING THE OPENING...
...OF THE ROYAL SELECTION?
—
LIKE I COULD FORGET.
LIKE I SHOULD EVER FORGET.
I REMEMBER EACH AND EVERY WORD.
MY NAME IS SUBARU NATSUKI.
A SERVANT AT ROSWAAL MANOR AND LADY EMILIA'S KNIGHT!!
YOUR MERITORIOUS SERVICES SHOULD BE REWARDED.
LET US MAKE THE WORDS YOU SPOKE THERE TRUE.

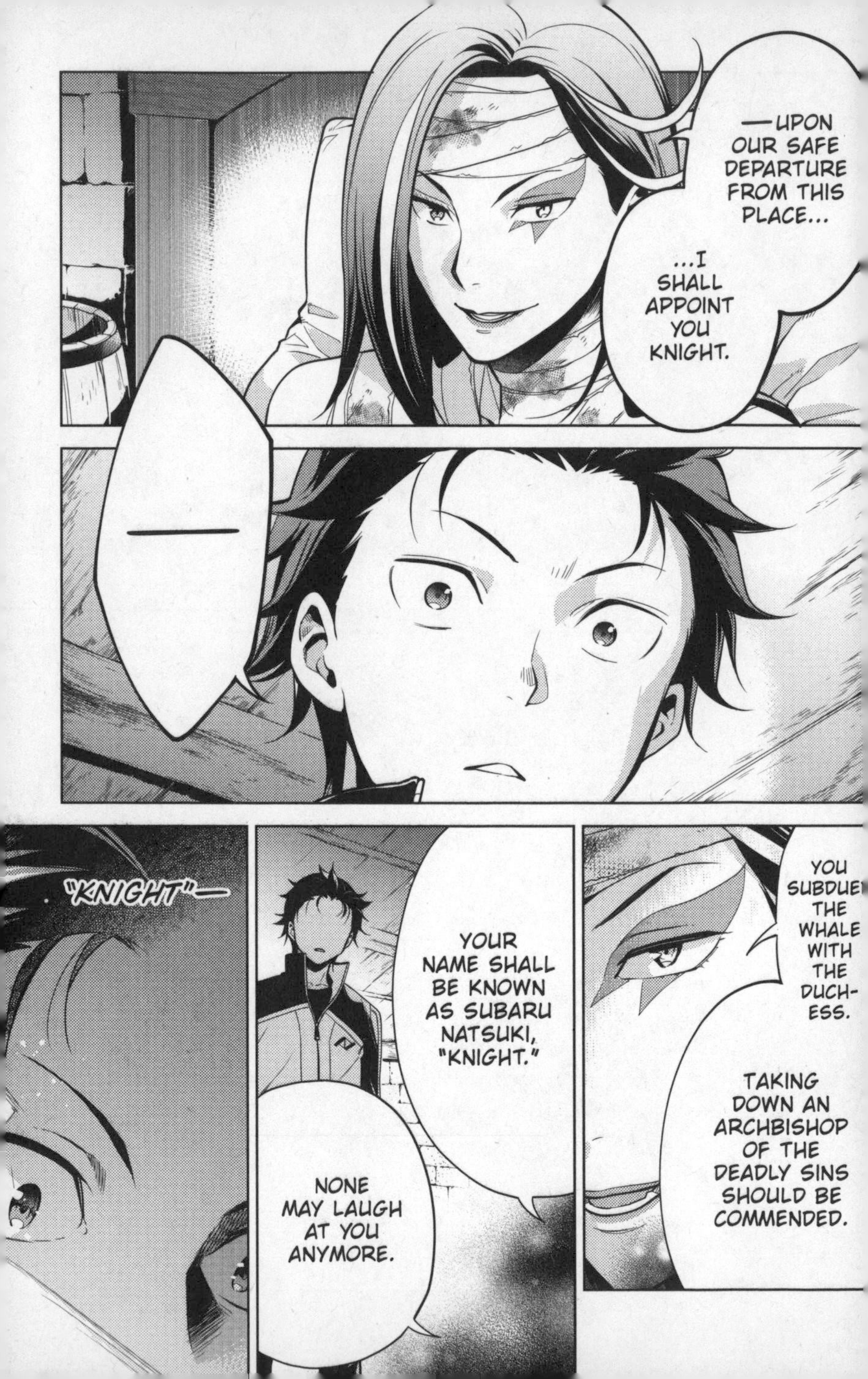
—UPON OUR SAFE DEPARTURE FROM THIS PLACE...
...I SHALL APPOINT YOU KNIGHT.
—
YOU SUBDUE THE WHALE WITH THE DUCH-ESS.
TAKING DOWN AN ARCHBISHOP OF THE DEADLY SINS SHOULD BE COMMENDED.
YOUR NAME SHALL BE KNOWN AS SUBARU NATSUKI, "KNIGHT."
NONE MAY LAUGH AT YOU ANYMORE.
"KNIGHT"—

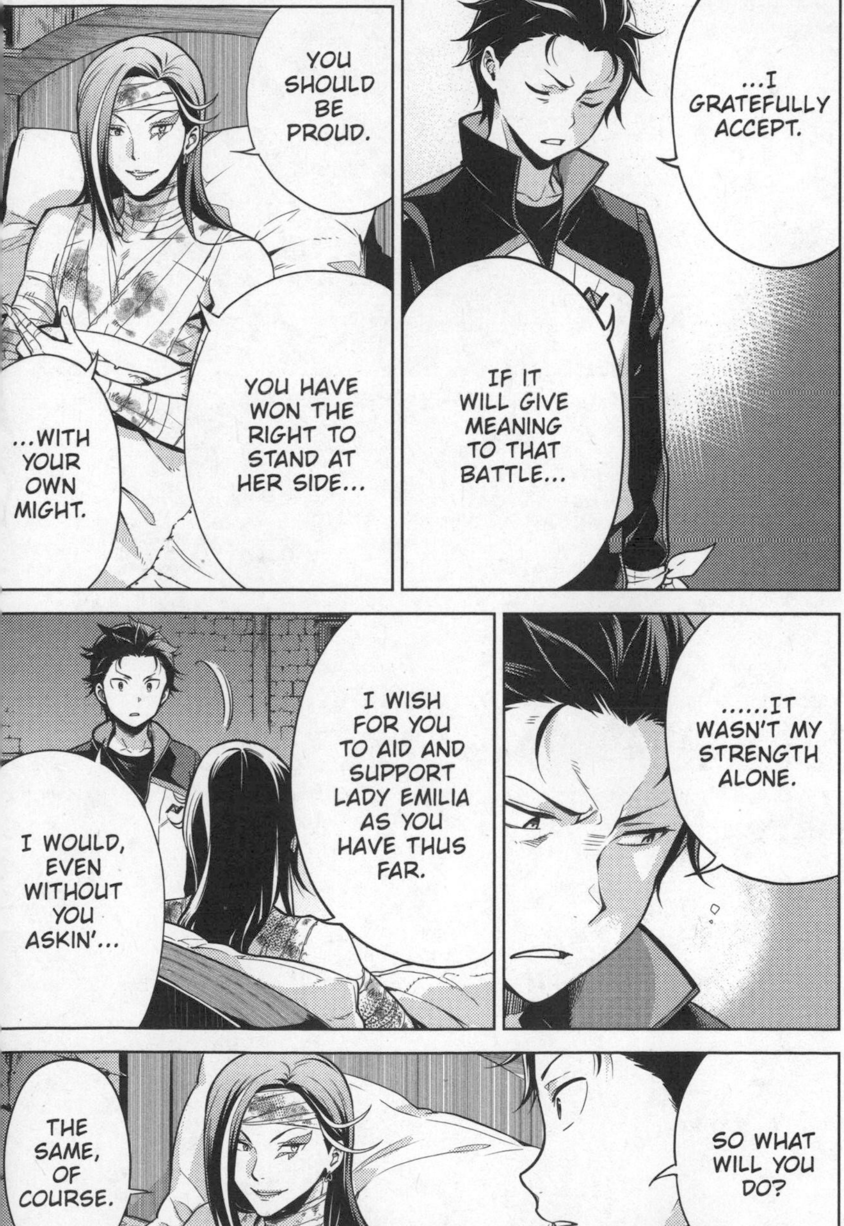
...I GRATEFULLY ACCEPT.
IF IT WILL GIVE MEANING TO THAT BATTLE...
YOU SHOULD BE PROUD.
YOU HAVE WON THE RIGHT TO STAND AT HER SIDE...
...WITH YOUR OWN MIGHT.
......IT WASN'T MY STRENGTH ALONE.
I WISH FOR YOU TO AID AND SUPPORT LADY EMILIA AS YOU HAVE THUS FAR.
I WOULD, EVEN WITHOUT YOU ASKIN'...
SO WHAT WILL YOU DO?
THE SAME, OF COURSE.

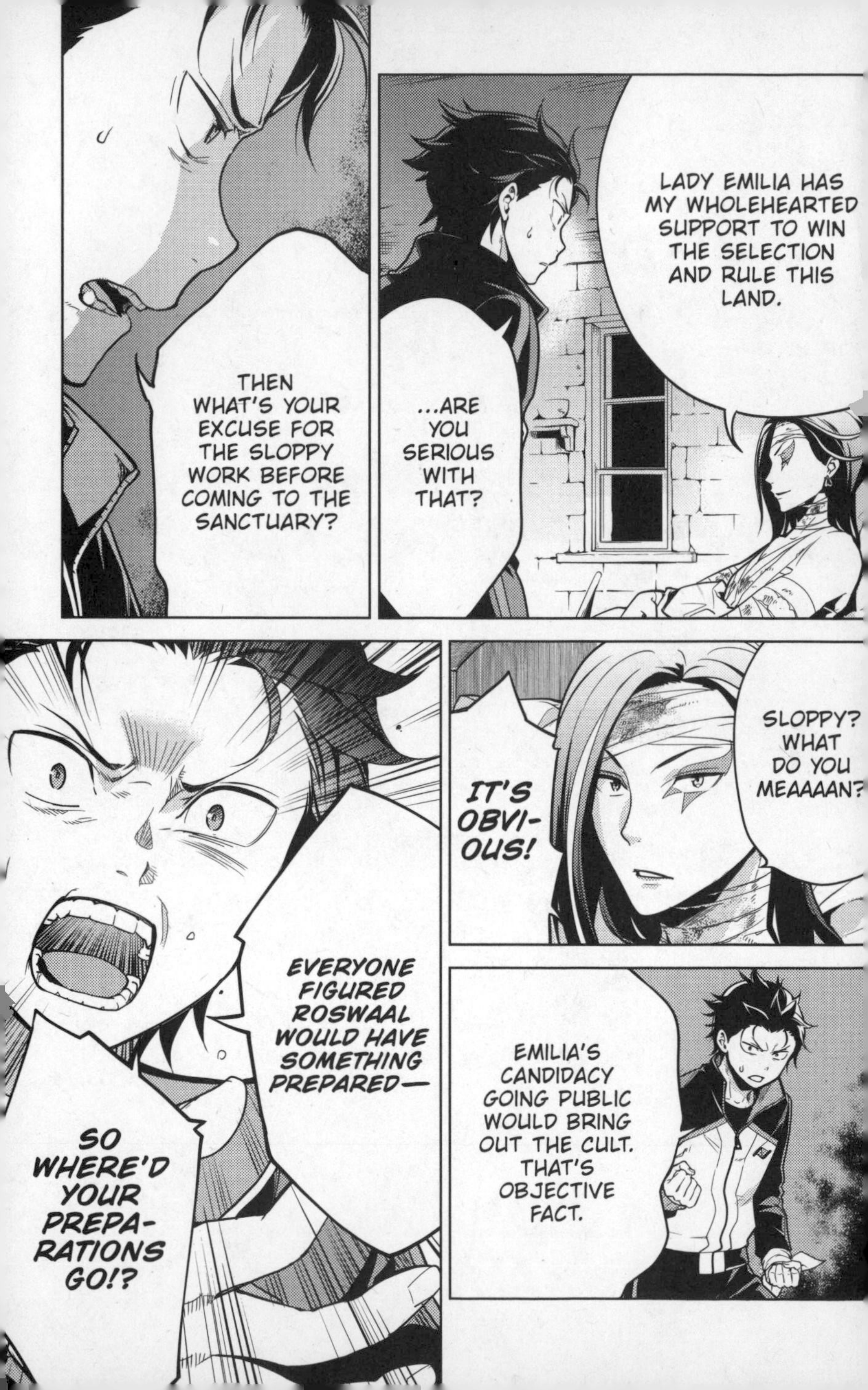
LADY EMILIA HAS MY WHOLEHEARTED SUPPORT TO WIN THE SELECTION AND RULE THIS LAND.
...ARE YOU SERIOUS WITH THAT?
THEN WHAT'S YOUR EXCUSE FOR THE SLOPPY WORK BEFORE COMING TO THE SANCTUARY?
SLOPPY? WHAT DO YOU MEAAAAN?
IT'S OBVI-OUS!
EMILIA'S CANDIDACY GOING PUBLIC WOULD BRING OUT THE CULT. THAT'S OBJECTIVE FACT.
EVERYONE FIGURED ROSWAAL WOULD HAVE SOMETHING PREPARED—
SO WHERE'D YOUR PREPA-RATIONS GO!?

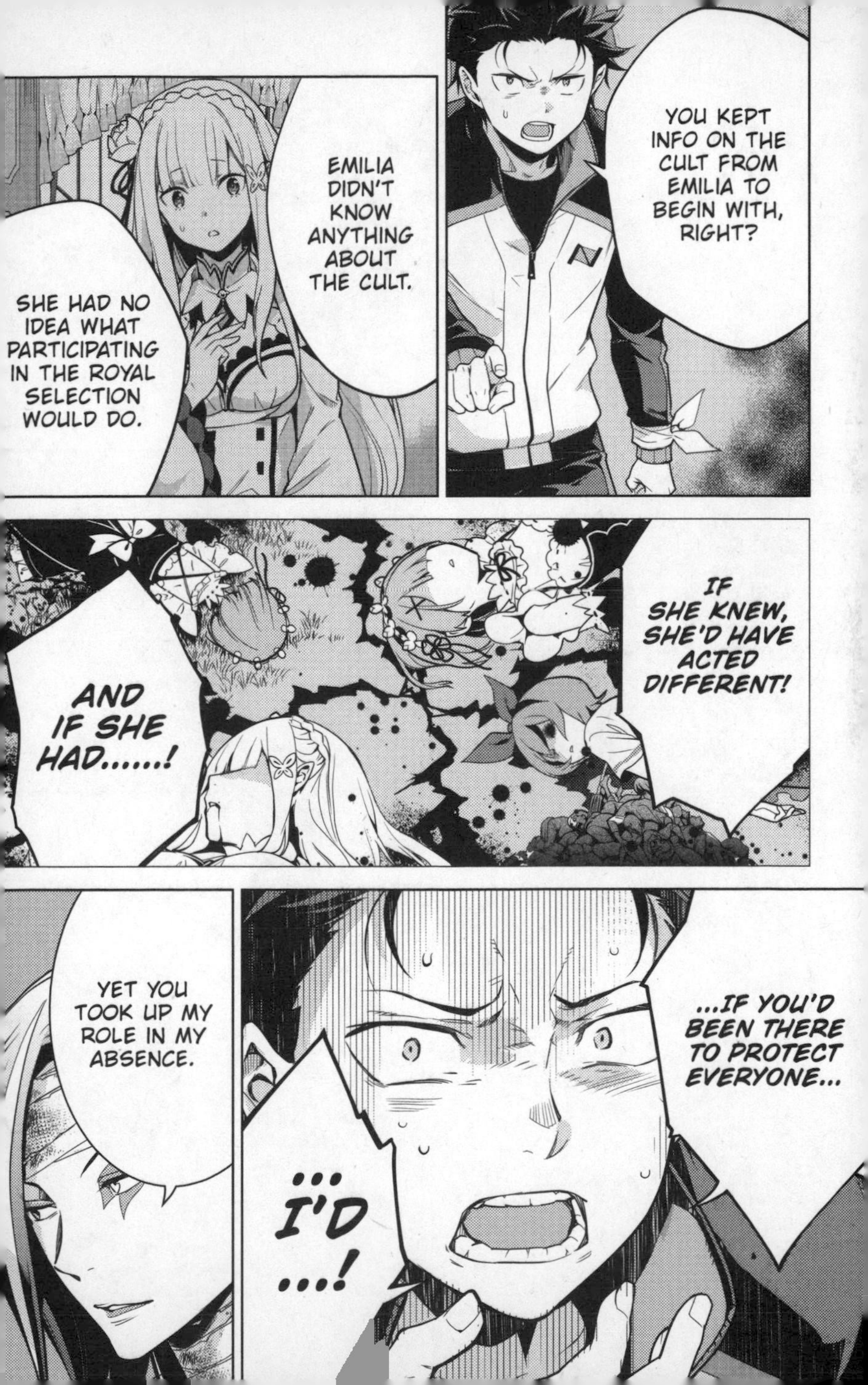
YOU KEPT INFO ON THE CULT FROM EMILIA TO BEGIN WITH, RIGHT?
EMILIA DIDN'T KNOW ANYTHING ABOUT THE CULT.
SHE HAD NO IDEA WHAT PARTICIPATING IN THE ROYAL SELECTION WOULD DO.
IF SHE KNEW, SHE'D HAVE ACTED DIFFERENT!
AND IF SHE HAD......!
...IF YOU'D BEEN THERE TO PROTECT EVERYONE...
...I'D ...!
YET YOU TOOK UP MY ROLE IN MY ABSENCE.

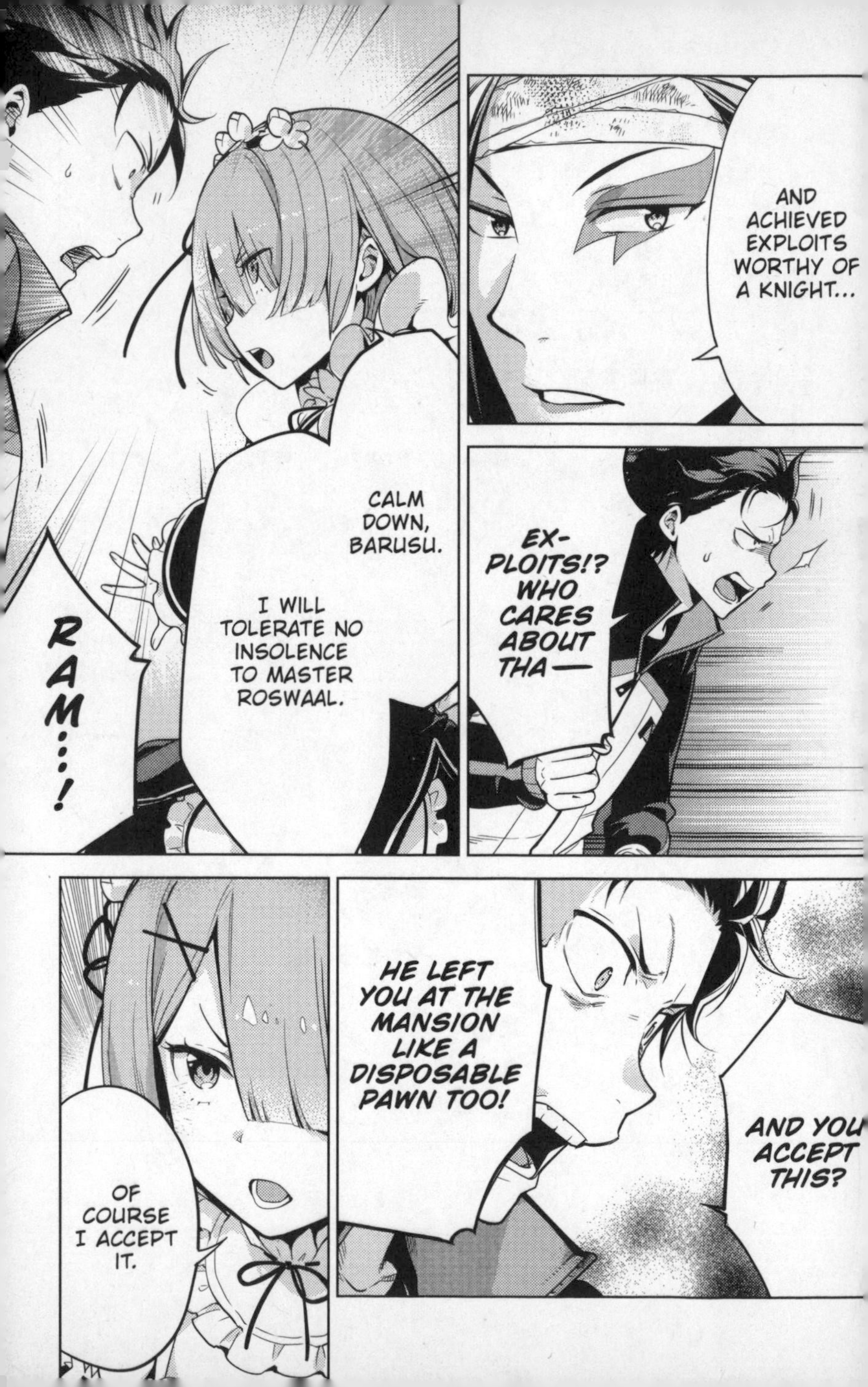
AND ACHIEVED EXPLOITS WORTHY OF A KNIGHT...
EX-PLOITS!? WHO CARES ABOUT THA—
CALM DOWN, BARUSU.
I WILL TOLERATE NO INSOLENCE TO MASTER ROSWAAL.
RAM...!
HE LEFT YOU AT THE MANSION LIKE A DISPOSABLE PAWN TOO!
AND YOU ACCEPT THIS?
OF COURSE I ACCEPT IT.

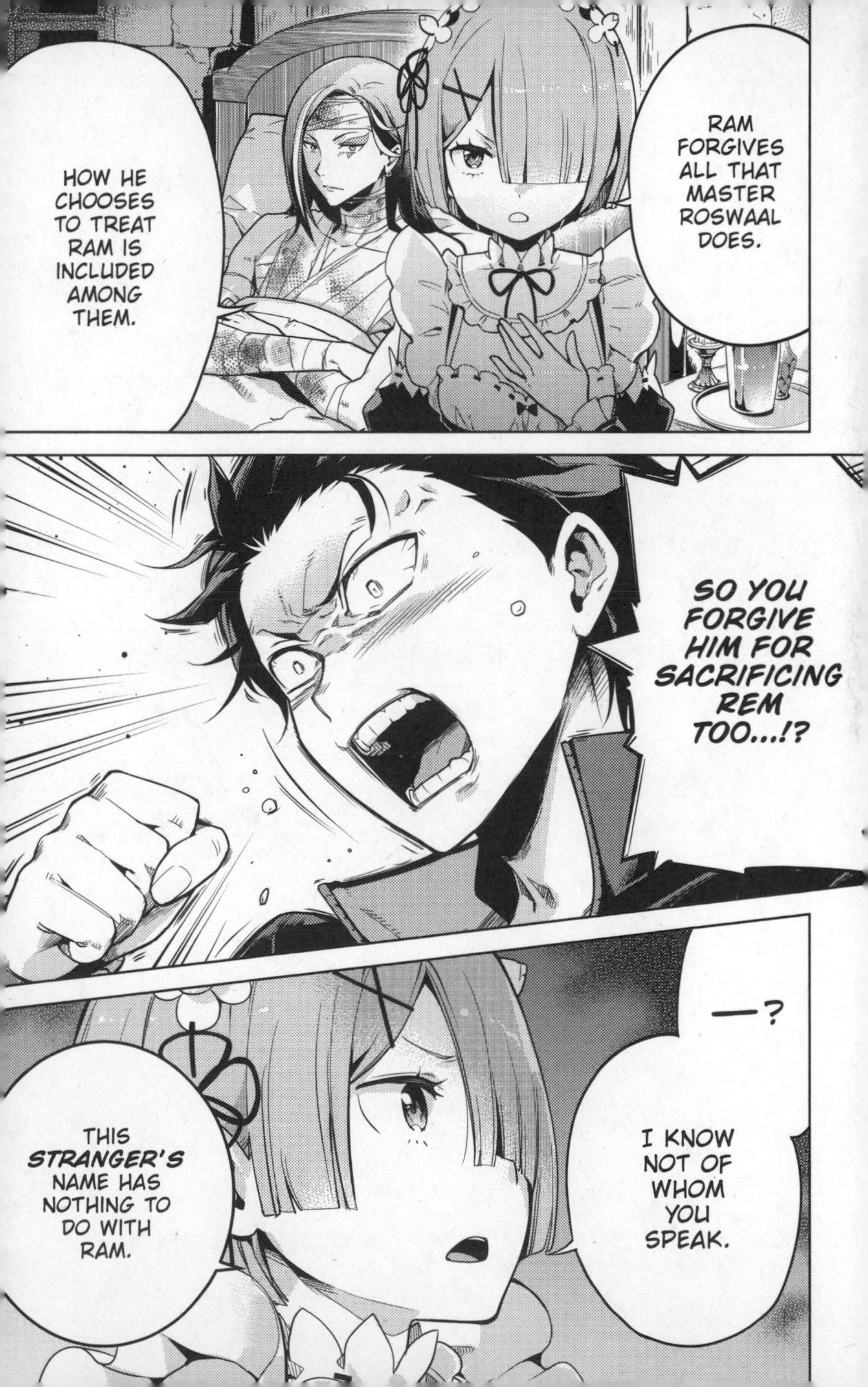
RAM FORGIVES ALL THAT MASTER ROSWAAL DOES.
HOW HE CHOOSES TO TREAT RAM IS INCLUDED AMONG THEM.
SO YOU FORGIVE HIM FOR SACRIFICING REM TOO...!?
—?
I KNOW NOT OF WHOM YOU SPEAK.
THIS STRANGER'S NAME HAS NOTHING TO DO WITH RAM.

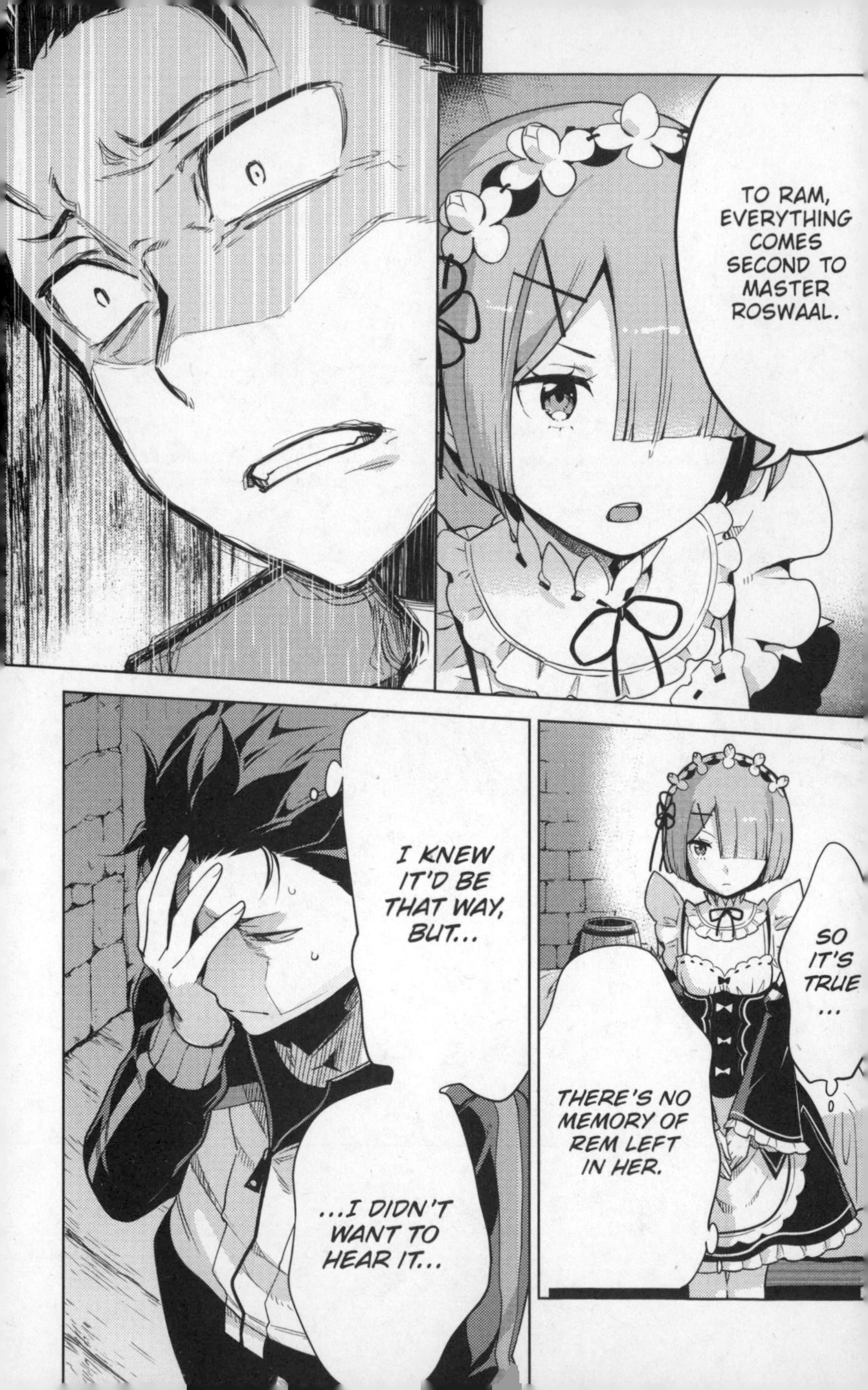
TO RAM, EVERYTHING COMES SECOND TO MASTER ROSWAAL.
SO IT'S TRUE ...
THERE'S NO MEMORY OF REM LEFT IN HER.
I KNEW IT'D BE THAT WAY, BUT...
...I DIDN'T WANT TO HEAR IT...

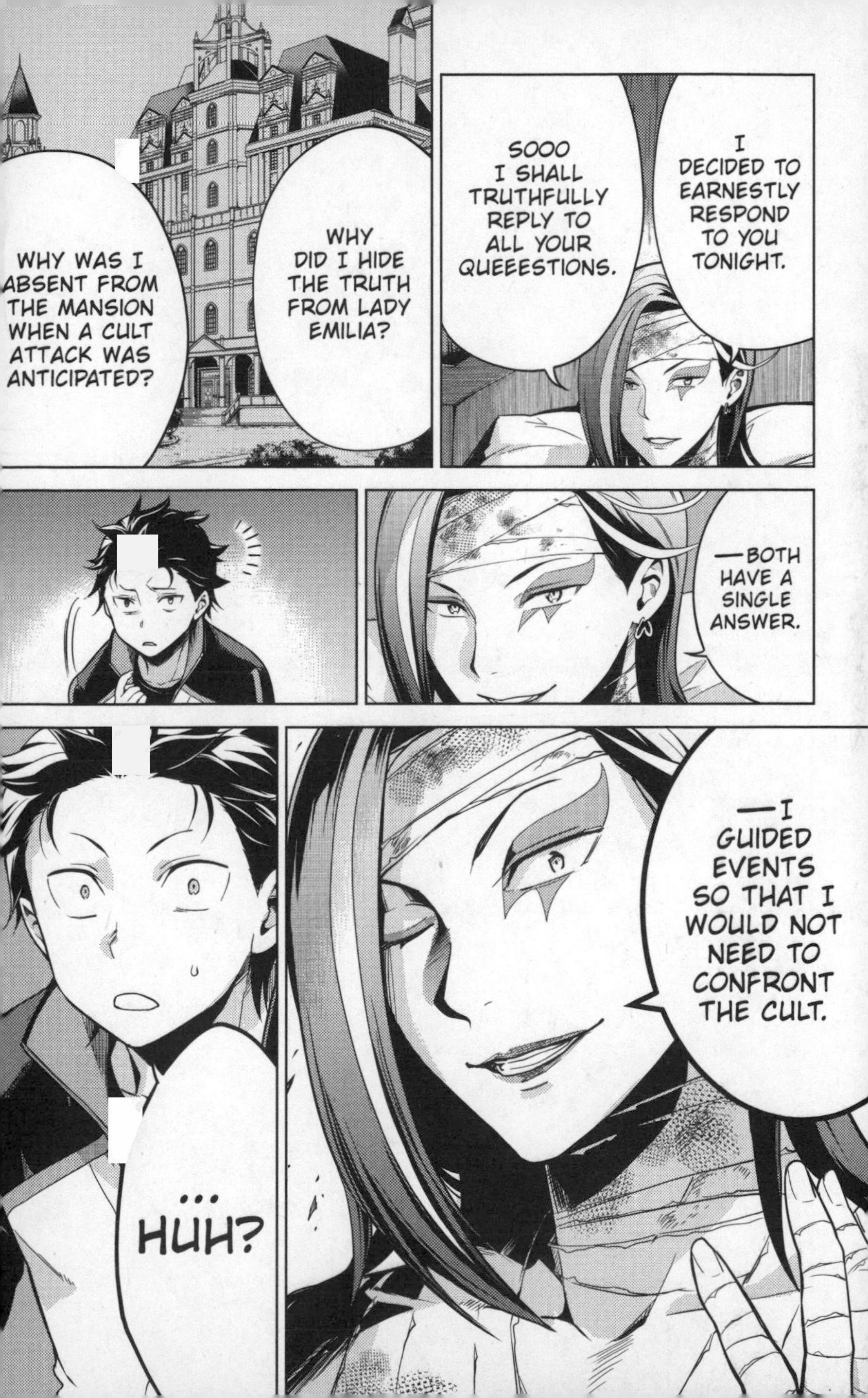
I DECIDED TO EARNESTLY RESPOND TO YOU TONIGHT.
SOOO I SHALL TRUTHFULLY REPLY TO ALL YOUR QUEEESTIONS.
WHY DID I HIDE THE TRUTH FROM LADY EMILIA?
WHY WAS I ABSENT FROM THE MANSION WHEN A CULT ATTACK WAS ANTICIPATED?
—BOTH HAVE A SINGLE ANSWER.
—I GUIDED EVENTS SO THAT I WOULD NOT NEED TO CONFRONT THE CULT.
... HUH?

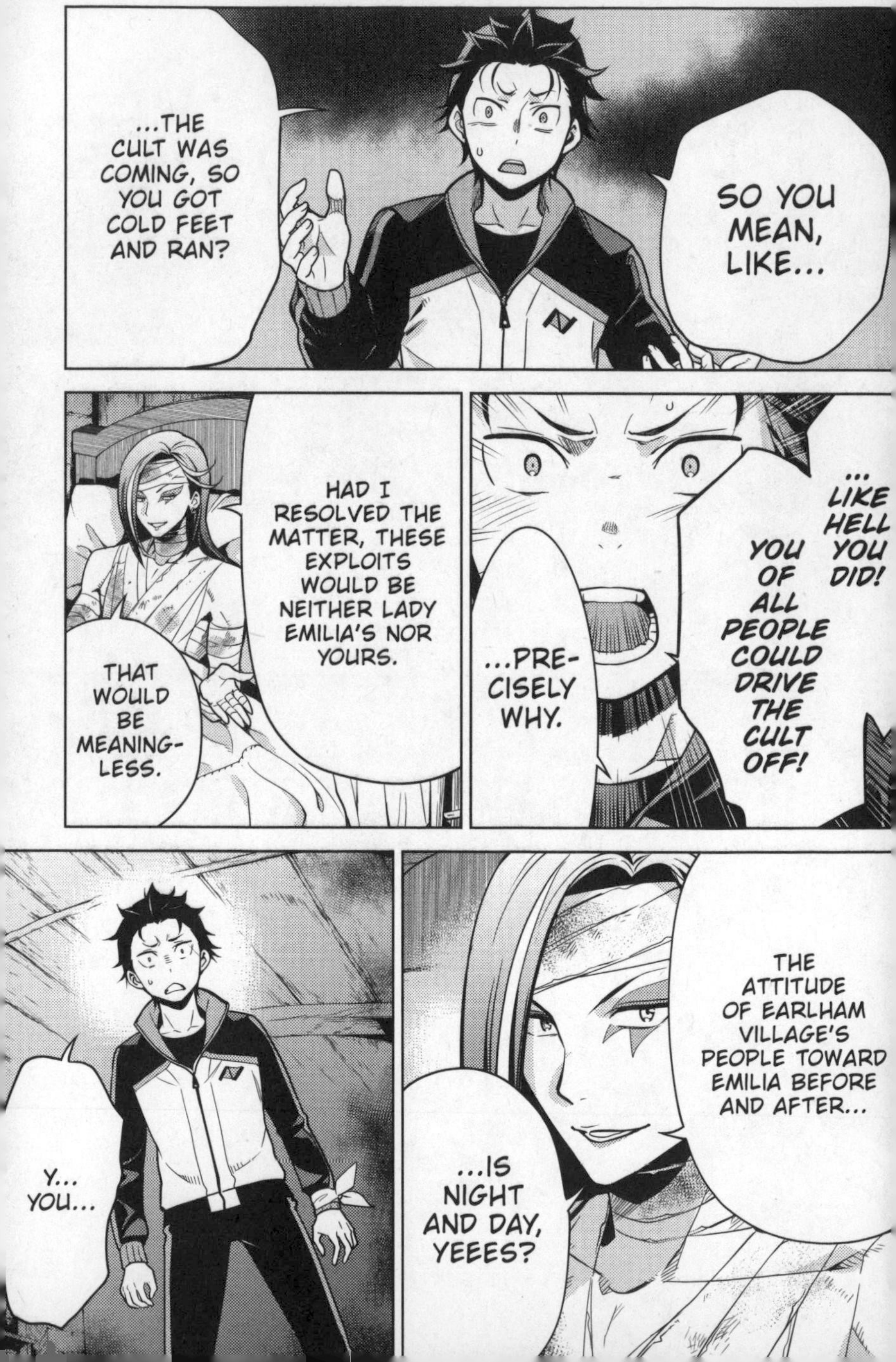
SO YOU MEAN, LIKE...
...THE CULT WAS COMING, SO YOU GOT COLD FEET AND RAN?
...LIKE HELL YOU DID!
YOU OF ALL PEOPLE COULD DRIVE THE CULT OFF!
...PRE-CISELY WHY.
HAD I RESOLVED THE MATTER, THESE EXPLOITS WOULD BE NEITHER LADY EMILIA'S NOR YOURS.
THAT WOULD BE MEANING-LESS.
THE ATTITUDE OF EARLHAM VILLAGE'S PEOPLE TOWARD EMILIA BEFORE AND AFTER...
...IS NIGHT AND DAY, YEEES?
Y... YOU...

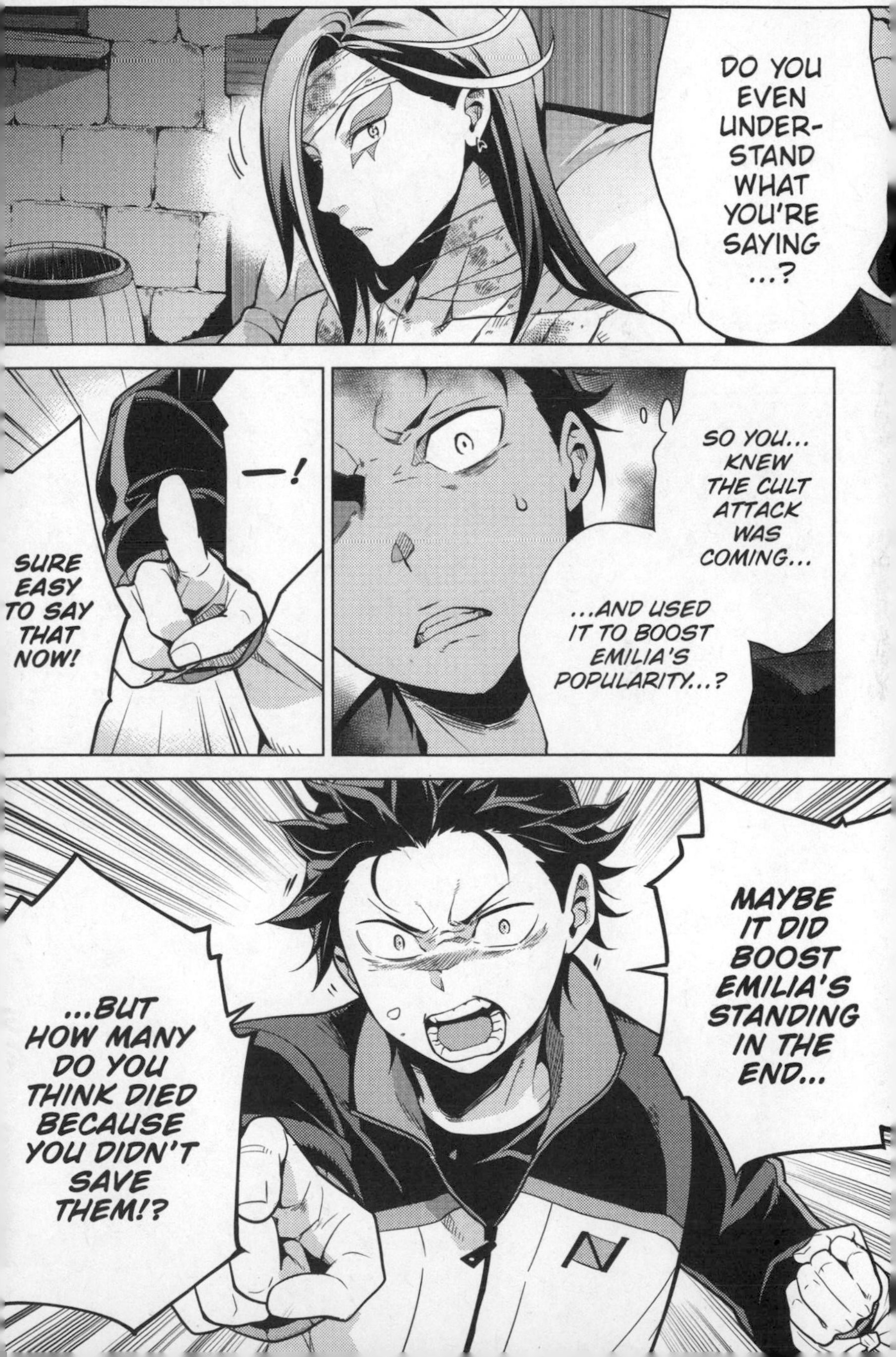
DO YOU EVEN UNDER-STAND WHAT YOU'RE SAYING ...?
SO YOU... KNEW THE CULT ATTACK WAS COMING...
...AND USED IT TO BOOST EMILIA'S POPULARITY...?
—!
SURE EASY TO SAY THAT NOW!
MAYBE IT DID BOOST EMILIA'S STANDING IN THE END...
...BUT HOW MANY DO YOU THINK DIED BECAUSE YOU DIDN'T SAVE THEM!?

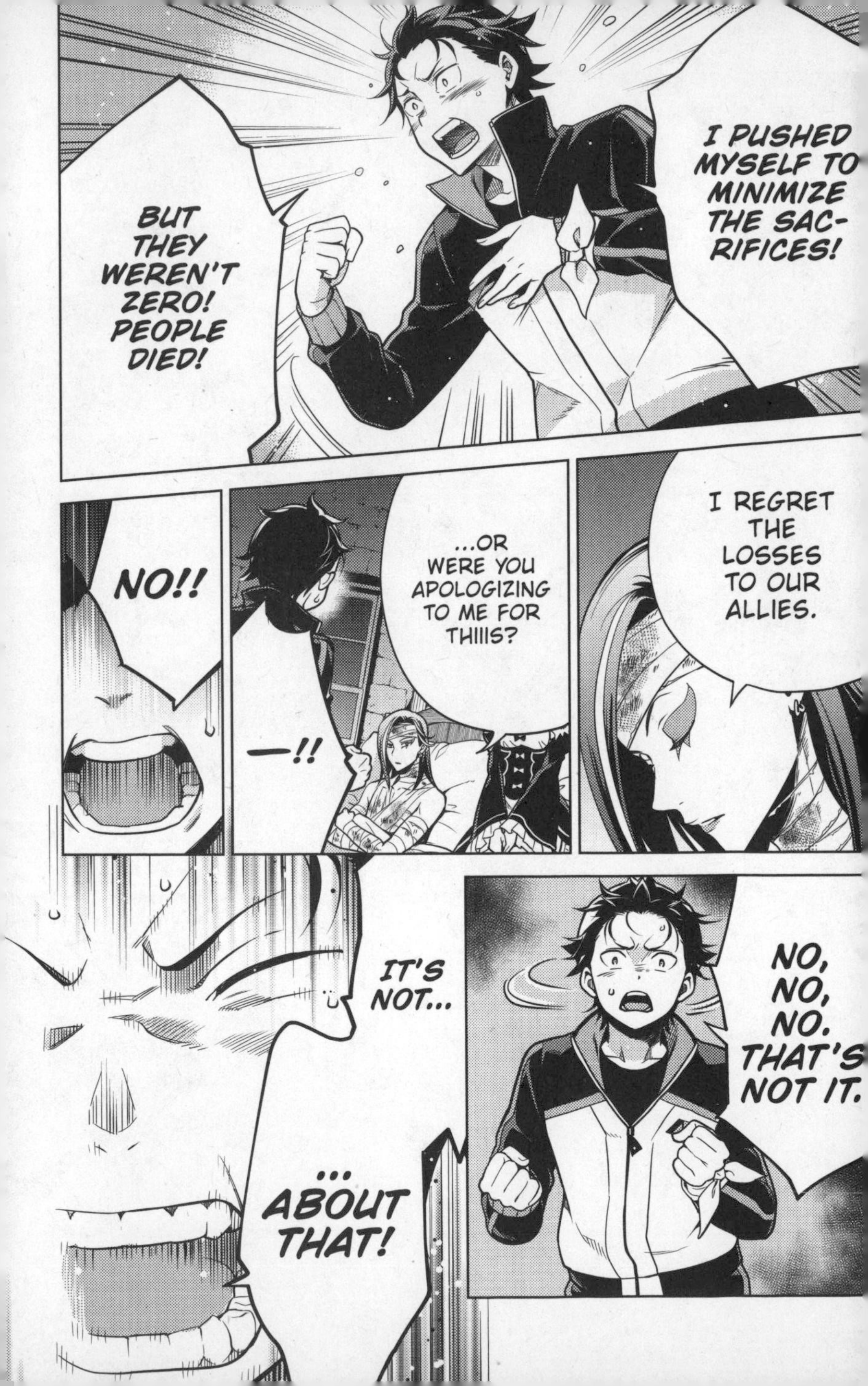
I PUSHED MYSELF TO MINIMIZE THE SAC-RIFICES!
BUT THEY WEREN'T ZERO! PEOPLE DIED!
I REGRET THE LOSSES TO OUR ALLIES.
...OR WERE YOU APOLOGIZING TO ME FOR THIIIS?
—!!
NO!!
NO, NO, NO. THAT'S NOT IT.
IT'S NOT...
...ABOUT THAT!

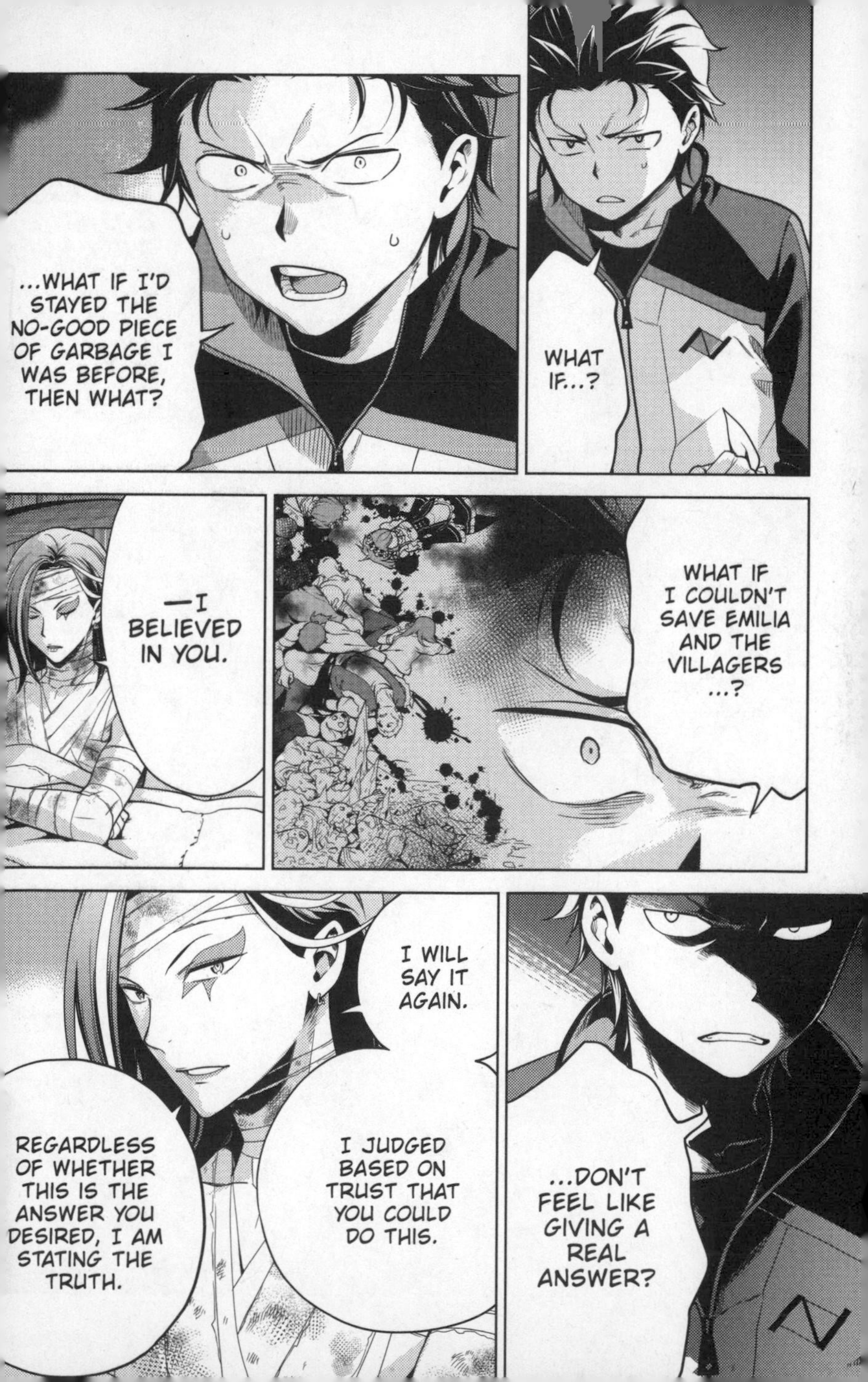
WHAT IF...?
...WHAT IF I'D STAYED THE NO-GOOD PIECE OF GARBAGE I WAS BEFORE, THEN WHAT?
WHAT IF I COULDN'T SAVE EMILIA AND THE VILLAGERS ...?
—I BELIEVED IN YOU.
...DON'T FEEL LIKE GIVING A REAL ANSWER?
I WILL SAY IT AGAIN.
I JUDGED BASED ON TRUST THAT YOU COULD DO THIS.
REGARDLESS OF WHETHER THIS IS THE ANSWER YOU DESIRED, I AM STATING THE TRUTH.

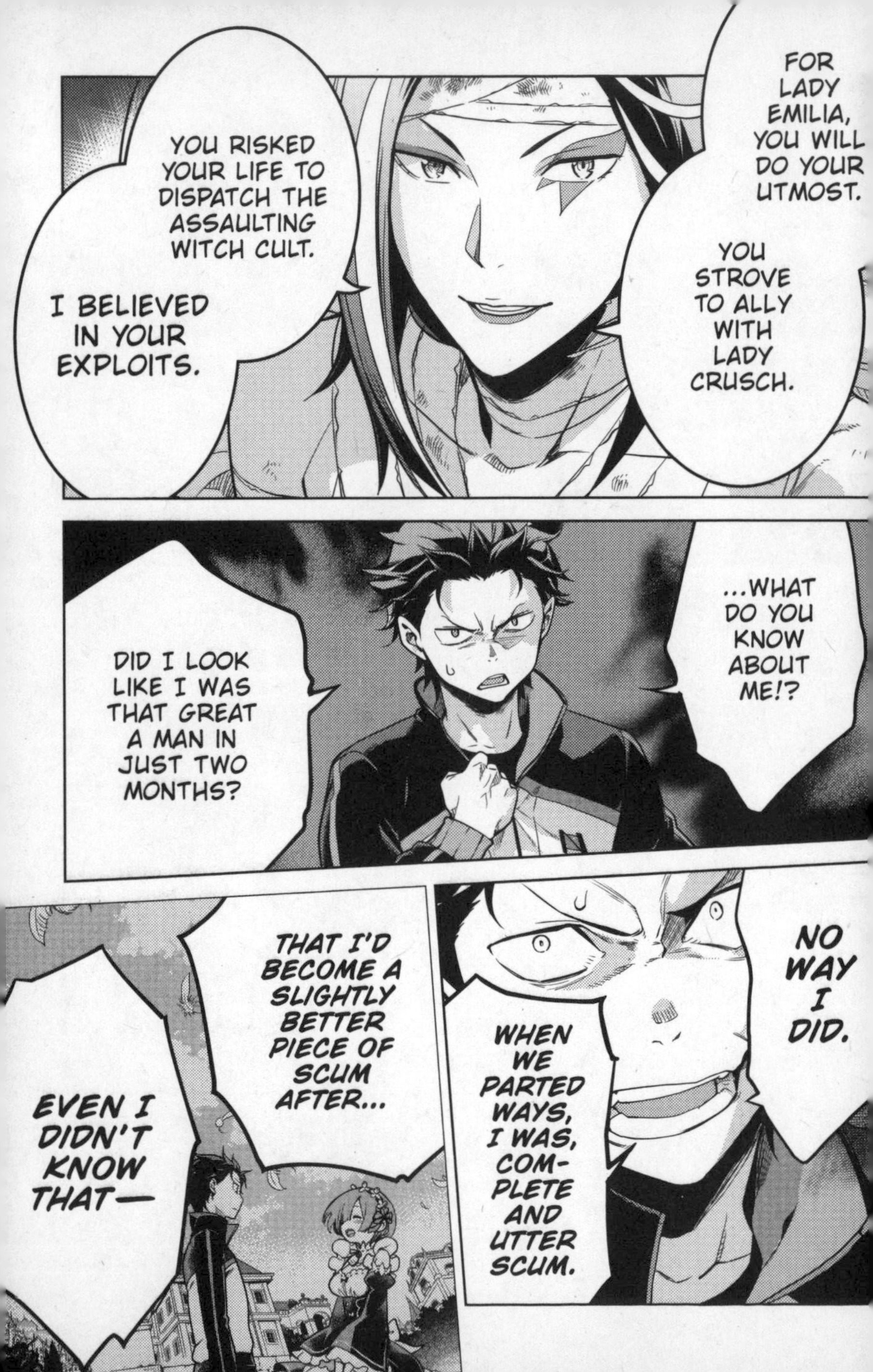
FOR LADY EMILIA, YOU WILL DO YOUR UTMOST.
YOU STROVE TO ALLY WITH LADY CRUSCH.
YOU RISKED YOUR LIFE TO DISPATCH THE ASSAULTING WITCH CULT.
I BELIEVED IN YOUR EXPLOITS.
...WHAT DO YOU KNOW ABOUT ME!?
DID I LOOK LIKE I WAS THAT GREAT A MAN IN JUST TWO MONTHS?
NO WAY I DID.
WHEN WE PARTED WAYS, I WAS, COM-PLETE AND UTTER SCUM.
THAT I'D BECOME A SLIGHTLY BETTER PIECE OF SCUM AFTER...
EVEN I DIDN'T KNOW THAT—

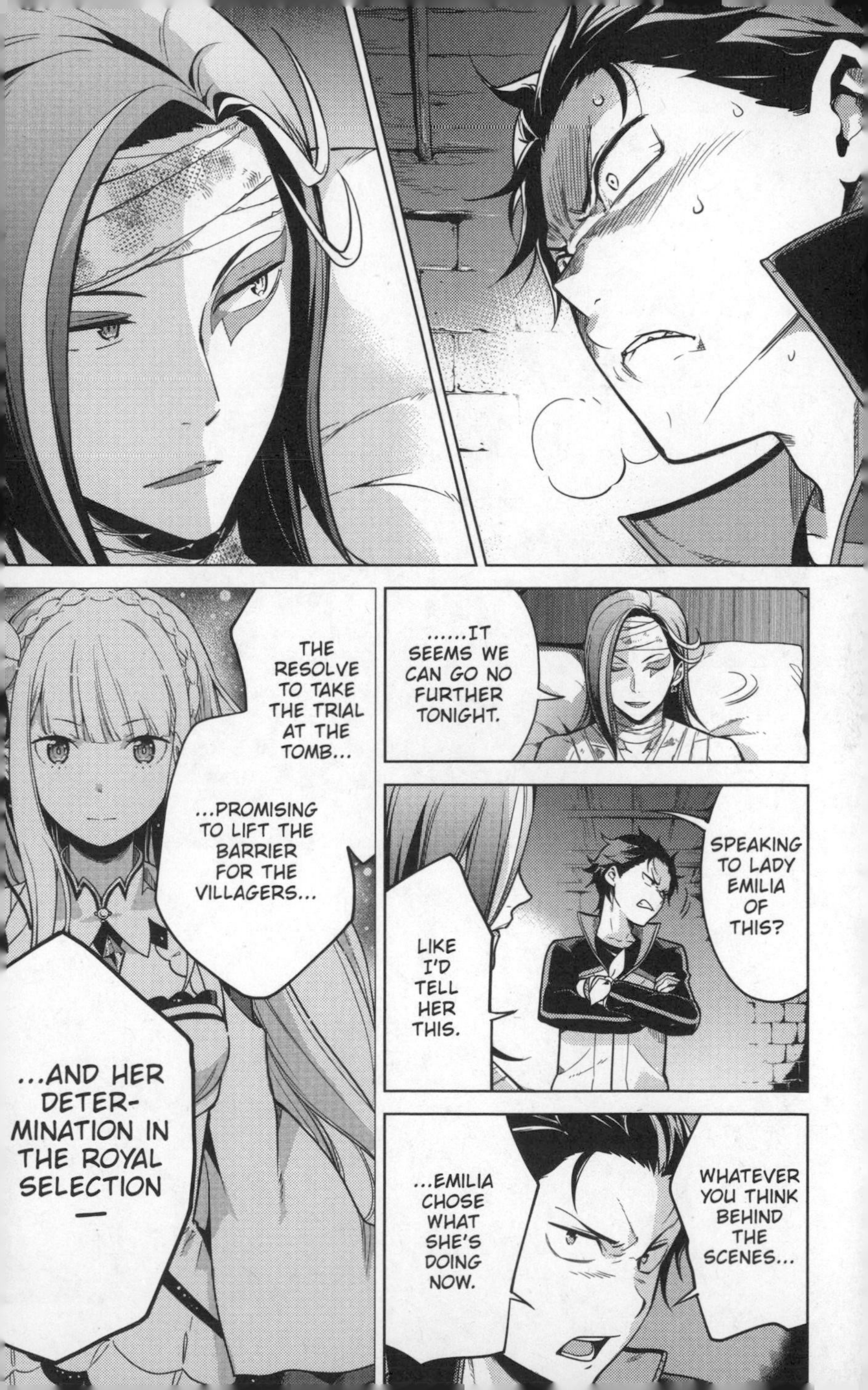
......IT SEEMS WE CAN GO NO FURTHER TONIGHT.
SPEAKING TO LADY EMILIA OF THIS?
LIKE I'D TELL HER THIS.
WHATEVER YOU THINK BEHIND THE SCENES...
...EMILIA CHOSE WHAT SHE'S DOING NOW.
THE RESOLVE TO TAKE THE TRIAL AT THE TOMB...
...PROMISING TO LIFT THE BARRIER FOR THE VILLAGERS...
...AND HER DETER-MINATION IN THE ROYAL SELECTION —

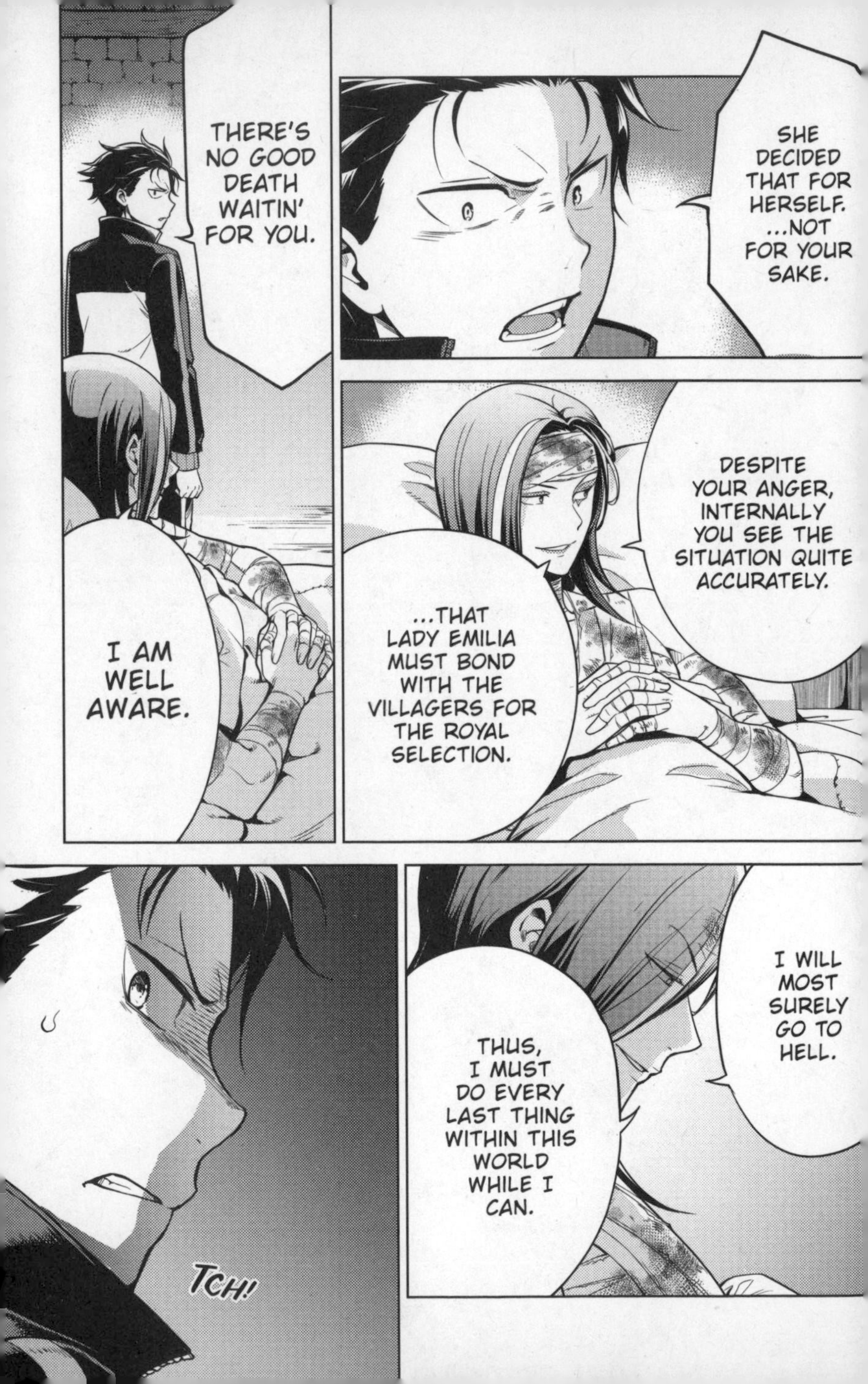
SHE DECIDED THAT FOR HERSELF. ...NOT FOR YOUR SAKE.
DESPITE YOUR ANGER, INTERNALLY YOU SEE THE SITUATION QUITE ACCURATELY.
...THAT LADY EMILIA MUST BOND WITH THE VILLAGERS FOR THE ROYAL SELECTION.
THERE'S NO GOOD DEATH WAITIN' FOR YOU.
I AM WELL AWARE.
I WILL MOST SURELY GO TO HELL.
THUS, I MUST DO EVERY LAST THING WITHIN THIS WORLD WHILE I CAN.
TCH!

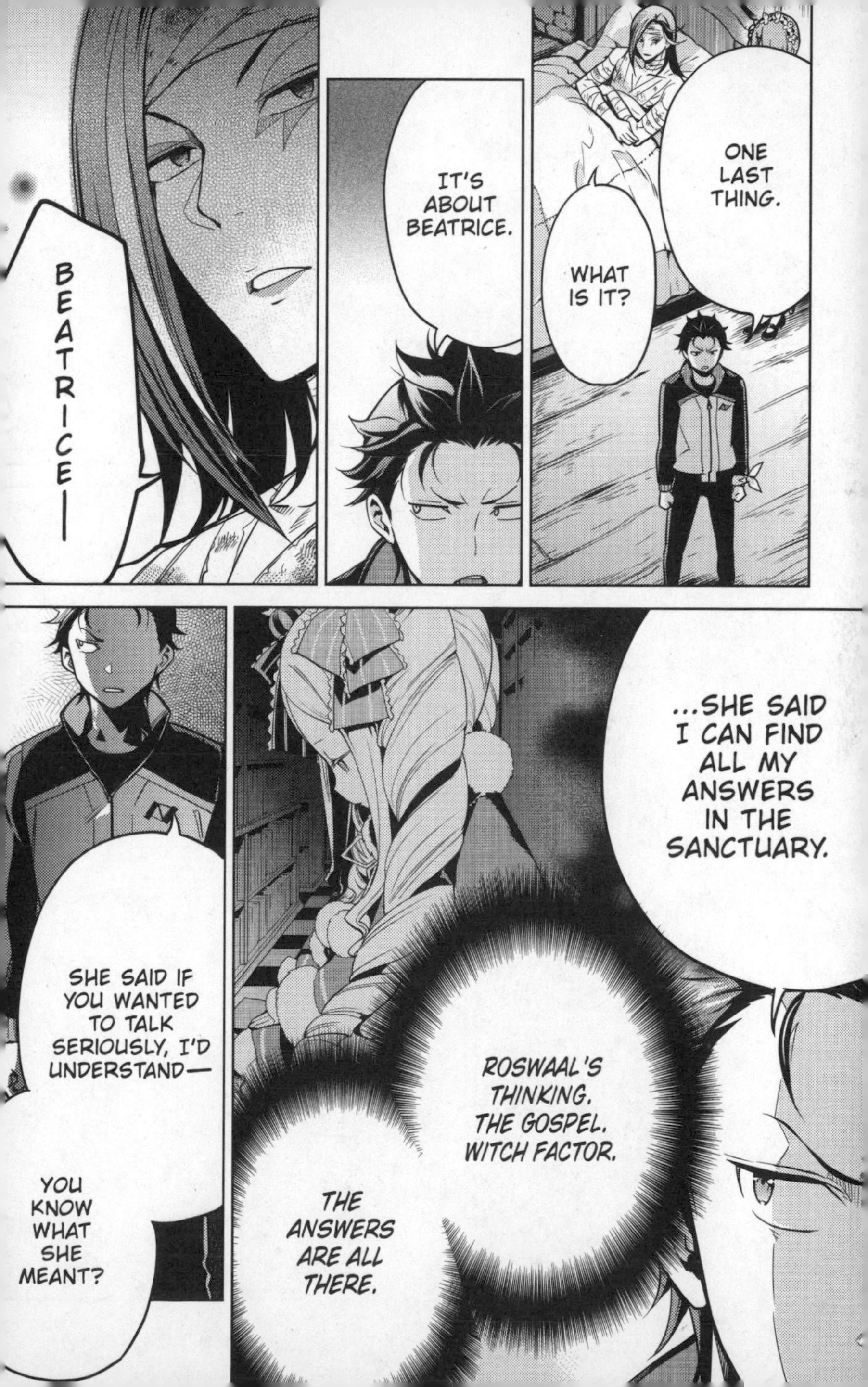
ONE LAST THING.
WHAT IS IT?
IT'S ABOUT BEATRICE.
BEATRICE—
...SHE SAID I CAN FIND ALL MY ANSWERS IN THE SANCTUARY.
ROSWAAL'S THINKING. THE GOSPEL. WITCH FACTOR.
THE ANSWERS ARE ALL THERE.
SHE SAID IF YOU WANTED TO TALK SERIOUSLY, I'D UNDERSTAND—
YOU KNOW WHAT SHE MEANT?

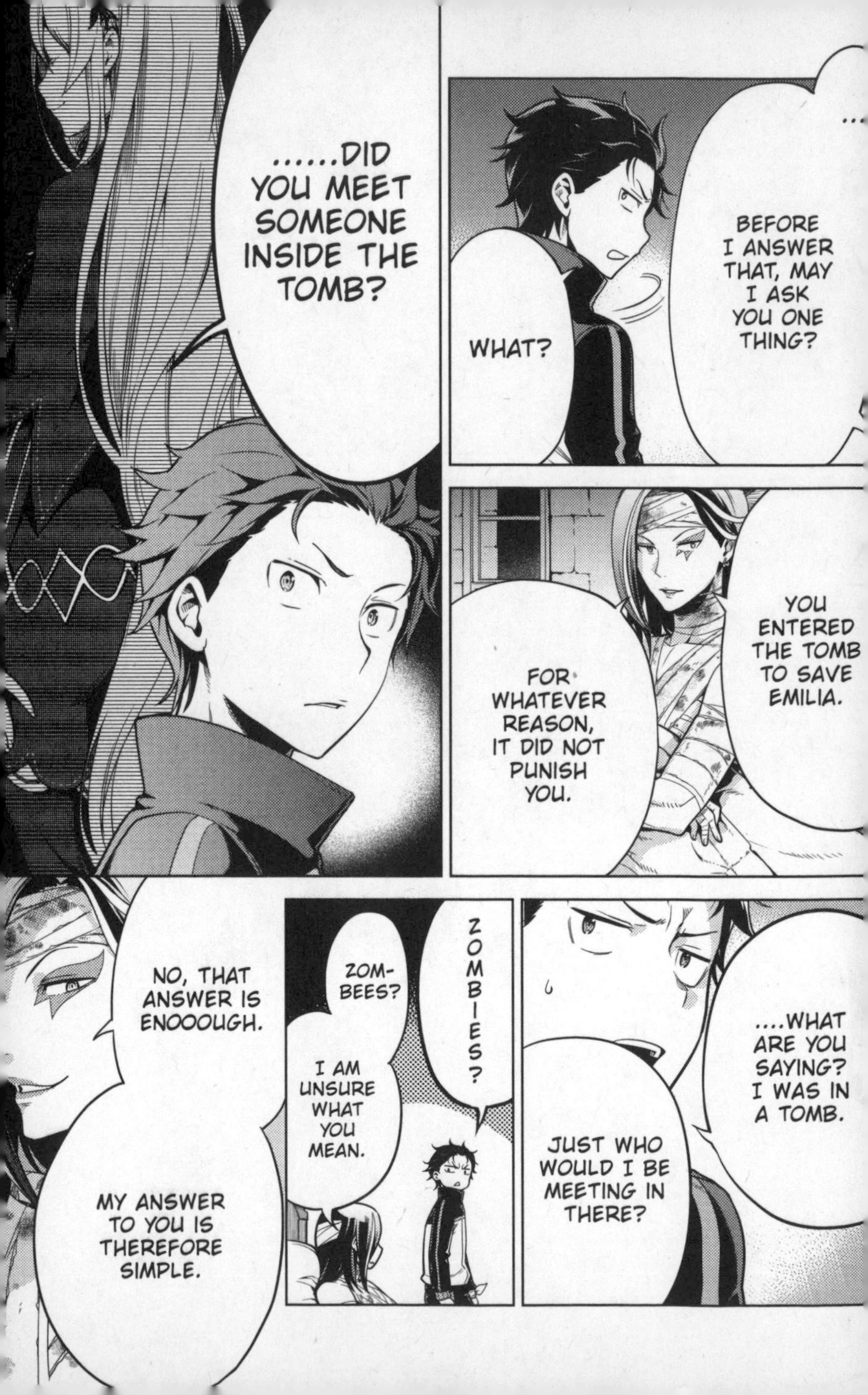
...
BEFORE I ANSWER THAT, MAY I ASK YOU ONE THING?
WHAT?
YOU ENTERED THE TOMB TO SAVE EMILIA.
FOR WHATEVER REASON, IT DID NOT PUNISH YOU.
......DID YOU MEET SOMEONE INSIDE THE TOMB?
....WHAT ARE YOU SAYING? I WAS IN A TOMB.
JUST WHO WOULD I BE MEETING IN THERE?
ZOMBIES?
ZOM-BEES?
I AM UNSURE WHAT YOU MEAN.
NO, THAT ANSWER IS ENOOOUGH.
MY ANSWER TO YOU IS THEREFORE SIMPLE.

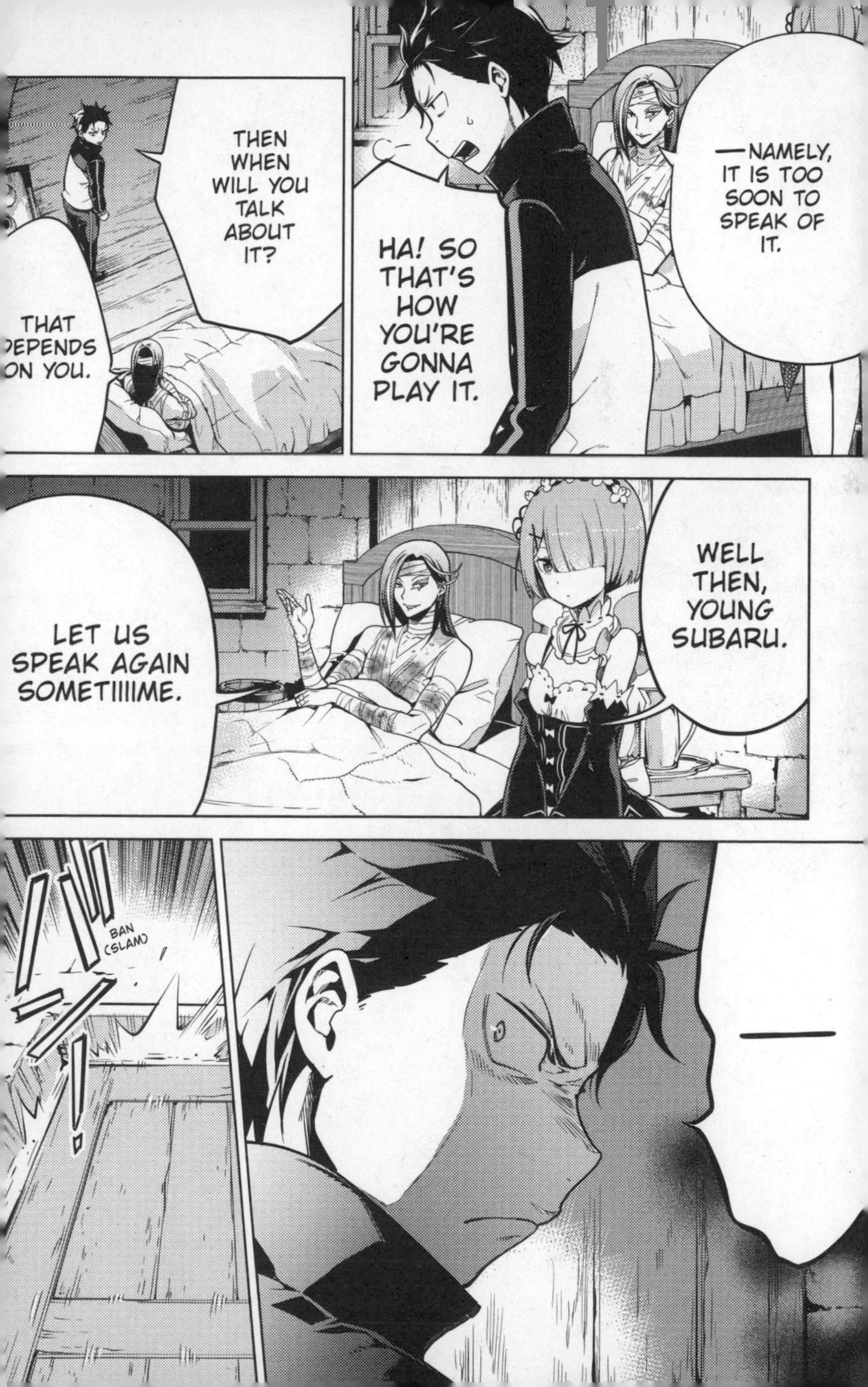
—NAMELY, IT IS TOO SOON TO SPEAK OF IT.
HA! SO THAT'S HOW YOU'RE GONNA PLAY IT.
THEN WHEN WILL YOU TALK ABOUT IT?
THAT DEPENDS ON YOU.
WELL THEN, YOUNG SUBARU.
LET US SPEAK AGAIN SOMETIIIIIME.
—
BAN (SLAM)

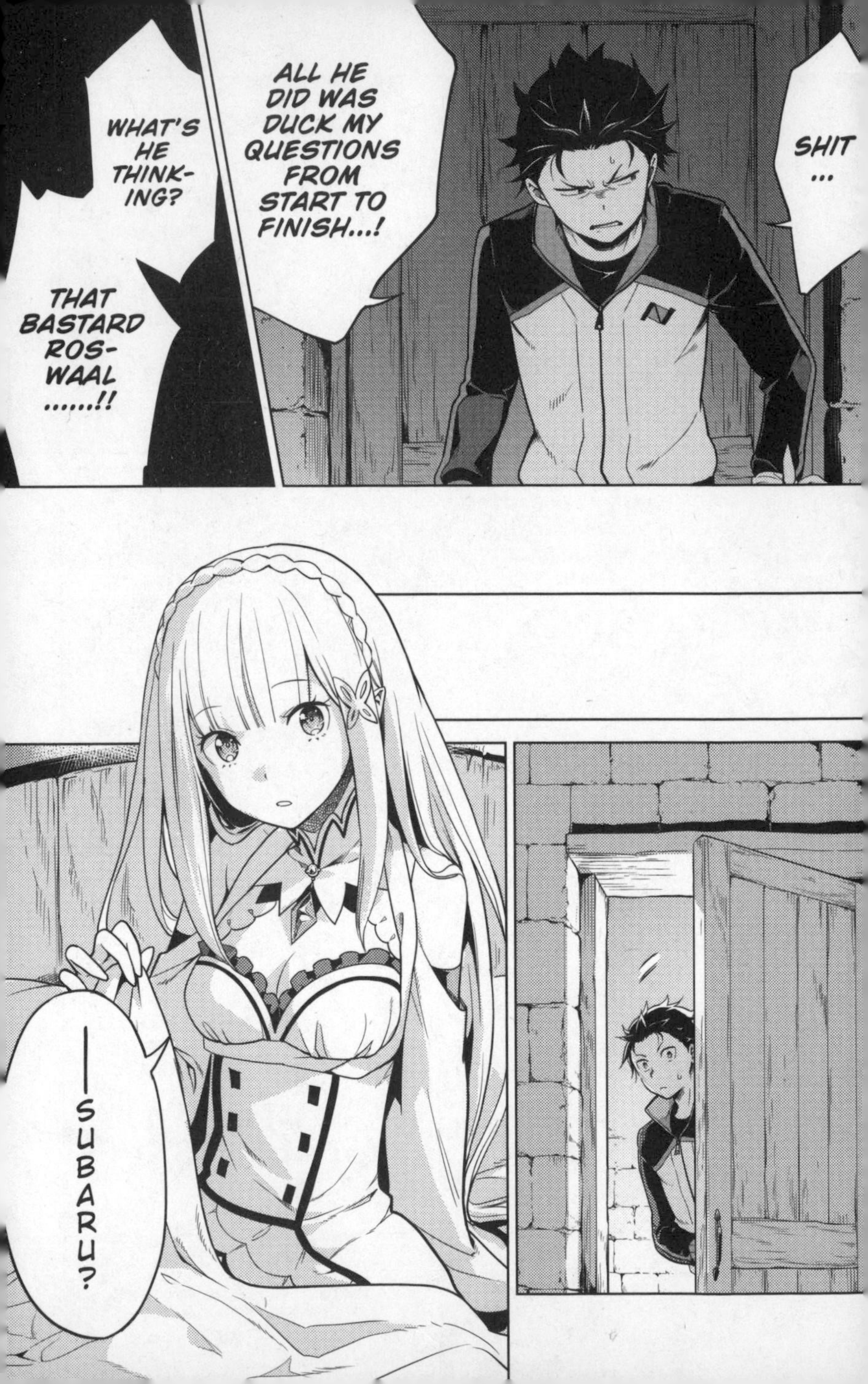
SHIT ...
ALL HE DID WAS DUCK MY QUESTIONS FROM START TO FINISH...!
WHAT'S HE THINK-ING?
THAT BASTARD ROS-WAAL ......!!
—SUBARU?

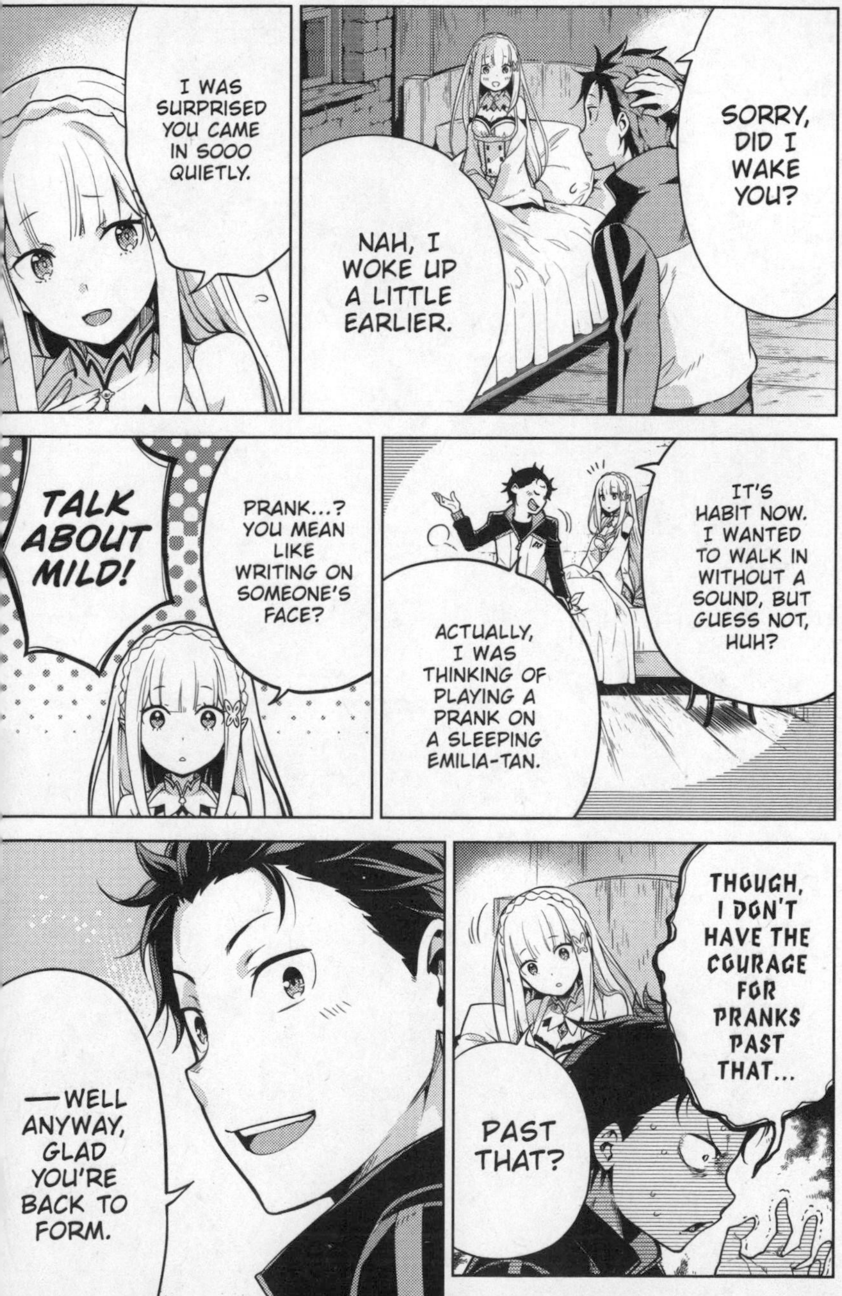
SORRY, DID I WAKE YOU?
NAH, I WOKE UP A LITTLE EARLIER.
I WAS SURPRISED YOU CAME IN SOOO QUIETLY.
IT'S HABIT NOW. I WANTED TO WALK IN WITHOUT A SOUND, BUT GUESS NOT, HUH?
ACTUALLY, I WAS THINKING OF PLAYING A PRANK ON A SLEEPING EMILIA-TAN.
PRANK...? YOU MEAN LIKE WRITING ON SOMEONE'S FACE?
TALK ABOUT MILD!
THOUGH, I DON'T HAVE THE COURAGE FOR PRANKS PAST THAT...
PAST THAT?
—WELL ANYWAY, GLAD YOU'RE BACK TO FORM.

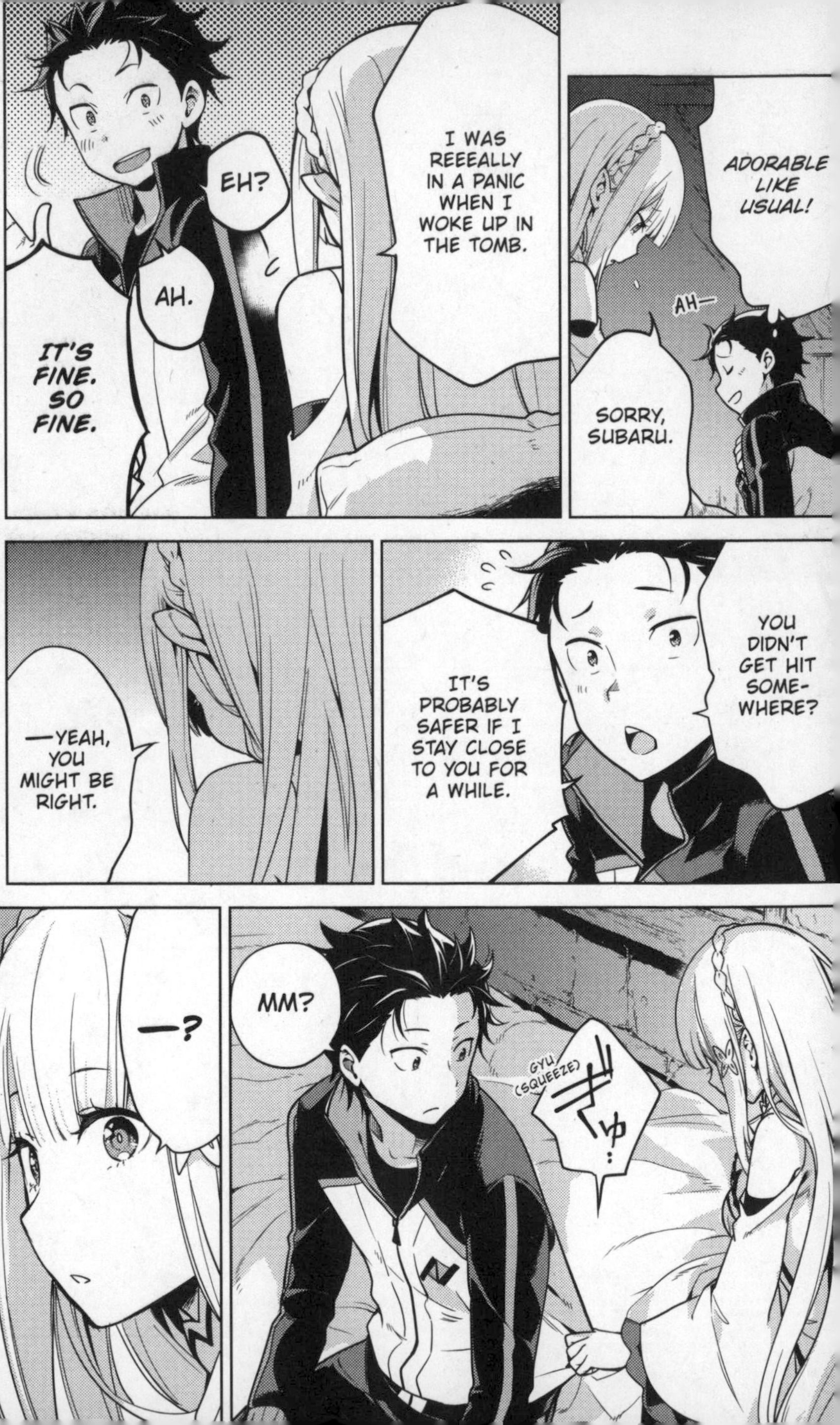
ADORABLE LIKE USUAL!
AH—
SORRY, SUBARU.
I WAS REEEALLY IN A PANIC WHEN I WOKE UP IN THE TOMB.
EH?
AH.
IT'S FINE. SO FINE.
YOU DIDN'T GET HIT SOME-WHERE?
IT'S PROBABLY SAFER IF I STAY CLOSE TO YOU FOR A WHILE.
—YEAH, YOU MIGHT BE RIGHT.
MM?
GYU (SQUEEZE)
ぎゅ
—?

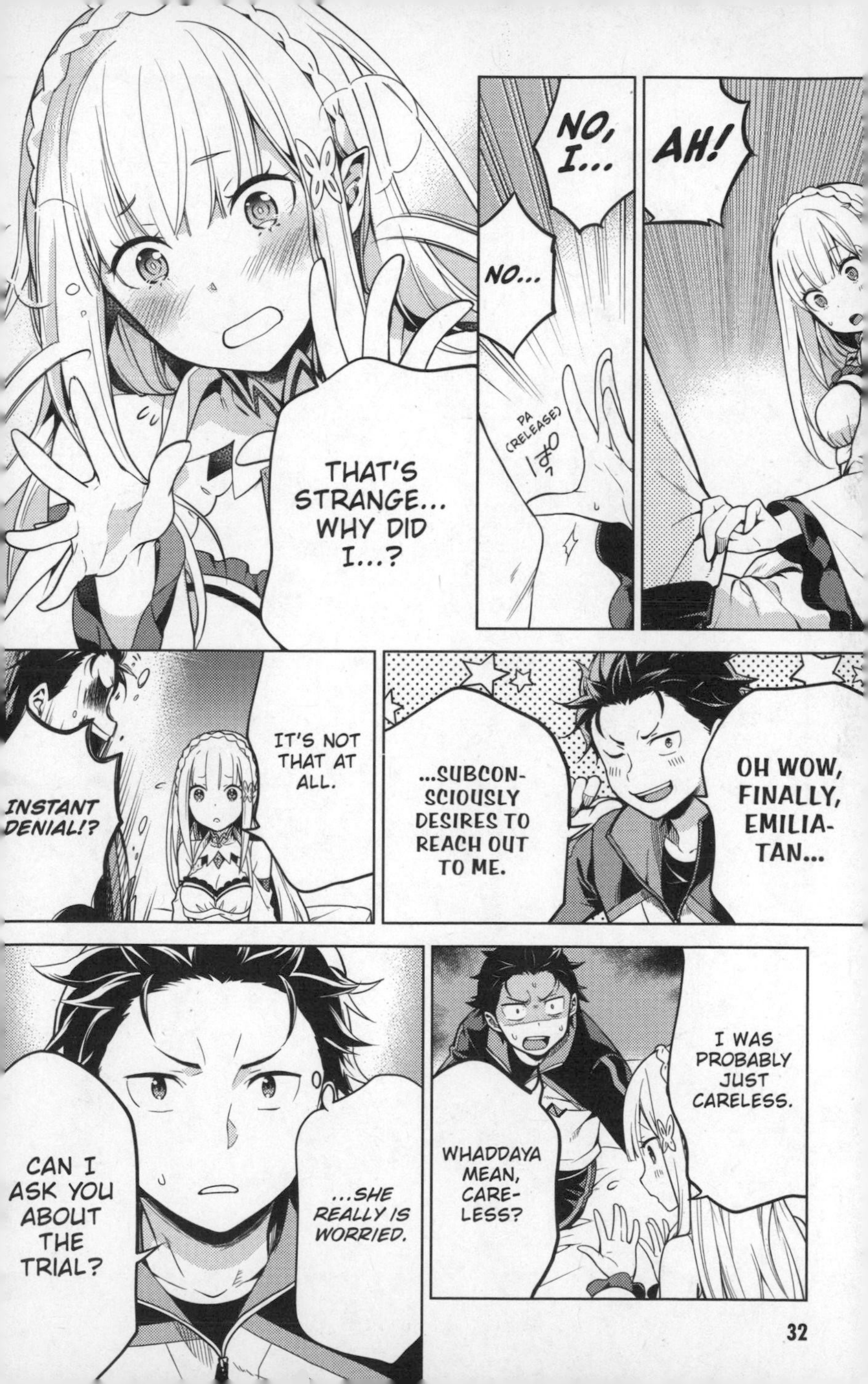
AH!
NO, I...
NO...
PA (RELEASE)
ぱ
THAT'S STRANGE... WHY DID I...?
OH WOW, FINALLY, EMILIA-TAN...
...SUBCONSCIOUSLY DESIRES TO REACH OUT TO ME.
IT'S NOT THAT AT ALL.
INSTANT DENIAL!?
I WAS PROBABLY JUST CARELESS.
WHADDAYA MEAN, CARELESS?
...SHE REALLY IS WORRIED.
CAN I ASK YOU ABOUT THE TRIAL?

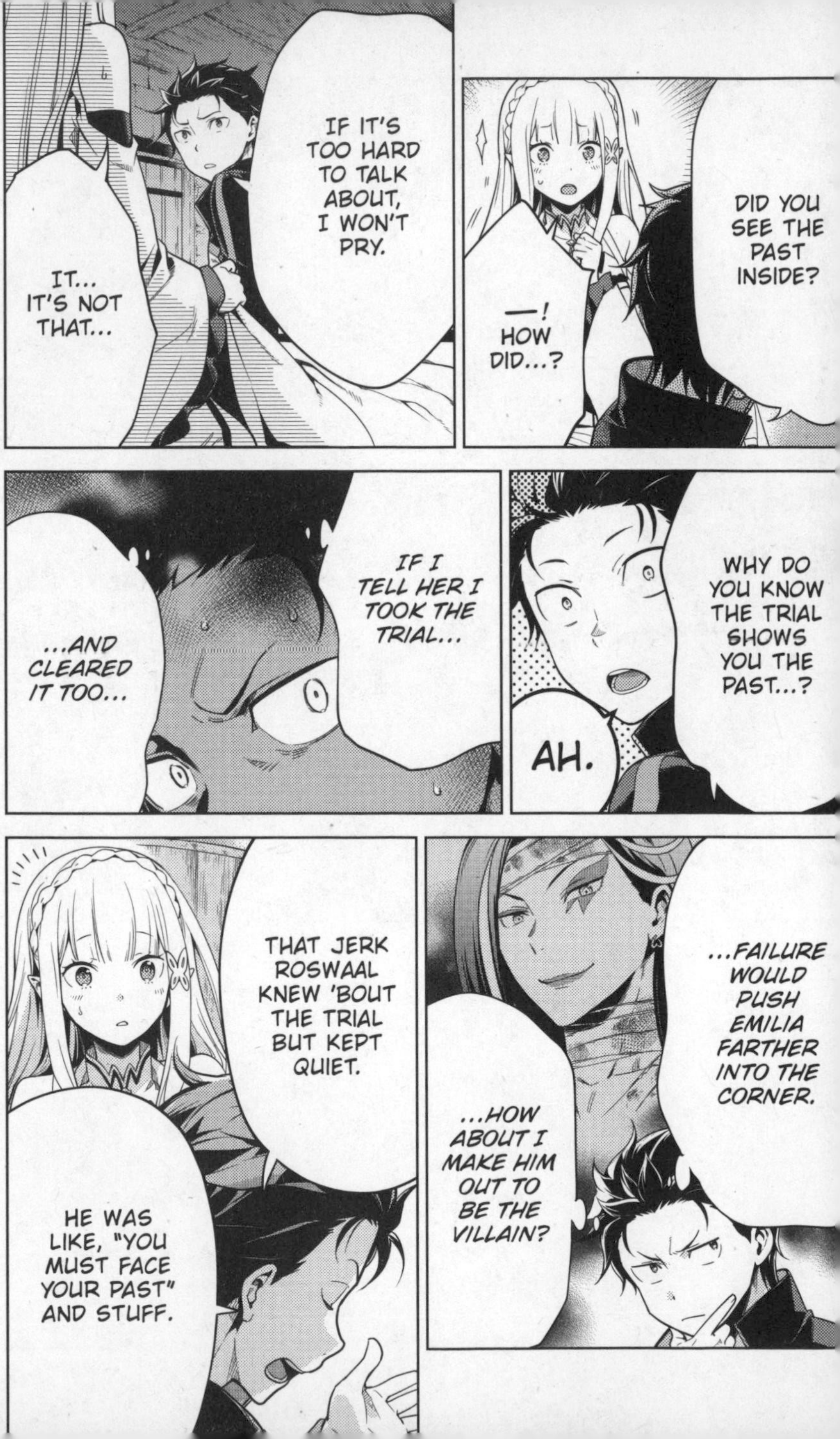
DID YOU SEE THE PAST INSIDE?
—! HOW DID...?
IF IT'S TOO HARD TO TALK ABOUT, I WON'T PRY.
IT... IT'S NOT THAT...
WHY DO YOU KNOW THE TRIAL SHOWS YOU THE PAST...?
AH.
IF I TELL HER I TOOK THE TRIAL...
...AND CLEARED IT TOO...
...FAILURE WOULD PUSH EMILIA FARTHER INTO THE CORNER.
...HOW ABOUT I MAKE HIM OUT TO BE THE VILLAIN?
THAT JERK ROSWAAL KNEW 'BOUT THE TRIAL BUT KEPT QUIET.
HE WAS LIKE, "YOU MUST FACE YOUR PAST" AND STUFF.

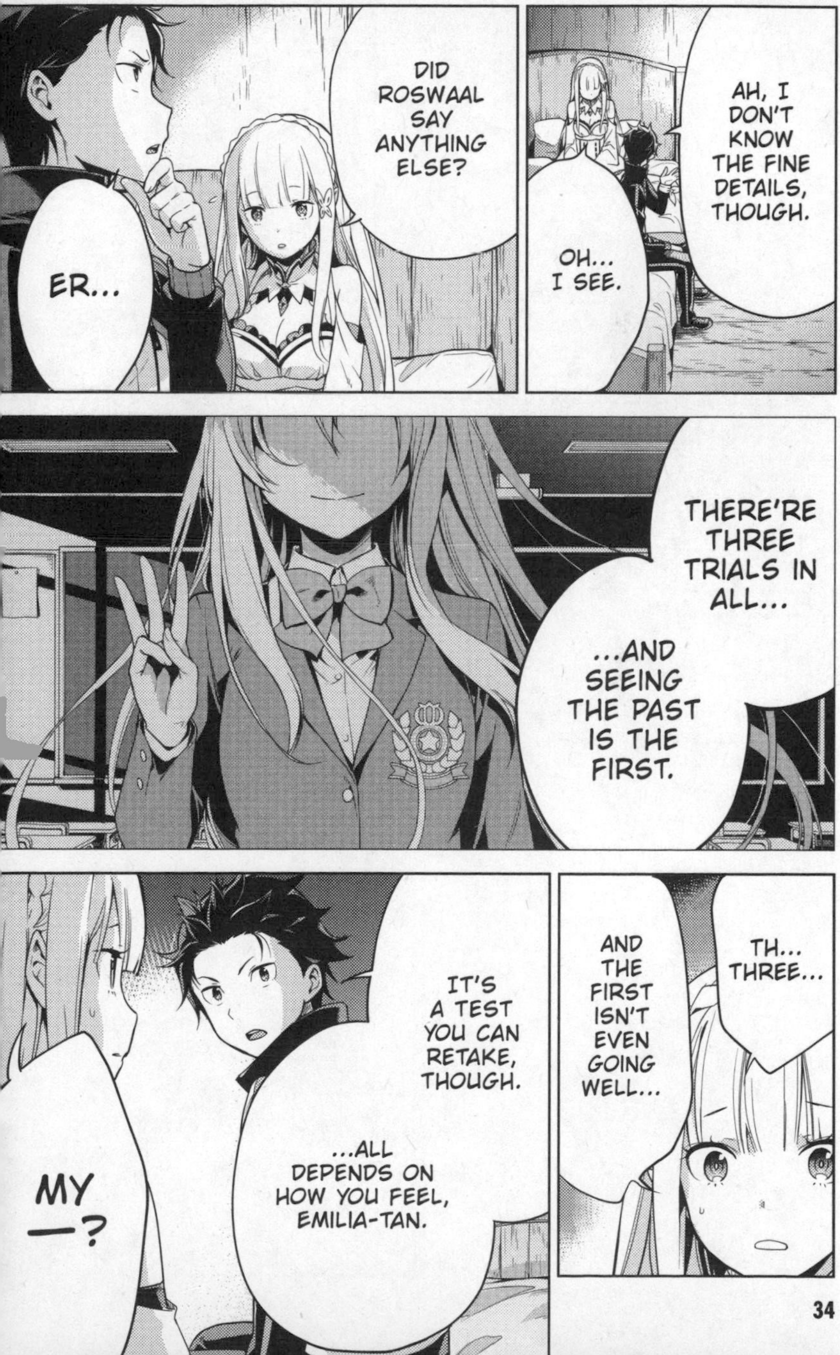
AH, I DON'T KNOW THE FINE DETAILS, THOUGH.
OH... I SEE.
DID ROSWAAL SAY ANYTHING ELSE?
ER...
THERE'RE THREE TRIALS IN ALL...
...AND SEEING THE PAST IS THE FIRST.
TH... THREE...
AND THE FIRST ISN'T EVEN GOING WELL...
IT'S A TEST YOU CAN RETAKE, THOUGH.
...ALL DEPENDS ON HOW YOU FEEL, EMILIA-TAN.
MY —?

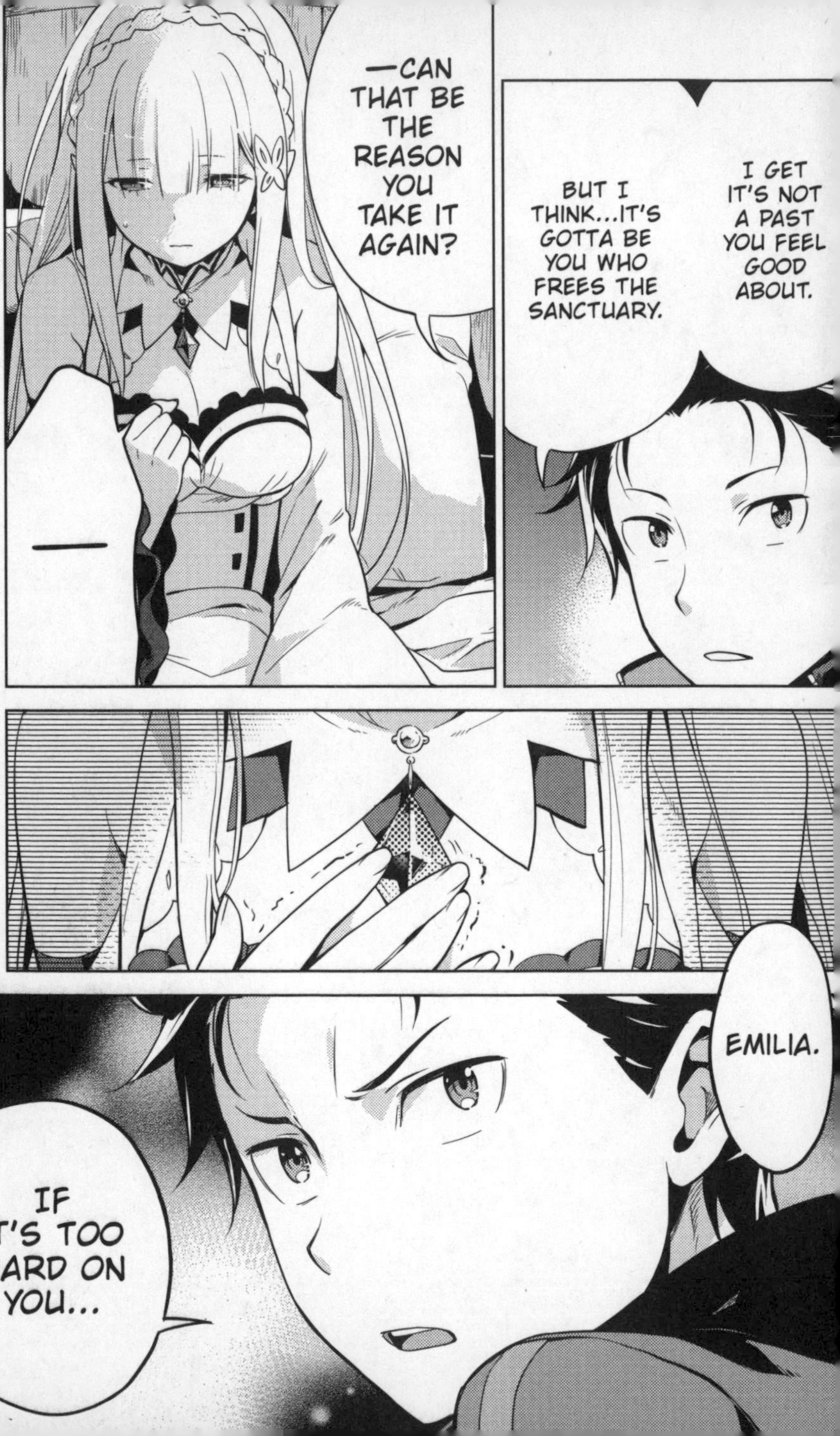
I GET IT'S NOT A PAST YOU FEEL GOOD ABOUT.
BUT I THINK...IT'S GOTTA BE YOU WHO FREES THE SANCTUARY.
—CAN THAT BE THE REASON YOU TAKE IT AGAIN?
—
EMILIA.
IF IT'S TOO HARD ON YOU...

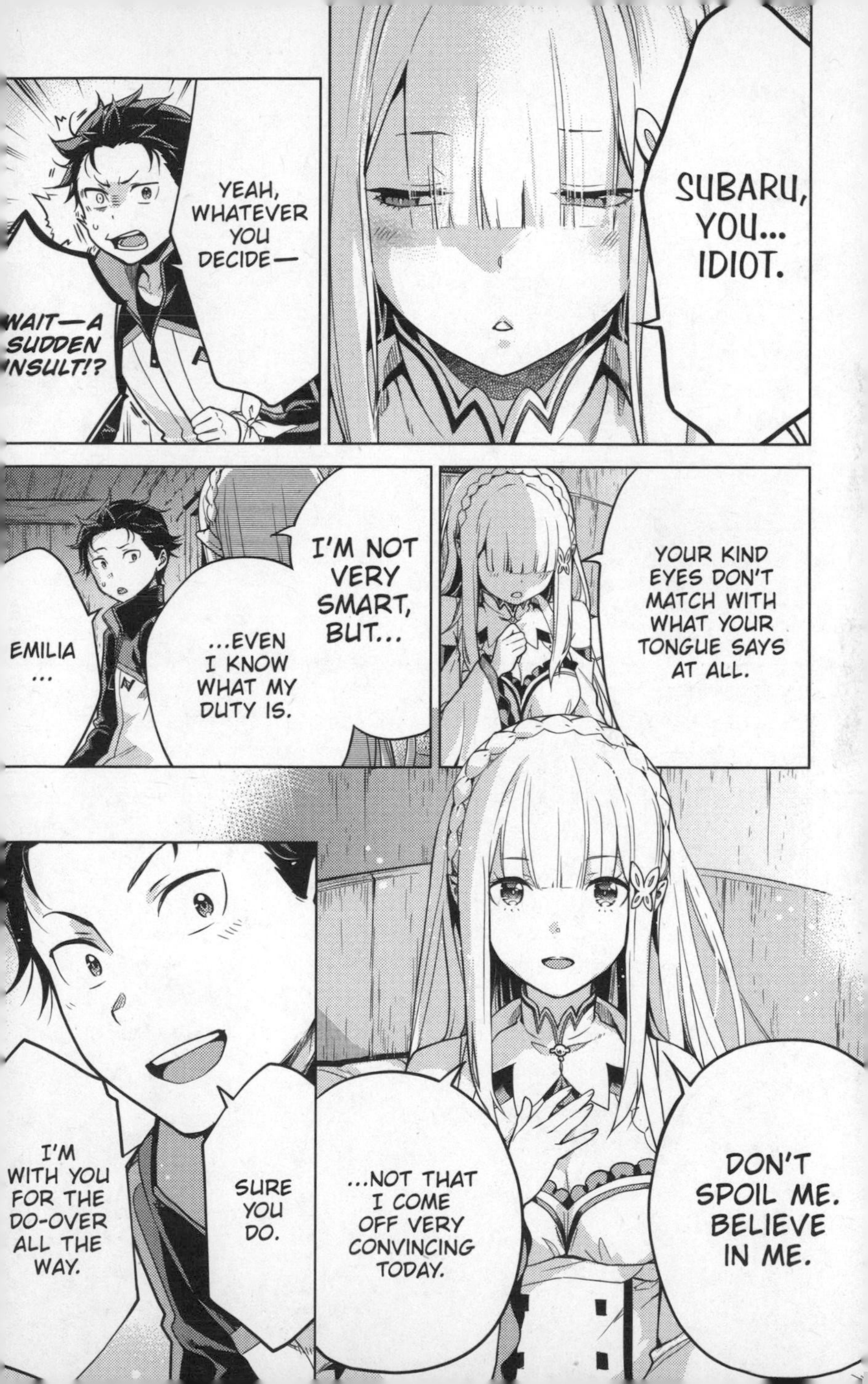
SUBARU, YOU... IDIOT.
YEAH, WHATEVER YOU DECIDE—
WAIT—A SUDDEN INSULT!?
YOUR KIND EYES DON'T MATCH WITH WHAT YOUR TONGUE SAYS AT ALL.
I'M NOT VERY SMART, BUT...
...EVEN I KNOW WHAT MY DUTY IS.
EMILIA...
DON'T SPOIL ME. BELIEVE IN ME.
...NOT THAT I COME OFF VERY CONVINCING TODAY.
SURE YOU DO.
I'M WITH YOU FOR THE DO-OVER ALL THE WAY.

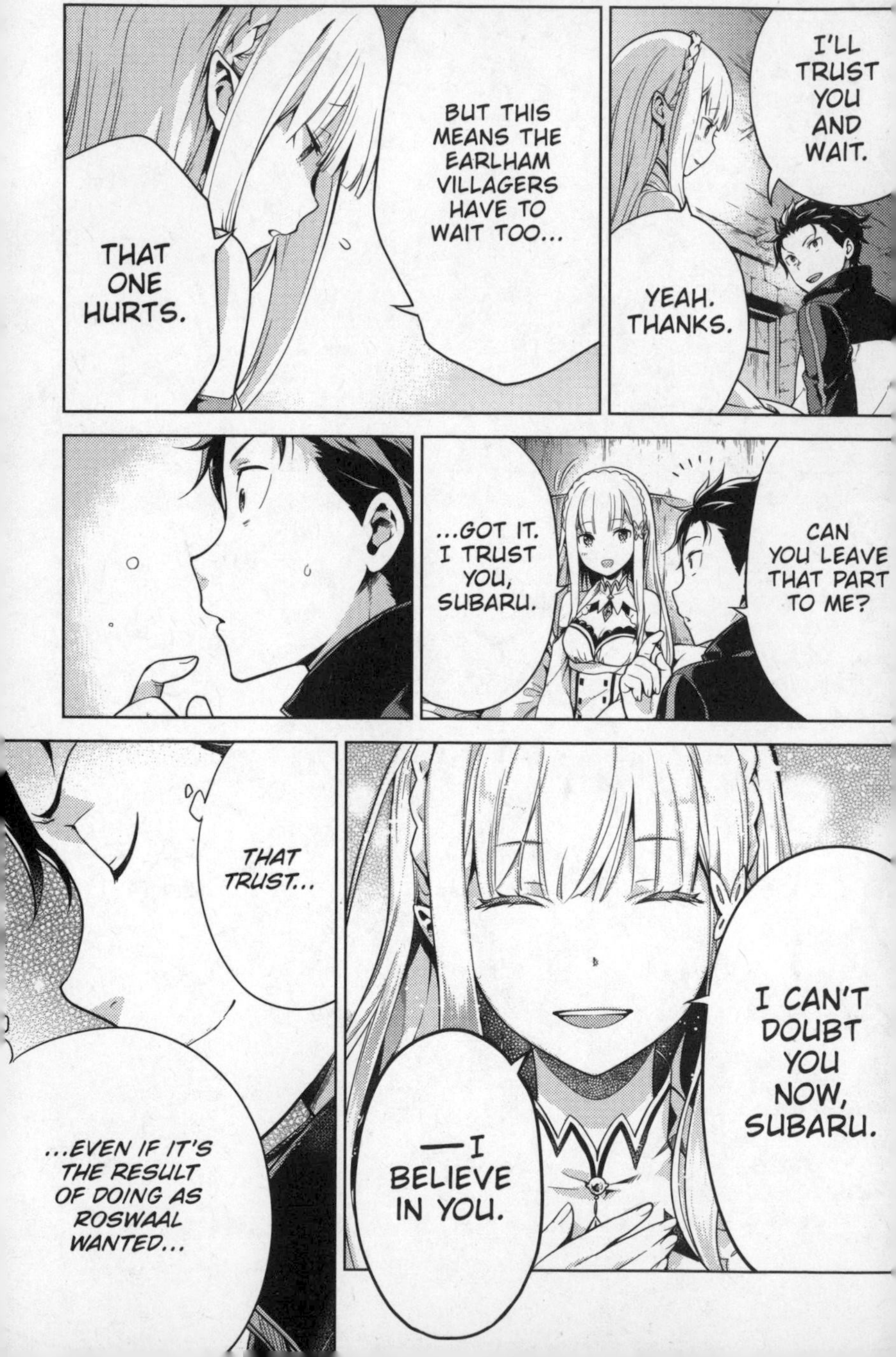
I'LL TRUST YOU AND WAIT.
YEAH. THANKS.
BUT THIS MEANS THE EARLHAM VILLAGERS HAVE TO WAIT TOO...
THAT ONE HURTS.
CAN YOU LEAVE THAT PART TO ME?
...GOT IT. I TRUST YOU, SUBARU.
I CAN'T DOUBT YOU NOW, SUBARU.
—I BELIEVE IN YOU.
THAT TRUST...
...EVEN IF IT'S THE RESULT OF DOING AS ROSWAAL WANTED...

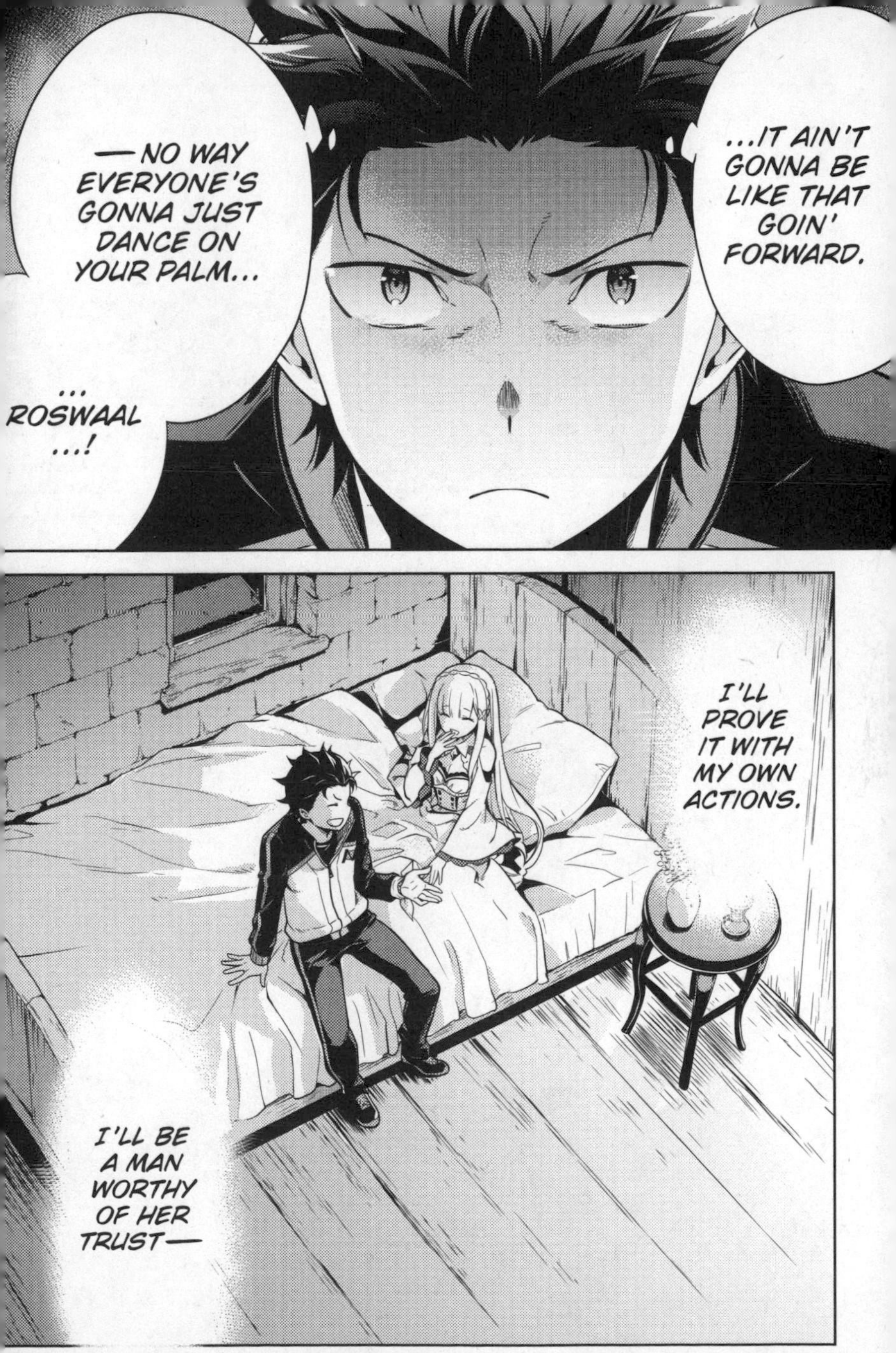
...IT AIN'T GONNA BE LIKE THAT GOIN' FORWARD.
—NO WAY EVERYONE'S GONNA JUST DANCE ON YOUR PALM...
... ROSWAAL ...!
I'LL PROVE IT WITH MY OWN ACTIONS.
I'LL BE A MAN WORTHY OF HER TRUST—

Episode 10
A New Loop

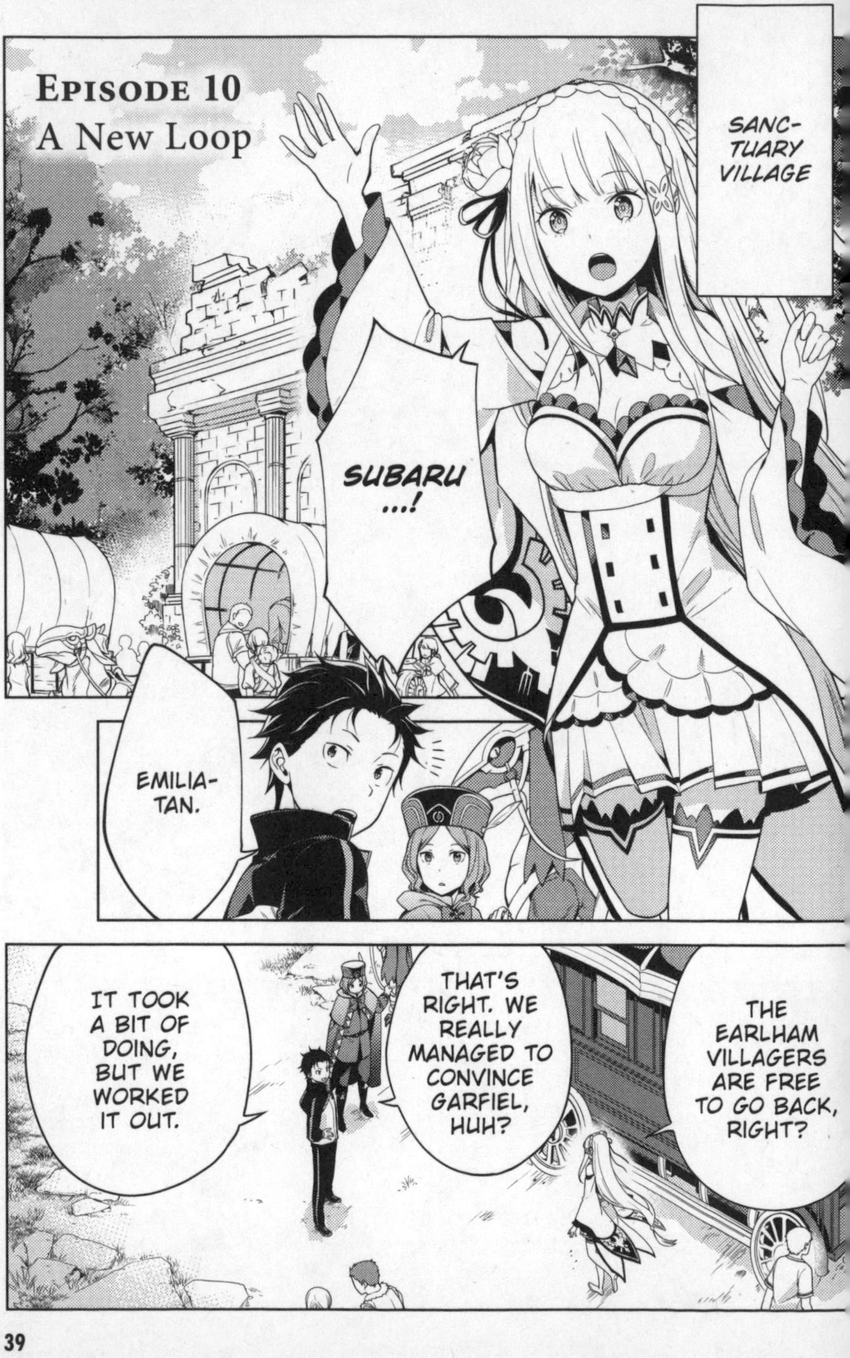
SANCTUARY VILLAGE
SUBARU ...!
EMILIA-TAN.
THE EARLHAM VILLAGERS ARE FREE TO GO BACK, RIGHT?
THAT'S RIGHT. WE REALLY MANAGED TO CONVINCE GARFIEL, HUH?
IT TOOK A BIT OF DOING, BUT WE WORKED IT OUT.

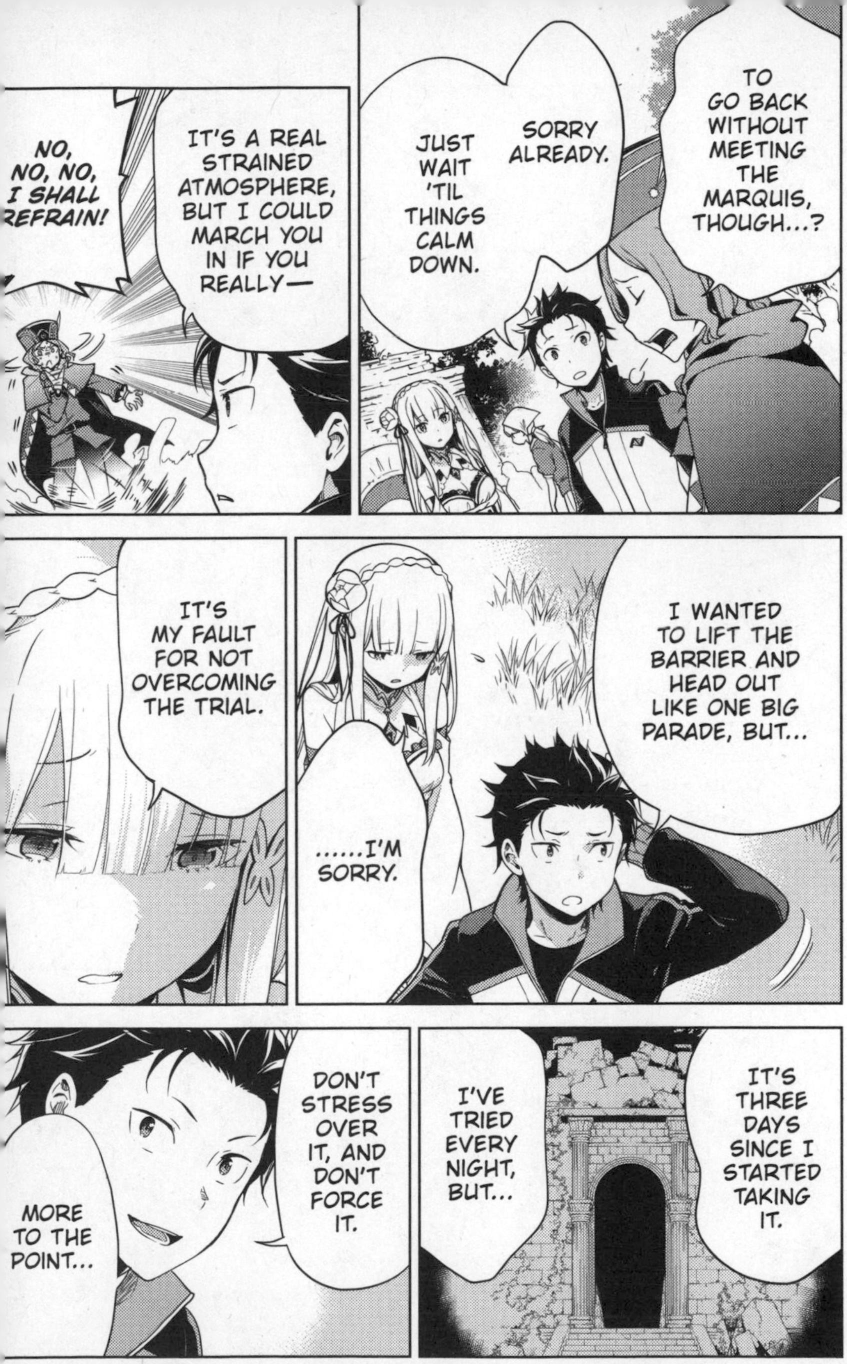
TO GO BACK WITHOUT MEETING THE MARQUIS, THOUGH...?
SORRY ALREADY.
JUST WAIT 'TIL THINGS CALM DOWN.
IT'S A REAL STRAINED ATMOSPHERE, BUT I COULD MARCH YOU IN IF YOU REALLY—
NO, NO, NO, I SHALL REFRAIN!
I WANTED TO LIFT THE BARRIER AND HEAD OUT LIKE ONE BIG PARADE, BUT...
......I'M SORRY.
IT'S MY FAULT FOR NOT OVERCOMING THE TRIAL.
IT'S THREE DAYS SINCE I STARTED TAKING IT.
I'VE TRIED EVERY NIGHT, BUT...
DON'T STRESS OVER IT, AND DON'T FORCE IT.
MORE TO THE POINT...

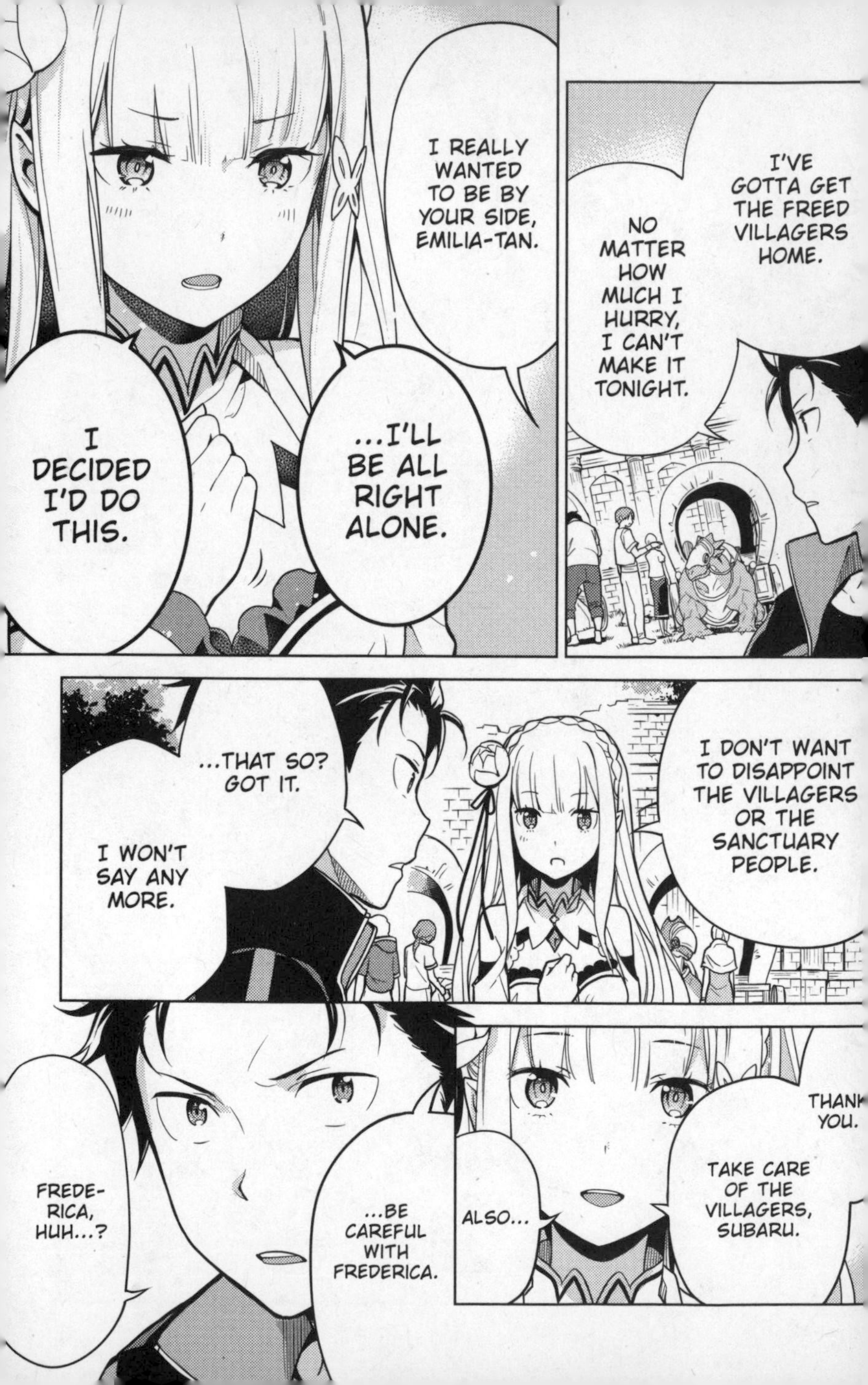
I'VE GOTTA GET THE FREED VILLAGERS HOME.
NO MATTER HOW MUCH I HURRY, I CAN'T MAKE IT TONIGHT.
I REALLY WANTED TO BE BY YOUR SIDE, EMILIA-TAN.
...I'LL BE ALL RIGHT ALONE.
I DECIDED I'D DO THIS.
I DON'T WANT TO DISAPPOINT THE VILLAGERS OR THE SANCTUARY PEOPLE.
...THAT SO? GOT IT.
I WON'T SAY ANY MORE.
THANK YOU.
TAKE CARE OF THE VILLAGERS, SUBARU.
ALSO...
...BE CAREFUL WITH FREDERICA.
FREDERICA, HUH...?

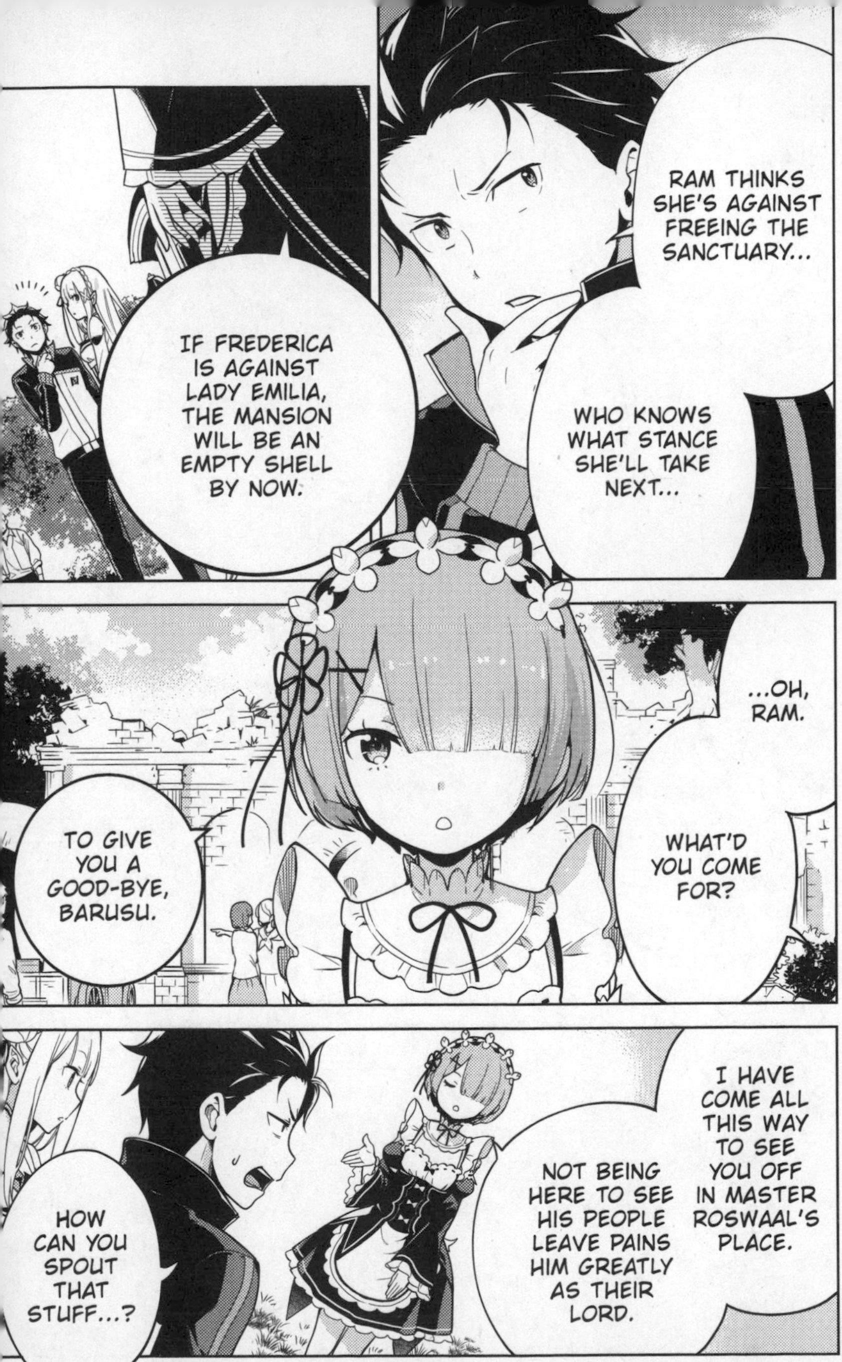
RAM THINKS SHE'S AGAINST FREEING THE SANCTUARY...
WHO KNOWS WHAT STANCE SHE'LL TAKE NEXT...
IF FREDERICA IS AGAINST LADY EMILIA, THE MANSION WILL BE AN EMPTY SHELL BY NOW.
...OH, RAM.
WHAT'D YOU COME FOR?
TO GIVE YOU A GOOD-BYE, BARUSU.
I HAVE COME ALL THIS WAY TO SEE YOU OFF IN MASTER ROSWAAL'S PLACE.
NOT BEING HERE TO SEE HIS PEOPLE LEAVE PAINS HIM GREATLY AS THEIR LORD.
HOW CAN YOU SPOUT THAT STUFF...?

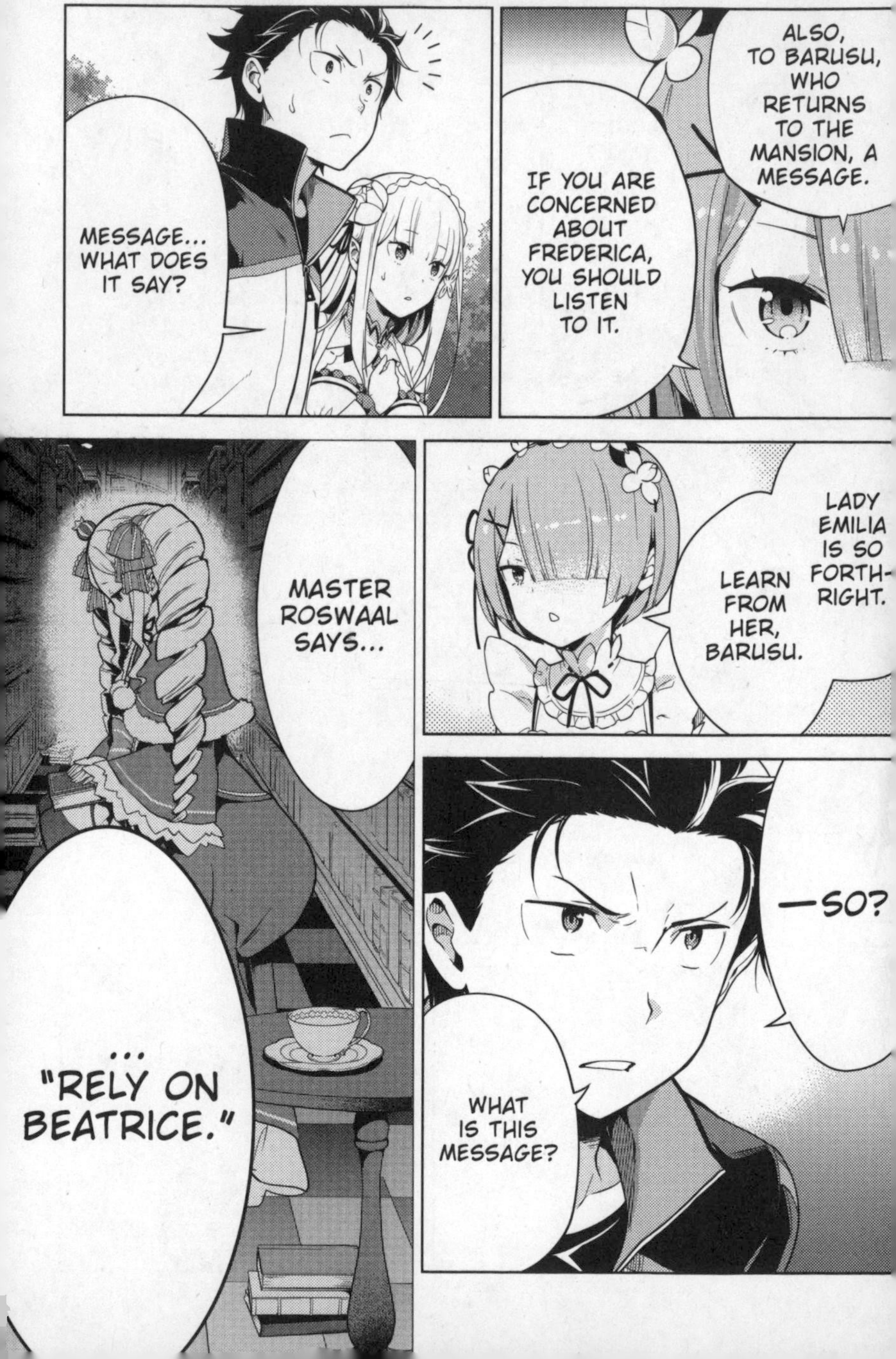
ALSO, TO BARUSU, WHO RETURNS TO THE MANSION, A MESSAGE.
IF YOU ARE CONCERNED ABOUT FREDERICA, YOU SHOULD LISTEN TO IT.
MESSAGE... WHAT DOES IT SAY?
LADY EMILIA IS SO FORTH-RIGHT.
LEARN FROM HER, BARUSU.
—SO?
WHAT IS THIS MESSAGE?
MASTER ROSWAAL SAYS...
... "RELY ON BEATRICE."

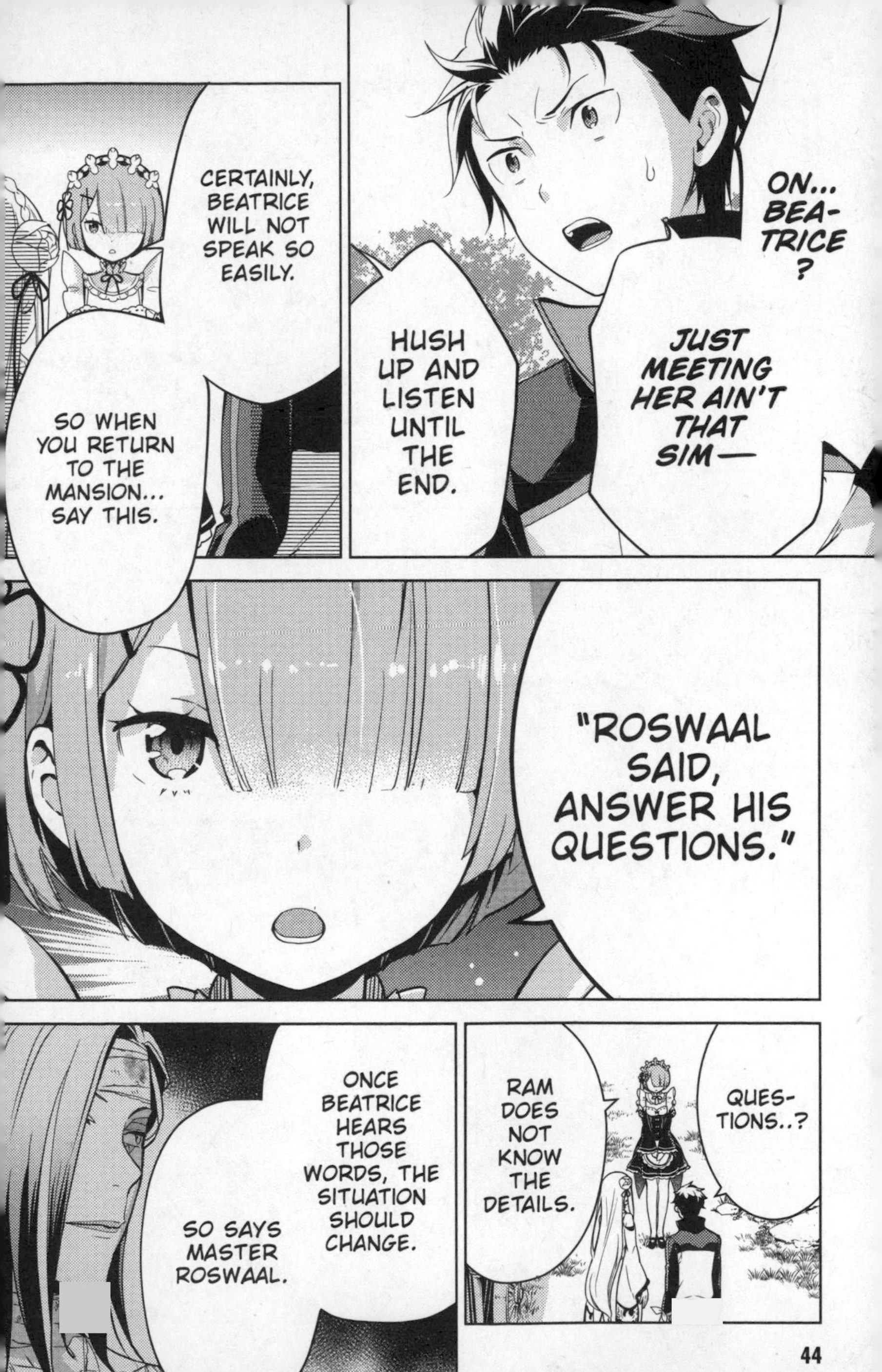
ON... BEA-TRICE?
JUST MEETING HER AIN'T THAT SIM—
HUSH UP AND LISTEN UNTIL THE END.
CERTAINLY, BEATRICE WILL NOT SPEAK SO EASILY.
SO WHEN YOU RETURN TO THE MANSION... SAY THIS.
"ROSWAAL SAID, ANSWER HIS QUESTIONS."
QUES-TIONS..?
RAM DOES NOT KNOW THE DETAILS.
ONCE BEATRICE HEARS THOSE WORDS, THE SITUATION SHOULD CHANGE.
SO SAYS MASTER ROSWAAL.

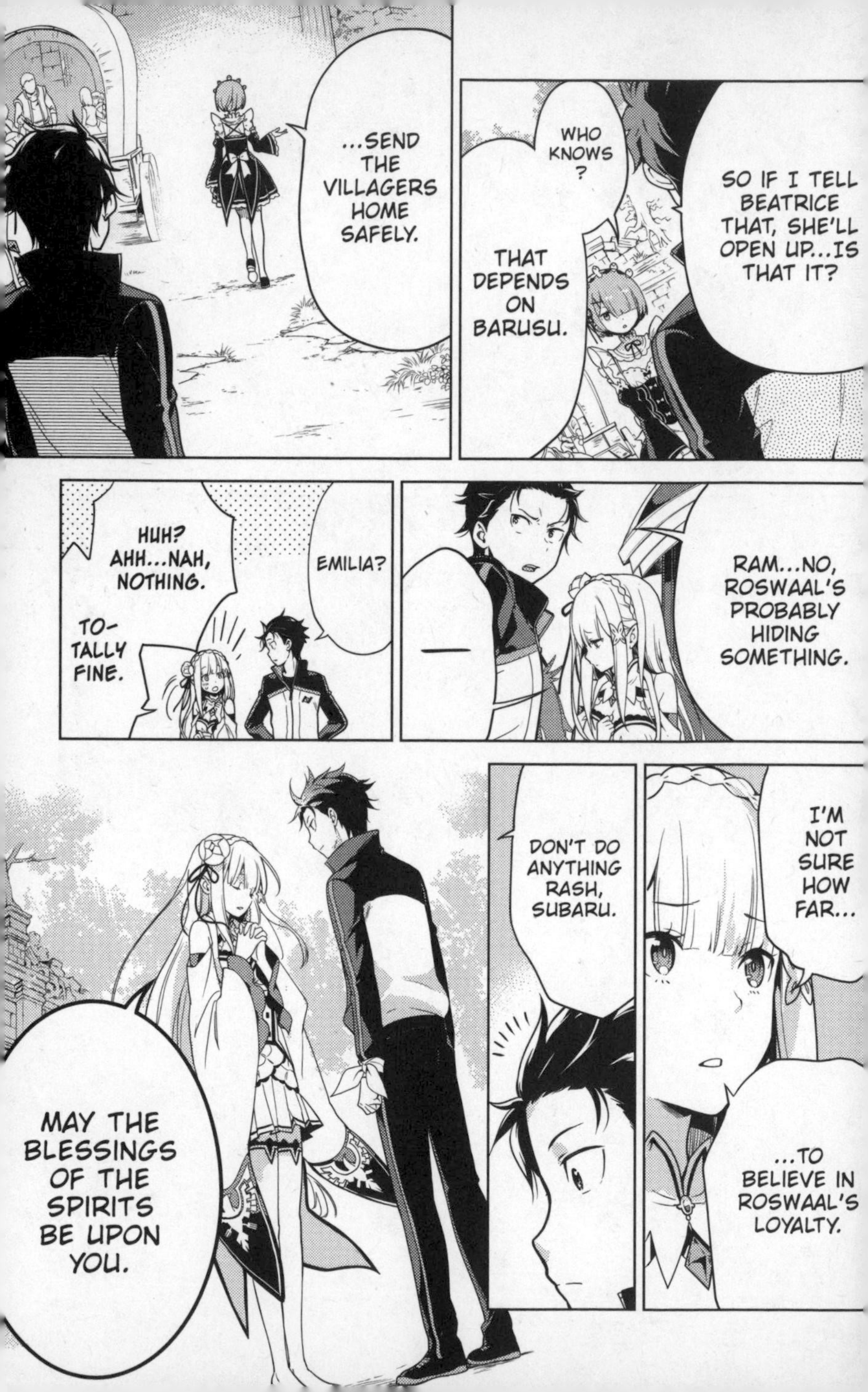
SO IF I TELL BEATRICE THAT, SHE'LL OPEN UP...IS THAT IT?
WHO KNOWS?
THAT DEPENDS ON BARUSU.
...SEND THE VILLAGERS HOME SAFELY.
RAM...NO, ROSWAAL'S PROBABLY HIDING SOMETHING.
—
EMILIA?
HUH? AHH...NAH, NOTHING.
TO-TALLY FINE.
I'M NOT SURE HOW FAR...
...TO BELIEVE IN ROSWAAL'S LOYALTY.
DON'T DO ANYTHING RASH, SUBARU.
MAY THE BLESSINGS OF THE SPIRITS BE UPON YOU.

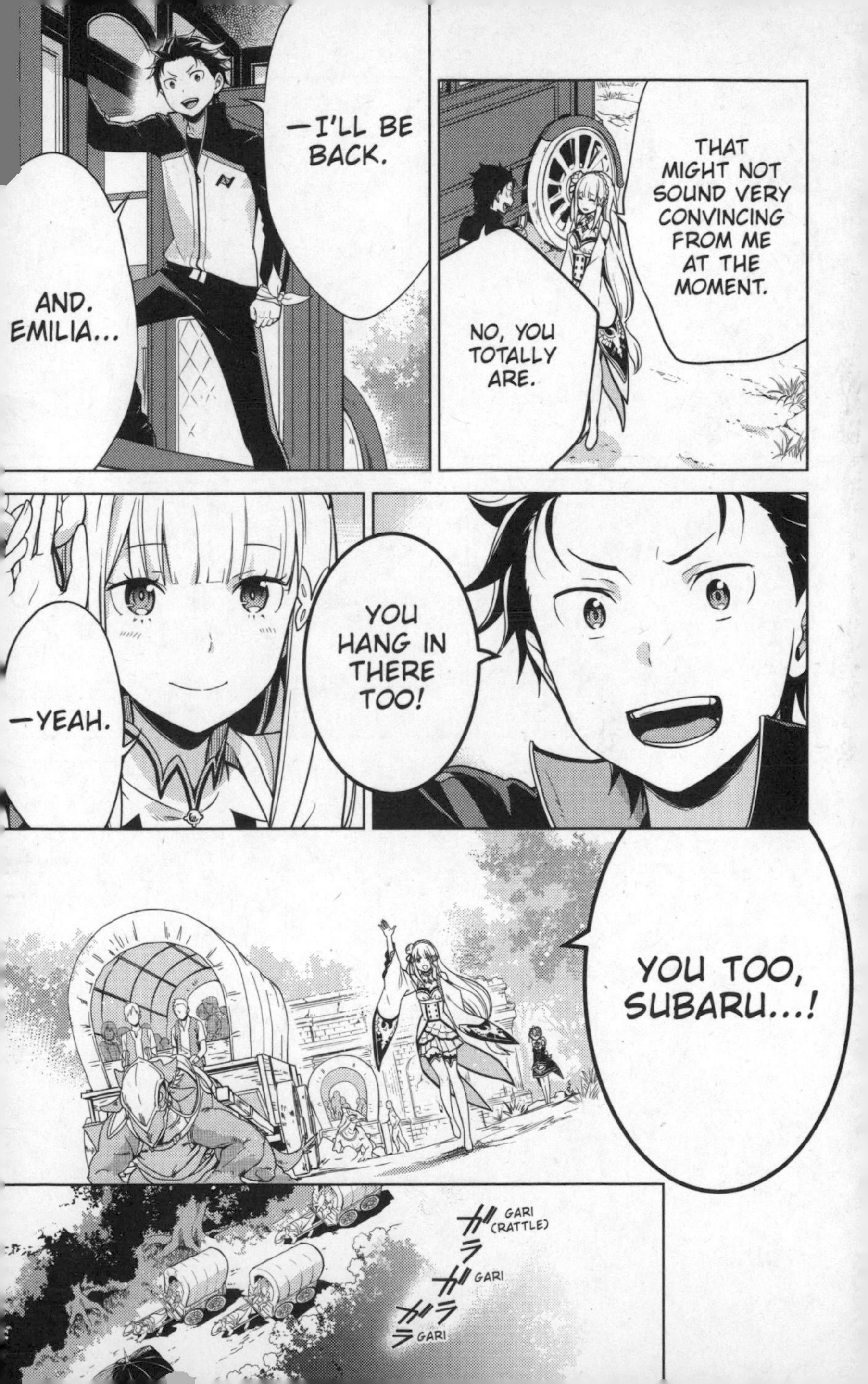
THAT MIGHT NOT SOUND VERY CONVINCING FROM ME AT THE MOMENT.
NO, YOU TOTALLY ARE.
—I'LL BE BACK.
AND. EMILIA...
YOU HANG IN THERE TOO!
—YEAH.
YOU TOO, SUBARU...!
GARI (RATTLE)
GARI
GARI

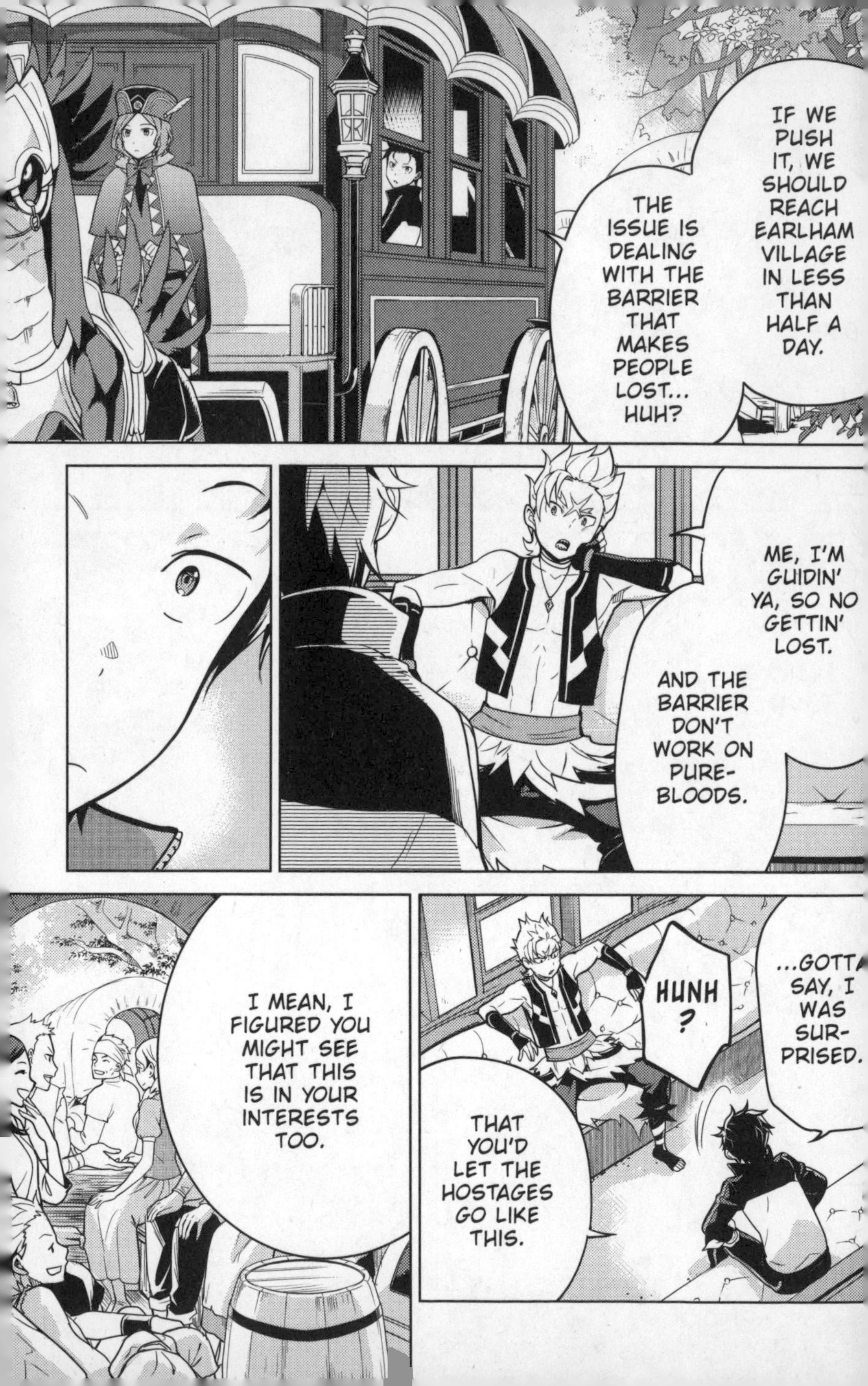
IF WE PUSH IT, WE SHOULD REACH EARLHAM VILLAGE IN LESS THAN HALF A DAY.
THE ISSUE IS DEALING WITH THE BARRIER THAT MAKES PEOPLE LOST... HUH?
ME, I'M GUIDIN' YA, SO NO GETTIN' LOST.
AND THE BARRIER DON'T WORK ON PURE-BLOODS.
...GOTTA SAY, I WAS SURPRISED.
HUNH?
THAT YOU'D LET THE HOSTAGES GO LIKE THIS.
I MEAN, I FIGURED YOU MIGHT SEE THAT THIS IS IN YOUR INTERESTS TOO.

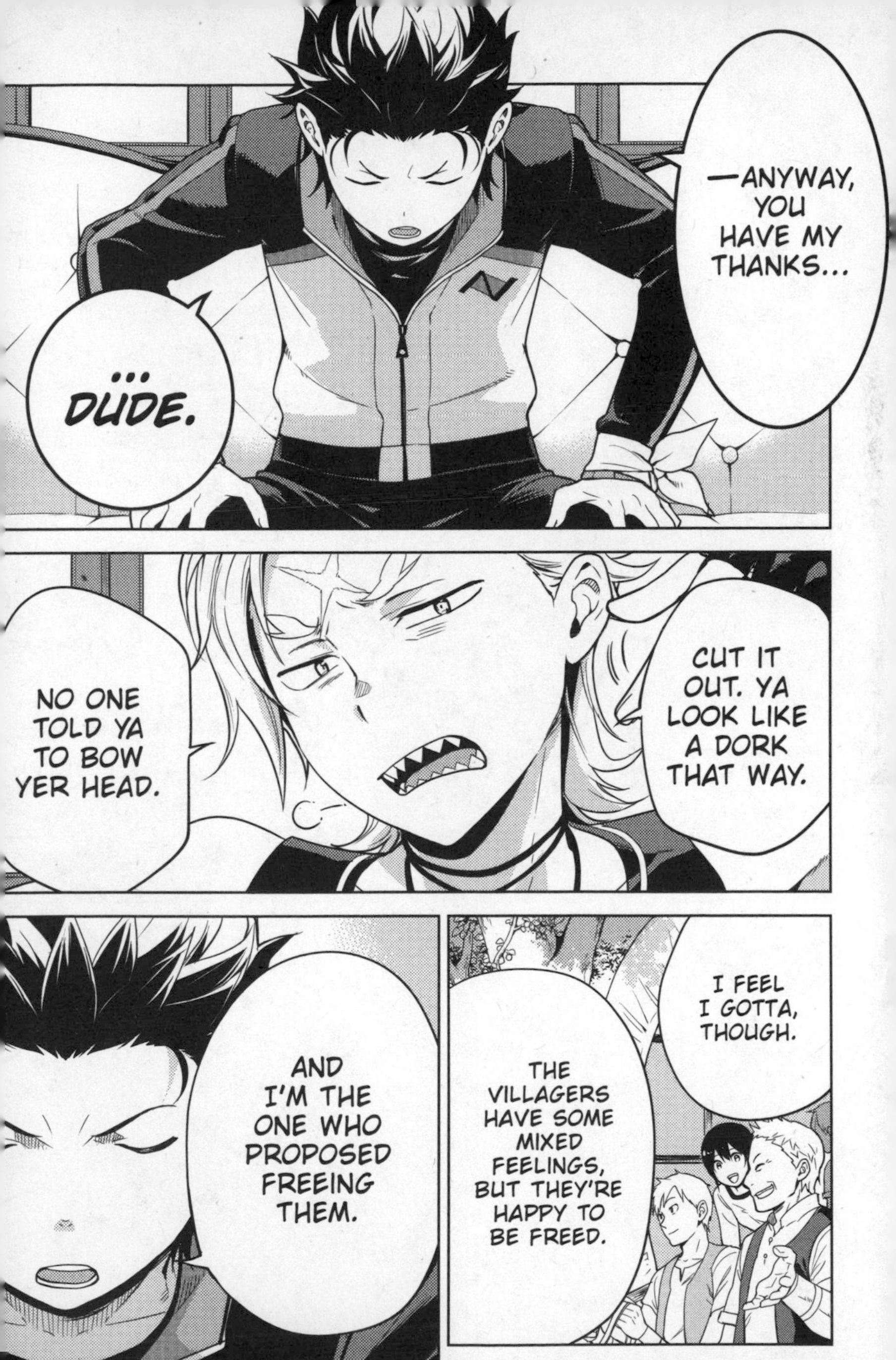
—ANYWAY, YOU HAVE MY THANKS...
... DUDE.
CUT IT OUT. YA LOOK LIKE A DORK THAT WAY.
NO ONE TOLD YA TO BOW YER HEAD.
I FEEL I GOTTA, THOUGH.
THE VILLAGERS HAVE SOME MIXED FEELINGS, BUT THEY'RE HAPPY TO BE FREED.
AND I'M THE ONE WHO PROPOSED FREEING THEM.

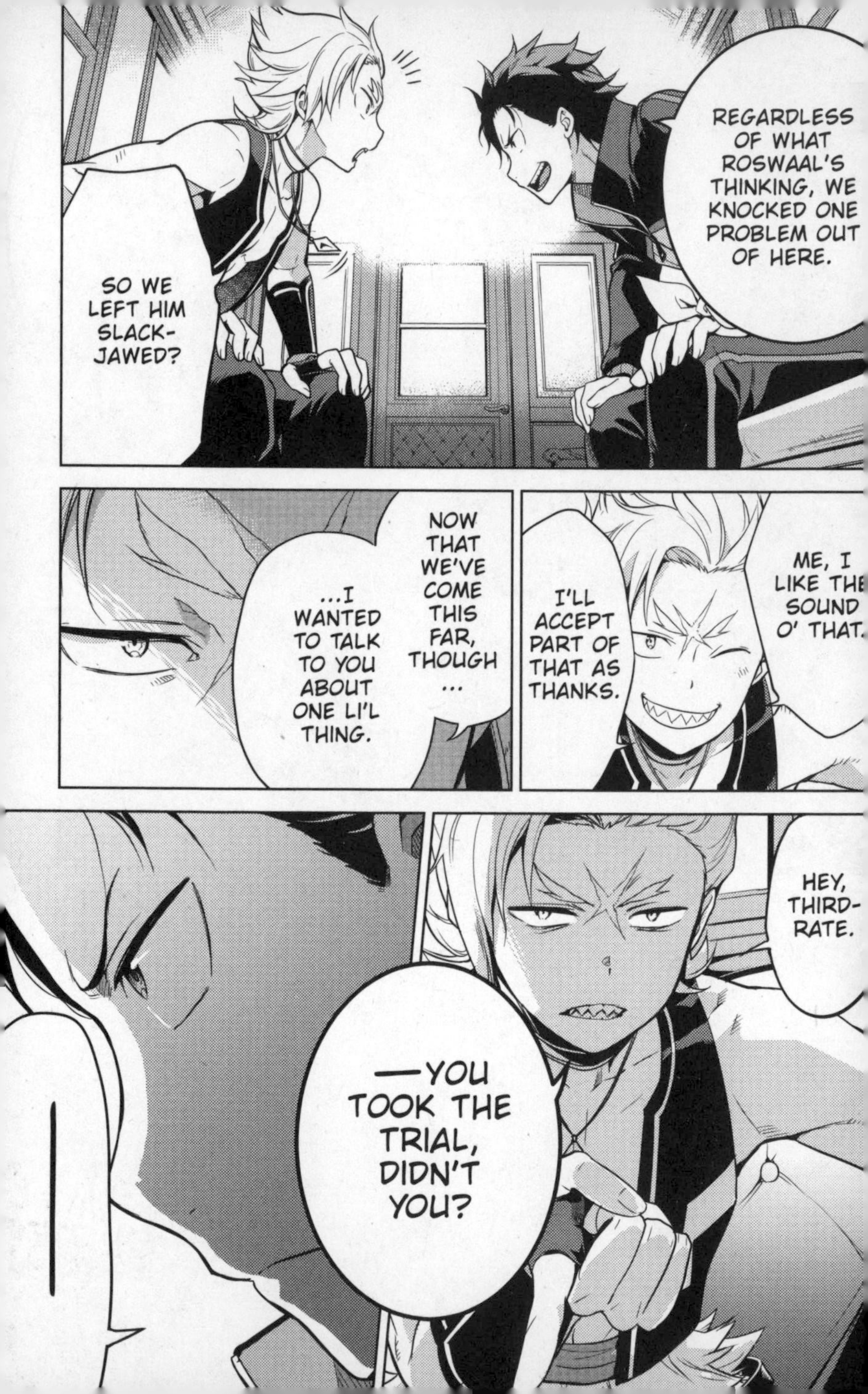
REGARDLESS OF WHAT ROSWAAL'S THINKING, WE KNOCKED ONE PROBLEM OUT OF HERE.
SO WE LEFT HIM SLACK-JAWED?
ME, I LIKE THE SOUND O' THAT.
I'LL ACCEPT PART OF THAT AS THANKS.
NOW THAT WE'VE COME THIS FAR, THOUGH...
...I WANTED TO TALK TO YOU ABOUT ONE LI'L THING.
HEY, THIRD-RATE.
—YOU TOOK THE TRIAL, DIDN'T YOU?

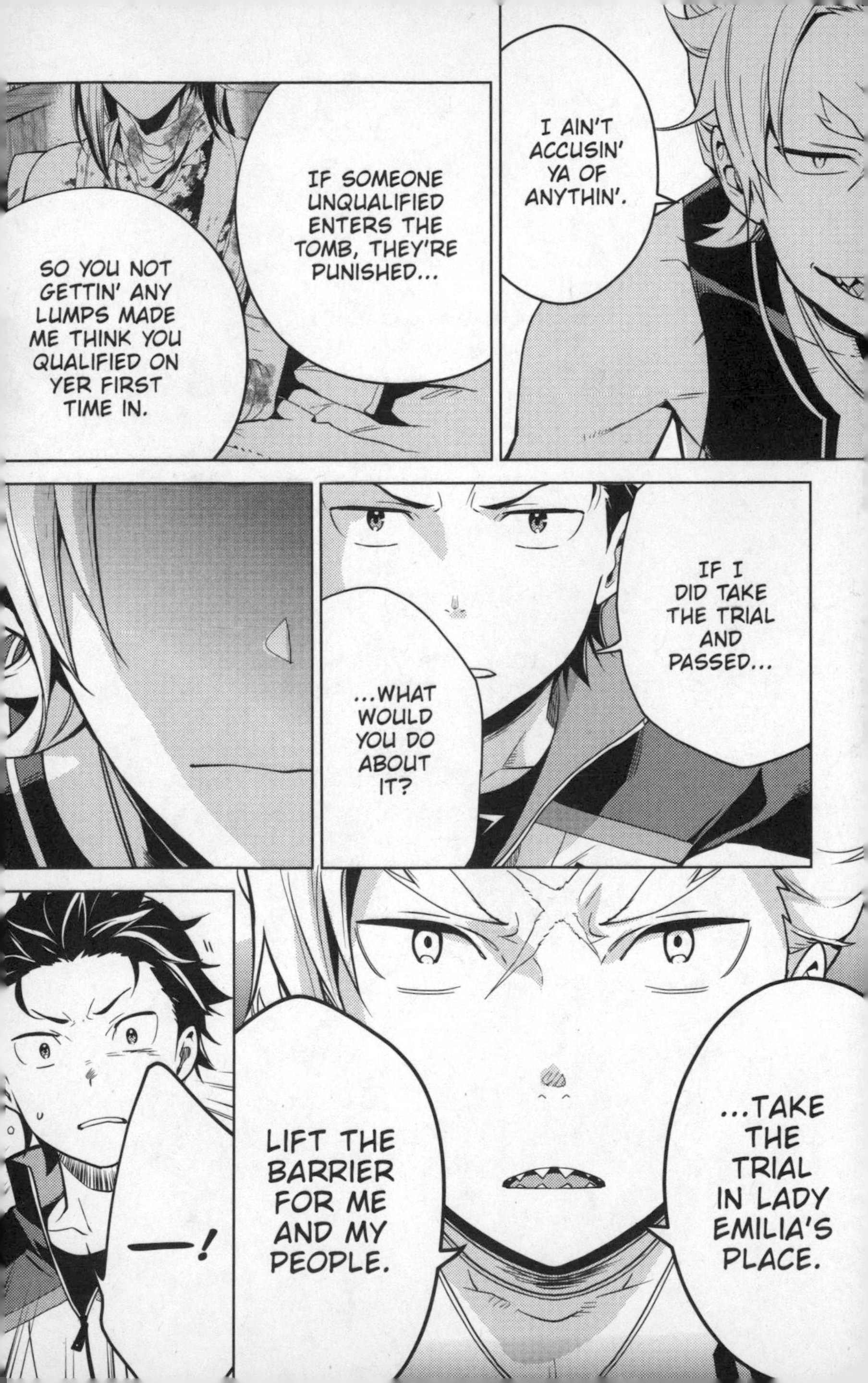
I AIN'T ACCUSIN' YA OF ANYTHIN'.
IF SOMEONE UNQUALIFIED ENTERS THE TOMB, THEY'RE PUNISHED...
SO YOU NOT GETTIN' ANY LUMPS MADE ME THINK YOU QUALIFIED ON YER FIRST TIME IN.
IF I DID TAKE THE TRIAL AND PASSED...
...WHAT WOULD YOU DO ABOUT IT?
...TAKE THE TRIAL IN LADY EMILIA'S PLACE.
LIFT THE BARRIER FOR ME AND MY PEOPLE.
—!

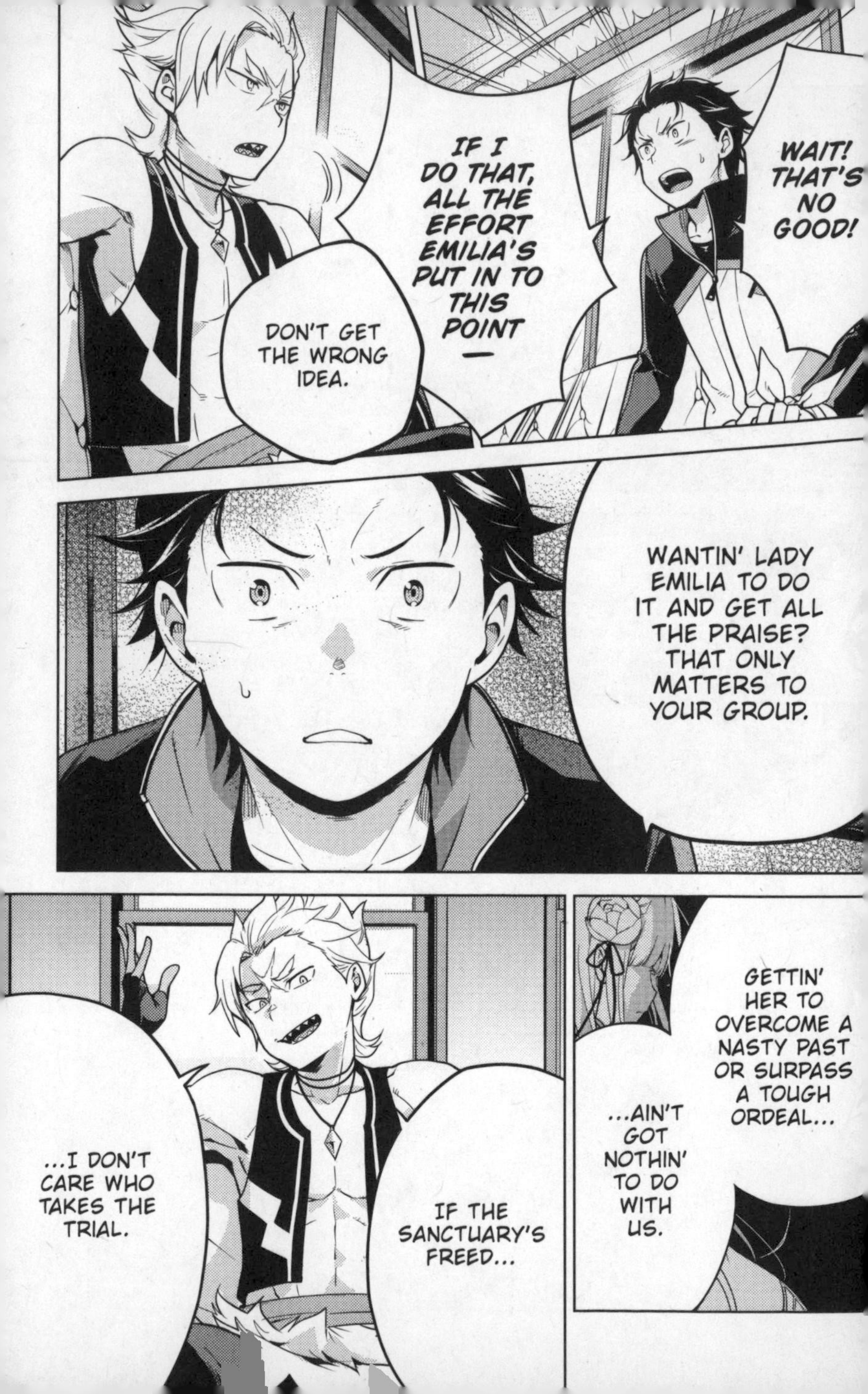
WAIT! THAT'S NO GOOD!
IF I DO THAT, ALL THE EFFORT EMILIA'S PUT IN TO THIS POINT —
DON'T GET THE WRONG IDEA.
WANTIN' LADY EMILIA TO DO IT AND GET ALL THE PRAISE? THAT ONLY MATTERS TO YOUR GROUP.
GETTIN' HER TO OVERCOME A NASTY PAST OR SURPASS A TOUGH ORDEAL...
...AIN'T GOT NOTHIN' TO DO WITH US.
IF THE SANCTUARY'S FREED...
...I DON'T CARE WHO TAKES THE TRIAL.

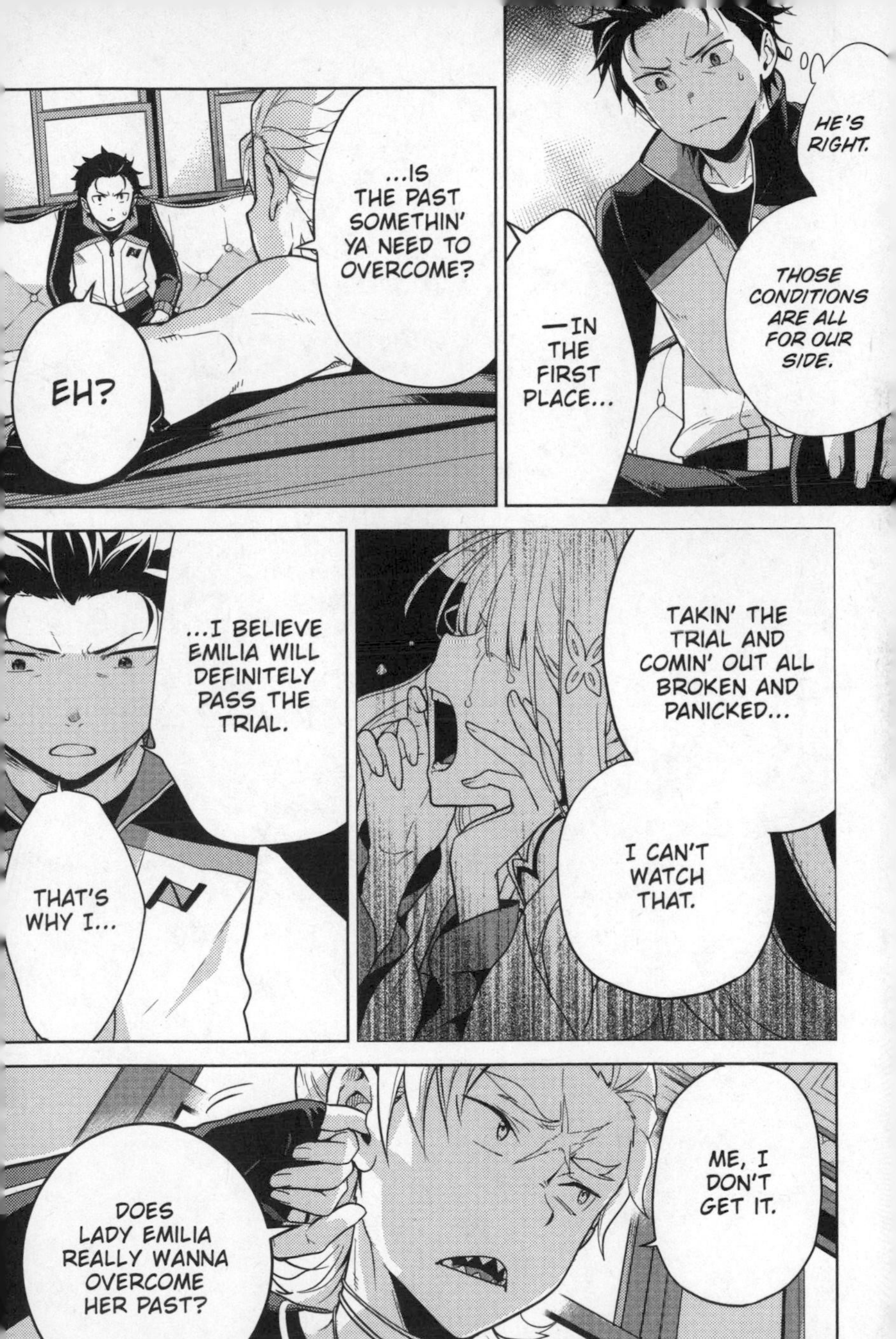
HE'S RIGHT.
THOSE CONDITIONS ARE ALL FOR OUR SIDE.
—IN THE FIRST PLACE...
...IS THE PAST SOMETHIN' YA NEED TO OVERCOME?
EH?
TAKIN' THE TRIAL AND COMIN' OUT ALL BROKEN AND PANICKED...
I CAN'T WATCH THAT.
...I BELIEVE EMILIA WILL DEFINITELY PASS THE TRIAL.
THAT'S WHY I...
ME, I DON'T GET IT.
DOES LADY EMILIA REALLY WANNA OVERCOME HER PAST?

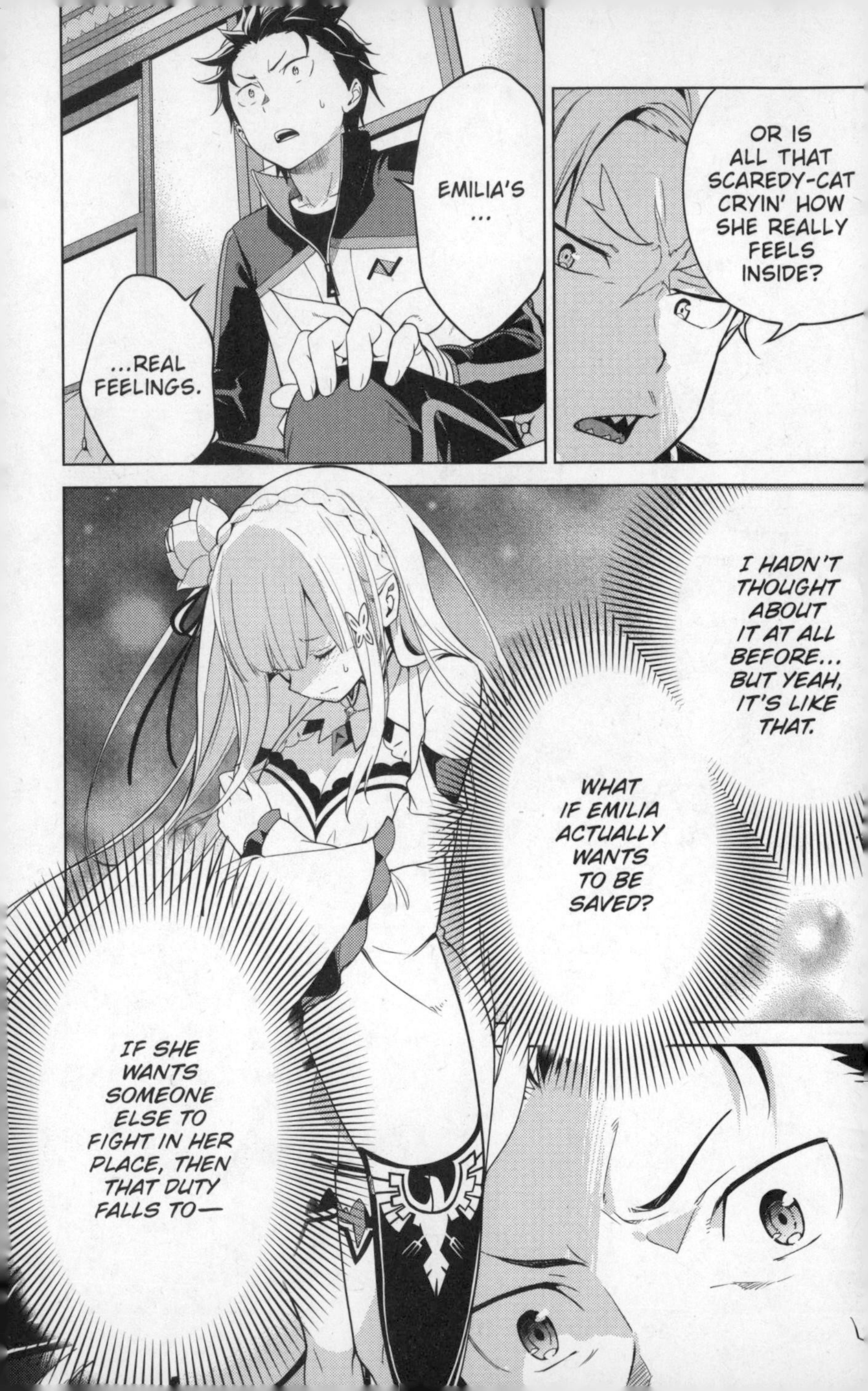
OR IS ALL THAT SCAREDY-CAT CRYIN' HOW SHE REALLY FEELS INSIDE?
EMILIA'S ...
...REAL FEELINGS.
I HADN'T THOUGHT ABOUT IT AT ALL BEFORE... BUT YEAH, IT'S LIKE THAT.
WHAT IF EMILIA ACTUALLY WANTS TO BE SAVED?
IF SHE WANTS SOMEONE ELSE TO FIGHT IN HER PLACE, THEN THAT DUTY FALLS TO—

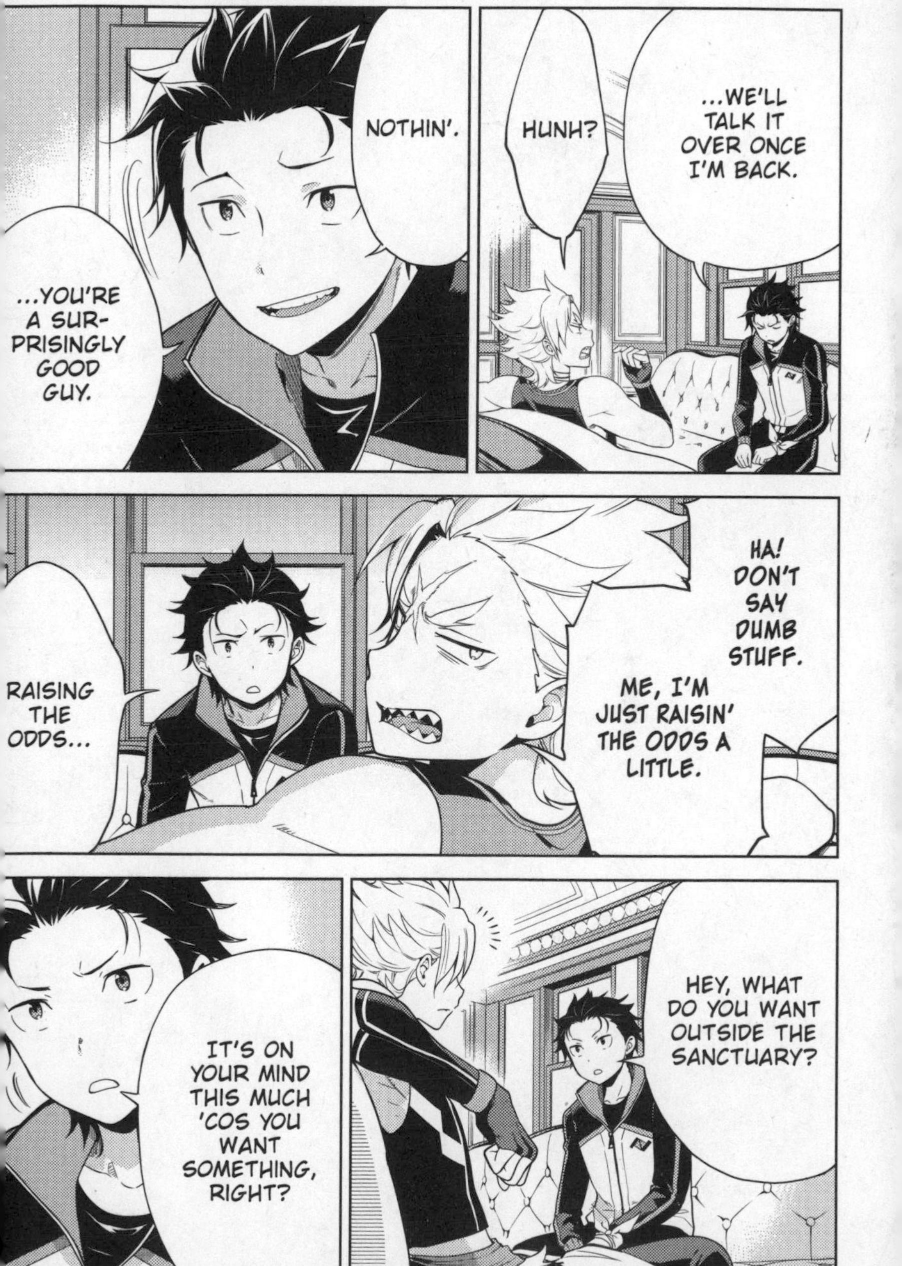
...WE'LL TALK IT OVER ONCE I'M BACK.
HUNH?
NOTHIN'.
...YOU'RE A SUR-PRISINGLY GOOD GUY.
HA! DON'T SAY DUMB STUFF.
ME, I'M JUST RAISIN' THE ODDS A LITTLE.
RAISING THE ODDS...
HEY, WHAT DO YOU WANT OUTSIDE THE SANCTUARY?
IT'S ON YOUR MIND THIS MUCH 'COS YOU WANT SOMETHING, RIGHT?

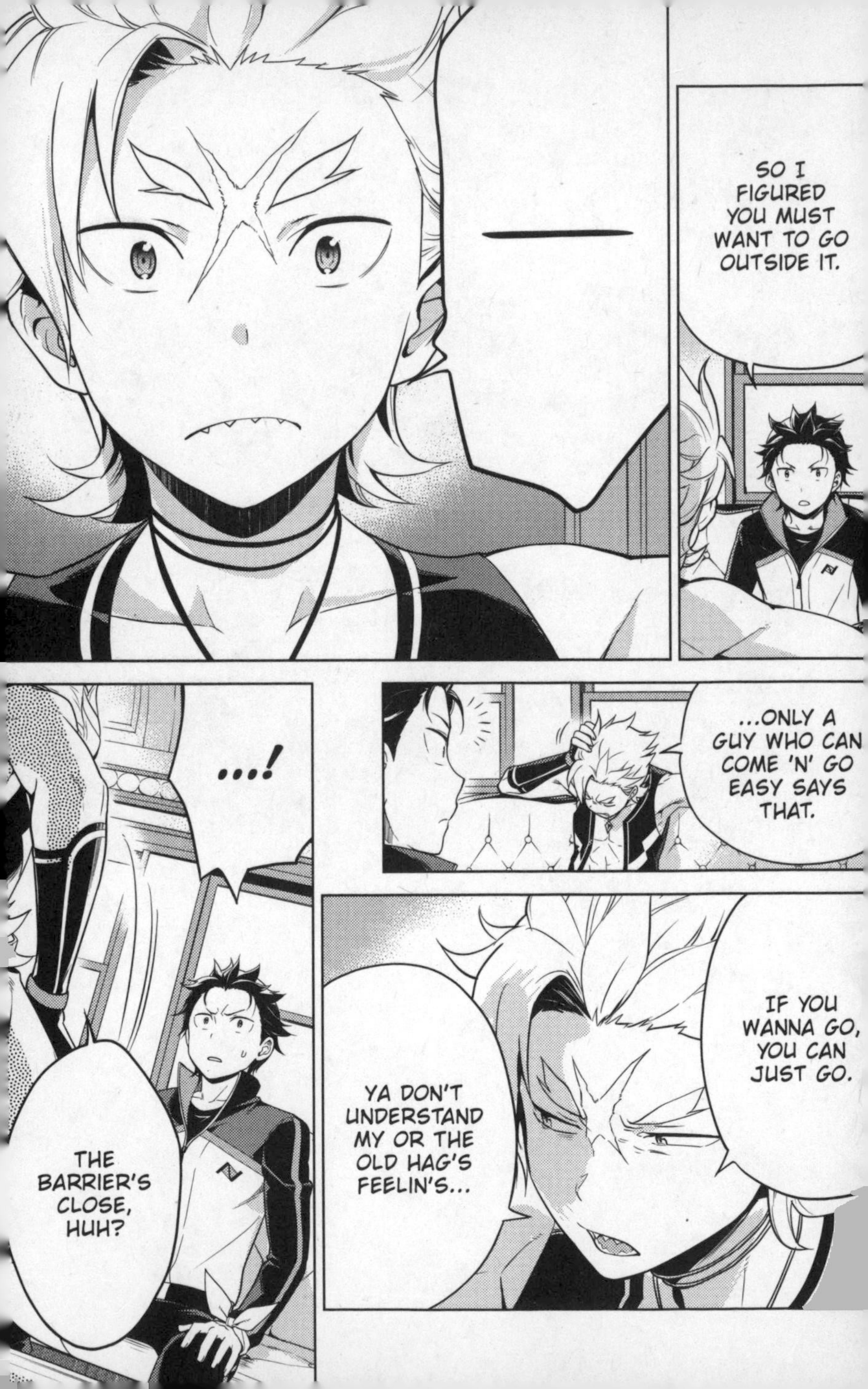
SO I FIGURED YOU MUST WANT TO GO OUTSIDE IT.
—
...ONLY A GUY WHO CAN COME 'N' GO EASY SAYS THAT.
...!
IF YOU WANNA GO, YOU CAN JUST GO.
YA DON'T UNDERSTAND MY OR THE OLD HAG'S FEELIN'S...
THE BARRIER'S CLOSE, HUH?

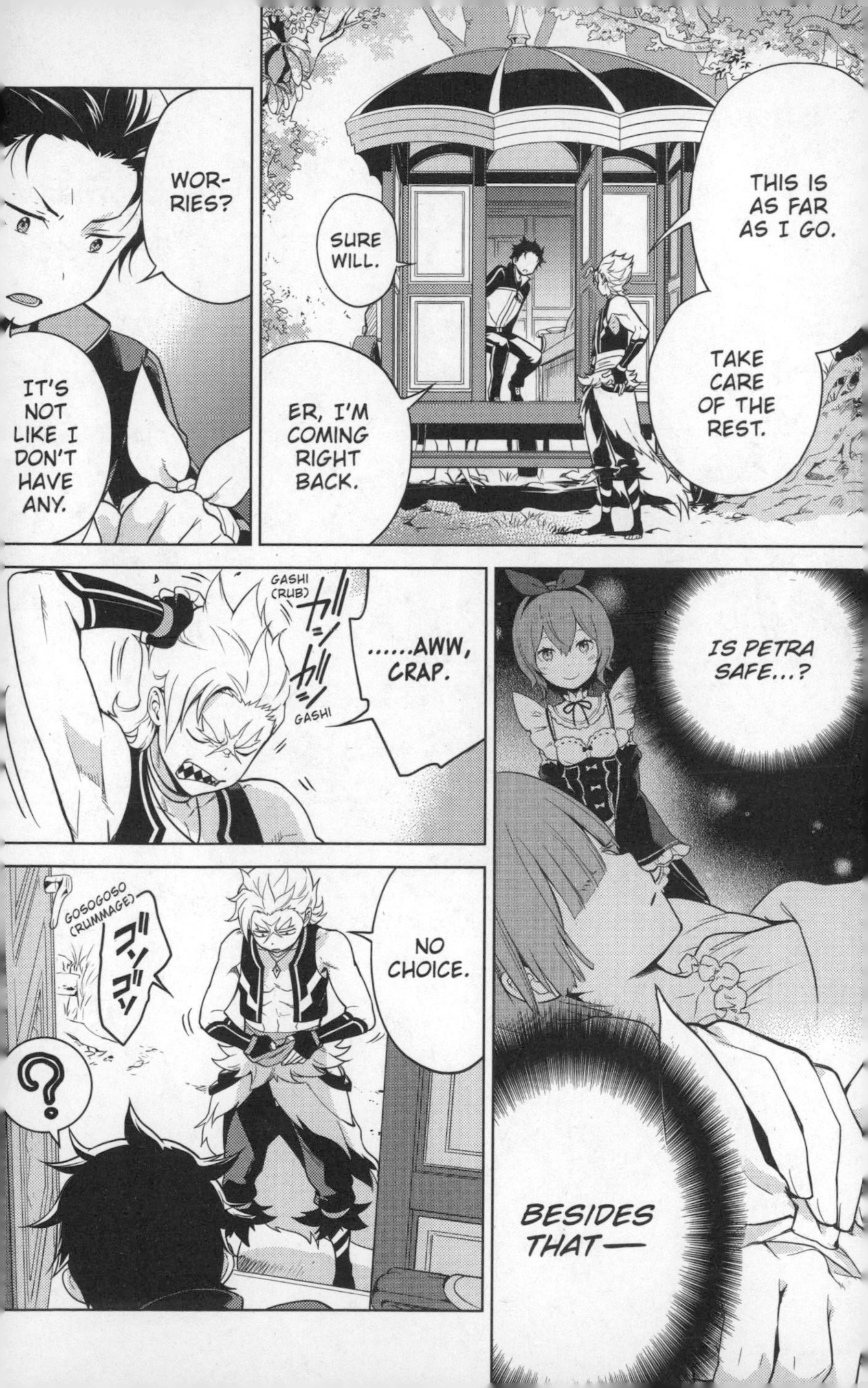
THIS IS AS FAR AS I GO.
TAKE CARE OF THE REST.
SURE WILL.
ER, I'M COMING RIGHT BACK.
WOR-RIES?
IT'S NOT LIKE I DON'T HAVE ANY.
IS PETRA SAFE...?
BESIDES THAT—
GASHI (RUB)
GASHI
......AWW, CRAP.
NO CHOICE.
GOSOGOSO (RUMMAGE)
?

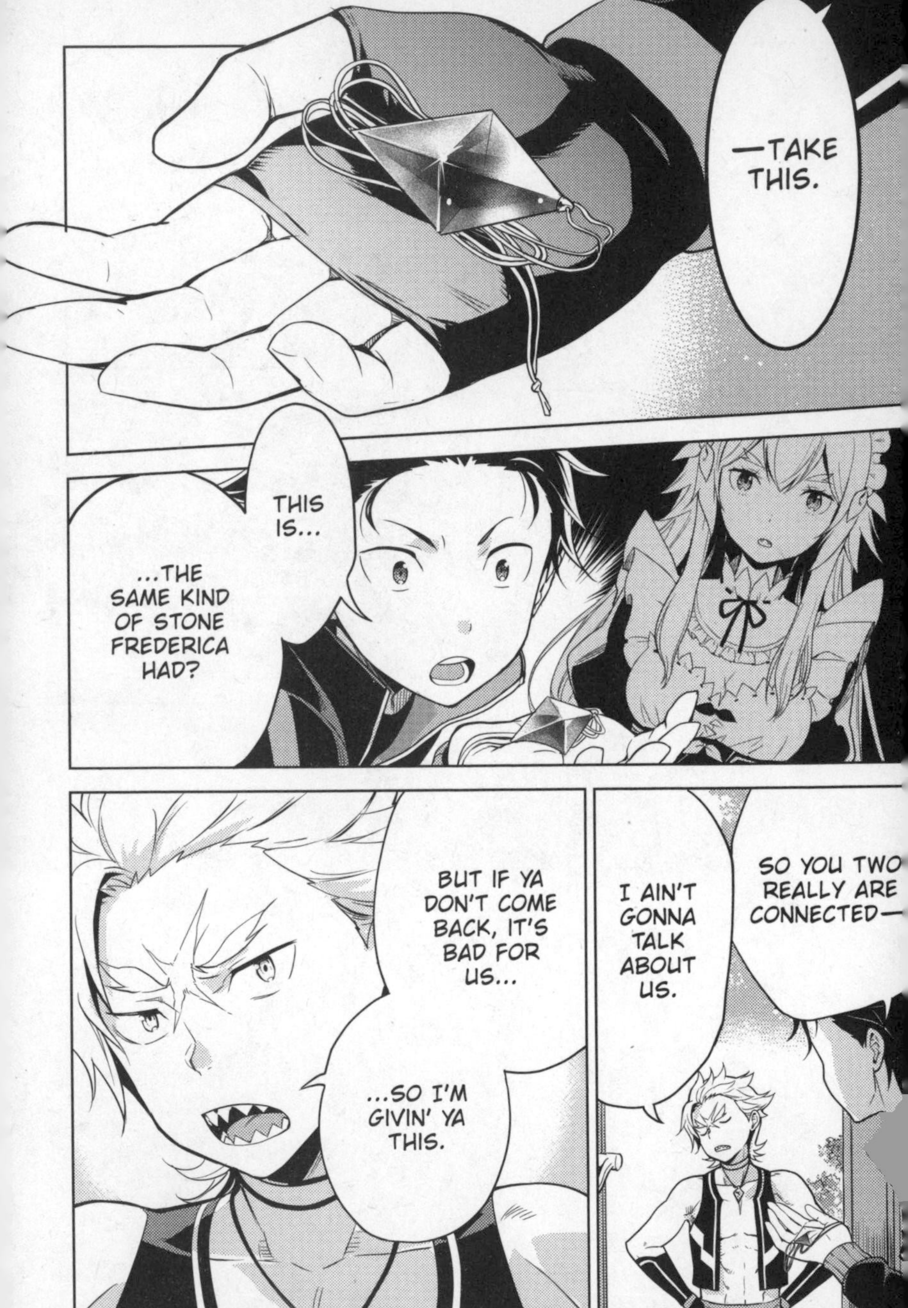
—TAKE THIS.
THIS IS...
...THE SAME KIND OF STONE FREDERICA HAD?
SO YOU TWO REALLY ARE CONNECTED—
I AIN'T GONNA TALK ABOUT US.
BUT IF YA DON'T COME BACK, IT'S BAD FOR US...
...SO I'M GIVIN' YA THIS.

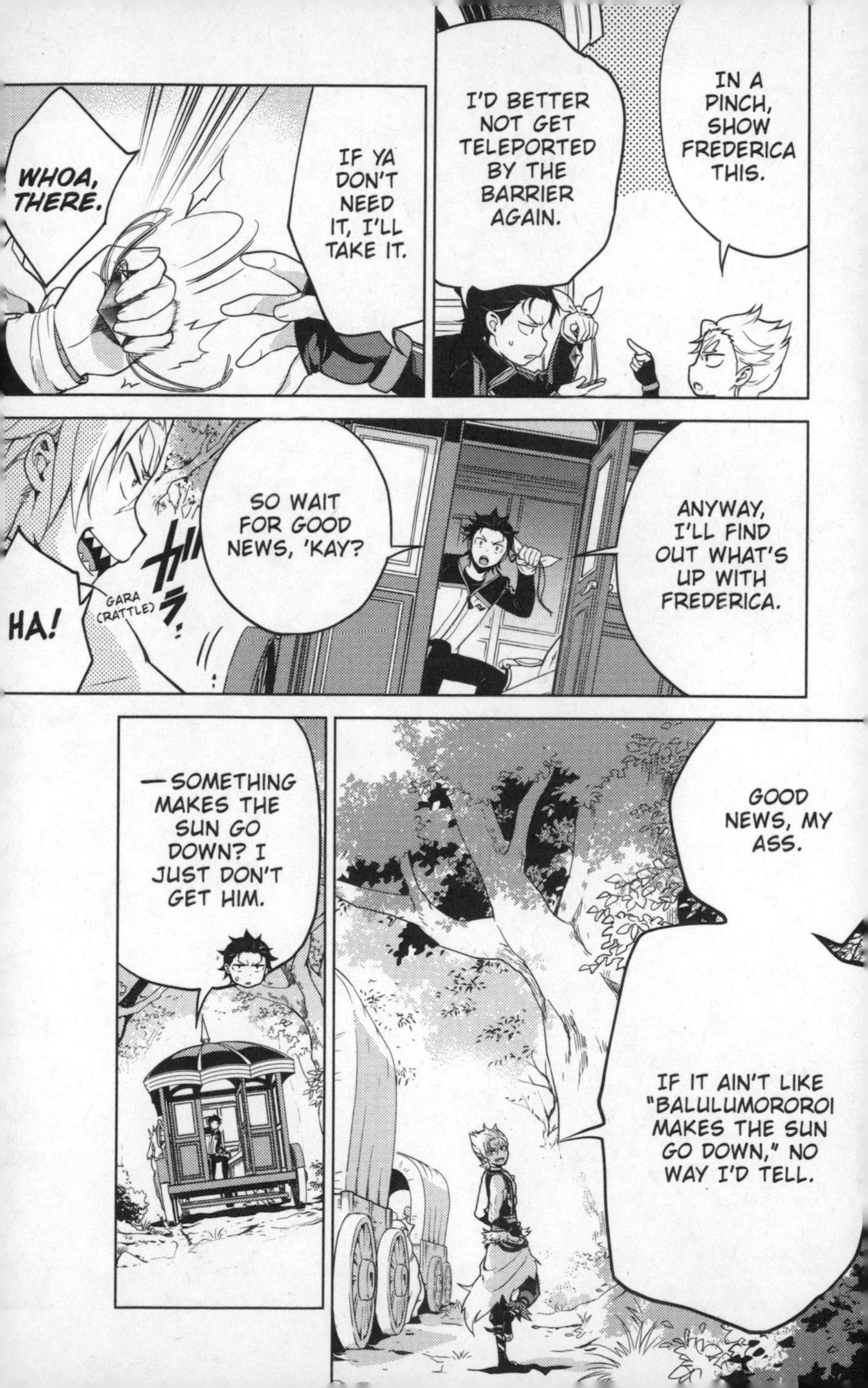
IN A PINCH, SHOW FREDERICA THIS.
I'D BETTER NOT GET TELEPORTED BY THE BARRIER AGAIN.
IF YA DON'T NEED IT, I'LL TAKE IT.
WHOA, THERE.
ANYWAY, I'LL FIND OUT WHAT'S UP WITH FREDERICA.
SO WAIT FOR GOOD NEWS, 'KAY?
GARA (RATTLE)
HA!
GOOD NEWS, MY ASS.
IF IT AIN'T LIKE "BALULUMOROROI MAKES THE SUN GO DOWN," NO WAY I'D TELL.
—SOMETHING MAKES THE SUN GO DOWN? I JUST DON'T GET HIM.

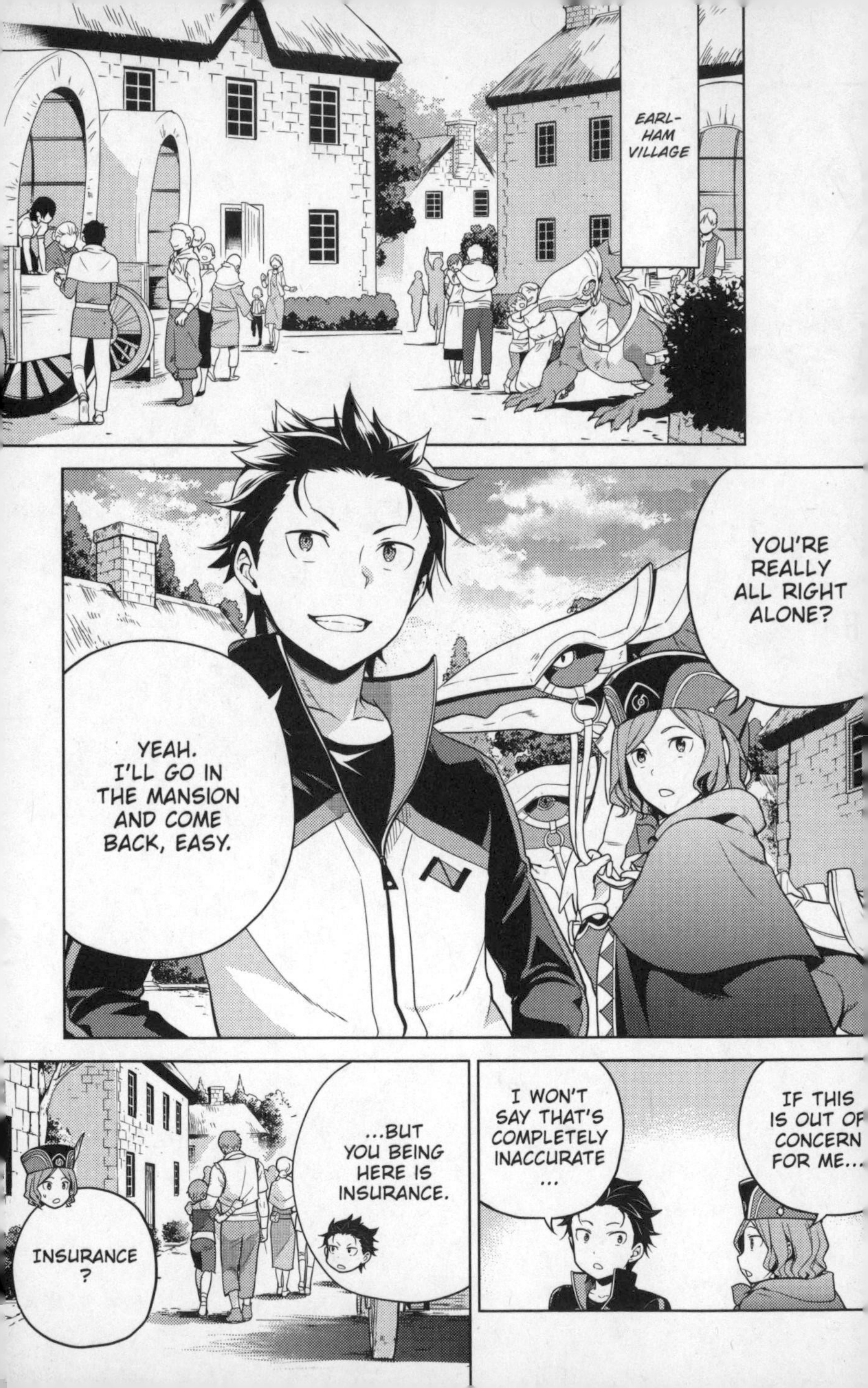
EARL-HAM VILLAGE
YOU'RE REALLY ALL RIGHT ALONE?
YEAH. I'LL GO IN THE MANSION AND COME BACK, EASY.
IF THIS IS OUT OF CONCERN FOR ME...
I WON'T SAY THAT'S COMPLETELY INACCURATE ...
...BUT YOU BEING HERE IS INSURANCE.
INSURANCE ?

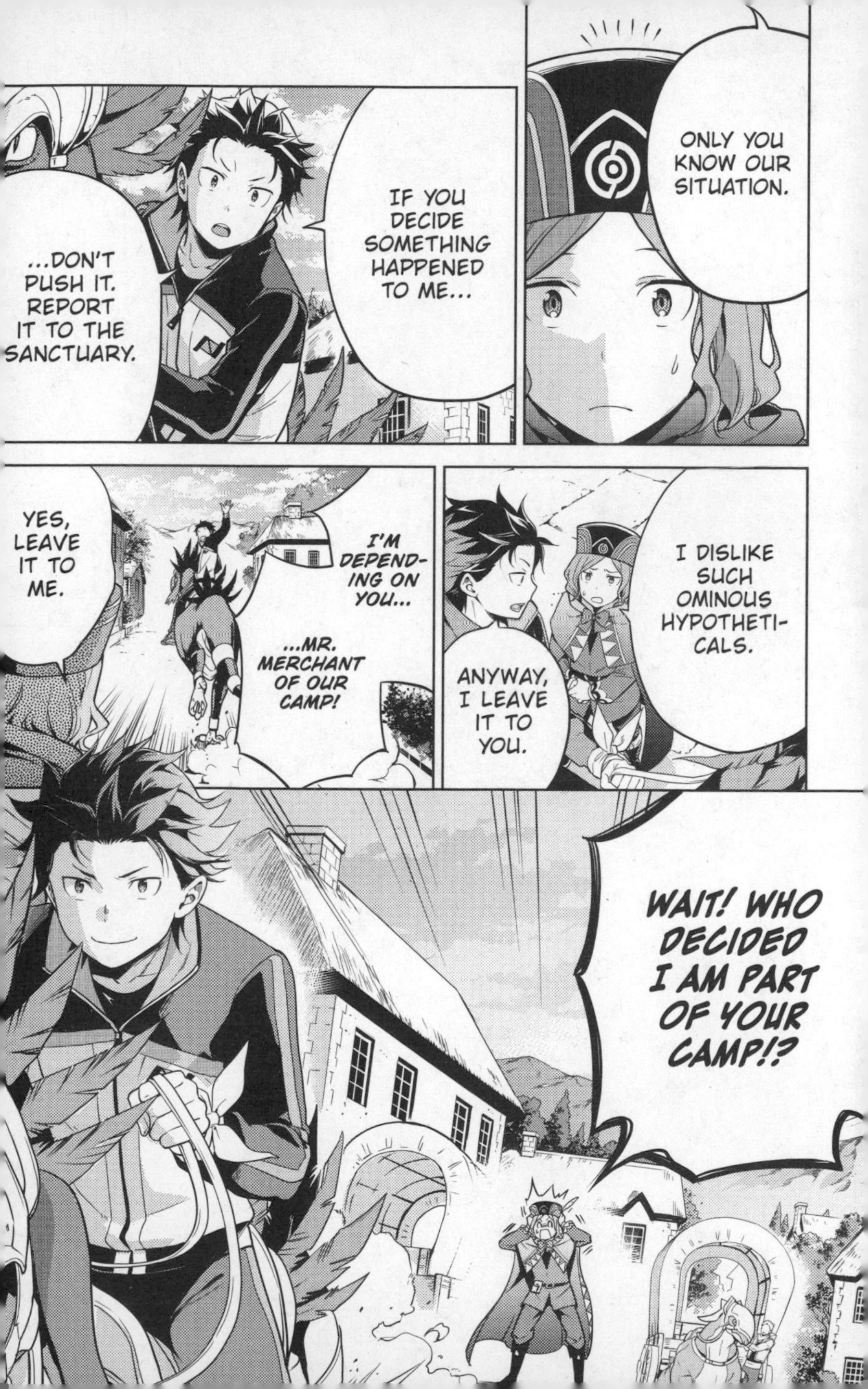
ONLY YOU KNOW OUR SITUATION.
IF YOU DECIDE SOMETHING HAPPENED TO ME...
...DON'T PUSH IT. REPORT IT TO THE SANCTUARY.
I DISLIKE SUCH OMINOUS HYPOTHETICALS.
ANYWAY, I LEAVE IT TO YOU.
YES, LEAVE IT TO ME.
I'M DEPENDING ON YOU...
...MR. MERCHANT OF OUR CAMP!
WAIT! WHO DECIDED I AM PART OF YOUR CAMP!?

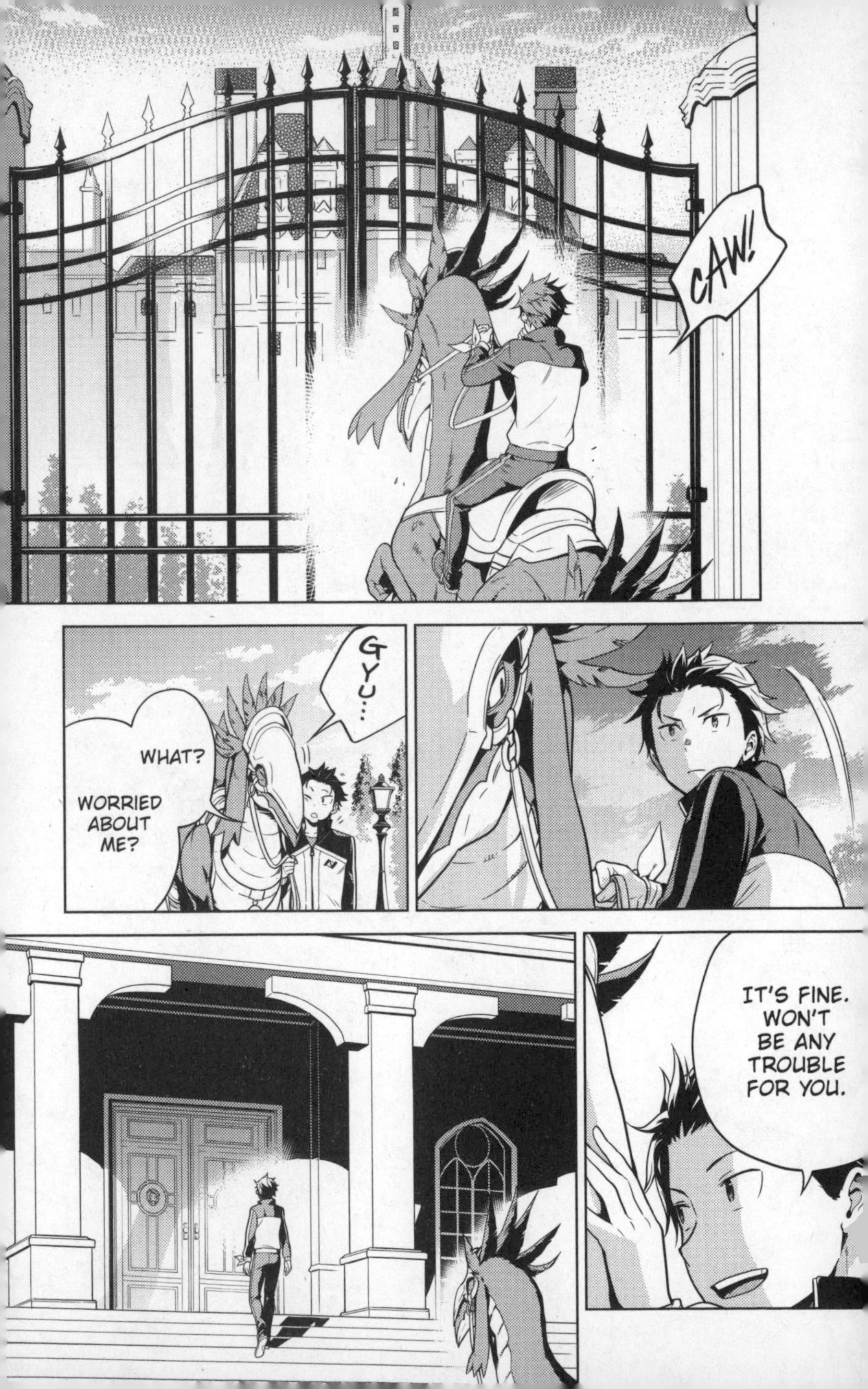
CAW!
GYU...
WHAT?
WORRIED ABOUT ME?
IT'S FINE. WON'T BE ANY TROUBLE FOR YOU.

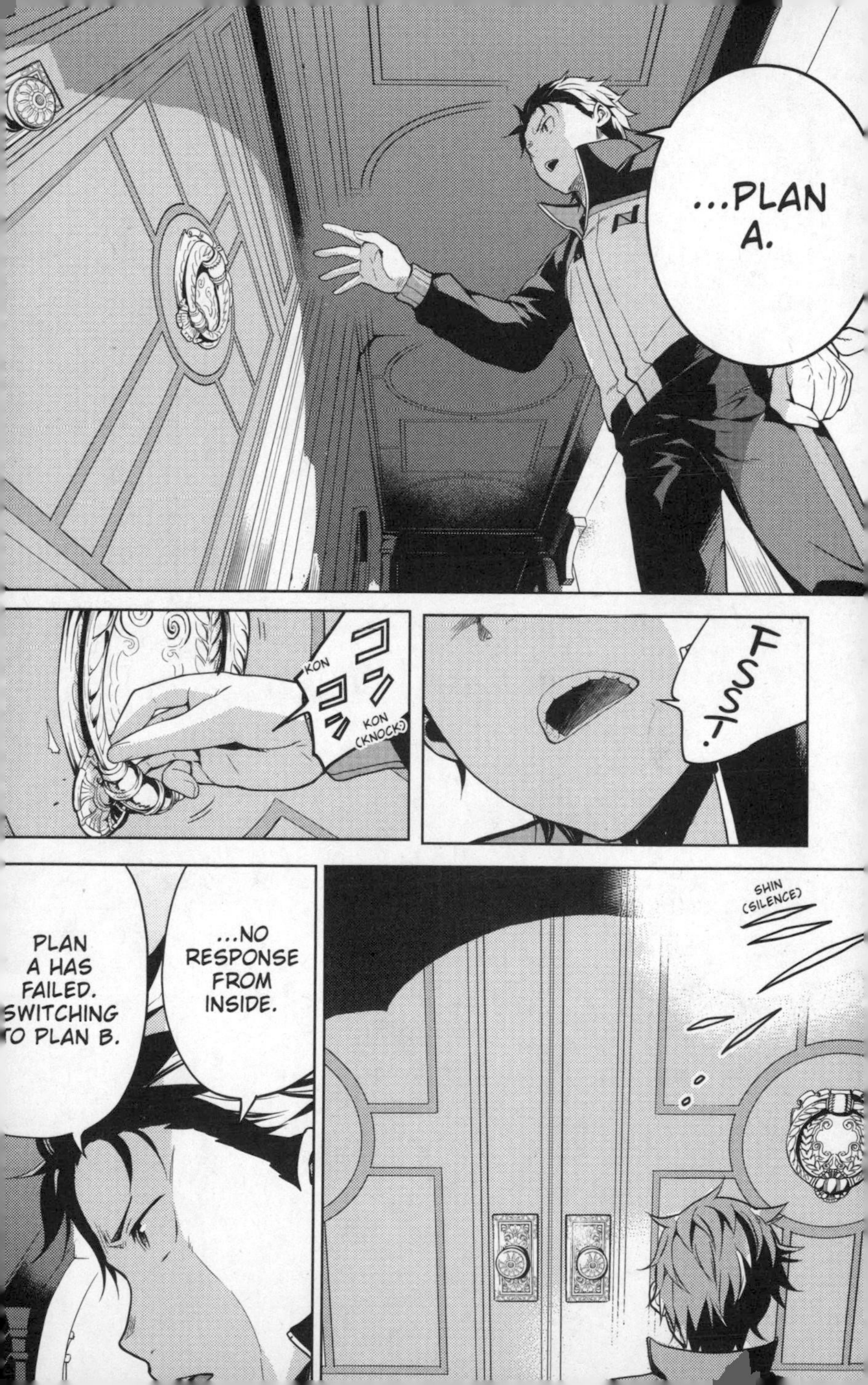
...PLAN A.
FSSX.
コンコン
KON KON (KNOCK)
SHIN (SILENCE)
...NO RESPONSE FROM INSIDE.
PLAN A HAS FAILED. SWITCHING TO PLAN B.

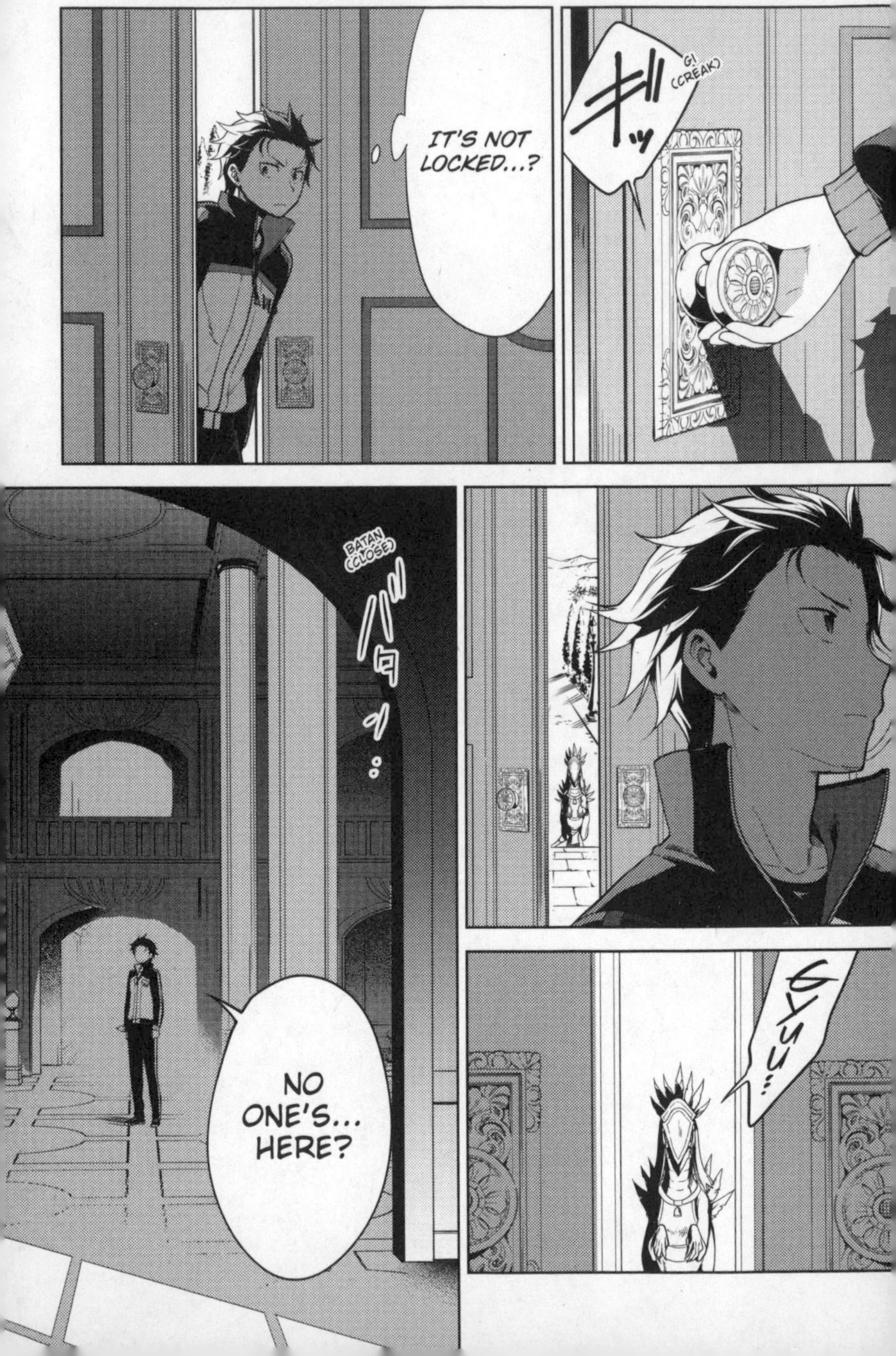
GI (CREAK)
IT'S NOT LOCKED...?
GYUU...
BATAN (CLOSE)
NO ONE'S... HERE?

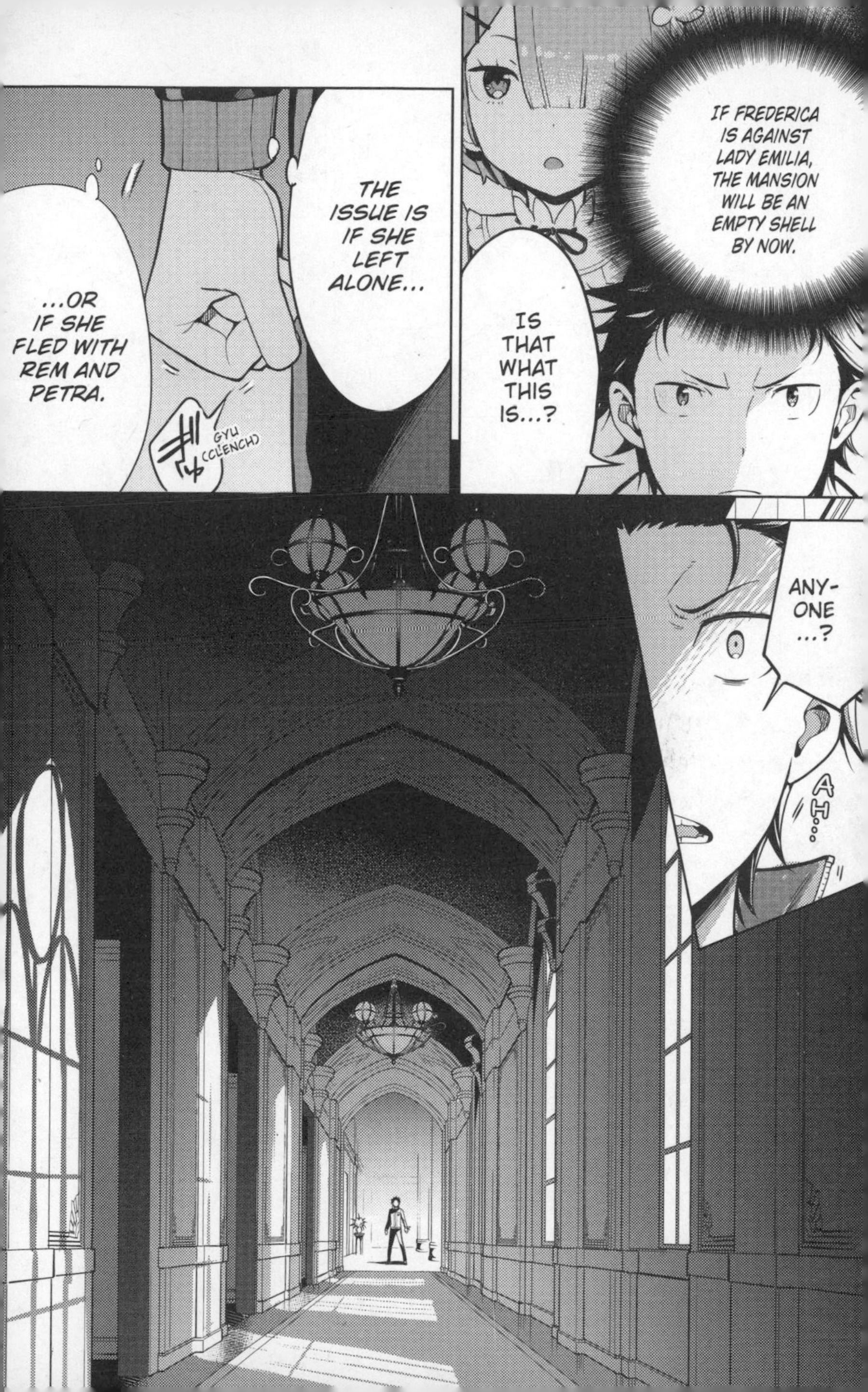
IF FREDERICA IS AGAINST LADY EMILIA, THE MANSION WILL BE AN EMPTY SHELL BY NOW.
IS THAT WHAT THIS IS...?
THE ISSUE IS IF SHE LEFT ALONE...
...OR IF SHE FLED WITH REM AND PETRA.
GYU (CLENCH)
ANY-ONE ...?
AH...

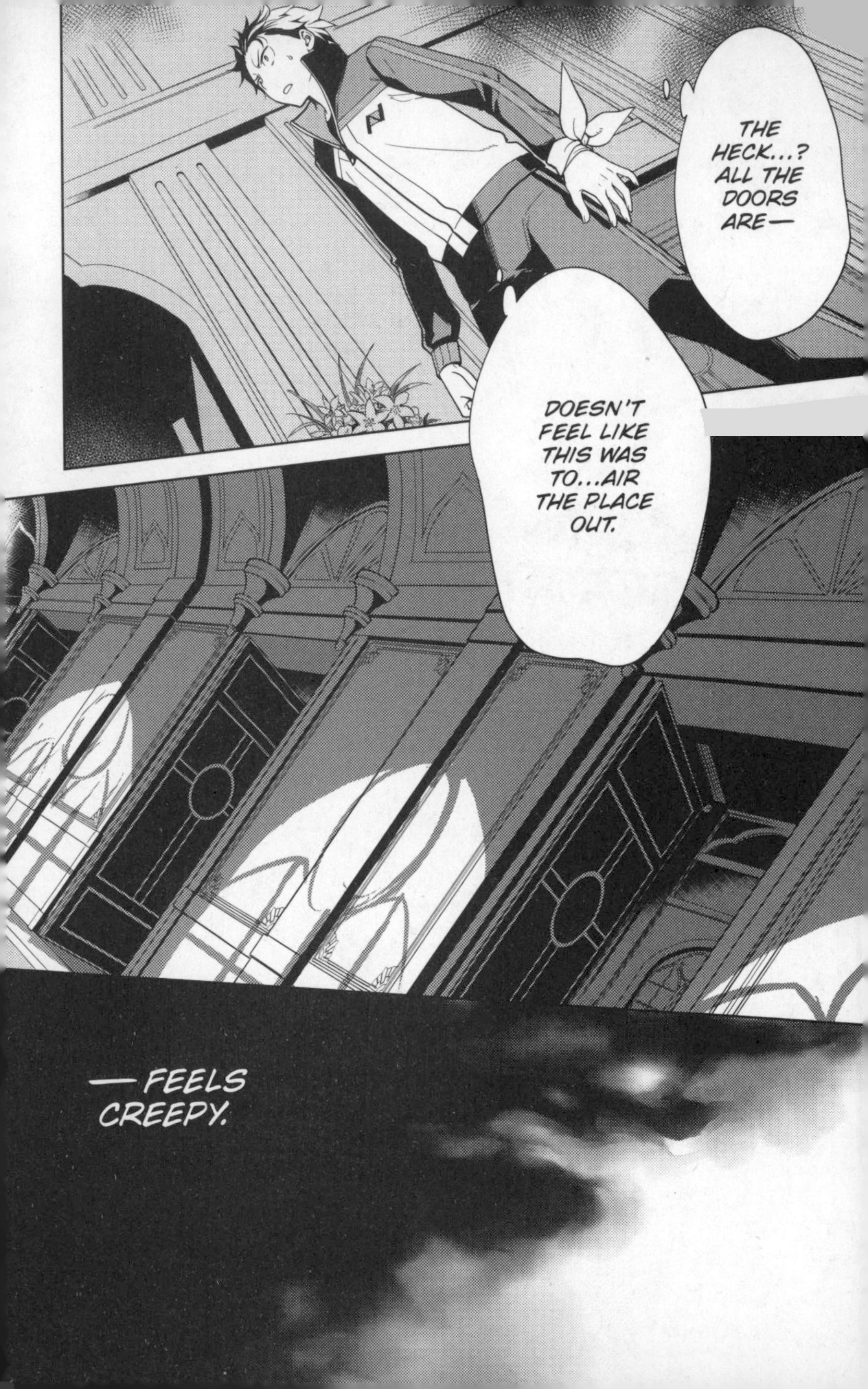
THE HECK...? ALL THE DOORS ARE—
DOESN'T FEEL LIKE THIS WAS TO...AIR THE PLACE OUT.
—FEELS CREEPY.

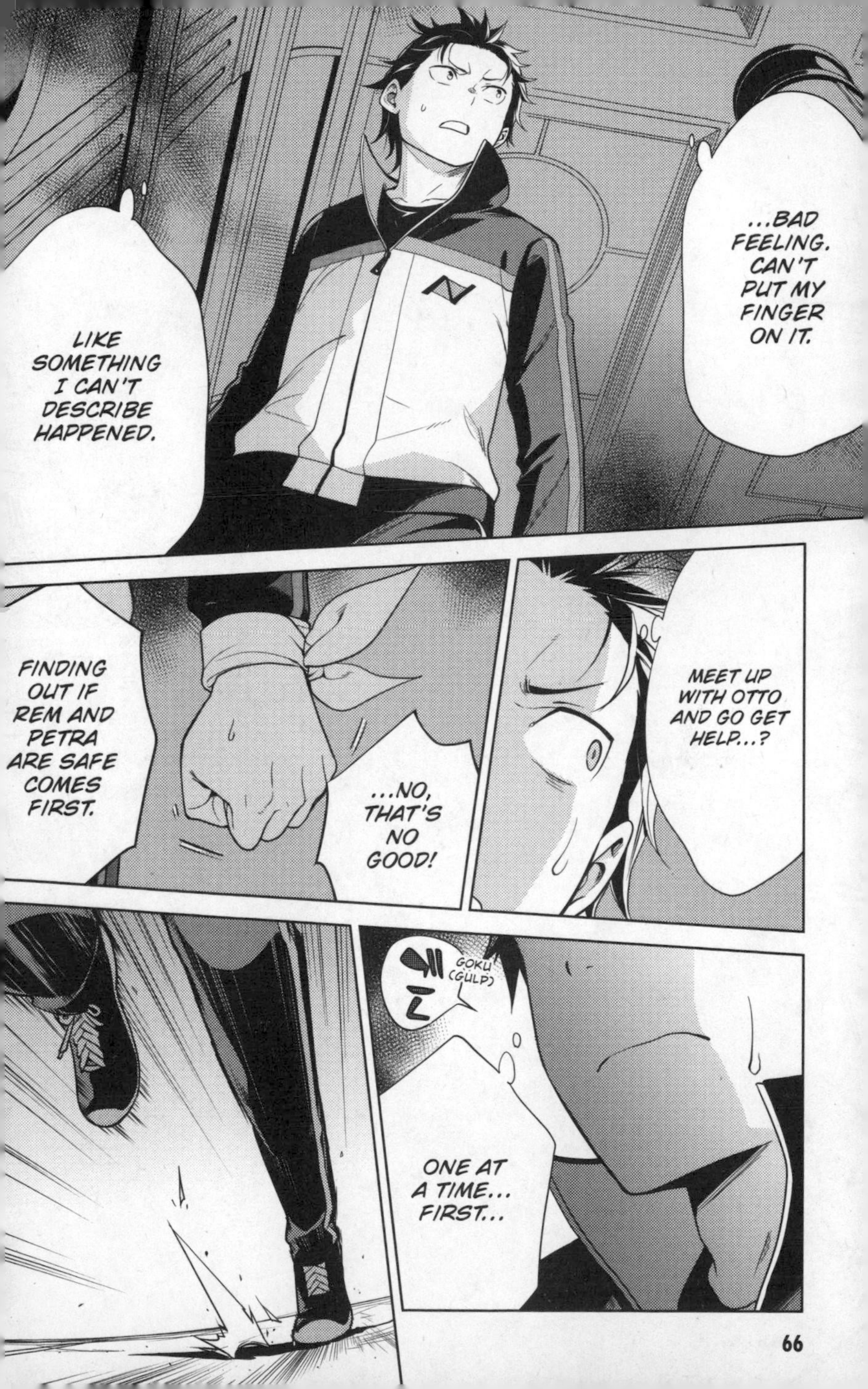
...BAD FEELING. CAN'T PUT MY FINGER ON IT.
LIKE SOMETHING I CAN'T DESCRIBE HAPPENED.
MEET UP WITH OTTO AND GO GET HELP...?
...NO, THAT'S NO GOOD!
FINDING OUT IF REM AND PETRA ARE SAFE COMES FIRST.
GOKU (GULP)
ONE AT A TIME... FIRST...

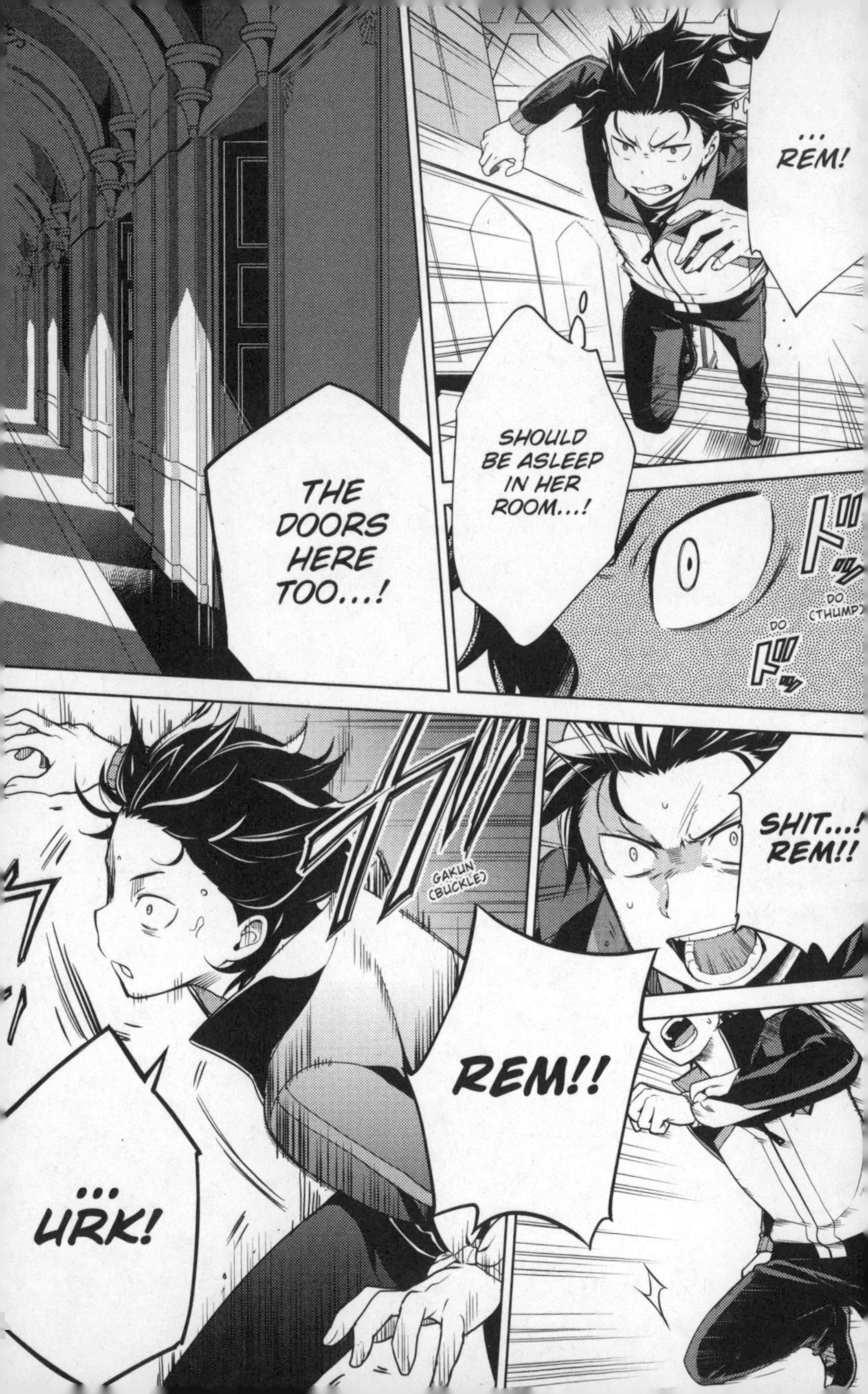

... REM!
SHOULD BE ASLEEP IN HER ROOM...!
DO (THUMP)
DO
THE DOORS HERE TOO...!
SHIT...! REM!!
REM!!
GAKUN (BUCKLE)
... URK!

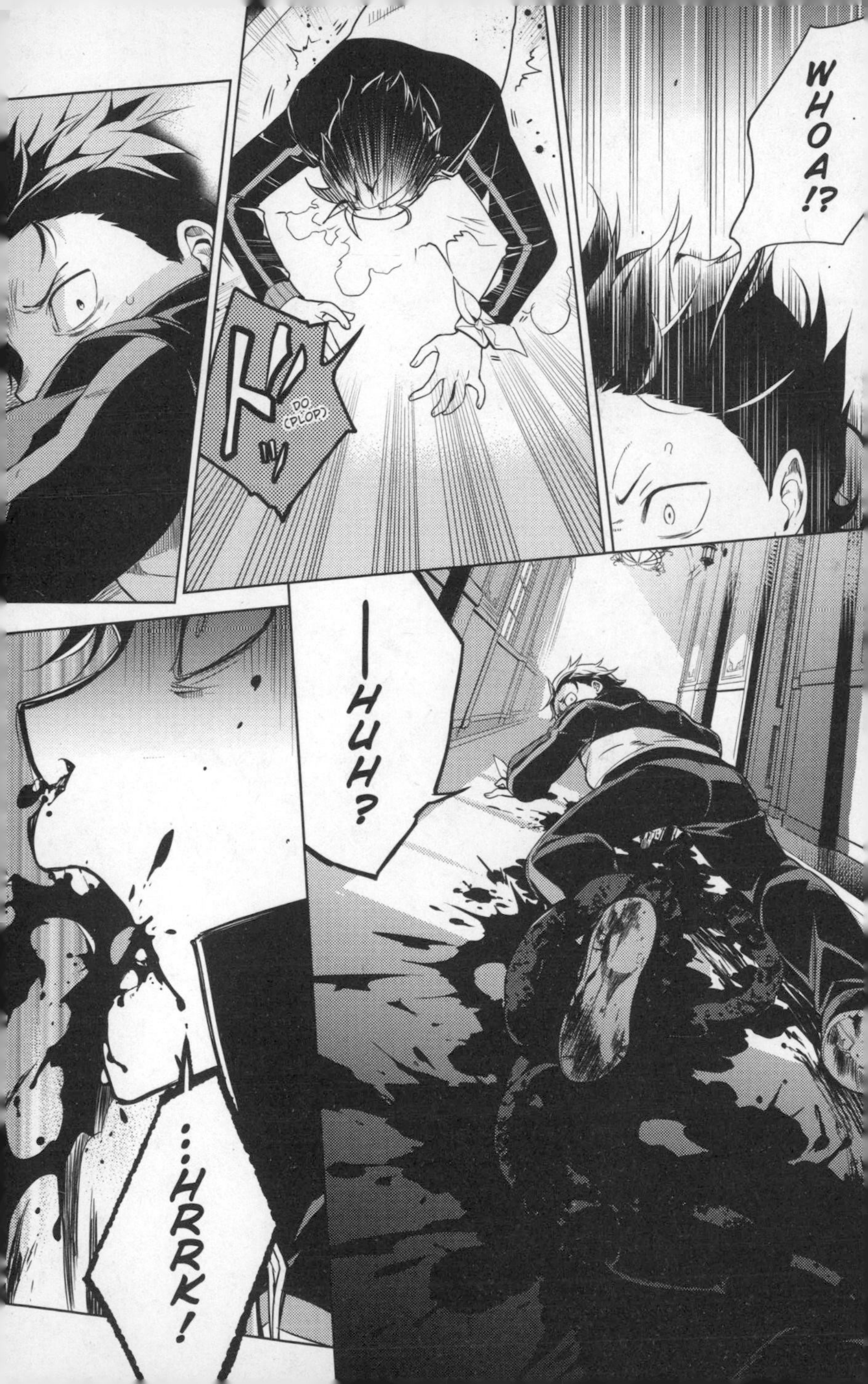
WHOA!?
ド
DO (PLOP)
HUH?
...HRRK!

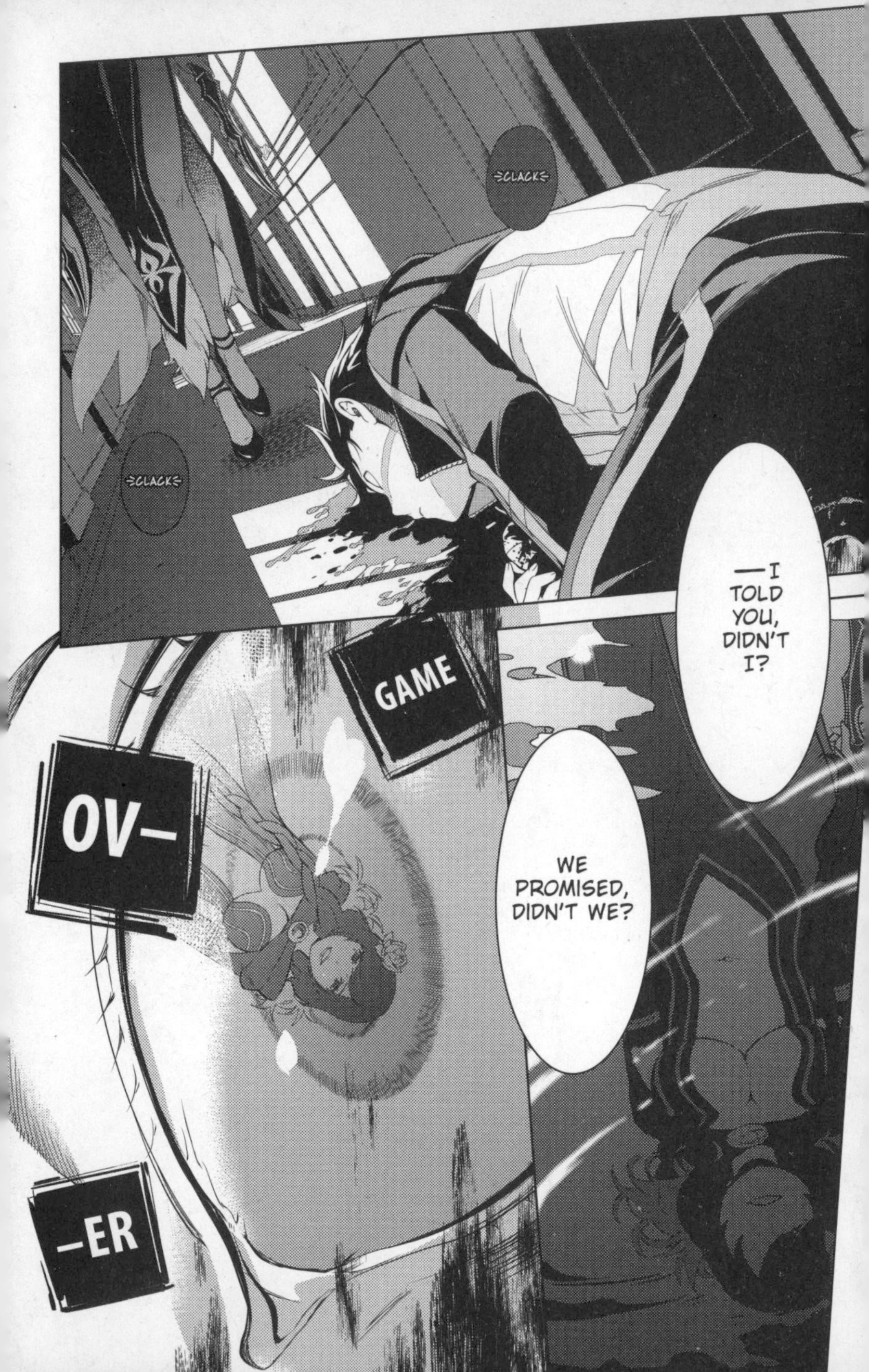
CLACK
CLACK
—I TOLD YOU, DIDN'T I?
WE PROMISED, DIDN'T WE?
GAME
OV—
—ER

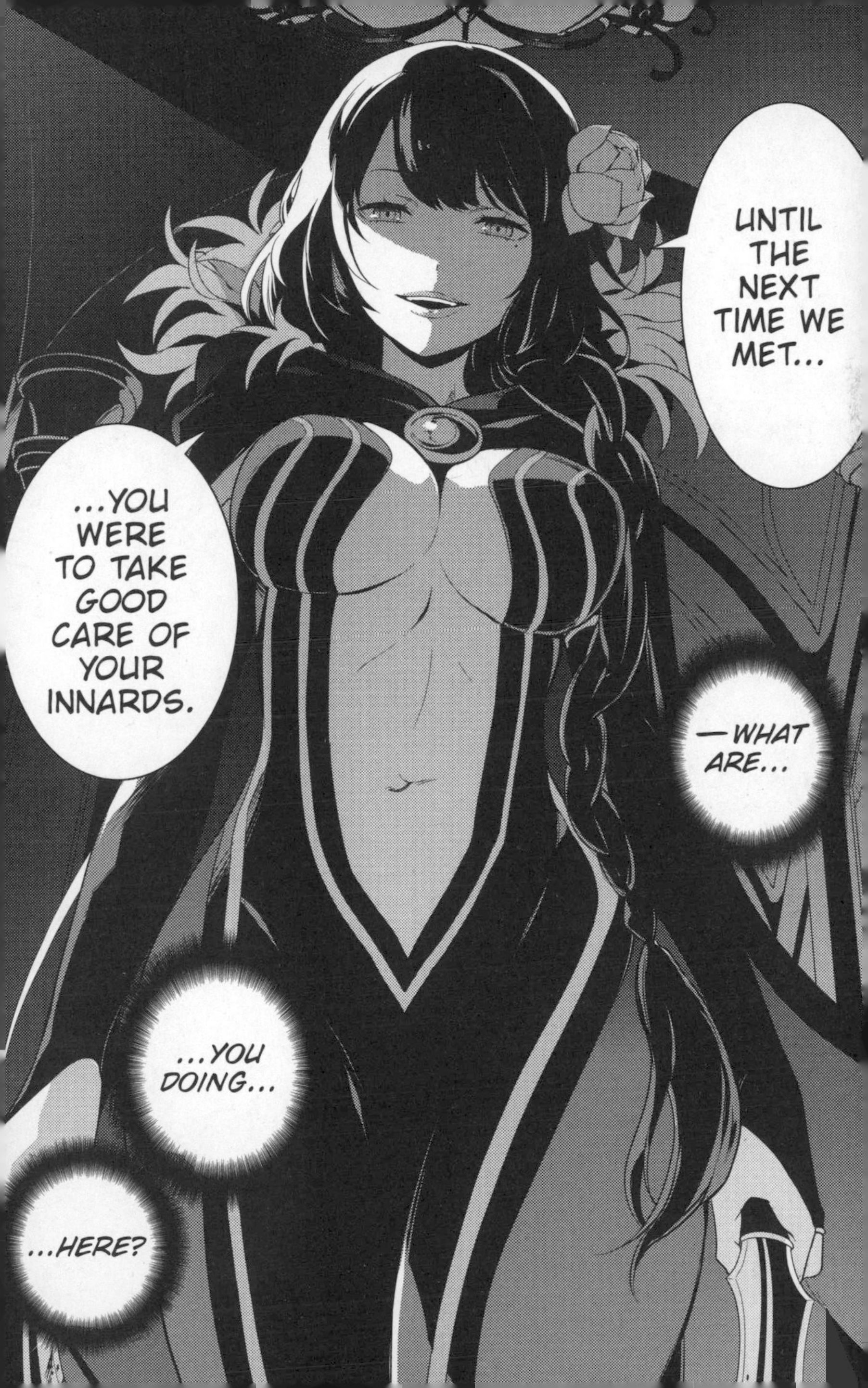
UNTIL THE NEXT TIME WE MET...
...YOU WERE TO TAKE GOOD CARE OF YOUR INNARDS.
—WHAT ARE...
...YOU DOING...
...HERE?

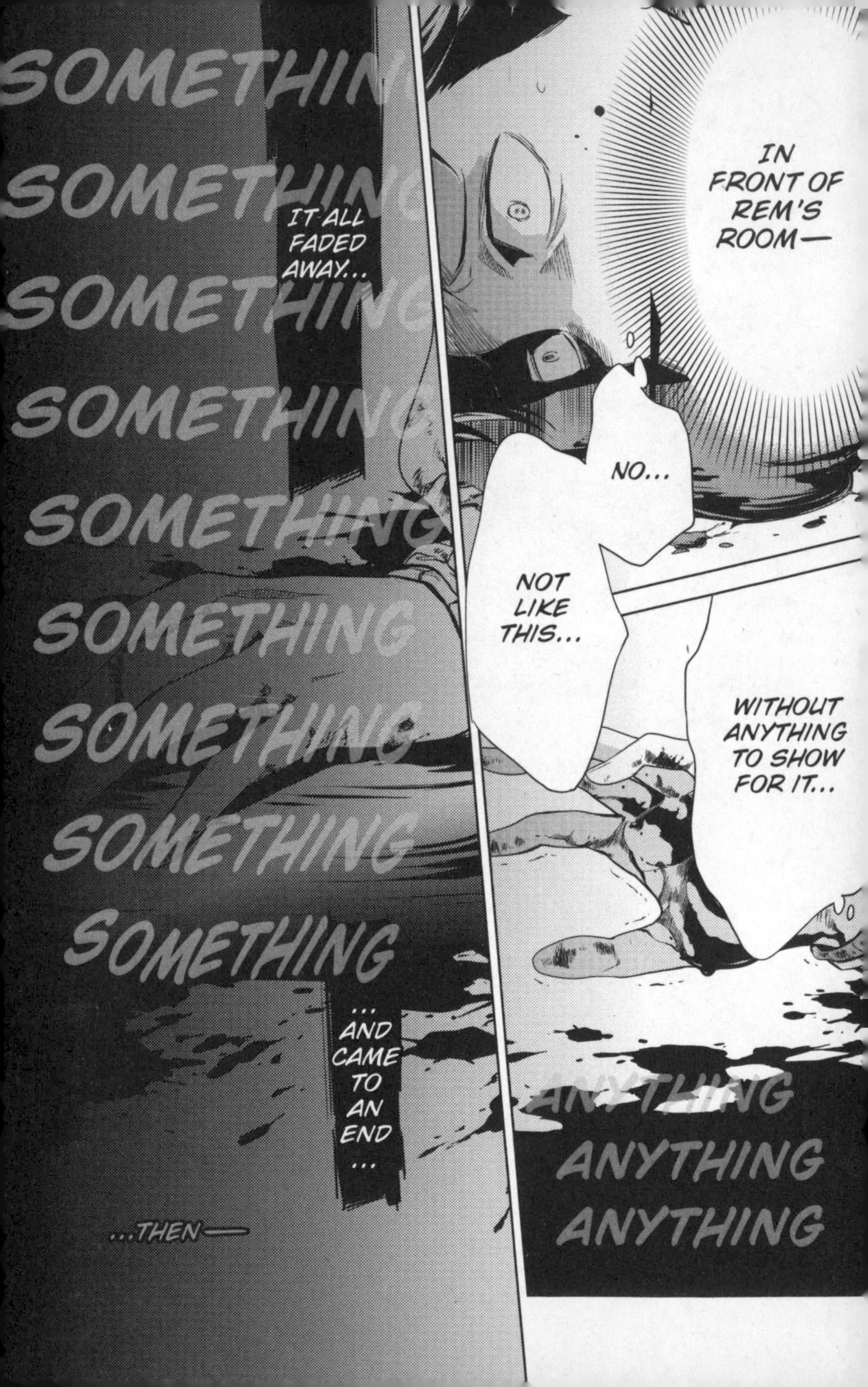
IN FRONT OF REM'S ROOM—
NO...
NOT LIKE THIS...
WITHOUT ANYTHING TO SHOW FOR IT...
ANYTHING
ANYTHING
ANYTHING
SOMETHIN
SOMETHING
IT ALL FADED AWAY...
SOMETHING
SOMETHING
SOMETHING
SOMETHING
SOMETHING
SOMETHING
SOMETHING
...AND CAME TO AN END...
...THEN—

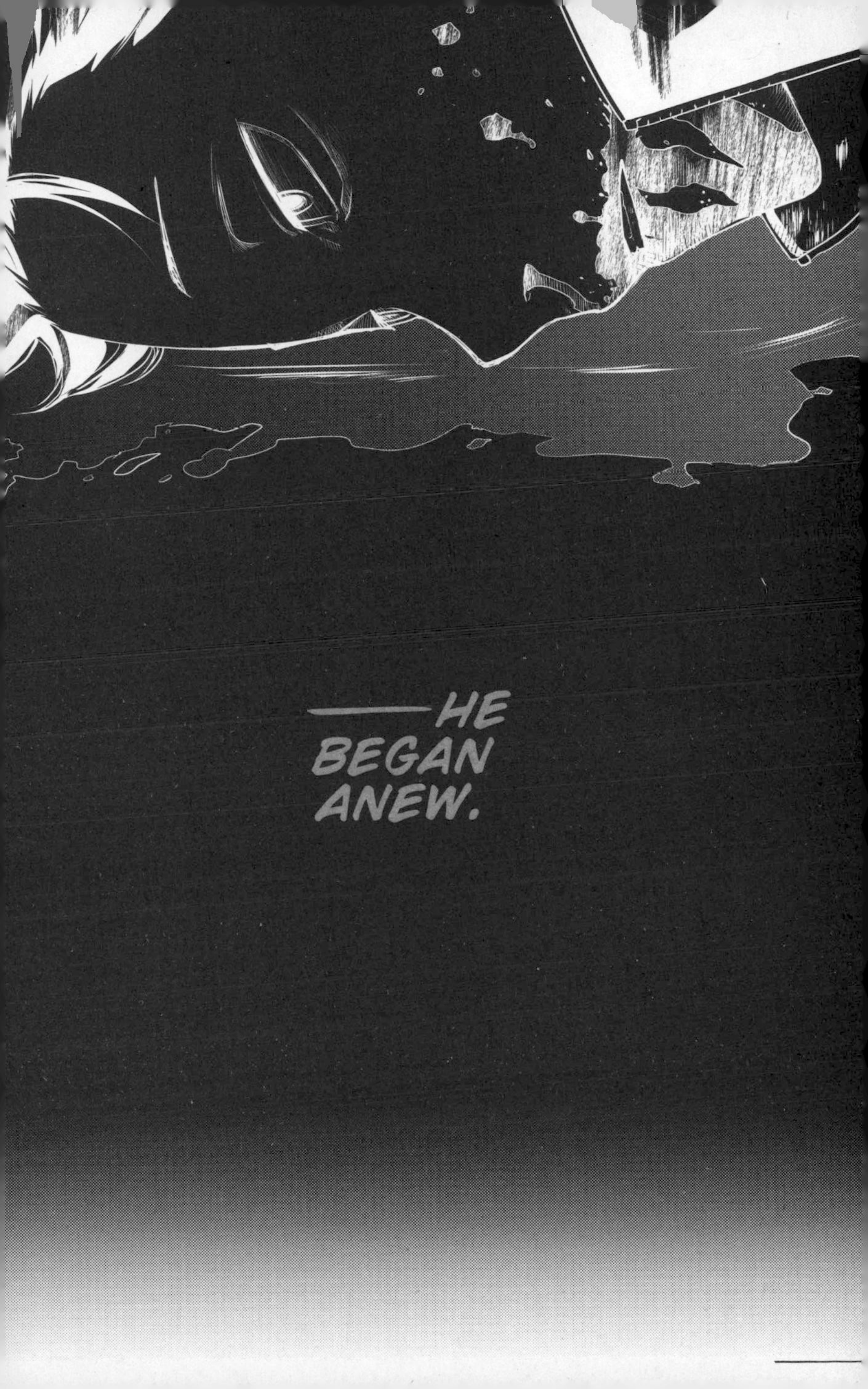
——HE BEGAN ANEW.

The only ability Subaru Natsuki gets when he's
summoned to another world is time travel via his own death.
But to save her, he'll die as many times as it takes.

Re:ZERO

-Starting Life in Another World-

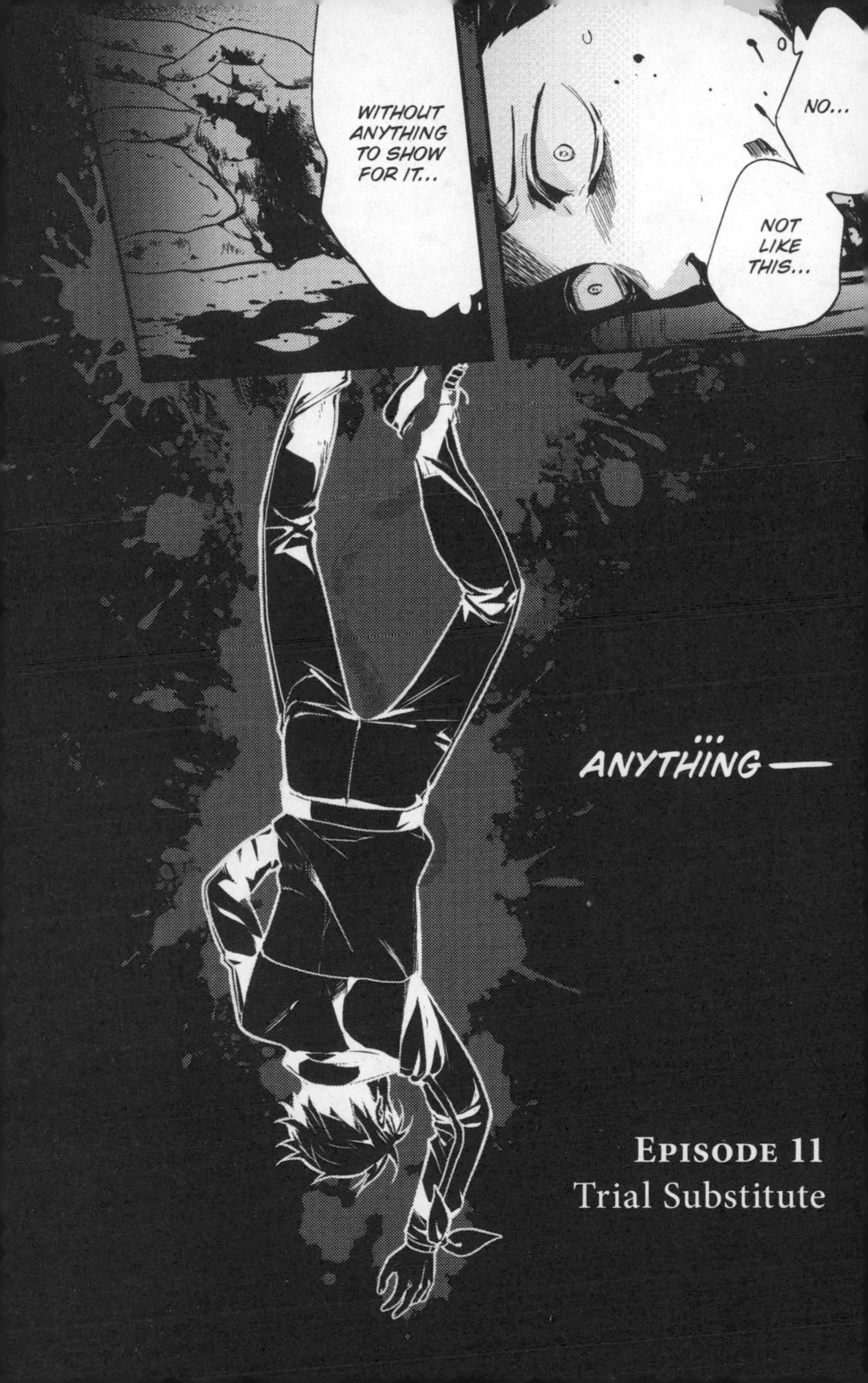
NO...
NOT LIKE THIS...
WITHOUT ANYTHING TO SHOW FOR IT...
ANYTHING—
EPISODE 11
Trial Substitute

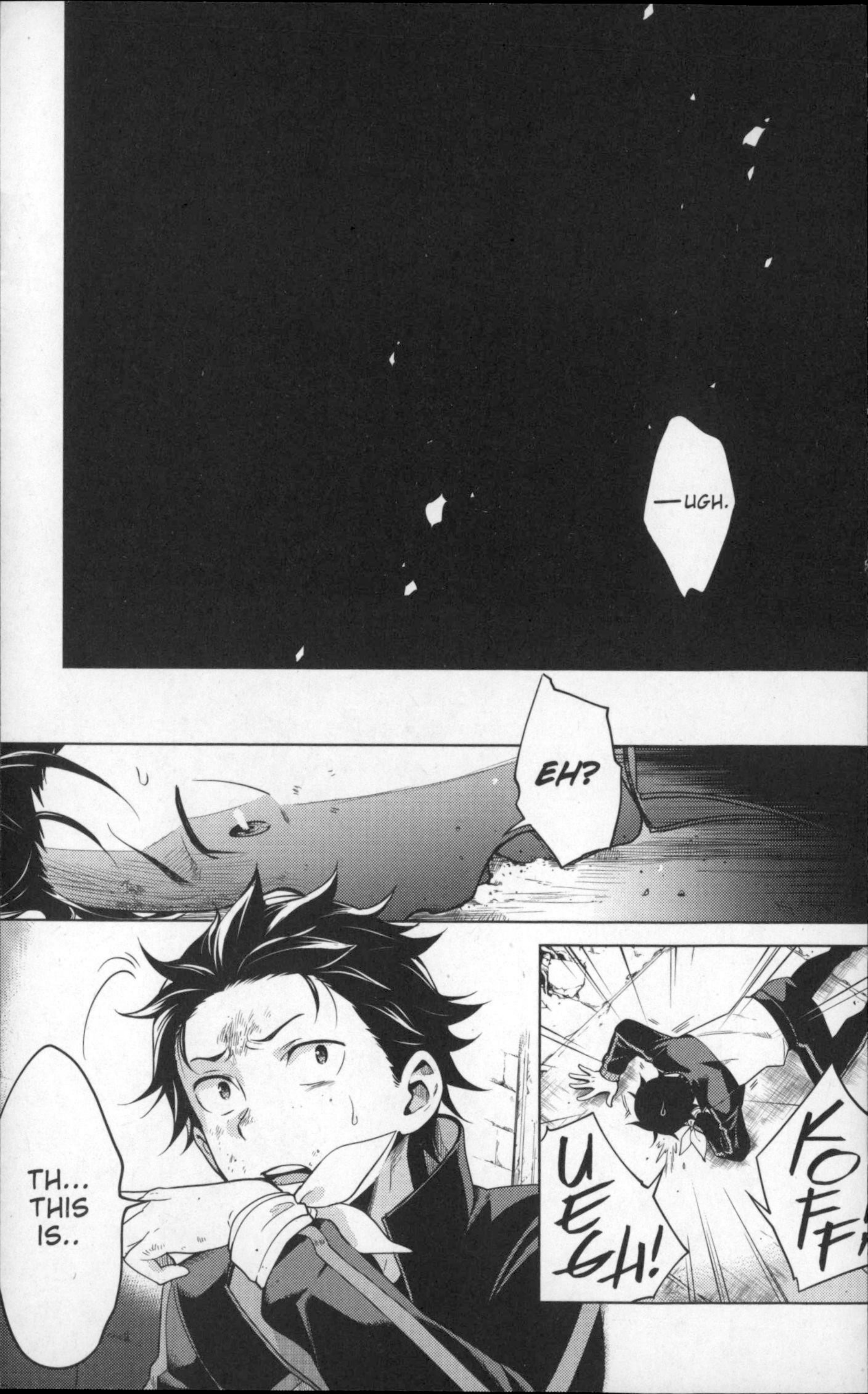
—UGH.
EH?
KOFF
UEGH!
TH... THIS IS..

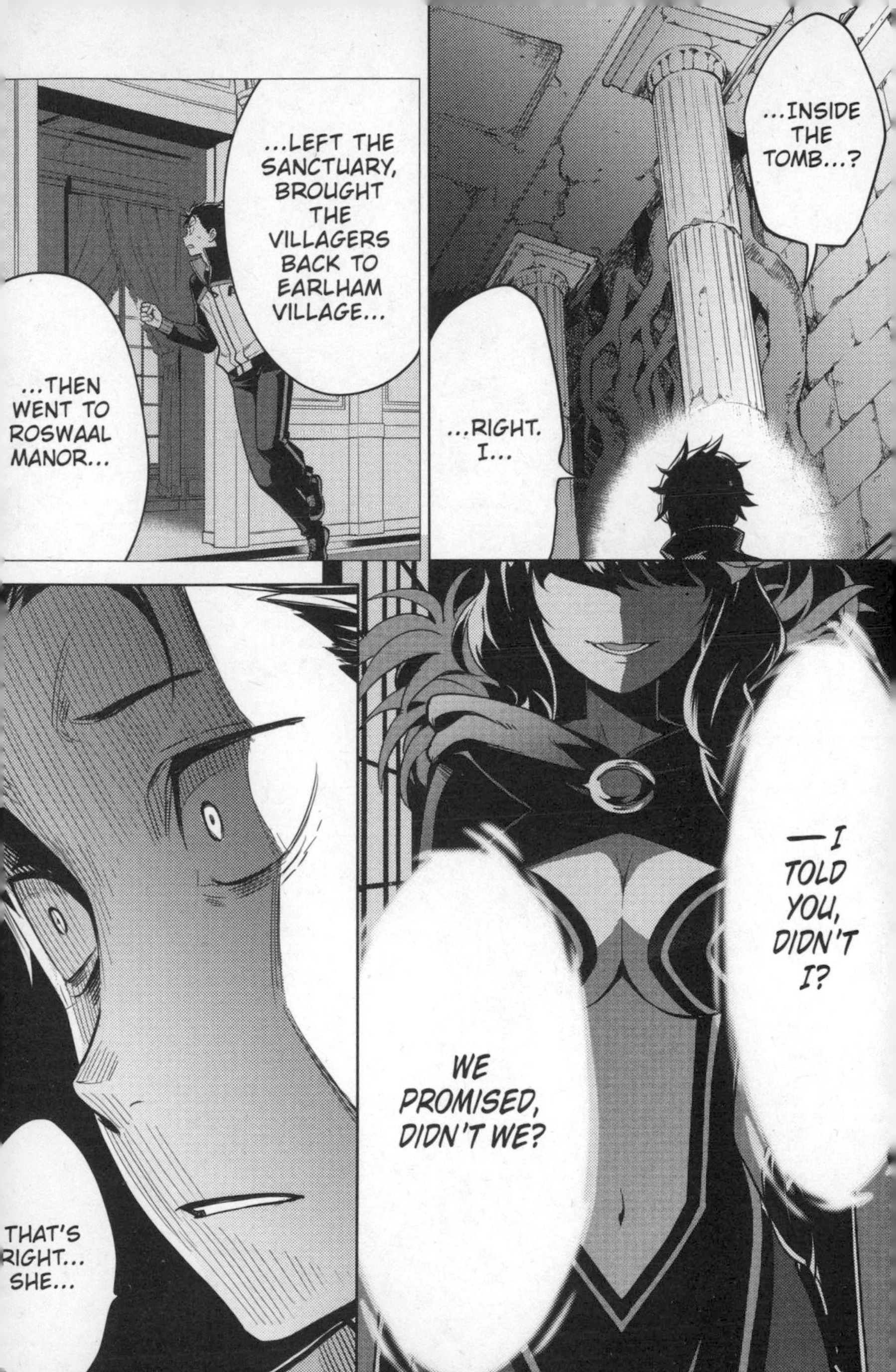
...INSIDE THE TOMB...?
...RIGHT. I...
...LEFT THE SANCTUARY, BROUGHT THE VILLAGERS BACK TO EARLHAM VILLAGE...
...THEN WENT TO ROSWAAL MANOR...
—I TOLD YOU, DIDN'T I?
WE PROMISED, DIDN'T WE?
THAT'S RIGHT... SHE...

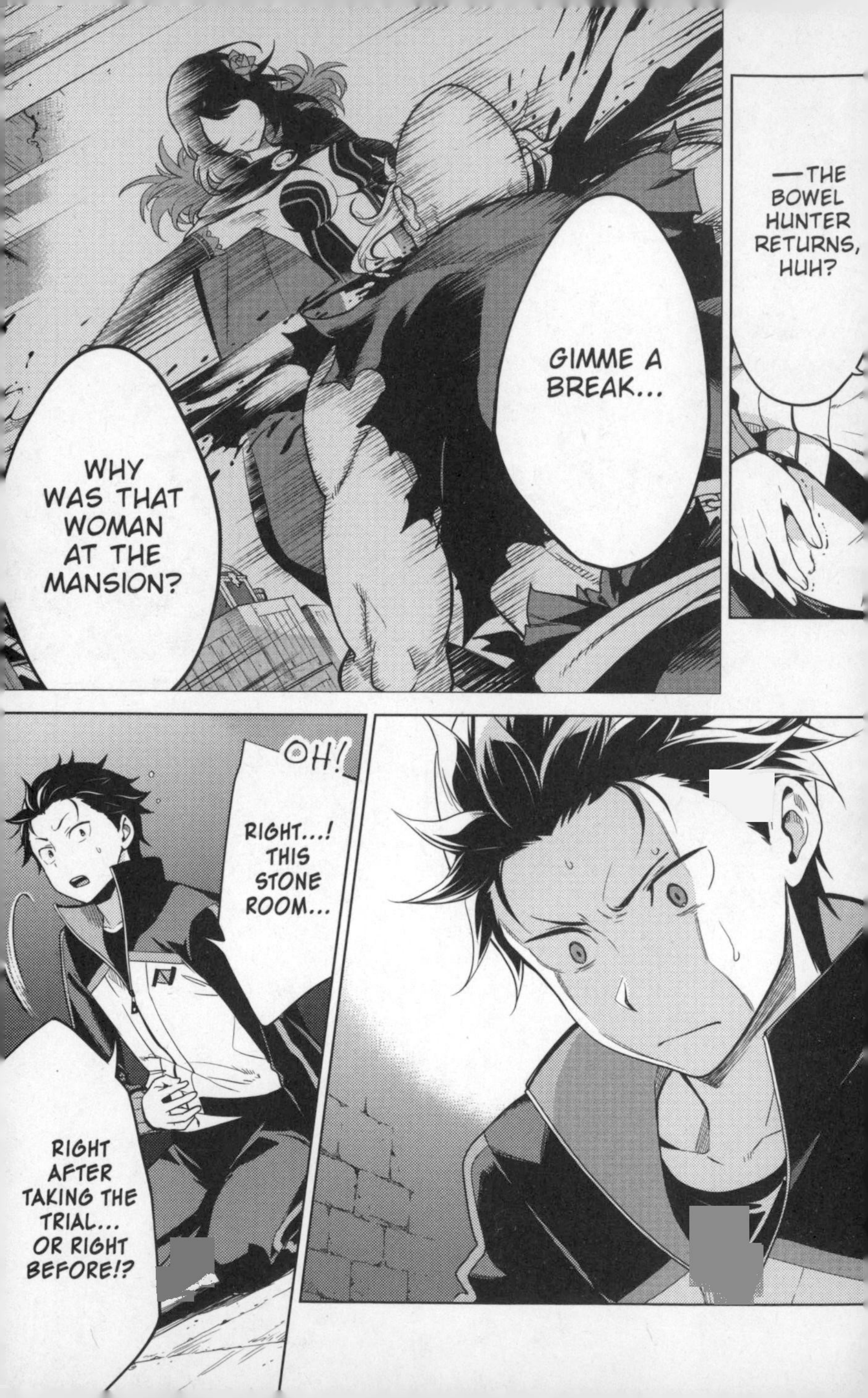
—THE BOWEL HUNTER RETURNS, HUH?
GIMME A BREAK...
WHY WAS THAT WOMAN AT THE MANSION?
OH!
RIGHT...! THIS STONE ROOM...
RIGHT AFTER TAKING THE TRIAL... OR RIGHT BEFORE!?

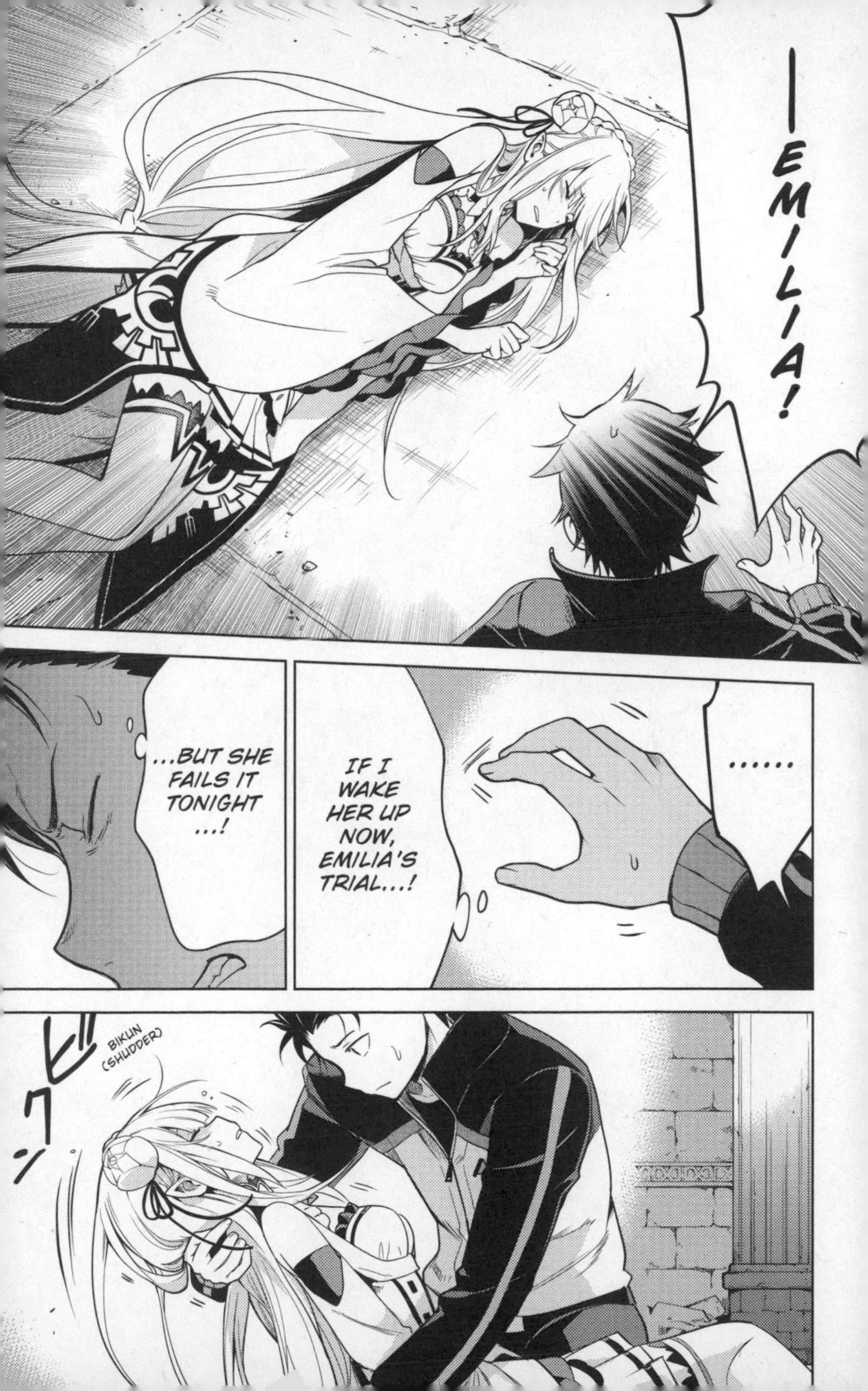
—EMILIA!
......
IF I WAKE HER UP NOW, EMILIA'S TRIAL...!
...BUT SHE FAILS IT TONIGHT ...!
ビクン
BIKUN (SHUDDER)

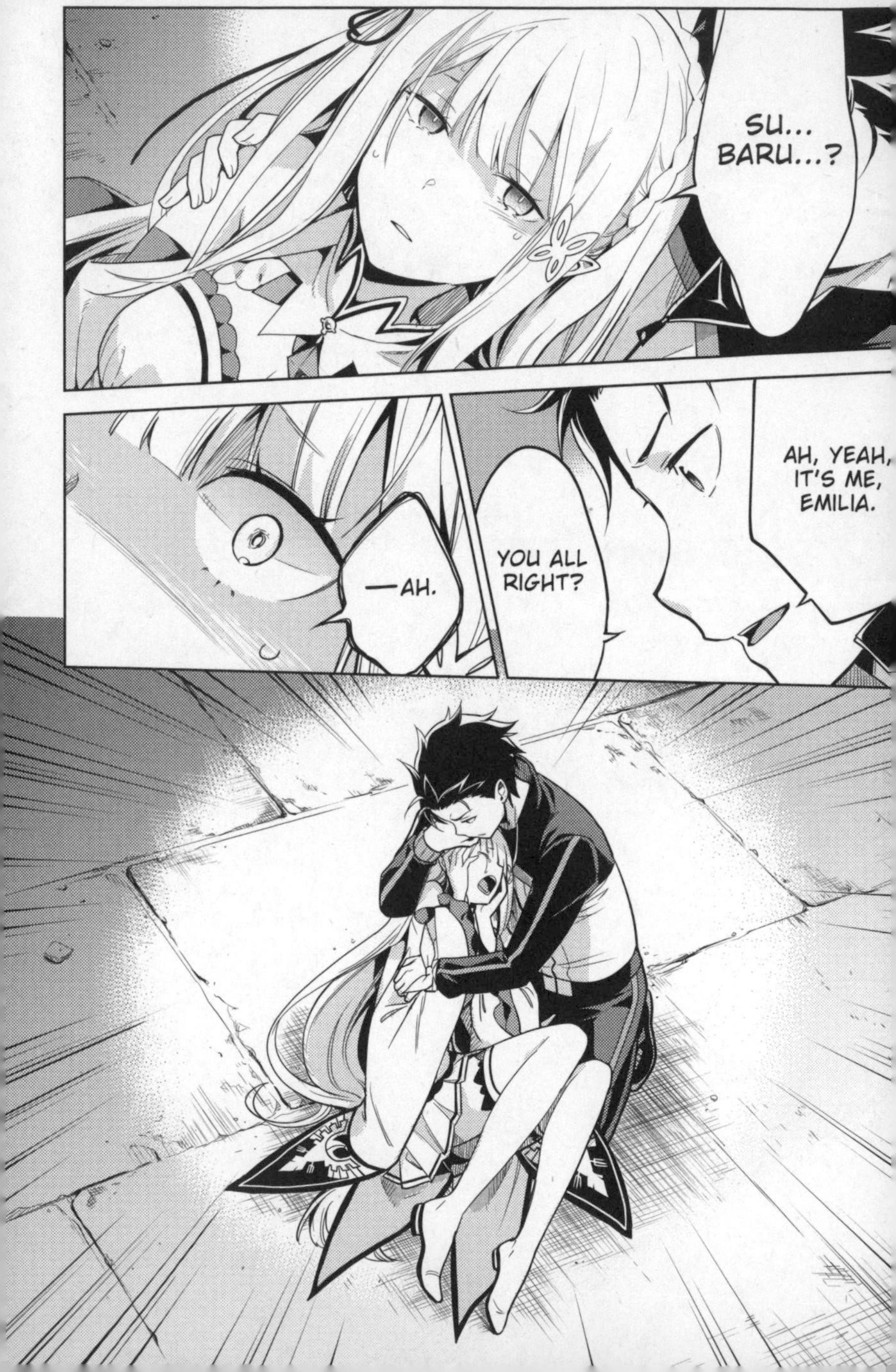
SU... BARU...?
AH, YEAH, IT'S ME, EMILIA.
YOU ALL RIGHT?
—AH.

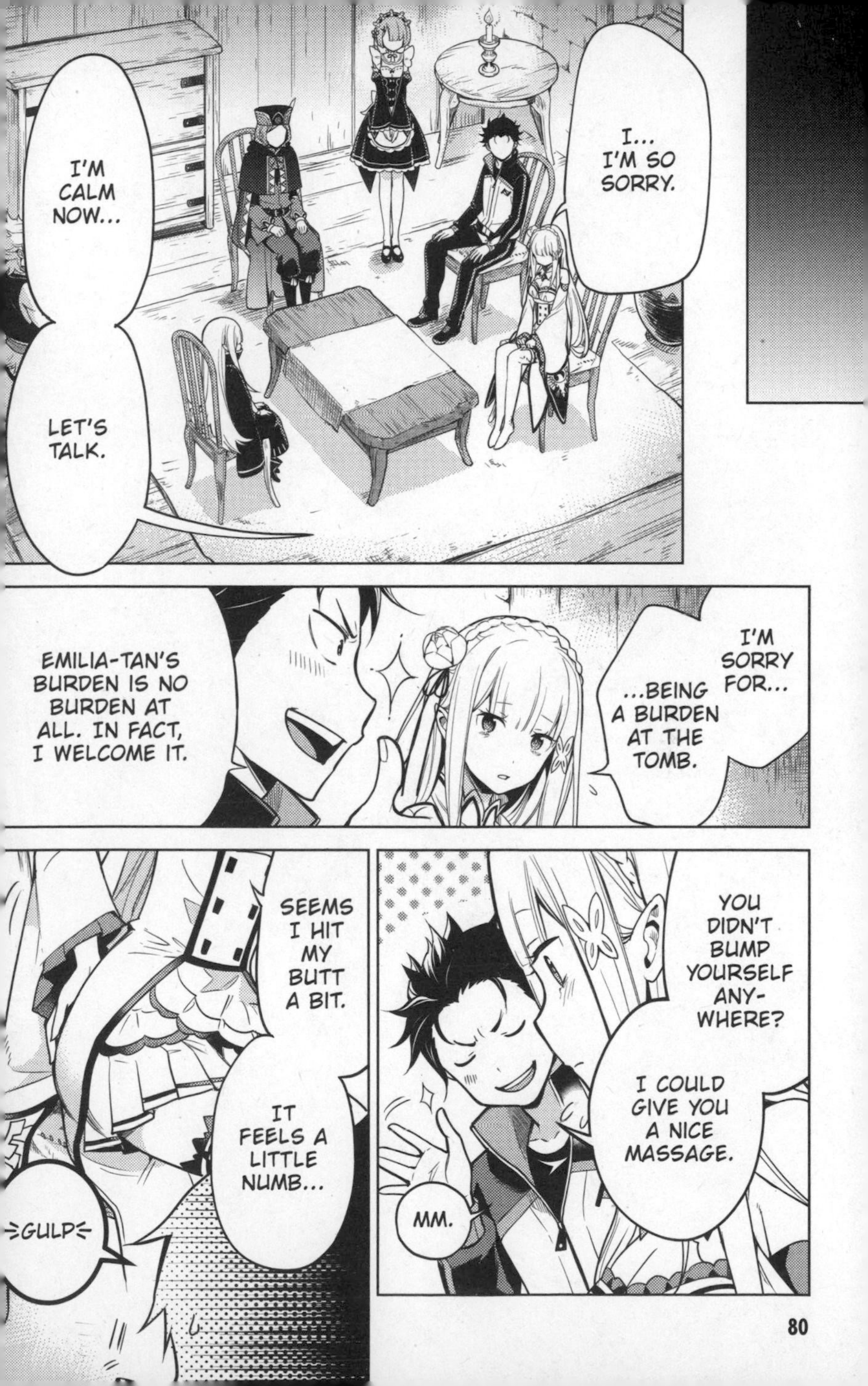
I... I'M SO SORRY.
I'M CALM NOW...
LET'S TALK.
I'M SORRY FOR...
...BEING A BURDEN AT THE TOMB.
EMILIA-TAN'S BURDEN IS NO BURDEN AT ALL. IN FACT, I WELCOME IT.
YOU DIDN'T BUMP YOURSELF ANY-WHERE?
I COULD GIVE YOU A NICE MASSAGE.
MM.
SEEMS I HIT MY BUTT A BIT.
IT FEELS A LITTLE NUMB...
⪤GULP⪤

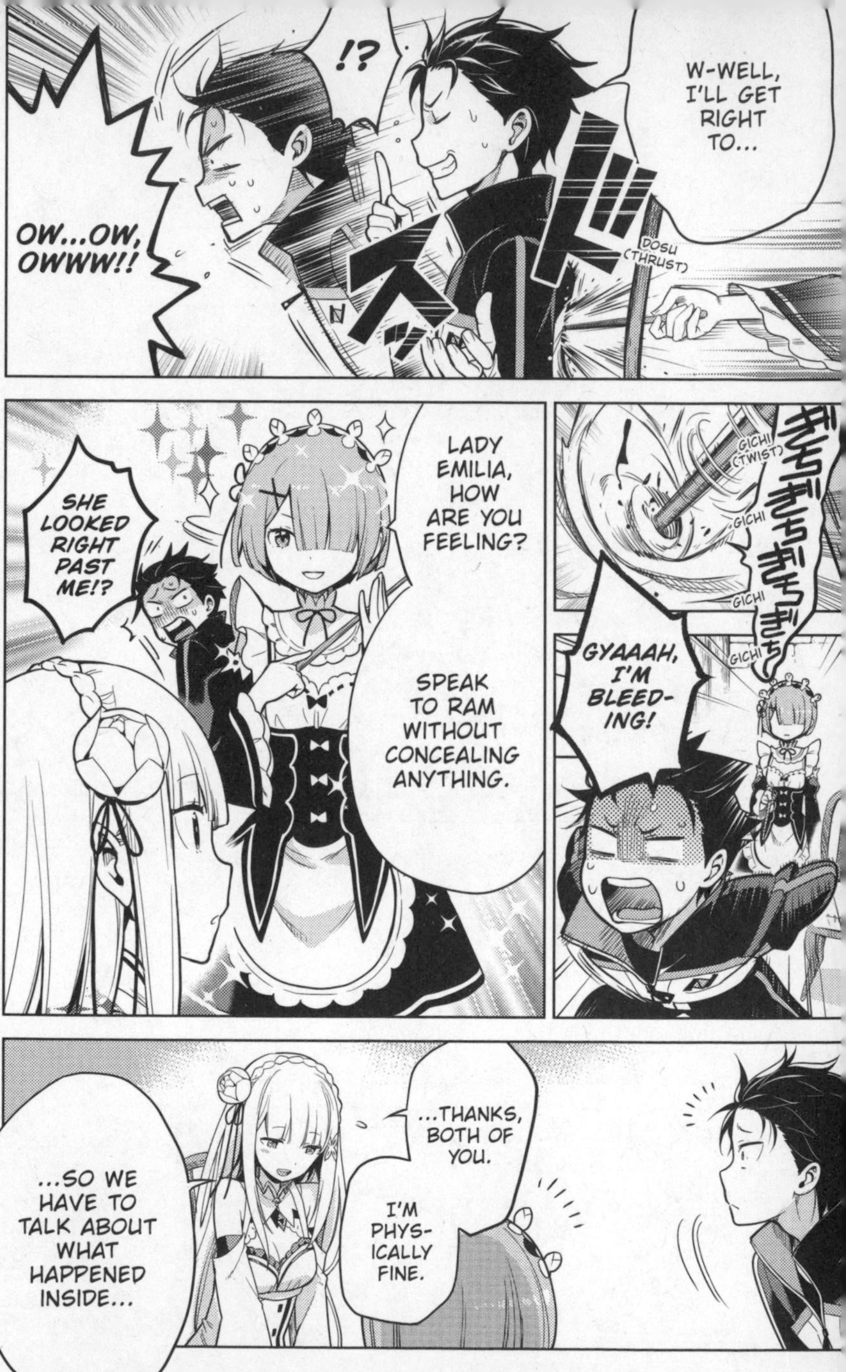

W-WELL, I'LL GET RIGHT TO...
!?
DOSU (THRUST)
OW...OW, OWWW!!
GICHI (TWIST)
GICHI
GICHI
GICHI
GYAAAH, I'M BLEED-ING!
LADY EMILIA, HOW ARE YOU FEELING?
SPEAK TO RAM WITHOUT CONCEALING ANYTHING.
SHE LOOKED RIGHT PAST ME!?
...THANKS, BOTH OF YOU.
I'M PHYS-ICALLY FINE.
...SO WE HAVE TO TALK ABOUT WHAT HAPPENED INSIDE...

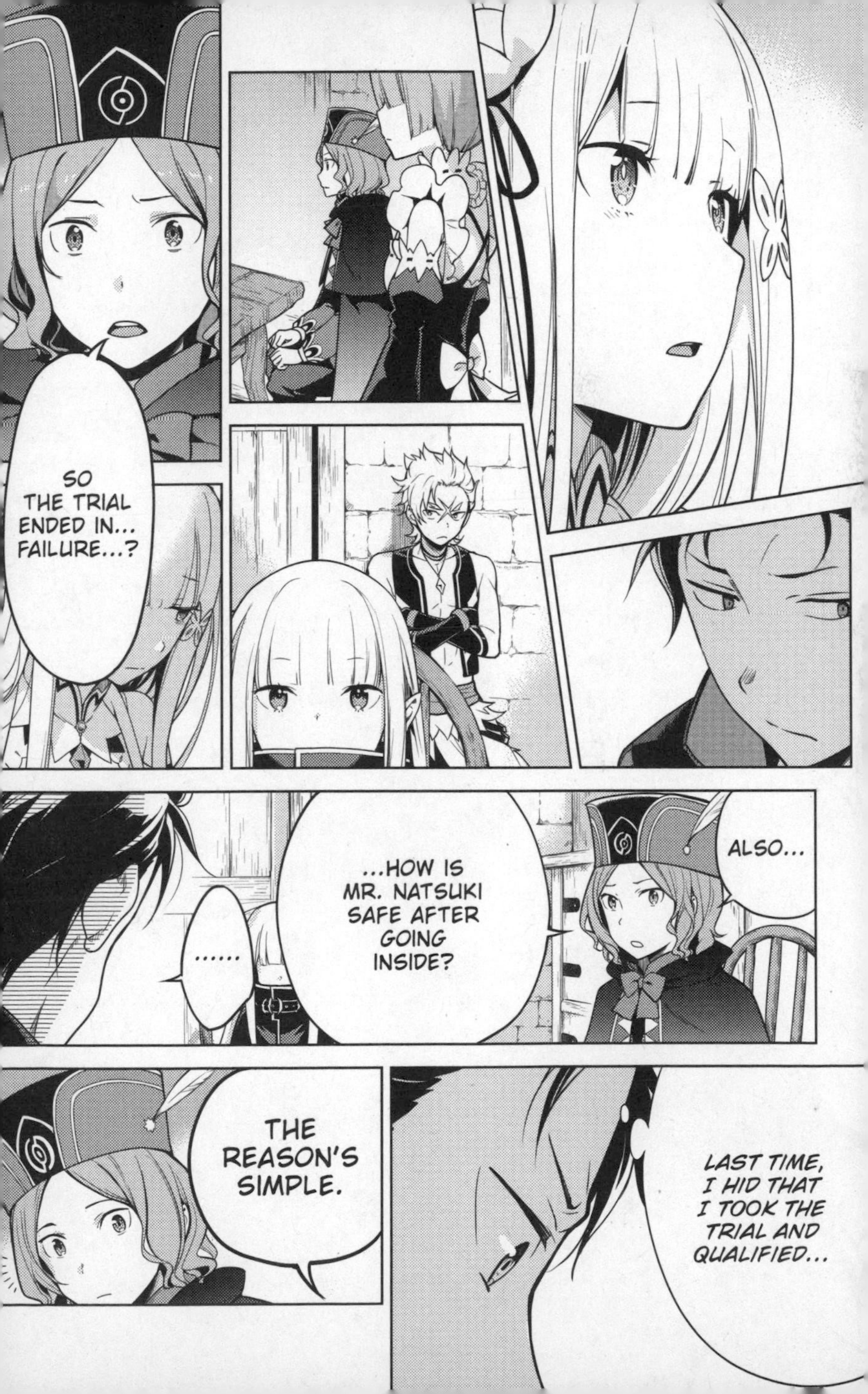
SO THE TRIAL ENDED IN... FAILURE...?
ALSO...
...HOW IS MR. NATSUKI SAFE AFTER GOING INSIDE?
......
LAST TIME, I HID THAT I TOOK THE TRIAL AND QUALIFIED...
THE REASON'S SIMPLE.

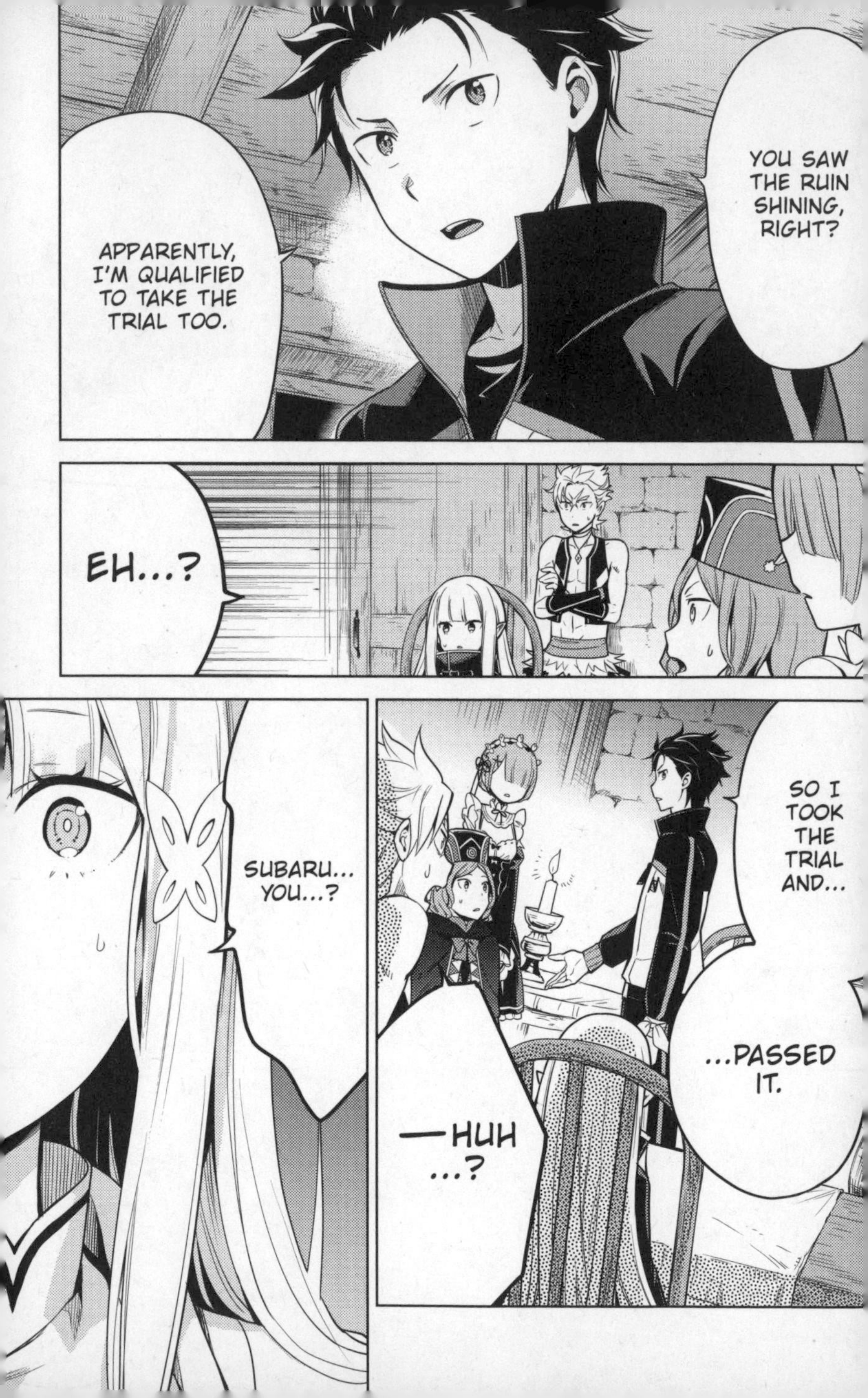
YOU SAW THE RUIN SHINING, RIGHT?
APPARENTLY, I'M QUALIFIED TO TAKE THE TRIAL TOO.
EH...?
SO I TOOK THE TRIAL AND...
...PASSED IT.
—HUH ...?
SUBARU... YOU...?

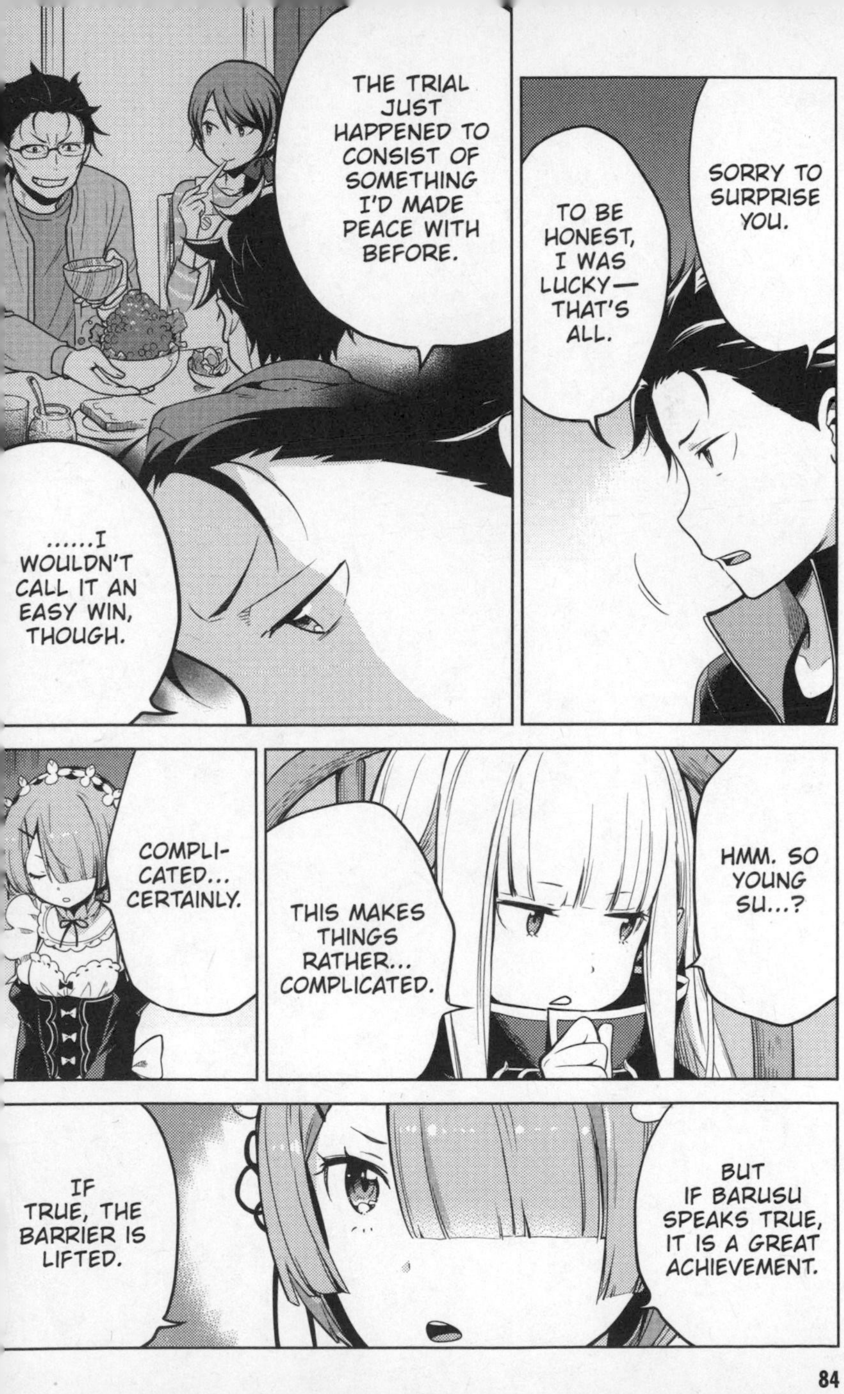
SORRY TO SURPRISE YOU.
TO BE HONEST, I WAS LUCKY—THAT'S ALL.
THE TRIAL JUST HAPPENED TO CONSIST OF SOMETHING I'D MADE PEACE WITH BEFORE.
......I WOULDN'T CALL IT AN EASY WIN, THOUGH.
HMM. SO YOUNG SU...?
THIS MAKES THINGS RATHER... COMPLICATED.
COMPLI-CATED... CERTAINLY.
BUT IF BARUSU SPEAKS TRUE, IT IS A GREAT ACHIEVEMENT.
IF TRUE, THE BARRIER IS LIFTED.

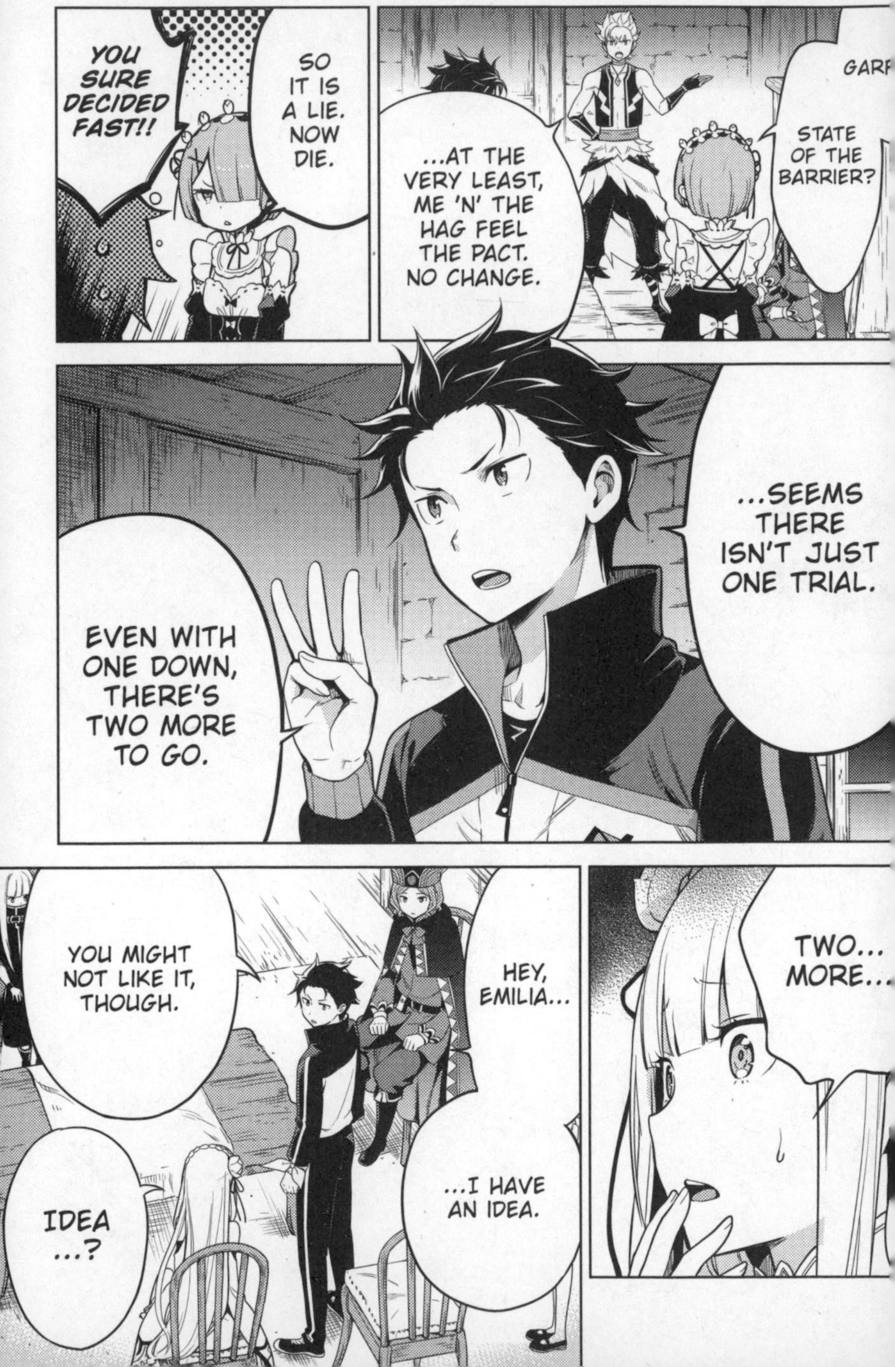
GARF
STATE OF THE BARRIER?
...AT THE VERY LEAST, ME 'N' THE HAG FEEL THE PACT. NO CHANGE.
SO IT IS A LIE. NOW DIE.
YOU SURE DECIDED FAST!!
...SEEMS THERE ISN'T JUST ONE TRIAL.
EVEN WITH ONE DOWN, THERE'S TWO MORE TO GO.
TWO... MORE...
HEY, EMILIA...
YOU MIGHT NOT LIKE IT, THOUGH.
...I HAVE AN IDEA.
IDEA ...?

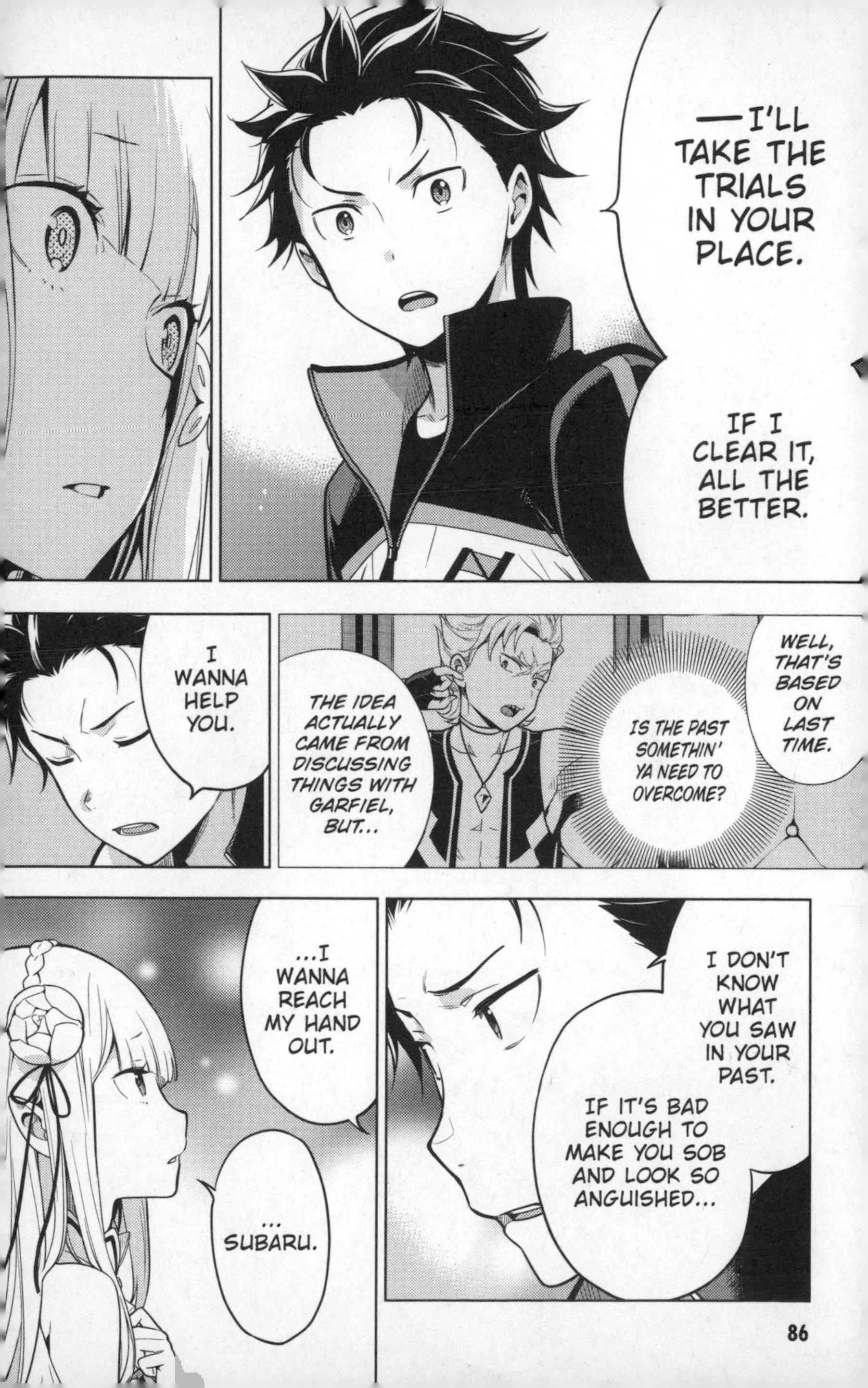
—I'LL TAKE THE TRIALS IN YOUR PLACE.
IF I CLEAR IT, ALL THE BETTER.
WELL, THAT'S BASED ON LAST TIME.
IS THE PAST SOMETHIN' YA NEED TO OVERCOME?
THE IDEA ACTUALLY CAME FROM DISCUSSING THINGS WITH GARFIEL, BUT...
I WANNA HELP YOU.
I DON'T KNOW WHAT YOU SAW IN YOUR PAST.
IF IT'S BAD ENOUGH TO MAKE YOU SOB AND LOOK SO ANGUISHED...
...I WANNA REACH MY HAND OUT.
... SUBARU.

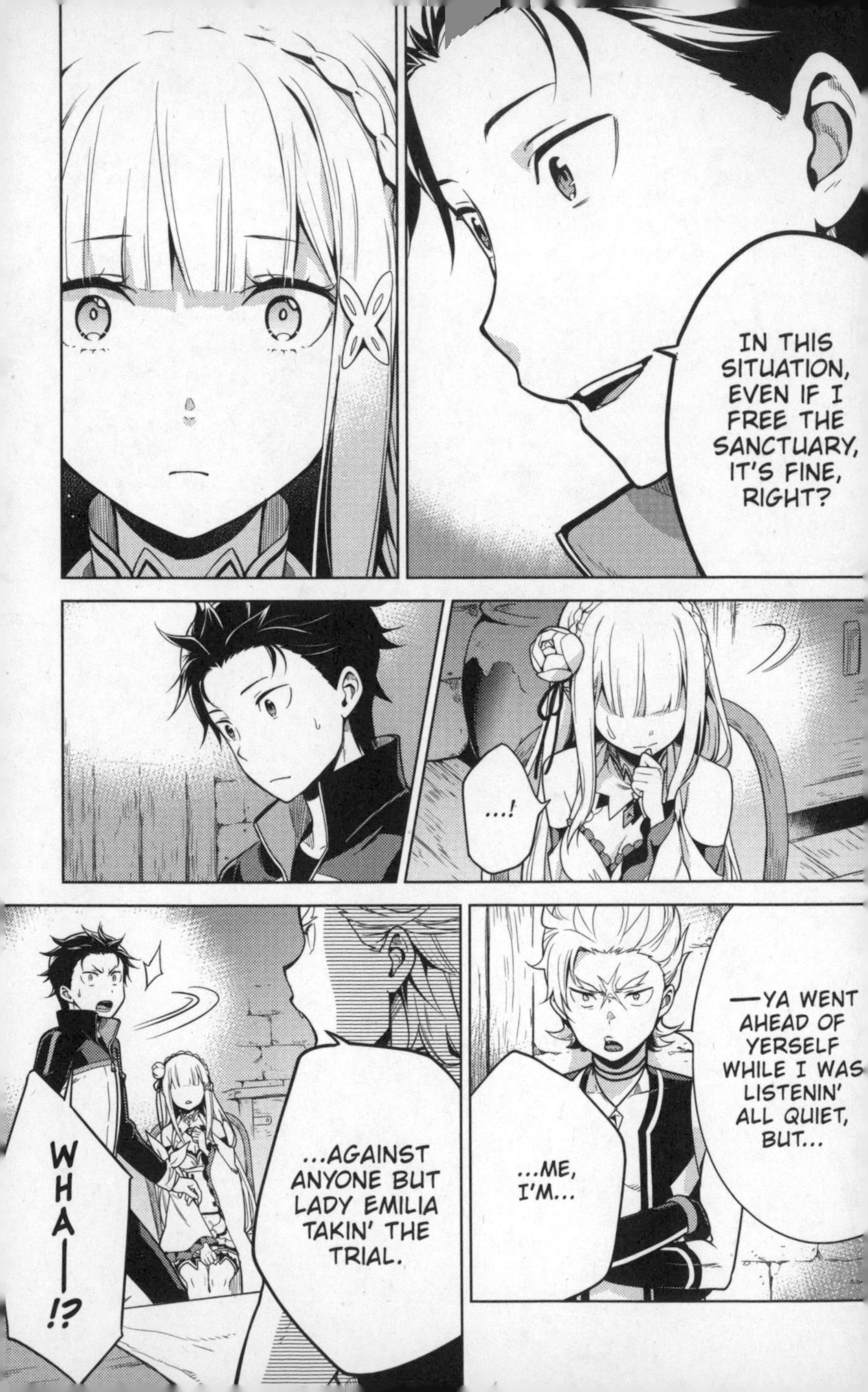
IN THIS SITUATION, EVEN IF I FREE THE SANCTUARY, IT'S FINE, RIGHT?
...!
—YA WENT AHEAD OF YERSELF WHILE I WAS LISTENIN' ALL QUIET, BUT...
...ME, I'M...
...AGAINST ANYONE BUT LADY EMILIA TAKIN' THE TRIAL.
WHA—!?

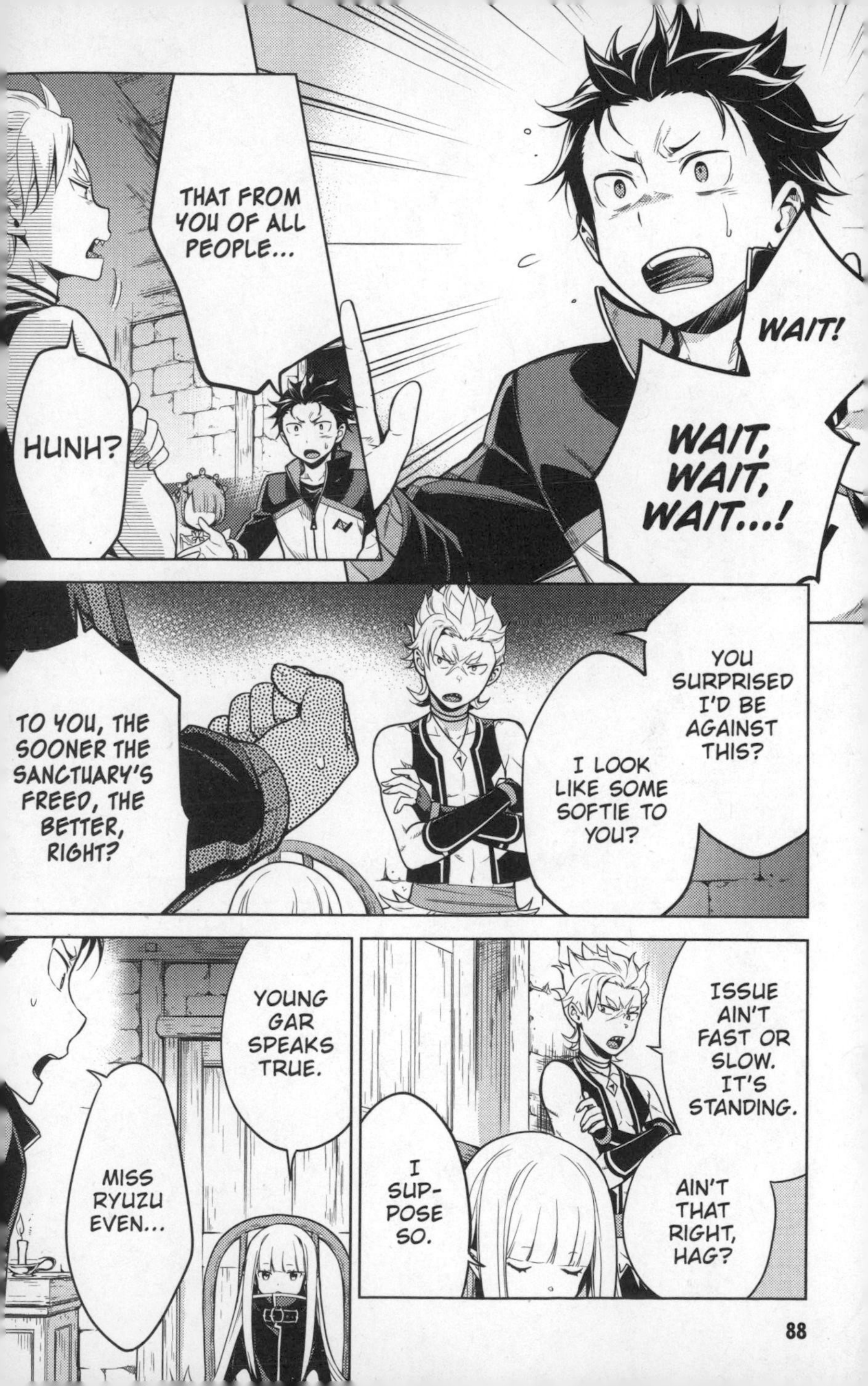
WAIT!
WAIT, WAIT, WAIT...!
THAT FROM YOU OF ALL PEOPLE...
HUNH?
YOU SURPRISED I'D BE AGAINST THIS?
I LOOK LIKE SOME SOFTIE TO YOU?
TO YOU, THE SOONER THE SANCTUARY'S FREED, THE BETTER, RIGHT?
ISSUE AIN'T FAST OR SLOW. IT'S STANDING.
AIN'T THAT RIGHT, HAG?
I SUP-POSE SO.
YOUNG GAR SPEAKS TRUE.
MISS RYUZU EVEN...

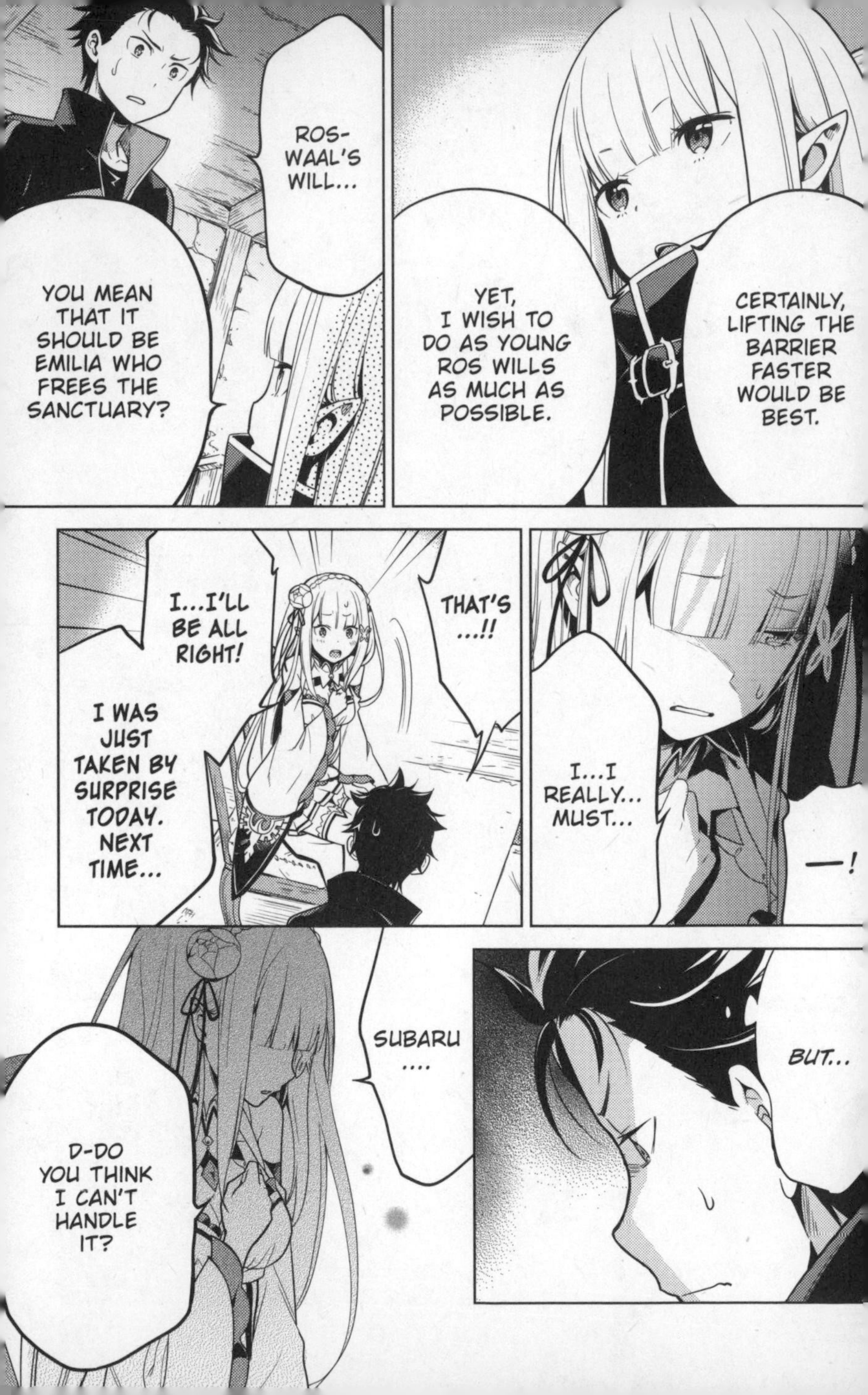
CERTAINLY, LIFTING THE BARRIER FASTER WOULD BE BEST.
YET, I WISH TO DO AS YOUNG ROS WILLS AS MUCH AS POSSIBLE.
ROS-WAAL'S WILL...
YOU MEAN THAT IT SHOULD BE EMILIA WHO FREES THE SANCTUARY?
—!
I...I REALLY... MUST...
THAT'S ...!!
I...I'LL BE ALL RIGHT!
I WAS JUST TAKEN BY SURPRISE TODAY. NEXT TIME...
BUT...
SUBARU ....
D-DO YOU THINK I CAN'T HANDLE IT?

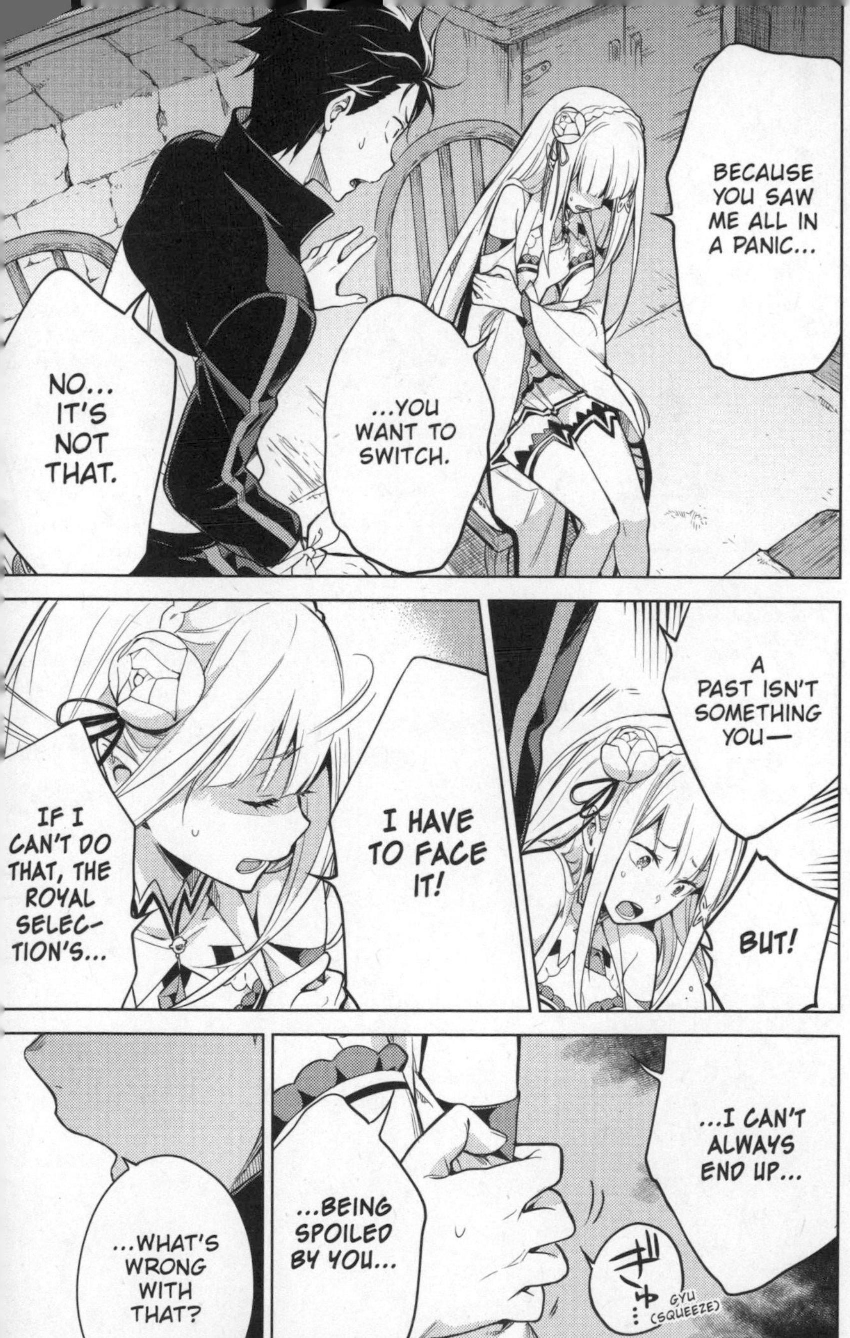
BECAUSE YOU SAW ME ALL IN A PANIC...
...YOU WANT TO SWITCH.
NO... IT'S NOT THAT.
A PAST ISN'T SOMETHING YOU—
BUT!
I HAVE TO FACE IT!
IF I CAN'T DO THAT, THE ROYAL SELEC-TION'S...
...I CAN'T ALWAYS END UP...
...BEING SPOILED BY YOU...
ぎゅ…
GYU (SQUEEZE)
...WHAT'S WRONG WITH THAT?

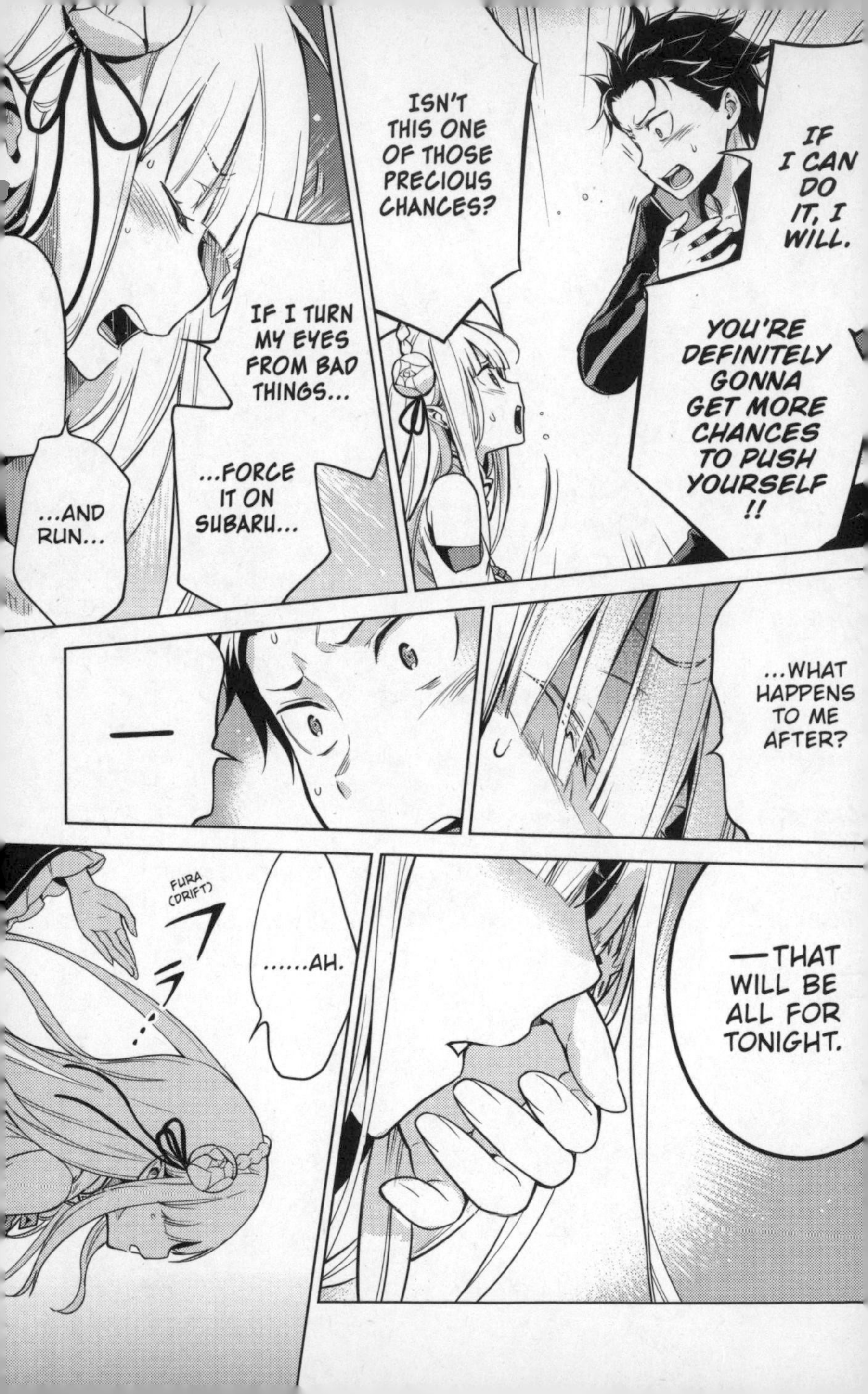
IF I CAN DO IT, I WILL.
YOU'RE DEFINITELY GONNA GET MORE CHANCES TO PUSH YOURSELF!!
ISN'T THIS ONE OF THOSE PRECIOUS CHANCES?
IF I TURN MY EYES FROM BAD THINGS...
...FORCE IT ON SUBARU...
...AND RUN...
...WHAT HAPPENS TO ME AFTER?
—
—THAT WILL BE ALL FOR TONIGHT.
......AH.
FURA (DRIFT)

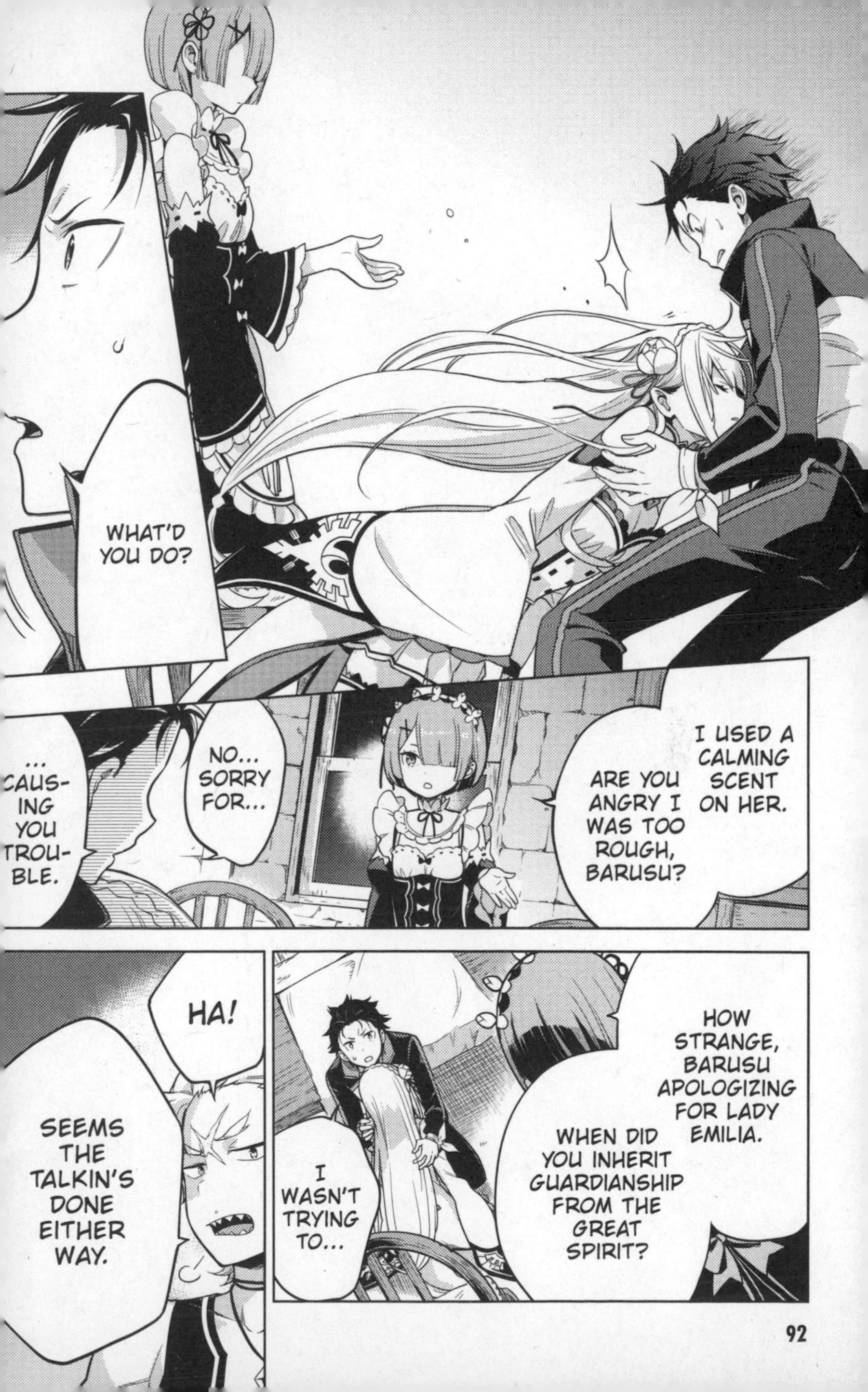
WHAT'D YOU DO?
I USED A CALMING SCENT ON HER.
ARE YOU ANGRY I WAS TOO ROUGH, BARUSU?
NO... SORRY FOR...
... CAUSING YOU TROUBLE.
HOW STRANGE, BARUSU APOLOGIZING FOR LADY EMILIA.
WHEN DID YOU INHERIT GUARDIANSHIP FROM THE GREAT SPIRIT?
I WASN'T TRYING TO...
HA!
SEEMS THE TALKIN'S DONE EITHER WAY.

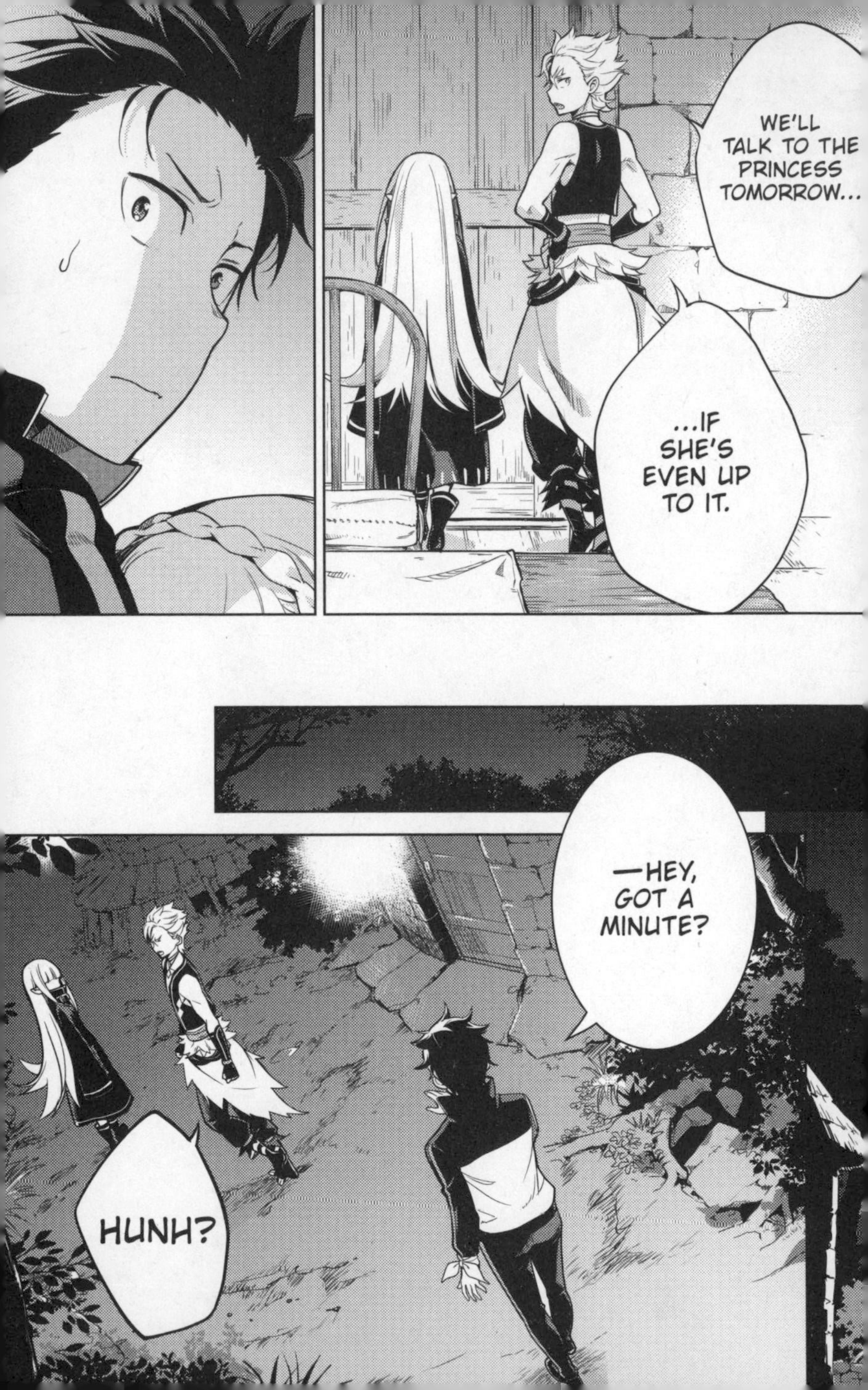
WE'LL TALK TO THE PRINCESS TOMORROW...
...IF SHE'S EVEN UP TO IT.
—HEY, GOT A MINUTE?
HUNH?

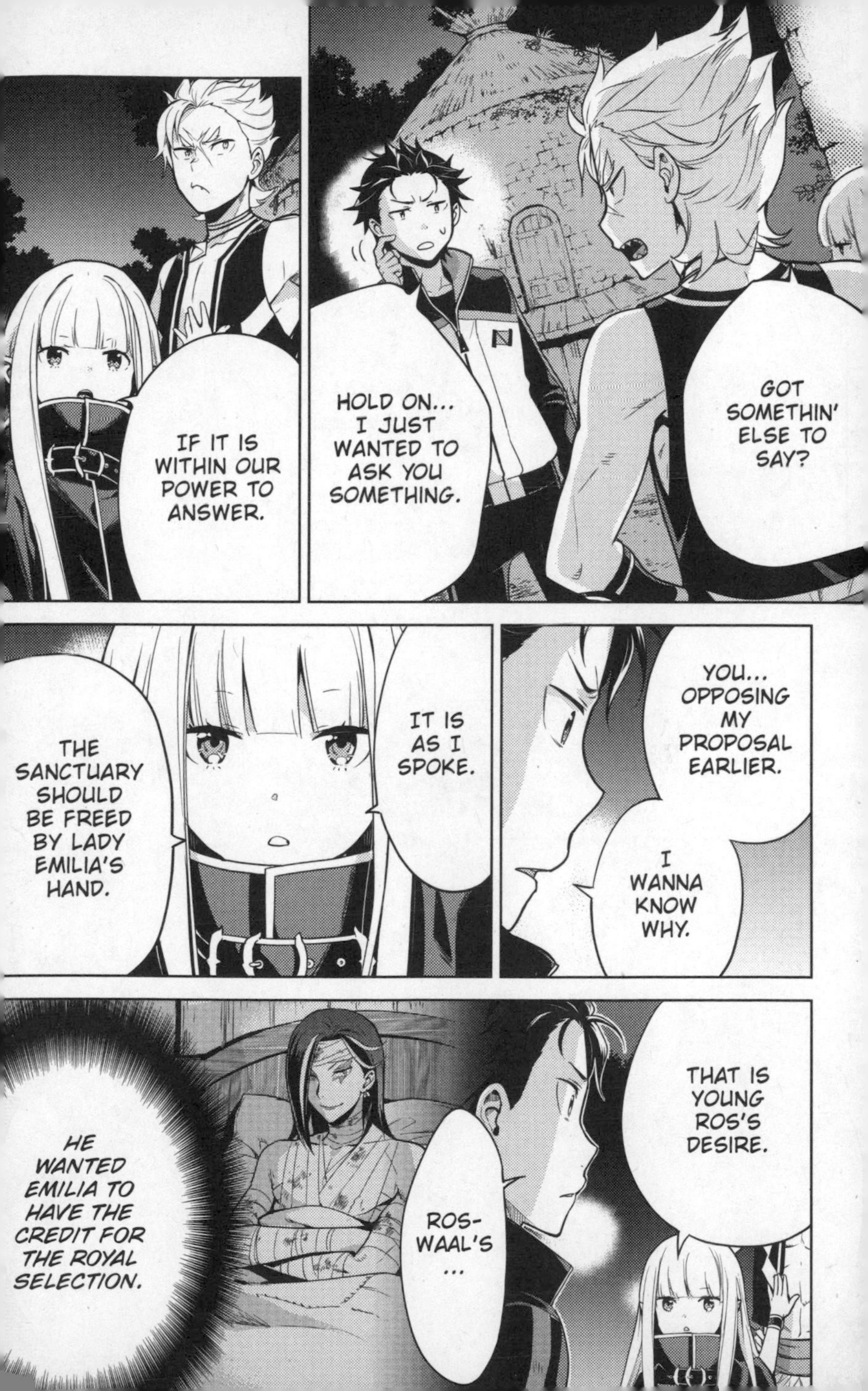
GOT SOMETHIN' ELSE TO SAY?
HOLD ON... I JUST WANTED TO ASK YOU SOMETHING.
IF IT IS WITHIN OUR POWER TO ANSWER.
YOU... OPPOSING MY PROPOSAL EARLIER.
I WANNA KNOW WHY.
IT IS AS I SPOKE.
THE SANCTUARY SHOULD BE FREED BY LADY EMILIA'S HAND.
THAT IS YOUNG ROS'S DESIRE.
ROS-WAAL'S ...
HE WANTED EMILIA TO HAVE THE CREDIT FOR THE ROYAL SELECTION.

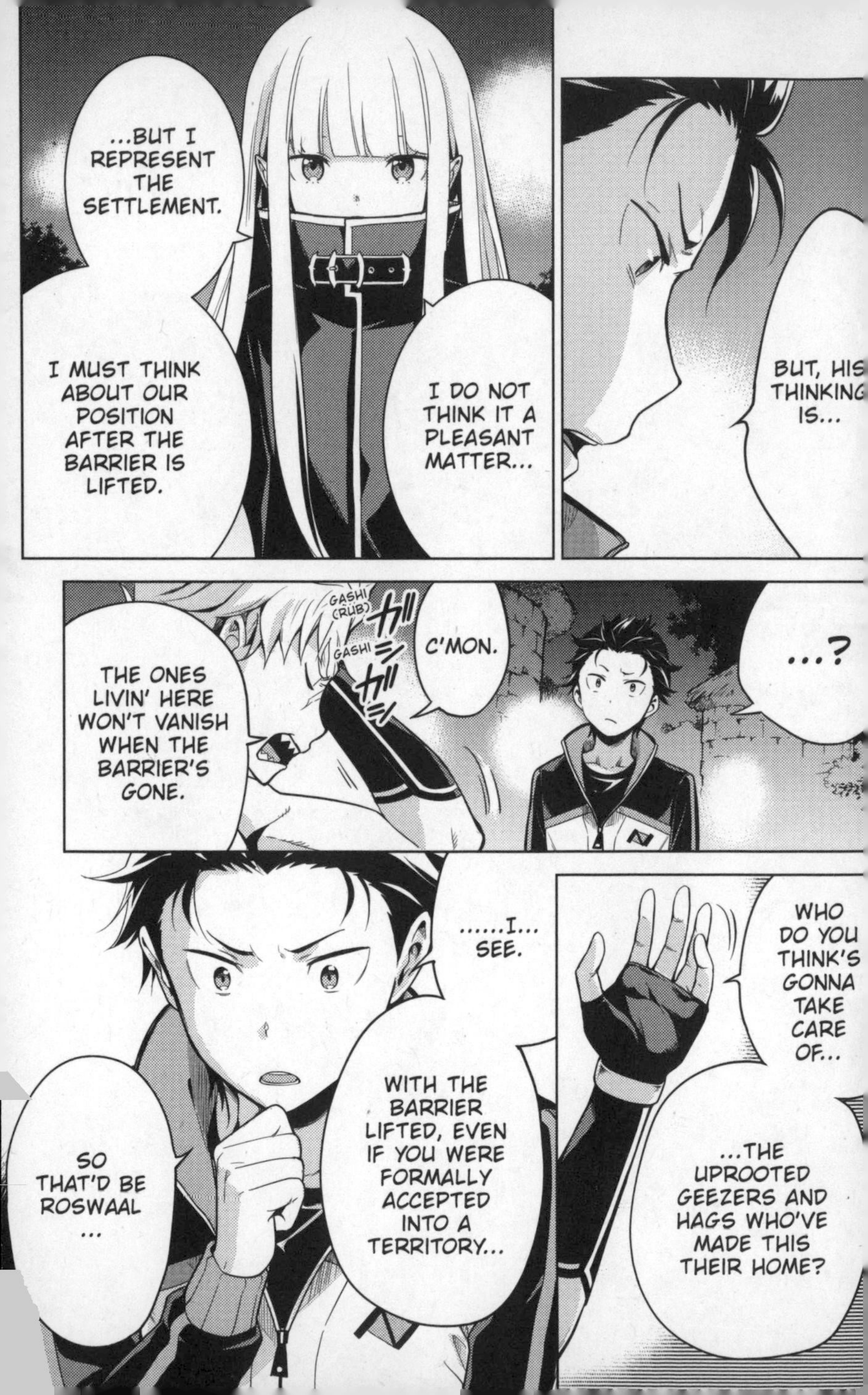
BUT, HIS THINKING IS...
...BUT I REPRESENT THE SETTLEMENT.
I DO NOT THINK IT A PLEASANT MATTER...
I MUST THINK ABOUT OUR POSITION AFTER THE BARRIER IS LIFTED.
...?
C'MON.
GASHI (RUB) GASHI
THE ONES LIVIN' HERE WON'T VANISH WHEN THE BARRIER'S GONE.
WHO DO YOU THINK'S GONNA TAKE CARE OF...
...THE UPROOTED GEEZERS AND HAGS WHO'VE MADE THIS THEIR HOME?
......I... SEE.
WITH THE BARRIER LIFTED, EVEN IF YOU WERE FORMALLY ACCEPTED INTO A TERRITORY...
SO THAT'D BE ROSWAAL ...

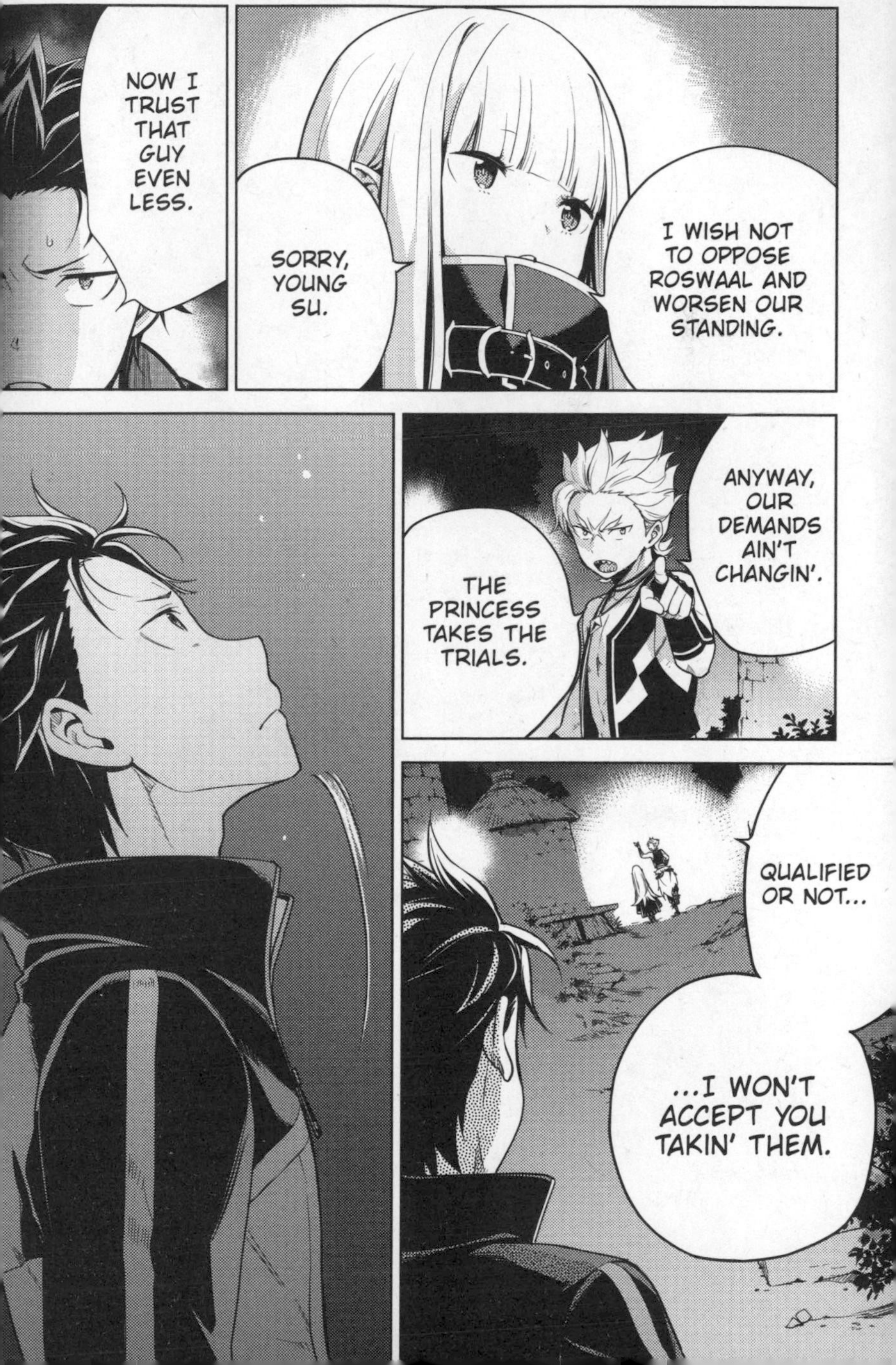
I WISH NOT TO OPPOSE ROSWAAL AND WORSEN OUR STANDING.
SORRY, YOUNG SU.
NOW I TRUST THAT GUY EVEN LESS.
ANYWAY, OUR DEMANDS AIN'T CHANGIN'.
THE PRINCESS TAKES THE TRIALS.
QUALIFIED OR NOT...
...I WON'T ACCEPT YOU TAKIN' THEM.

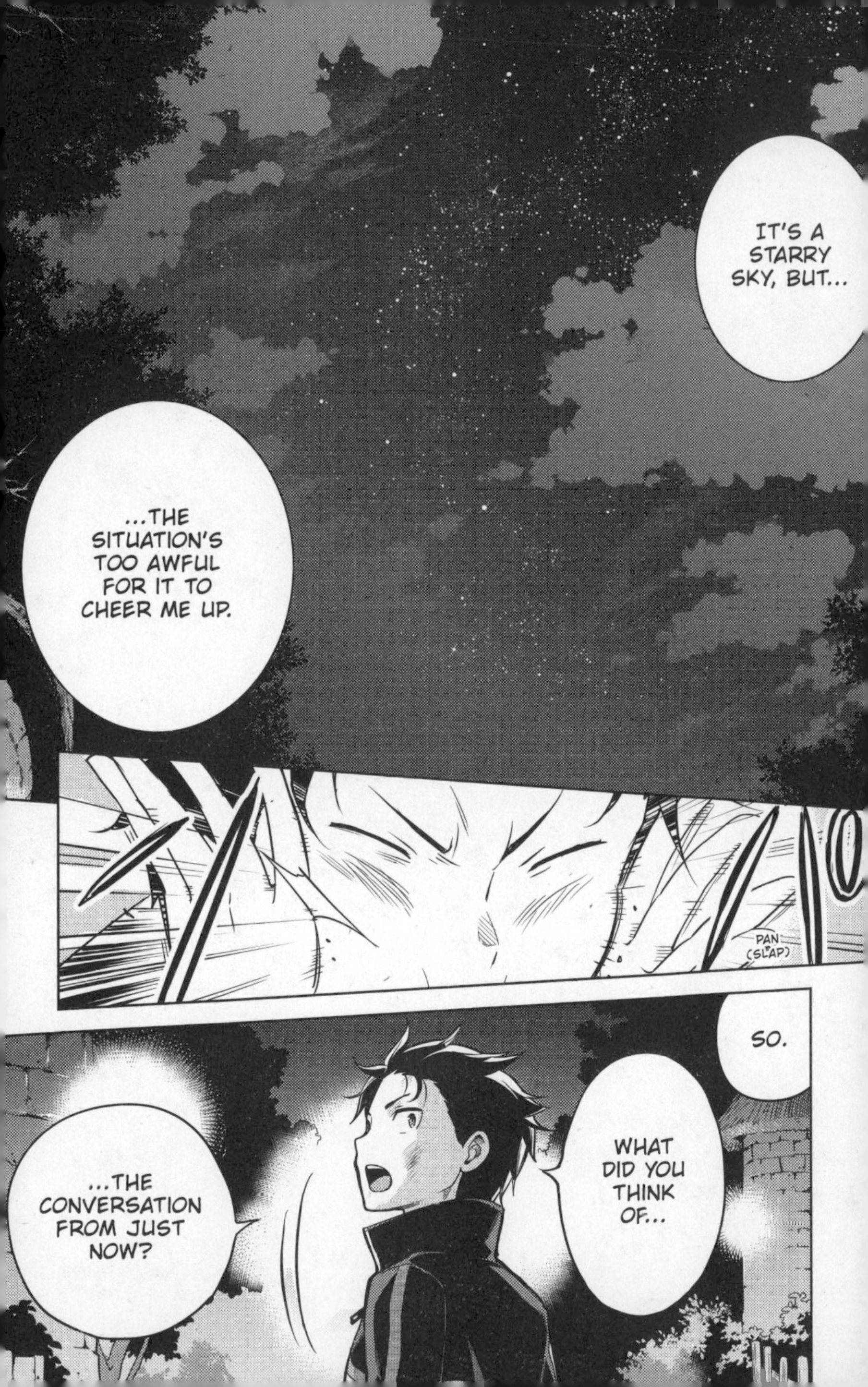
IT'S A STARRY SKY, BUT...
...THE SITUATION'S TOO AWFUL FOR IT TO CHEER ME UP.
PAN (SLAP)
SO.
WHAT DID YOU THINK OF...
...THE CONVERSATION FROM JUST NOW?

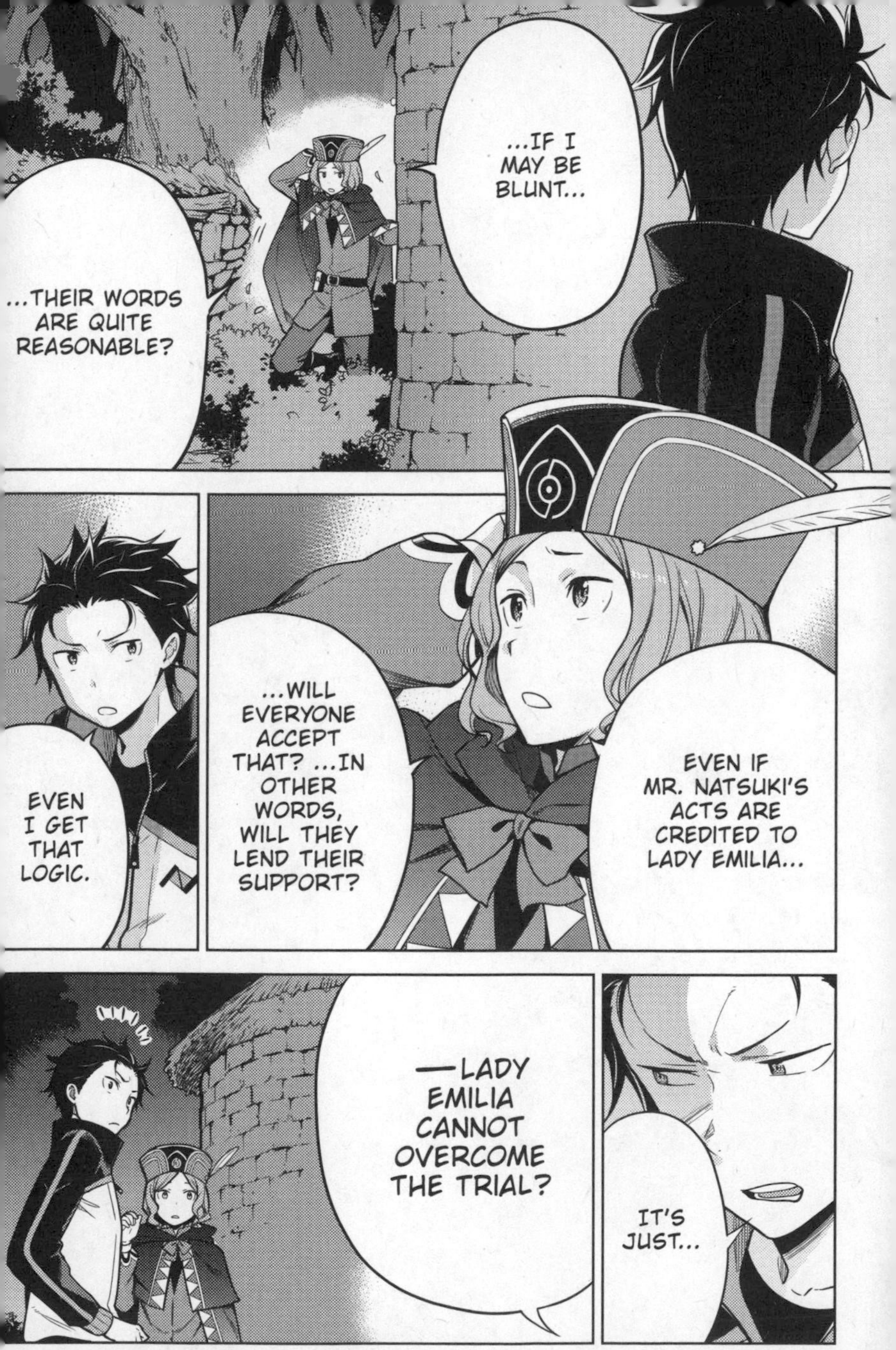
...IF I MAY BE BLUNT...
...THEIR WORDS ARE QUITE REASONABLE?
EVEN IF MR. NATSUKI'S ACTS ARE CREDITED TO LADY EMILIA...
...WILL EVERYONE ACCEPT THAT? ...IN OTHER WORDS, WILL THEY LEND THEIR SUPPORT?
EVEN I GET THAT LOGIC.
IT'S JUST...
—LADY EMILIA CANNOT OVERCOME THE TRIAL?

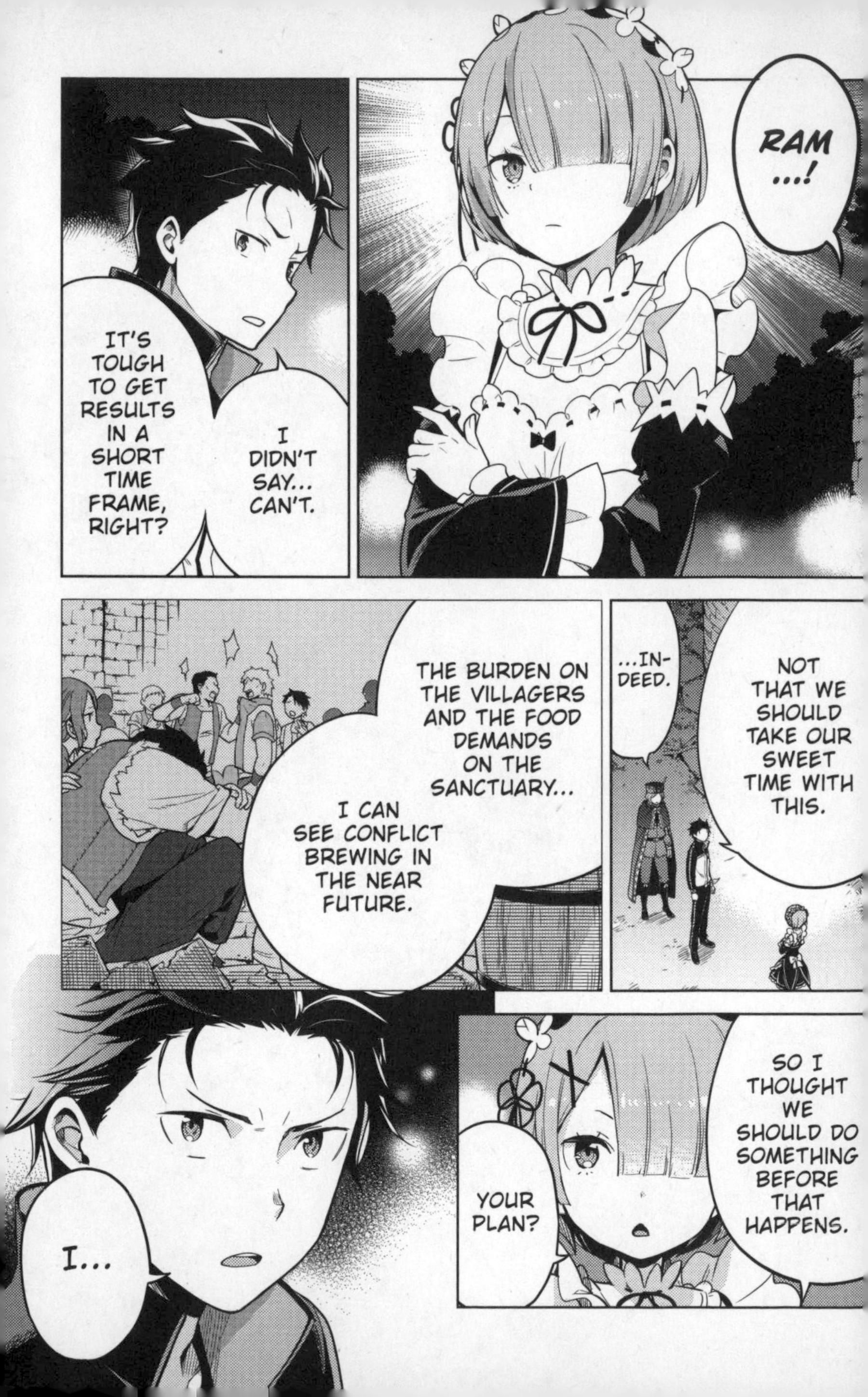
RAM ...!
IT'S TOUGH TO GET RESULTS IN A SHORT TIME FRAME, RIGHT?
I DIDN'T SAY... CAN'T.
NOT THAT WE SHOULD TAKE OUR SWEET TIME WITH THIS.
...IN-DEED.
THE BURDEN ON THE VILLAGERS AND THE FOOD DEMANDS ON THE SANCTUARY...
I CAN SEE CONFLICT BREWING IN THE NEAR FUTURE.
SO I THOUGHT WE SHOULD DO SOMETHING BEFORE THAT HAPPENS.
YOUR PLAN?
I...

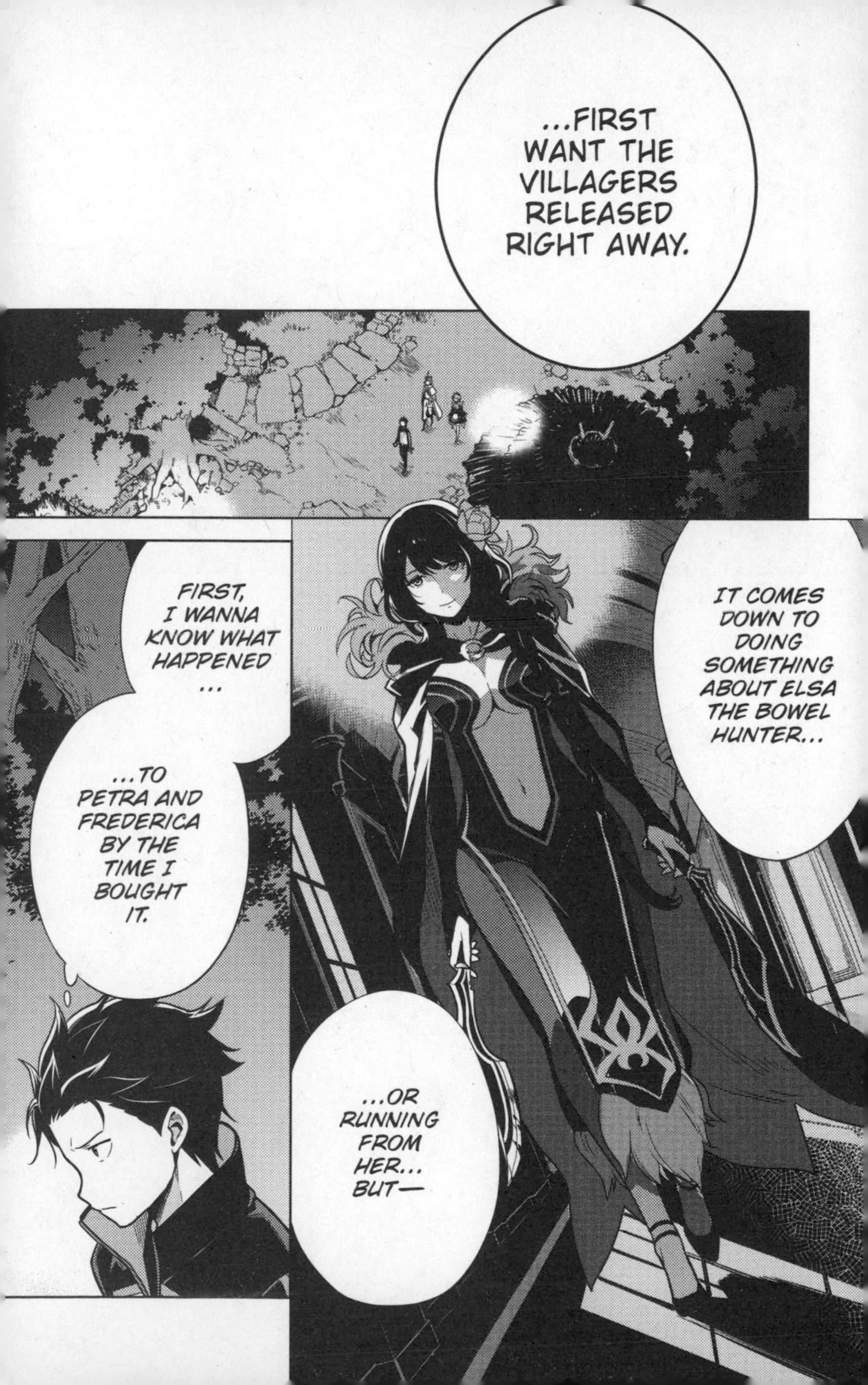
...FIRST WANT THE VILLAGERS RELEASED RIGHT AWAY.
IT COMES DOWN TO DOING SOMETHING ABOUT ELSA THE BOWEL HUNTER...
...OR RUNNING FROM HER... BUT—
FIRST, I WANNA KNOW WHAT HAPPENED ...
...TO PETRA AND FREDERICA BY THE TIME I BOUGHT IT.

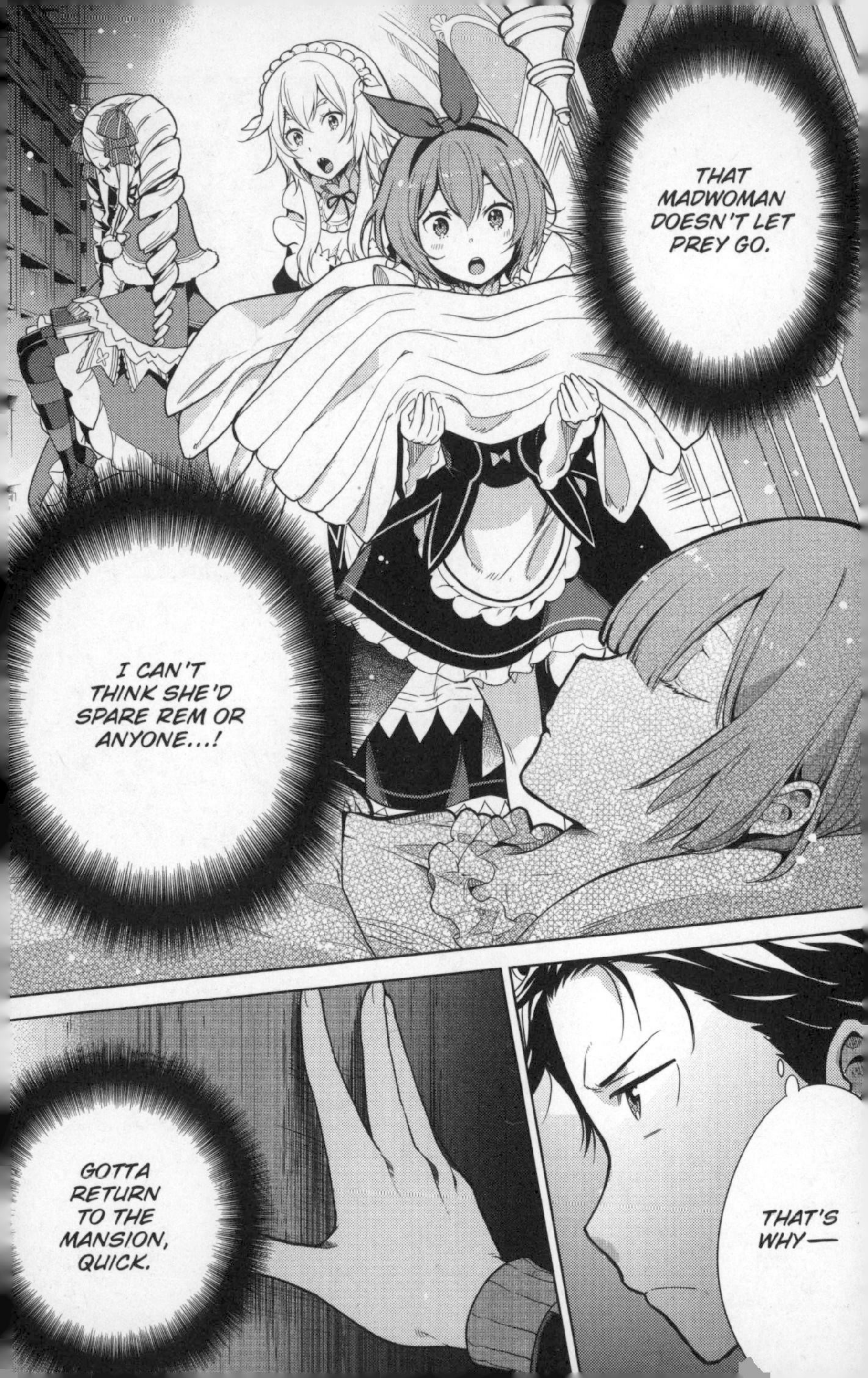
THAT MADWOMAN DOESN'T LET PREY GO.
I CAN'T THINK SHE'D SPARE REM OR ANYONE...!
THAT'S WHY—
GOTTA RETURN TO THE MANSION, QUICK.

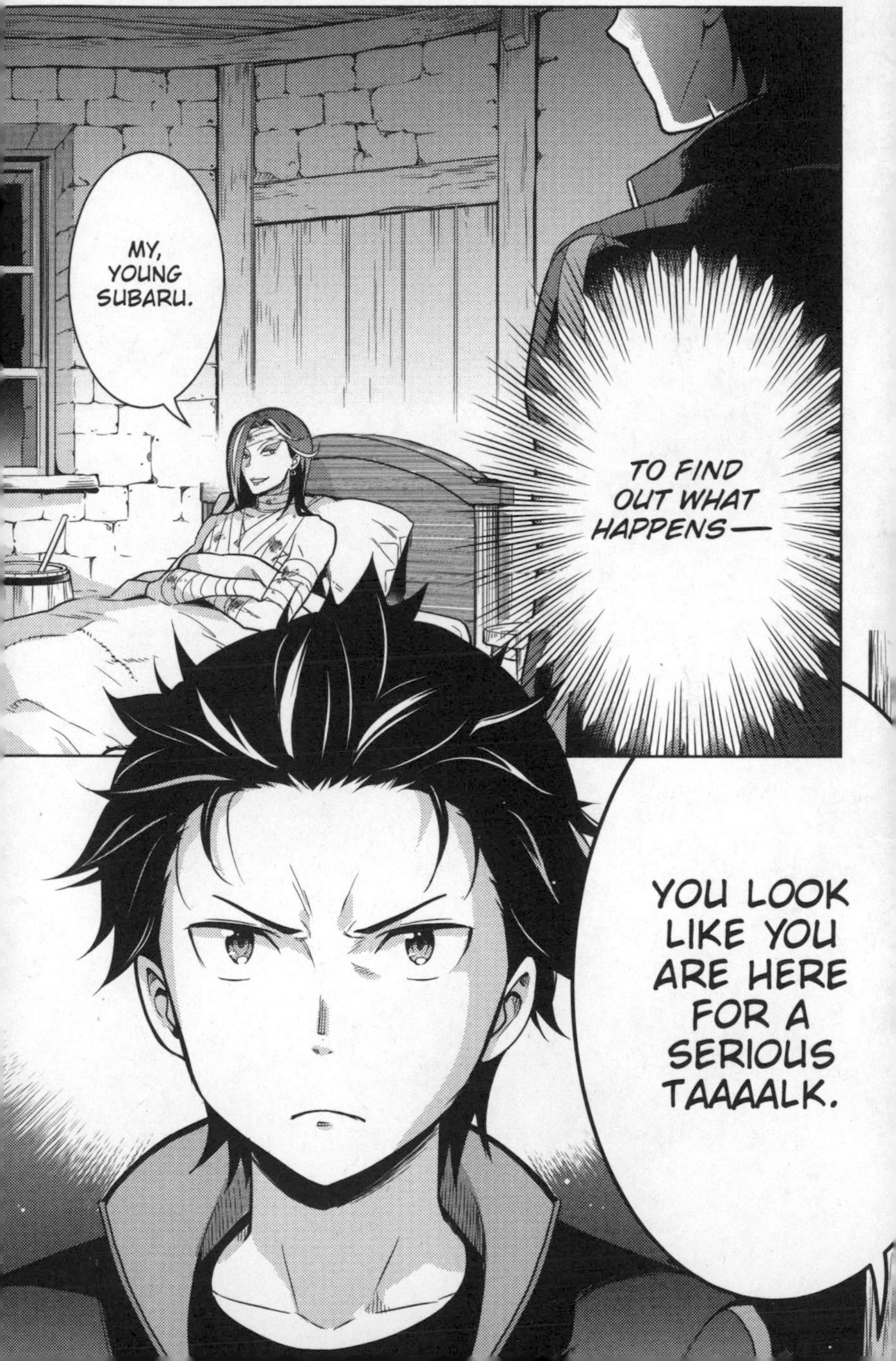
TO FIND OUT WHAT HAPPENS—
MY, YOUNG SUBARU.
YOU LOOK LIKE YOU ARE HERE FOR A SERIOUS TAAAALK.

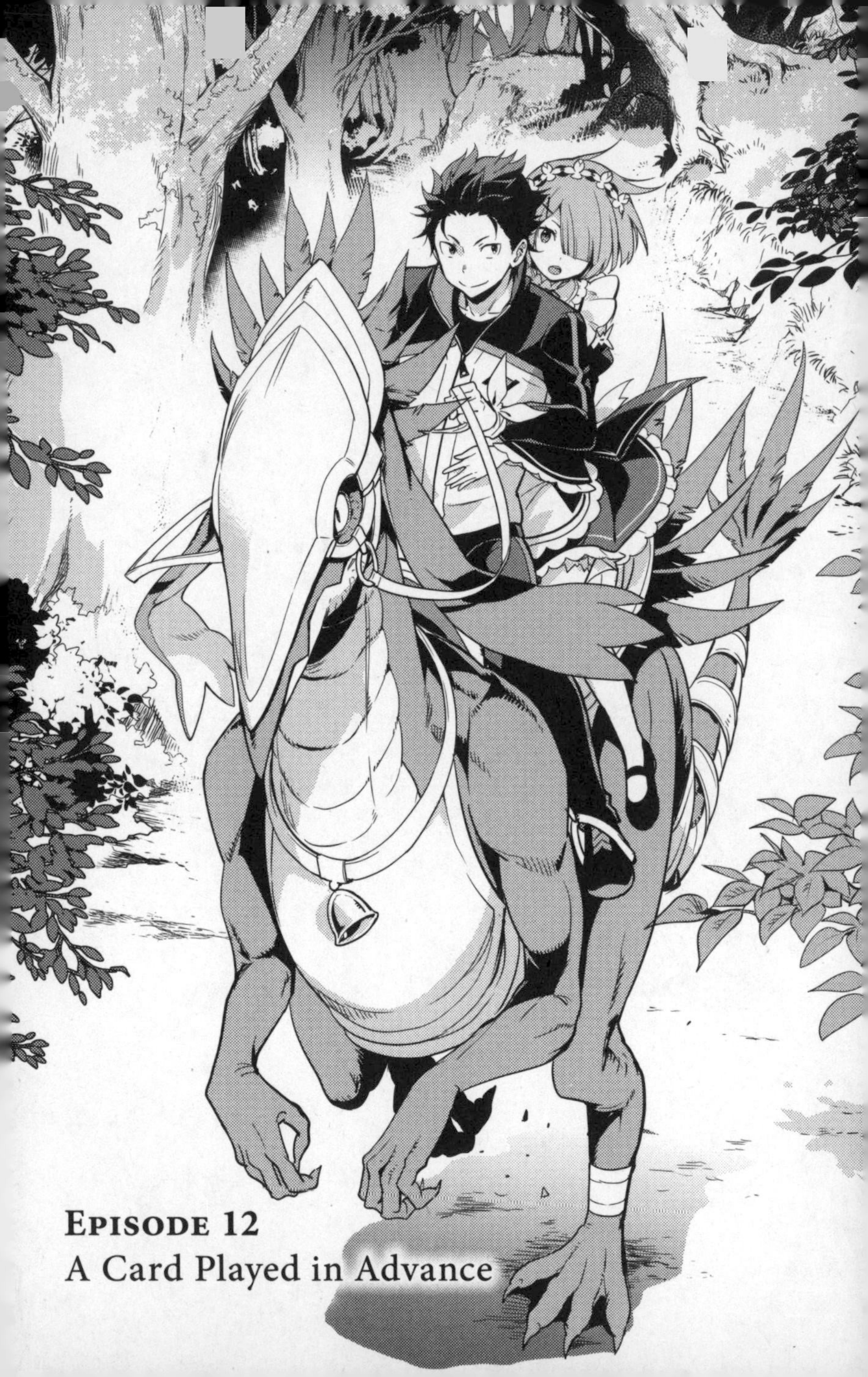

Episode 12
A Card Played in Advance

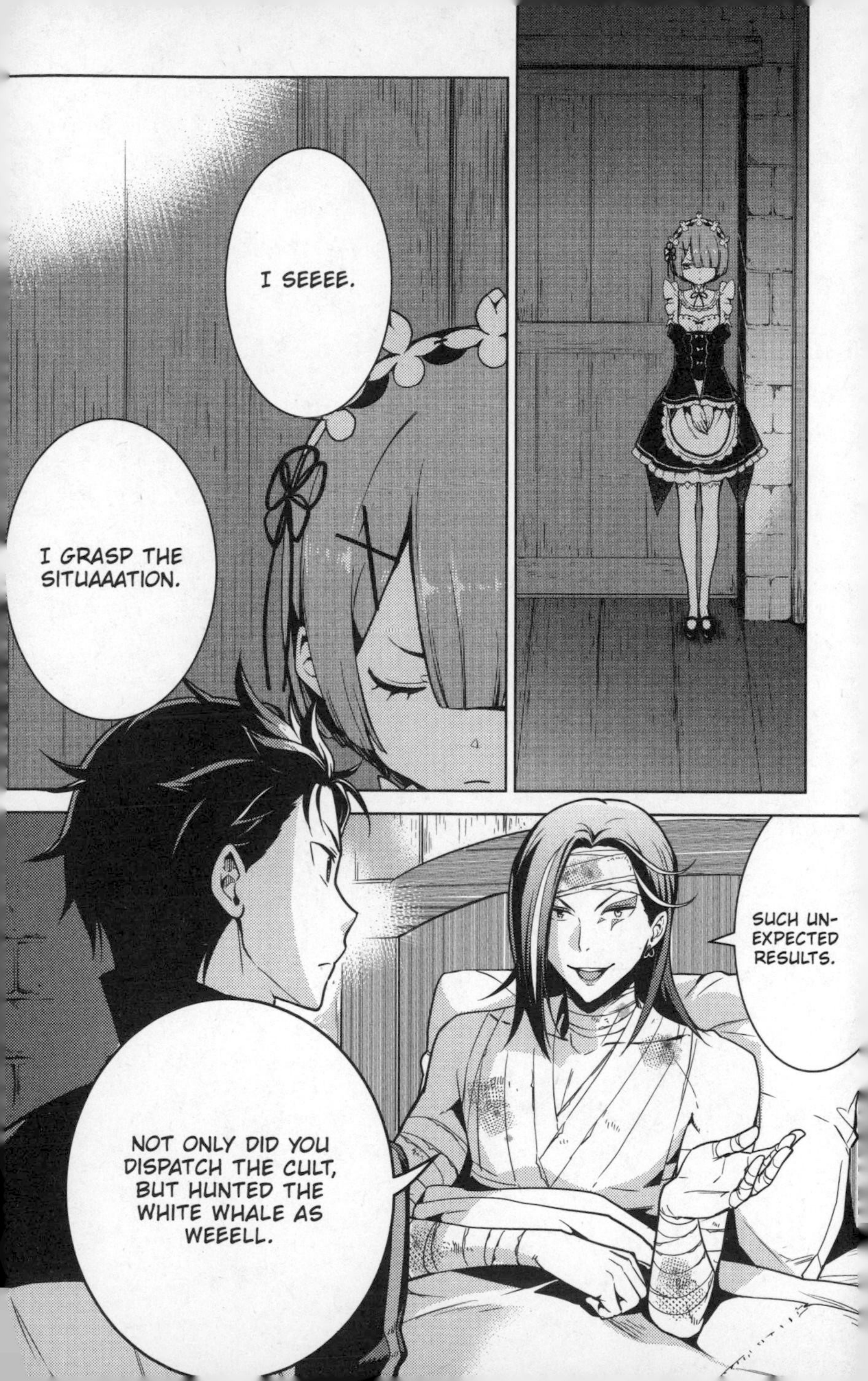
I SEEEE.
I GRASP THE SITUAAATION.
SUCH UN-EXPECTED RESULTS.
NOT ONLY DID YOU DISPATCH THE CULT, BUT HUNTED THE WHITE WHALE AS WEEELL.

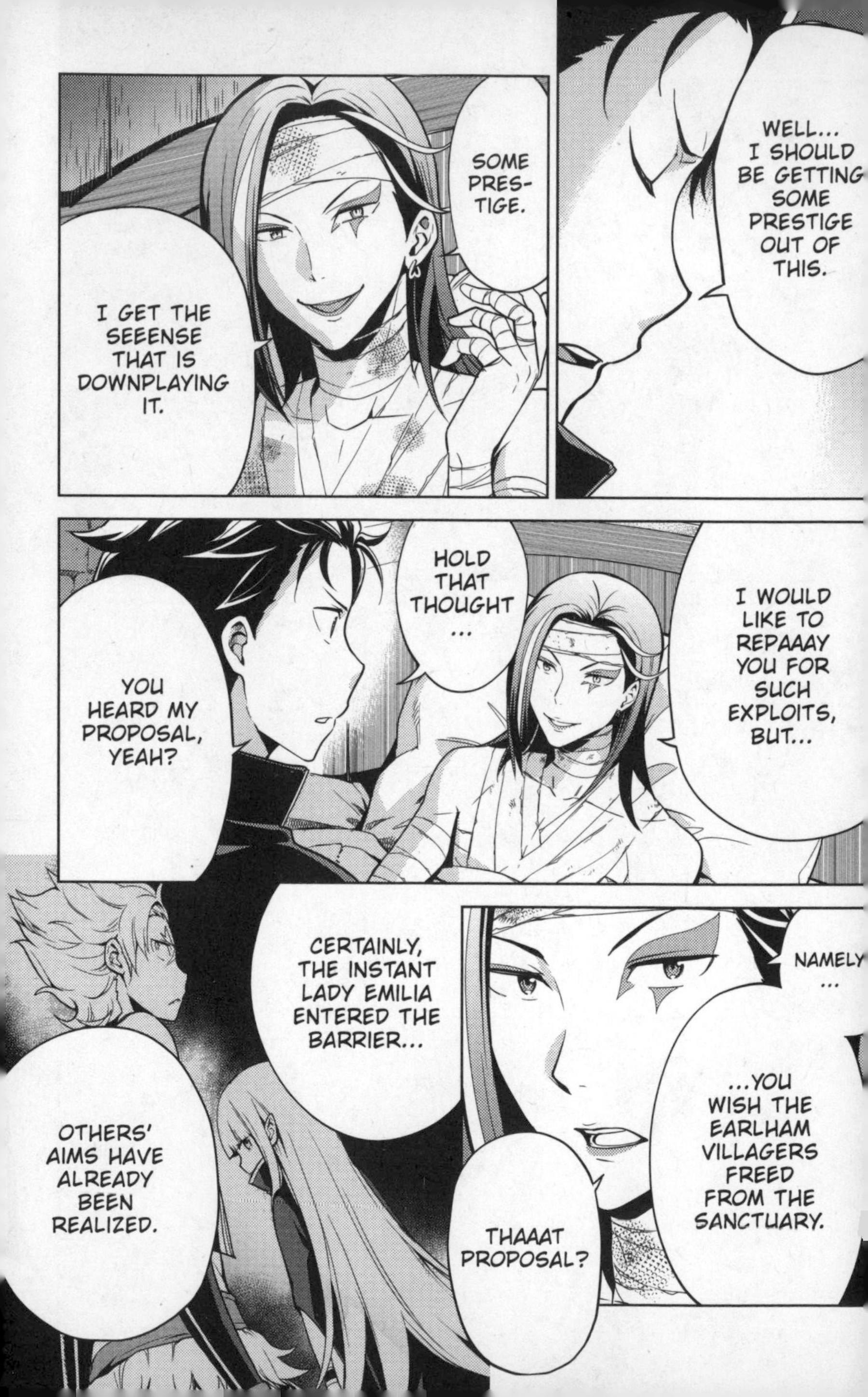
WELL... I SHOULD BE GETTING SOME PRESTIGE OUT OF THIS.
SOME PRES-TIGE.
I GET THE SEEENSE THAT IS DOWNPLAYING IT.
I WOULD LIKE TO REPAAAY YOU FOR SUCH EXPLOITS, BUT...
HOLD THAT THOUGHT...
YOU HEARD MY PROPOSAL, YEAH?
NAMELY...
...YOU WISH THE EARLHAM VILLAGERS FREED FROM THE SANCTUARY.
THAAAT PROPOSAL?
CERTAINLY, THE INSTANT LADY EMILIA ENTERED THE BARRIER...
OTHERS' AIMS HAVE ALREADY BEEN REALIZED.

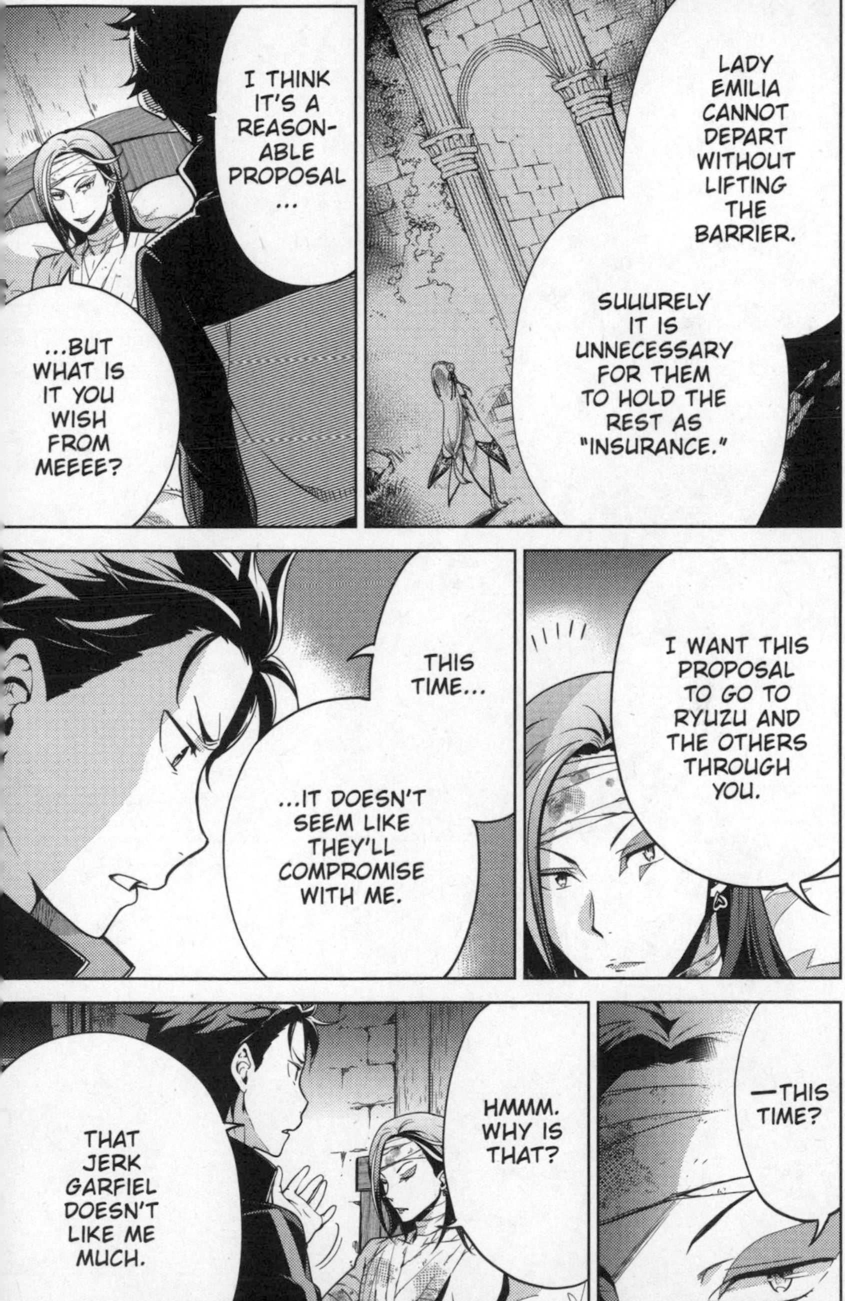
LADY EMILIA CANNOT DEPART WITHOUT LIFTING THE BARRIER.
SUUURELY IT IS UNNECESSARY FOR THEM TO HOLD THE REST AS "INSURANCE."
I THINK IT'S A REASON-ABLE PROPOSAL ...
...BUT WHAT IS IT YOU WISH FROM MEEEE?
I WANT THIS PROPOSAL TO GO TO RYUZU AND THE OTHERS THROUGH YOU.
THIS TIME...
...IT DOESN'T SEEM LIKE THEY'LL COMPROMISE WITH ME.
—THIS TIME?
HMMM. WHY IS THAT?
THAT JERK GARFIEL DOESN'T LIKE ME MUCH.

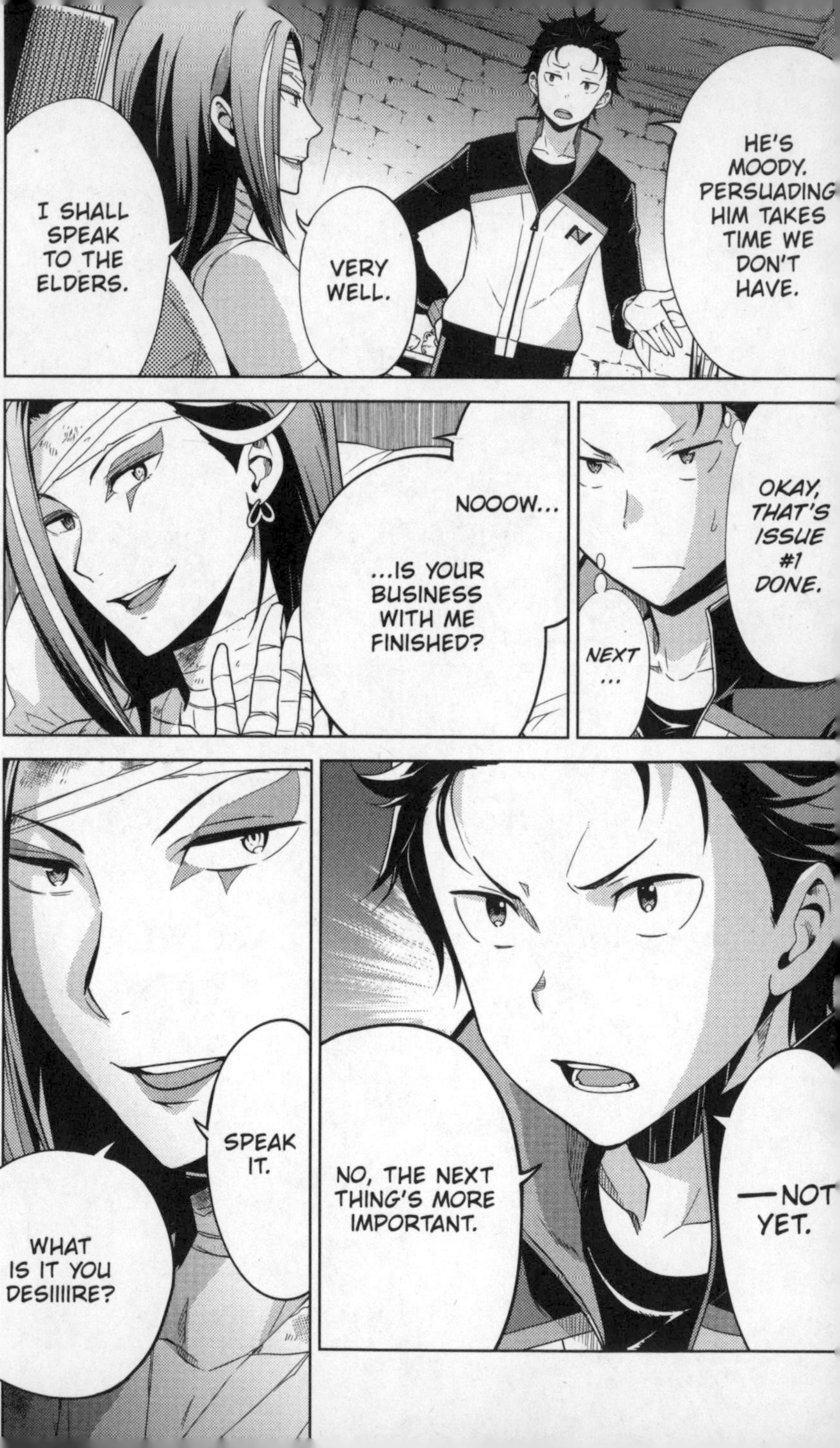
HE'S MOODY. PERSUADING HIM TAKES TIME WE DON'T HAVE.
VERY WELL.
I SHALL SPEAK TO THE ELDERS.
OKAY, THAT'S ISSUE #1 DONE.
NEXT ...
NOOOW...
...IS YOUR BUSINESS WITH ME FINISHED?
—NOT YET.
NO, THE NEXT THING'S MORE IMPORTANT.
SPEAK IT.
WHAT IS IT YOU DESIIIIRE?

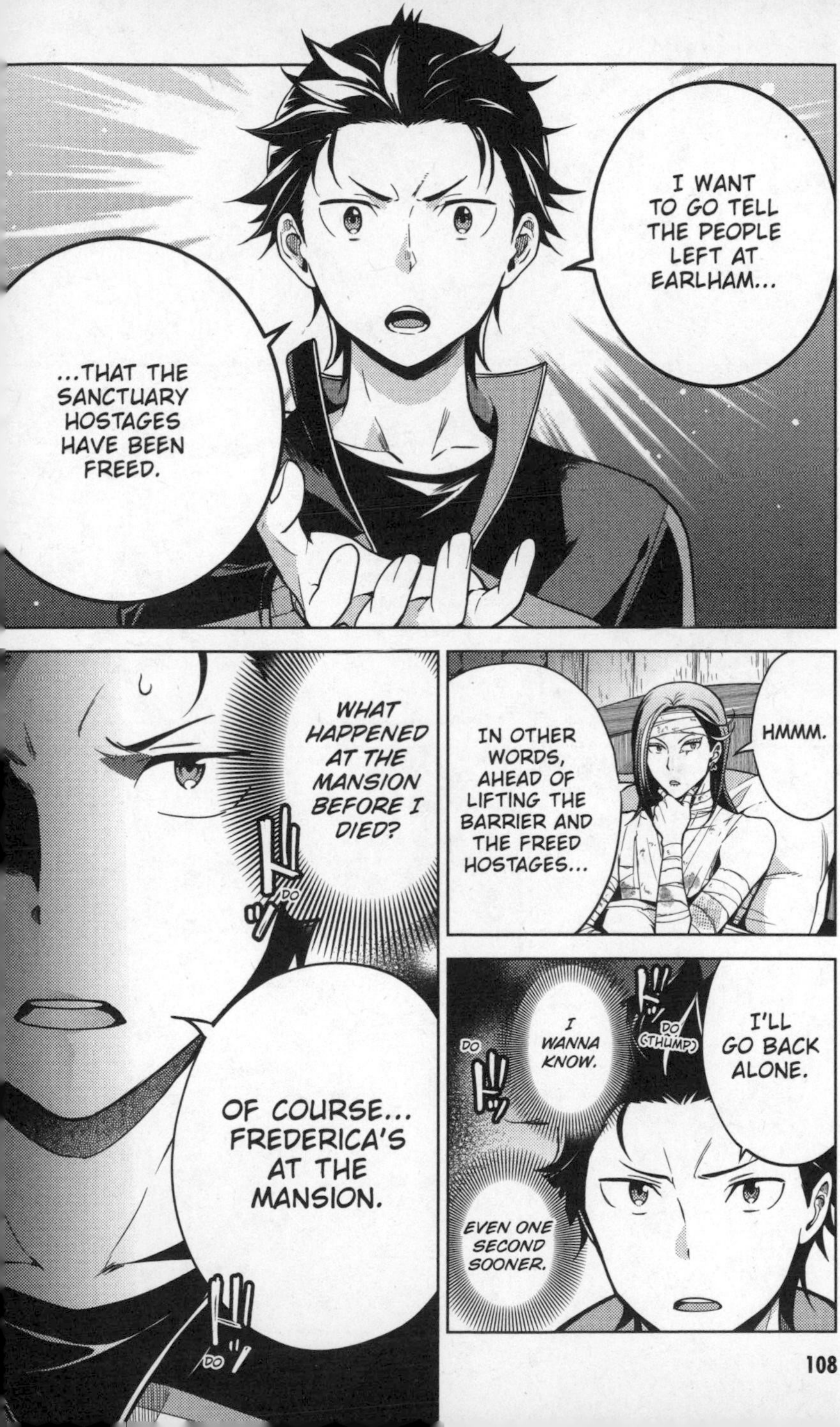
I WANT TO GO TELL THE PEOPLE LEFT AT EARLHAM...
...THAT THE SANCTUARY HOSTAGES HAVE BEEN FREED.
HMMM.
IN OTHER WORDS, AHEAD OF LIFTING THE BARRIER AND THE FREED HOSTAGES...
I'LL GO BACK ALONE.
DO (THUMP)
I WANNA KNOW.
DO
EVEN ONE SECOND SOONER.
WHAT HAPPENED AT THE MANSION BEFORE I DIED?
DO
OF COURSE... FREDERICA'S AT THE MANSION.
DO

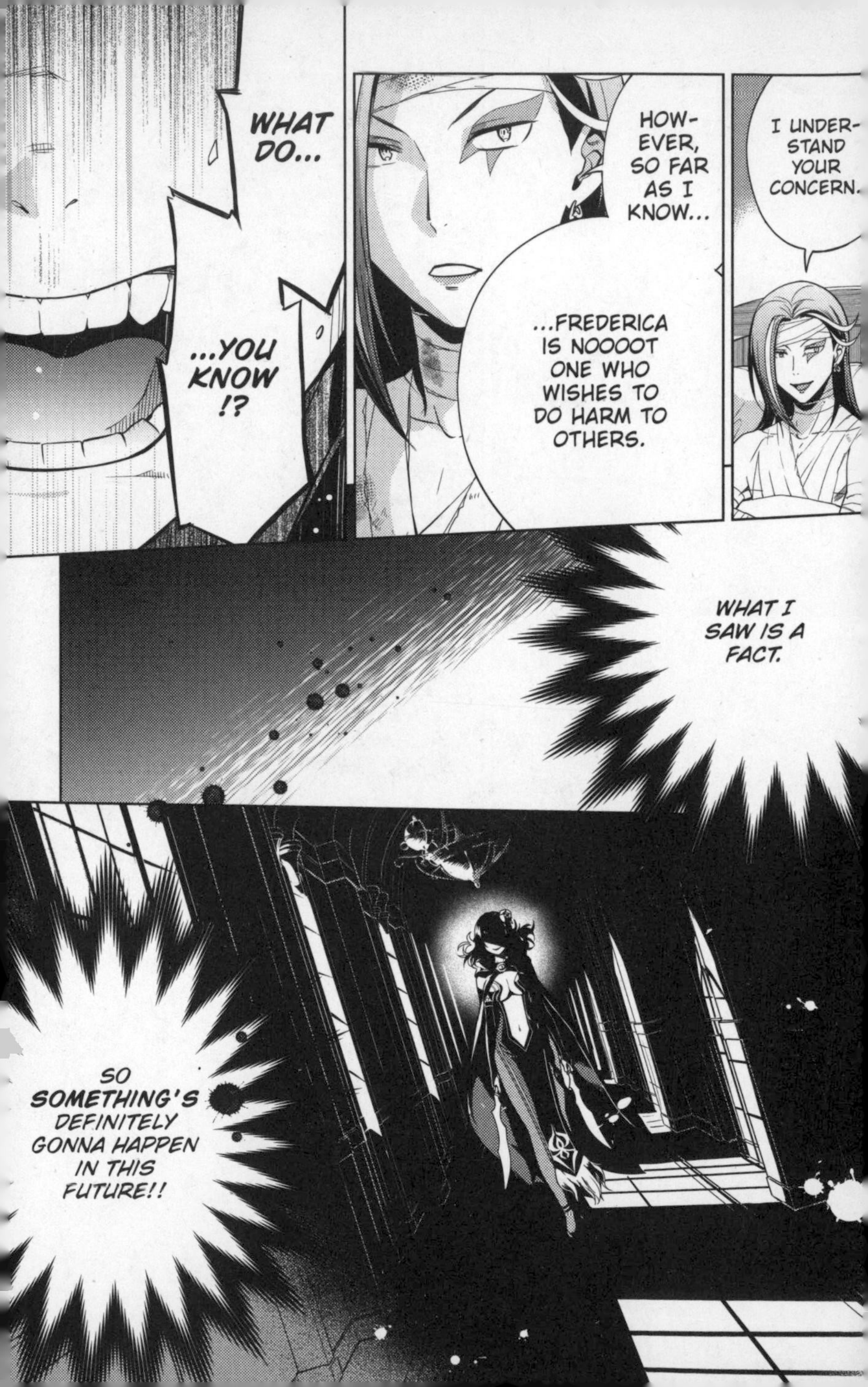
I UNDER-STAND YOUR CONCERN.
HOW-EVER, SO FAR AS I KNOW...
...FREDERICA IS NOOOOT ONE WHO WISHES TO DO HARM TO OTHERS.
WHAT DO...
...YOU KNOW!?
WHAT I SAW IS A FACT.
SO SOMETHING'S DEFINITELY GONNA HAPPEN IN THIS FUTURE!!

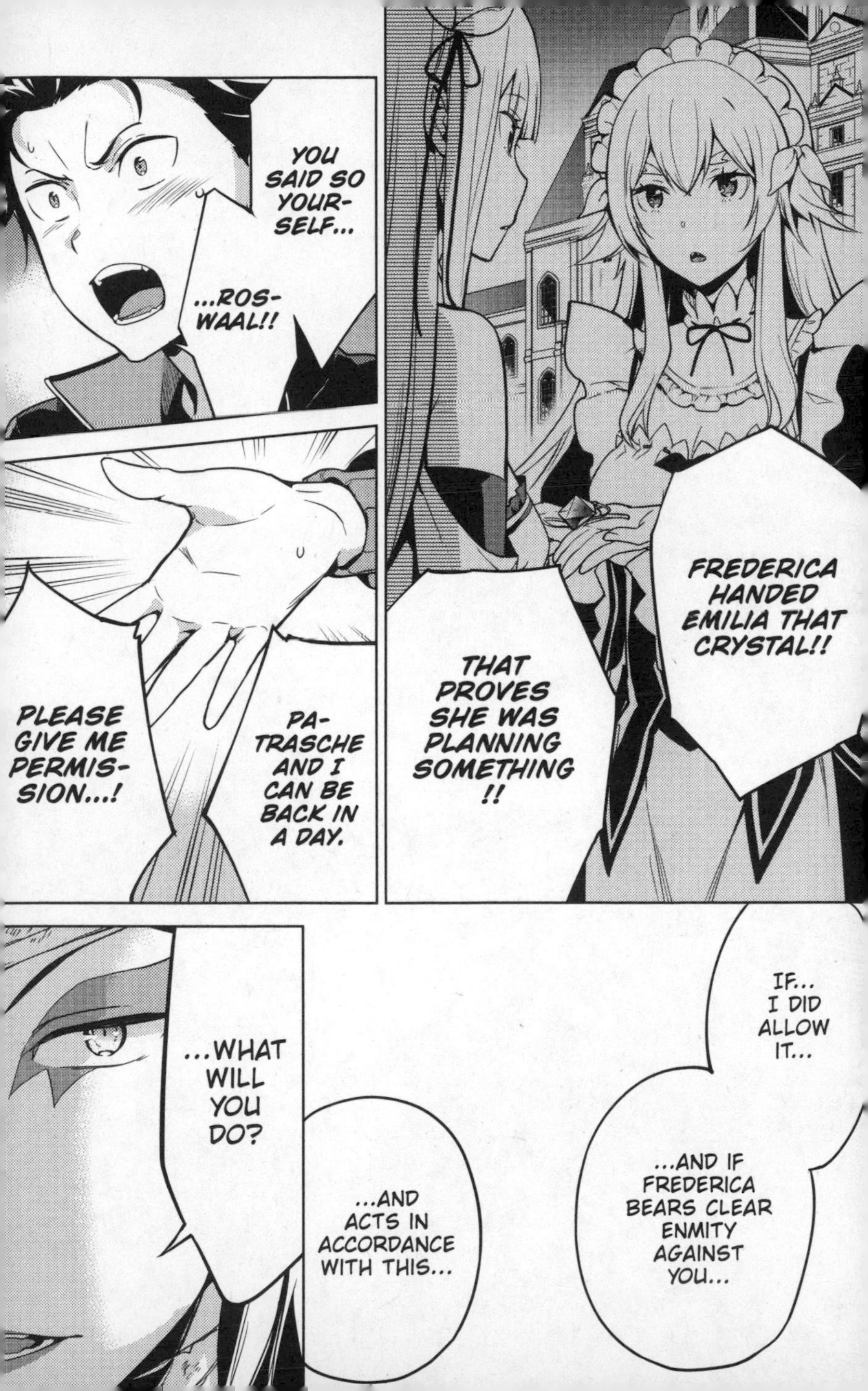
FREDERICA HANDED EMILIA THAT CRYSTAL!!
THAT PROVES SHE WAS PLANNING SOMETHING!!
YOU SAID SO YOUR-SELF...
...ROS-WAAL!!
PA-TRASCHE AND I CAN BE BACK IN A DAY.
PLEASE GIVE ME PERMIS-SION...!
IF... I DID ALLOW IT...
...AND IF FREDERICA BEARS CLEAR ENMITY AGAINST YOU...
...AND ACTS IN ACCORDANCE WITH THIS...
...WHAT WILL YOU DO?

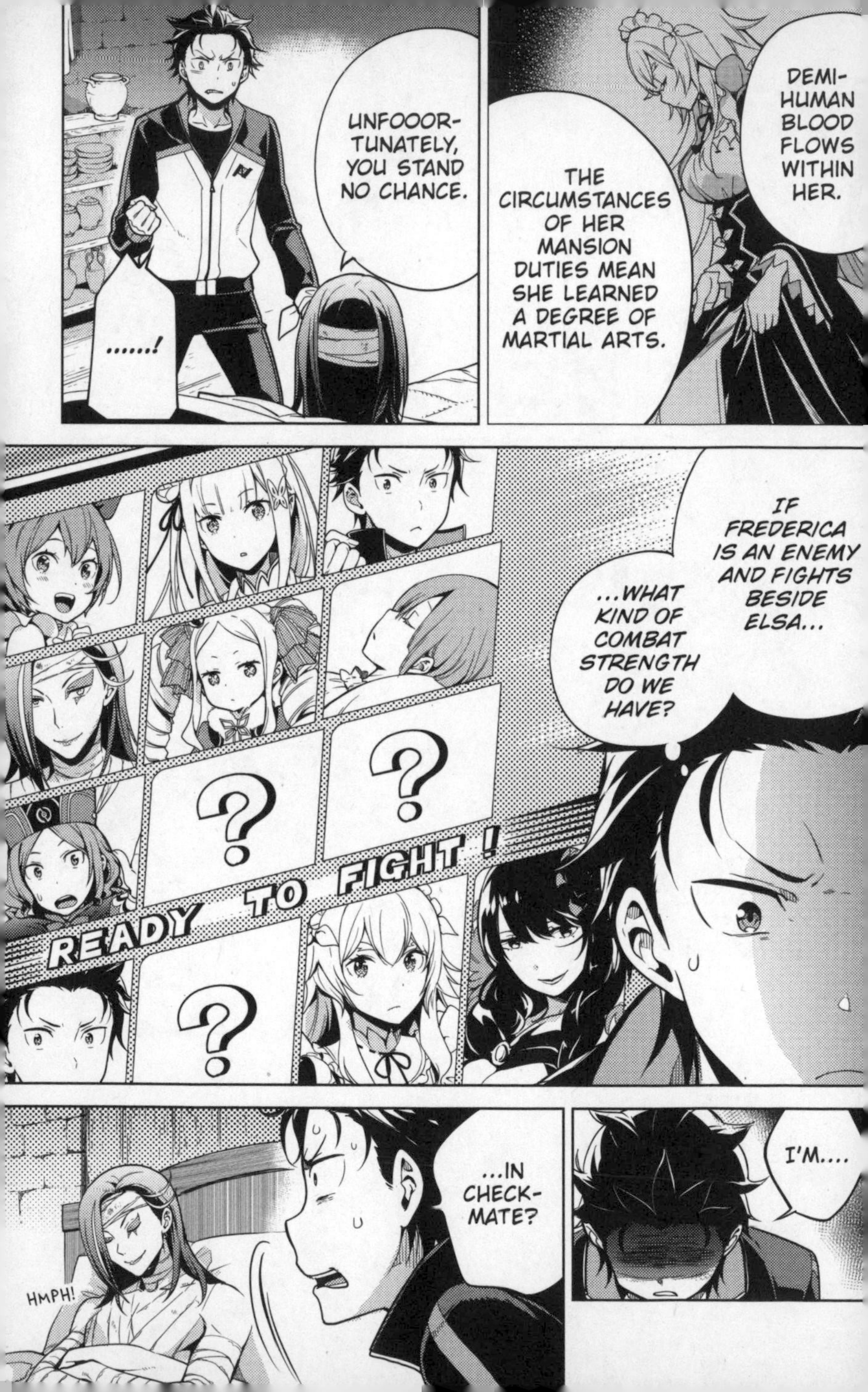
DEMI-HUMAN BLOOD FLOWS WITHIN HER.
THE CIRCUMSTANCES OF HER MANSION DUTIES MEAN SHE LEARNED A DEGREE OF MARTIAL ARTS.
UNFOOOR-TUNATELY, YOU STAND NO CHANCE.
......!
IF FREDERICA IS AN ENEMY AND FIGHTS BESIDE ELSA...
...WHAT KIND OF COMBAT STRENGTH DO WE HAVE?
READY TO FIGHT!
I'M....
...IN CHECK-MATE?
HMPH!

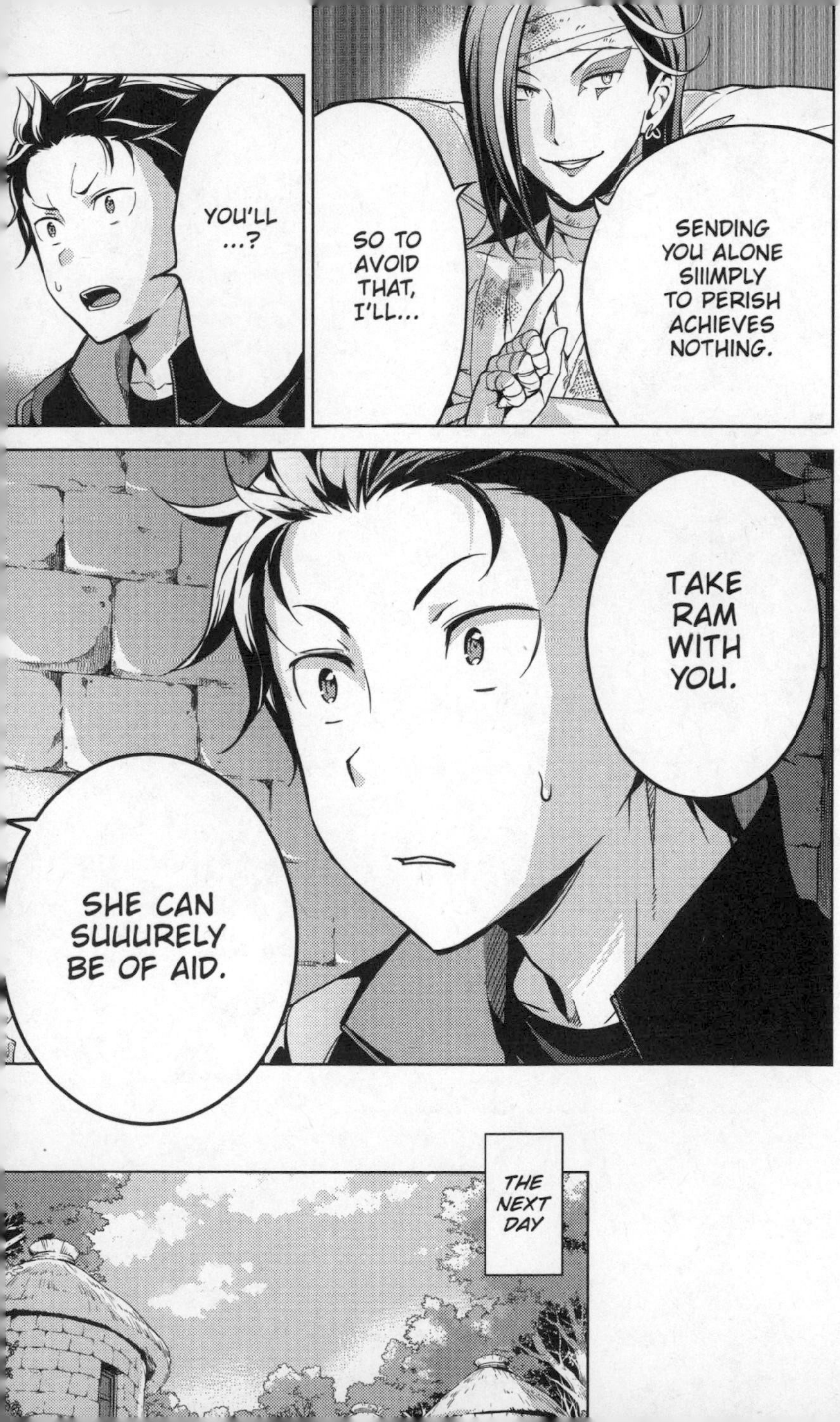
SENDING YOU ALONE SIIIMPLY TO PERISH ACHIEVES NOTHING.
SO TO AVOID THAT, I'LL...
YOU'LL ...?
TAKE RAM WITH YOU.
SHE CAN SUUURELY BE OF AID.
THE NEXT DAY

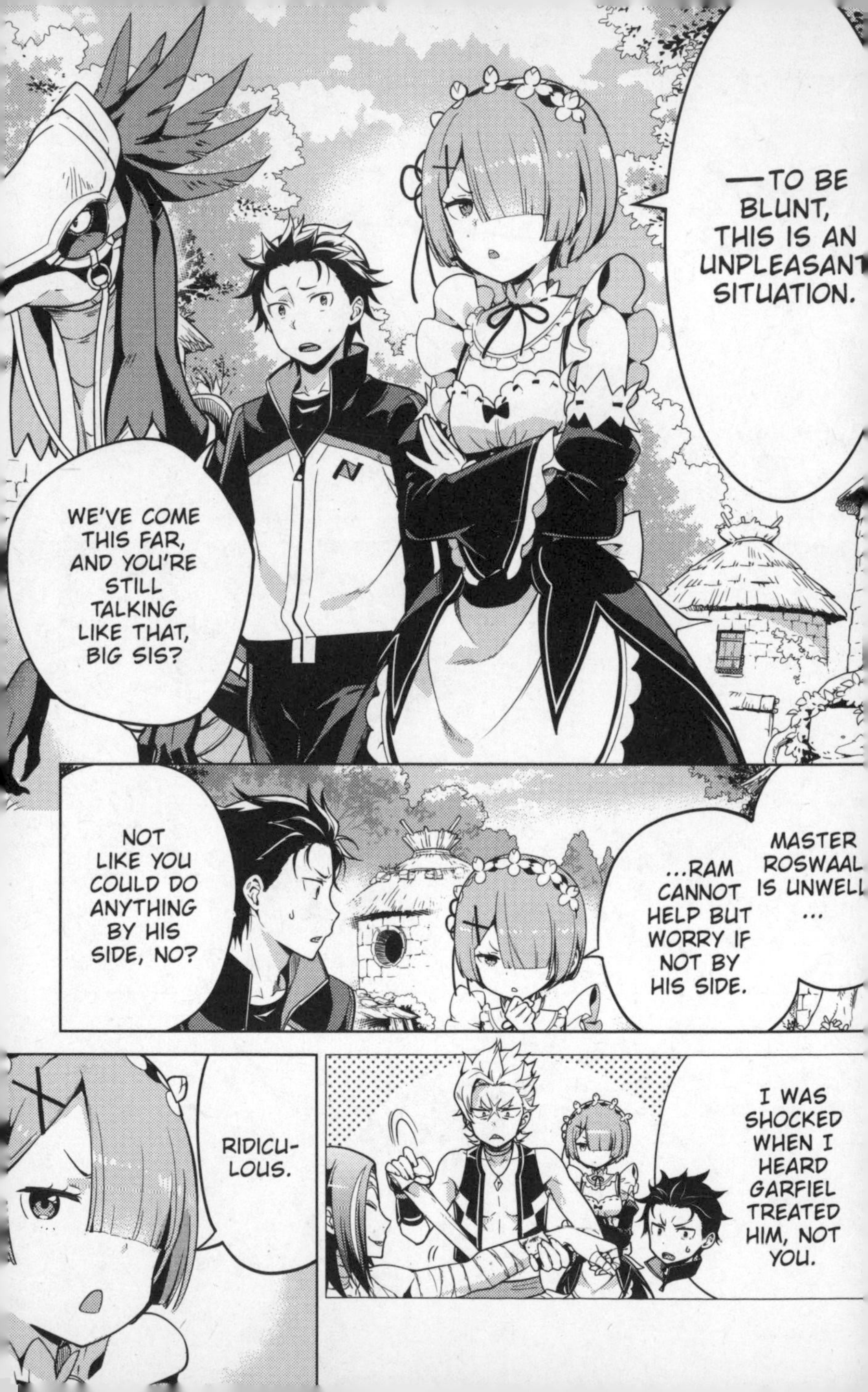
—TO BE BLUNT, THIS IS AN UNPLEASANT SITUATION.
WE'VE COME THIS FAR, AND YOU'RE STILL TALKING LIKE THAT, BIG SIS?
MASTER ROSWAAL IS UNWELL ...
...RAM CANNOT HELP BUT WORRY IF NOT BY HIS SIDE.
NOT LIKE YOU COULD DO ANYTHING BY HIS SIDE, NO?
I WAS SHOCKED WHEN I HEARD GARFIEL TREATED HIM, NOT YOU.
RIDICU-LOUS.

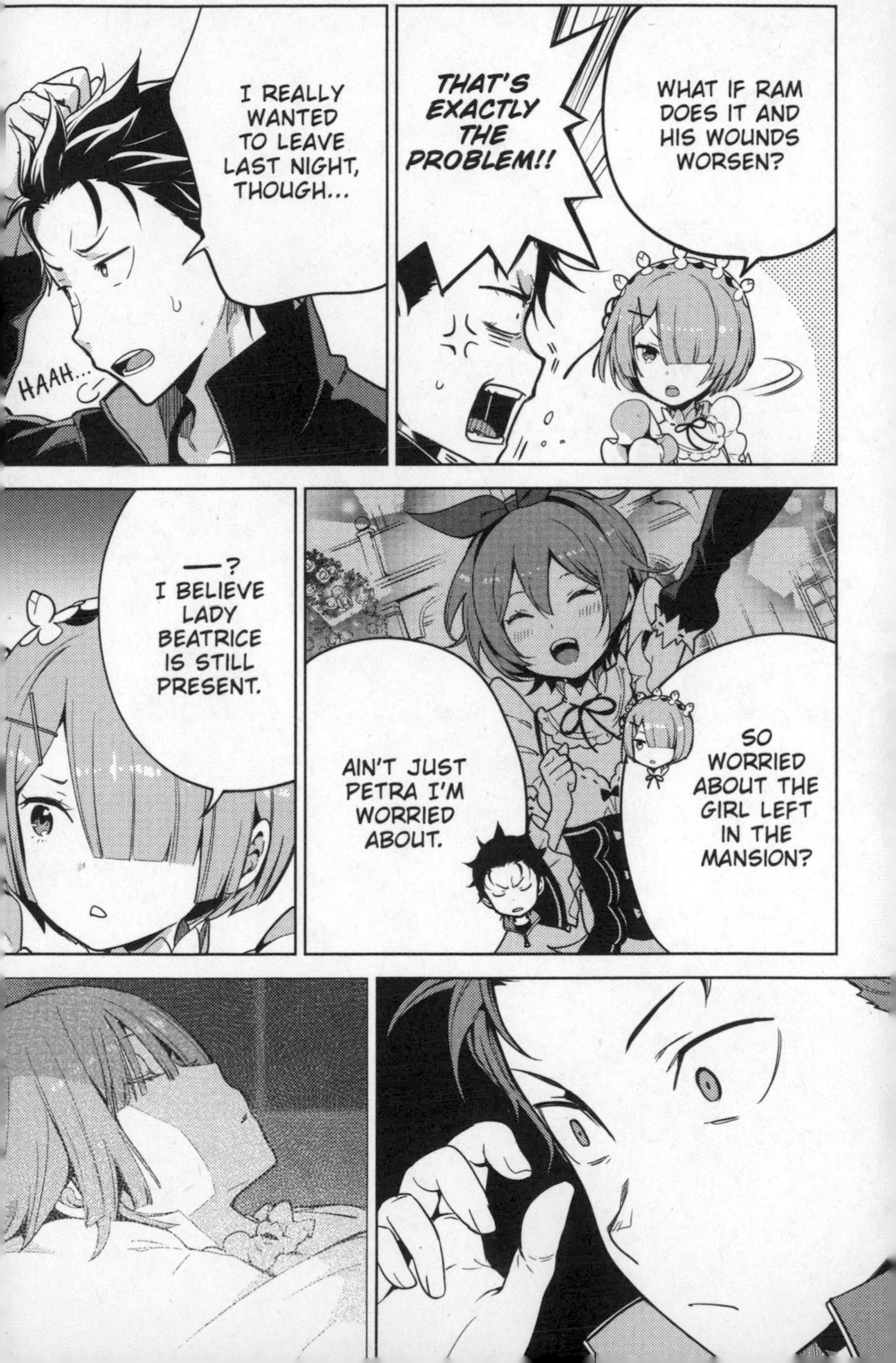
WHAT IF RAM DOES IT AND HIS WOUNDS WORSEN?
THAT'S EXACTLY THE PROBLEM!!
I REALLY WANTED TO LEAVE LAST NIGHT, THOUGH...
HAAH...
SO WORRIED ABOUT THE GIRL LEFT IN THE MANSION?
AIN'T JUST PETRA I'M WORRIED ABOUT.
—? I BELIEVE LADY BEATRICE IS STILL PRESENT.

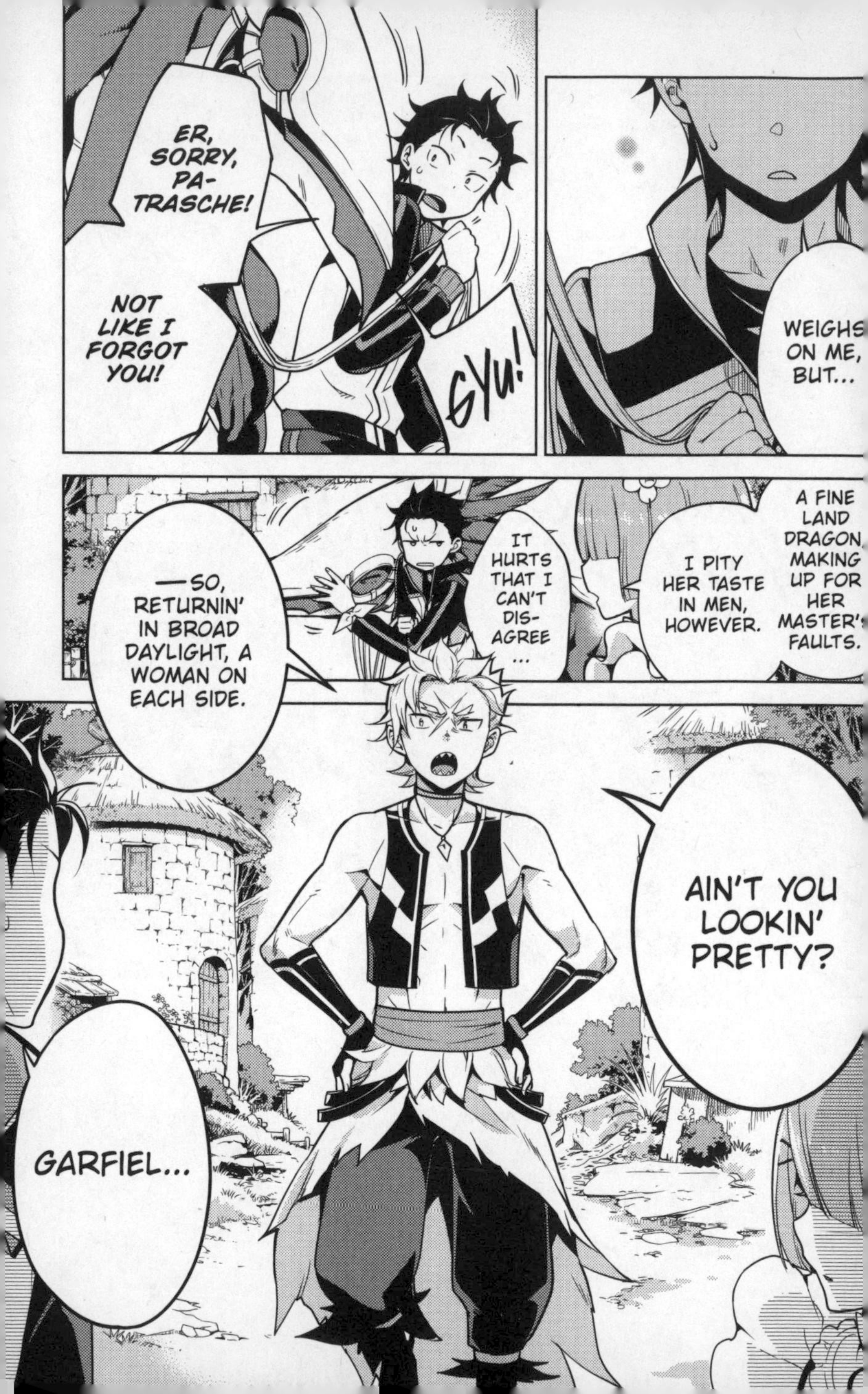
WEIGHS ON ME, BUT...
ER, SORRY, PA-TRASCHE!
NOT LIKE I FORGOT YOU!
GYU!
A FINE LAND DRAGON, MAKING UP FOR HER MASTER'S FAULTS.
I PITY HER TASTE IN MEN, HOWEVER.
IT HURTS THAT I CAN'T DIS-AGREE...
—SO, RETURNIN' IN BROAD DAYLIGHT, A WOMAN ON EACH SIDE.
AIN'T YOU LOOKIN' PRETTY?
GARFIEL...

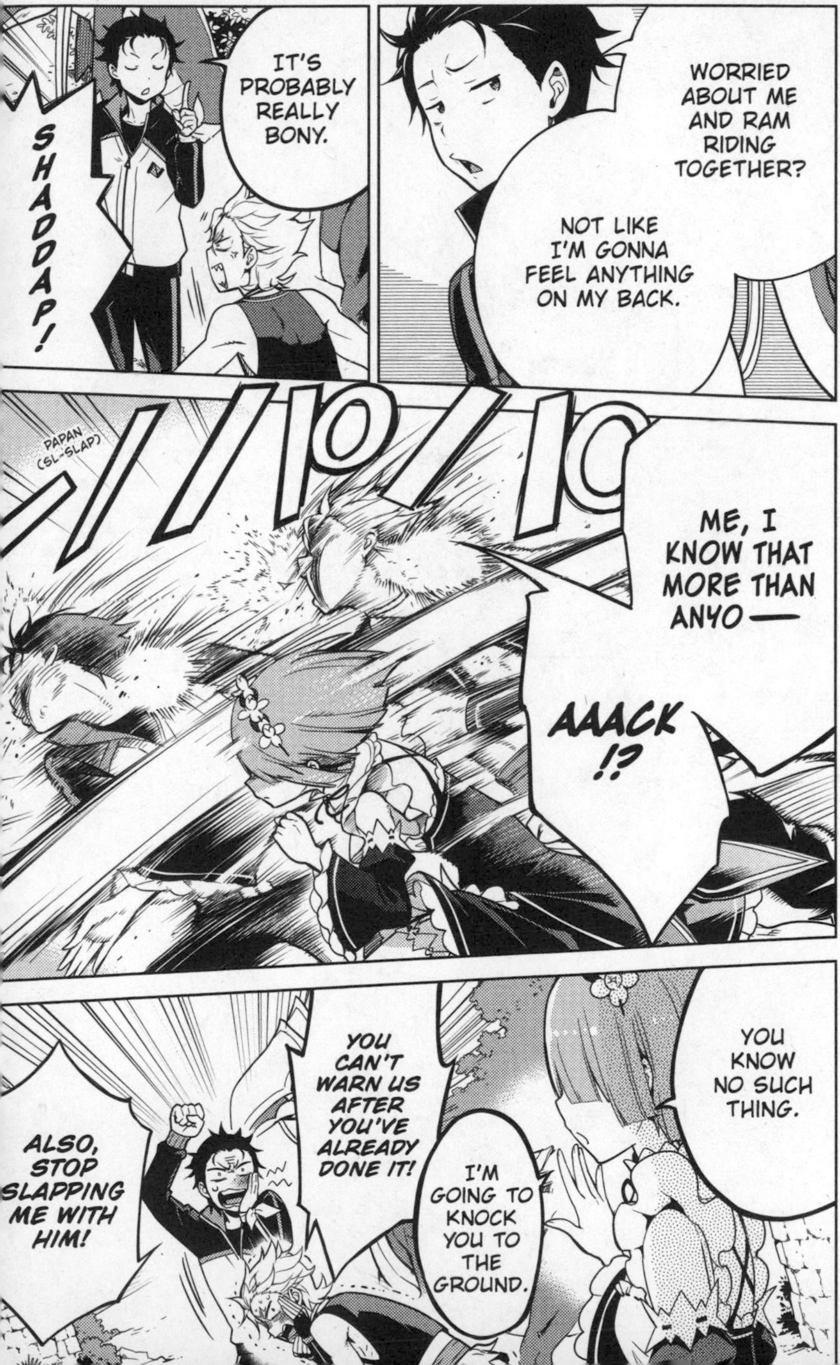
WORRIED ABOUT ME AND RAM RIDING TOGETHER?
NOT LIKE I'M GONNA FEEL ANYTHING ON MY BACK.
IT'S PROBABLY REALLY BONY.
SHADDAP!
ME, I KNOW THAT MORE THAN ANYO—
AAACK!?
PAPAN (SL-SLAP)
YOU KNOW NO SUCH THING.
I'M GOING TO KNOCK YOU TO THE GROUND.
YOU CAN'T WARN US AFTER YOU'VE ALREADY DONE IT!
ALSO, STOP SLAPPING ME WITH HIM!

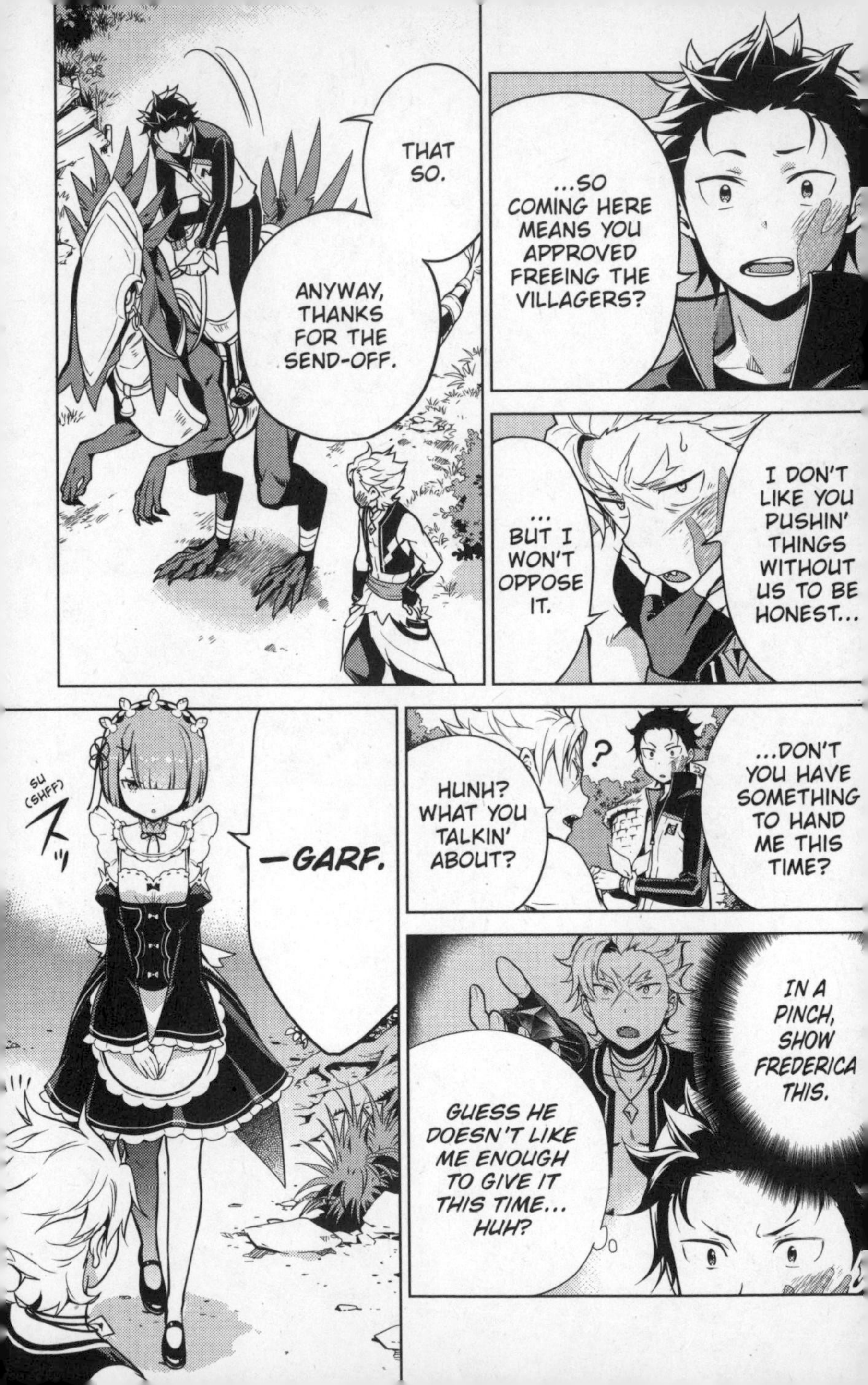
...SO COMING HERE MEANS YOU APPROVED FREEING THE VILLAGERS?
I DON'T LIKE YOU PUSHIN' THINGS WITHOUT US TO BE HONEST...
... BUT I WON'T OPPOSE IT.
THAT SO.
ANYWAY, THANKS FOR THE SEND-OFF.
...DON'T YOU HAVE SOMETHING TO HAND ME THIS TIME?
HUNH? WHAT YOU TALKIN' ABOUT?
IN A PINCH, SHOW FREDERICA THIS.
GUESS HE DOESN'T LIKE ME ENOUGH TO GIVE IT THIS TIME... HUH?
—GARF.
SU (SHFF)

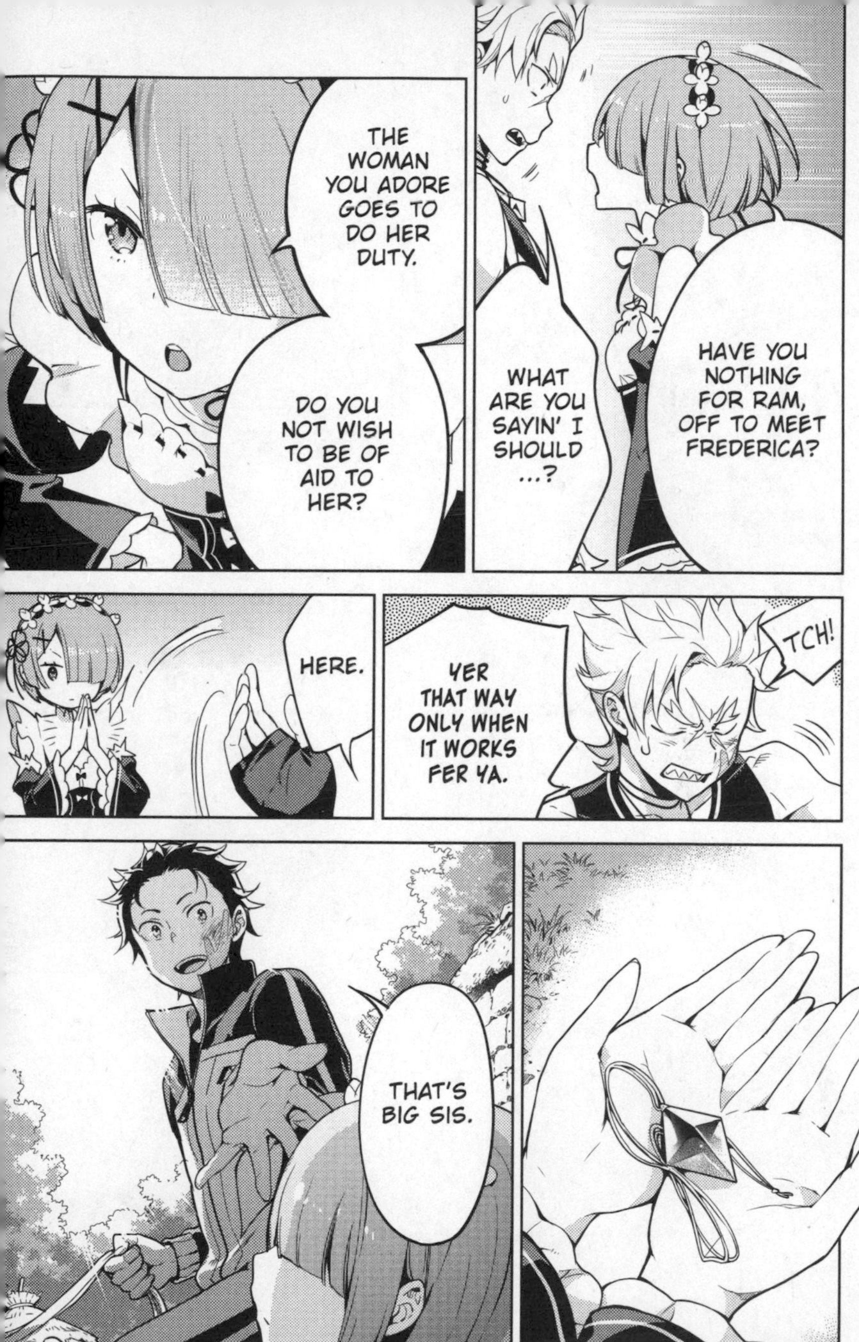
HAVE YOU NOTHING FOR RAM, OFF TO MEET FREDERICA?
WHAT ARE YOU SAYIN' I SHOULD ...?
THE WOMAN YOU ADORE GOES TO DO HER DUTY.
DO YOU NOT WISH TO BE OF AID TO HER?
TCH!
YER THAT WAY ONLY WHEN IT WORKS FER YA.
HERE.
THAT'S BIG SIS.

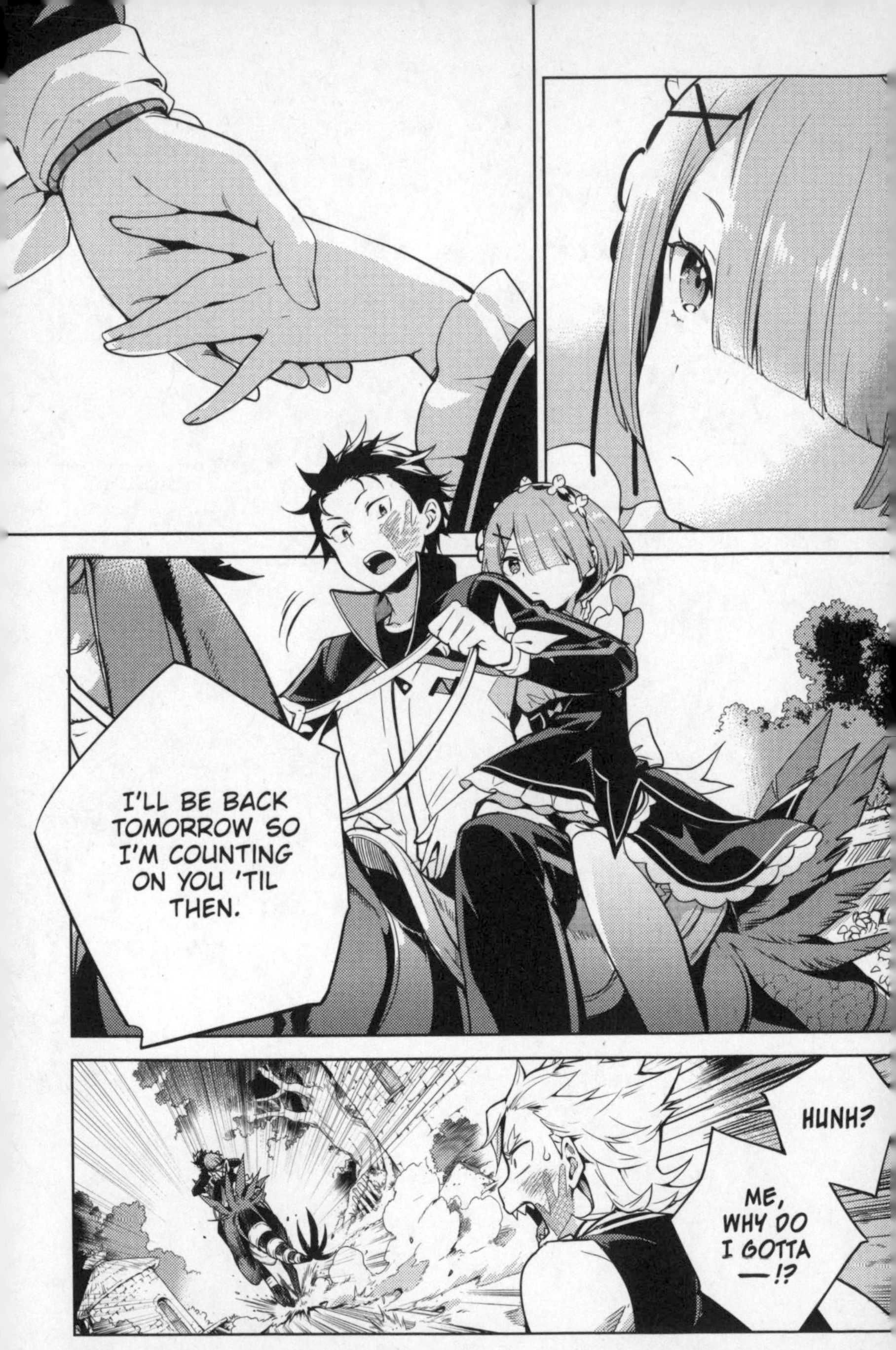
I'LL BE BACK TOMORROW SO I'M COUNTING ON YOU 'TIL THEN.
HUNH?
ME, WHY DO I GOTTA —!?

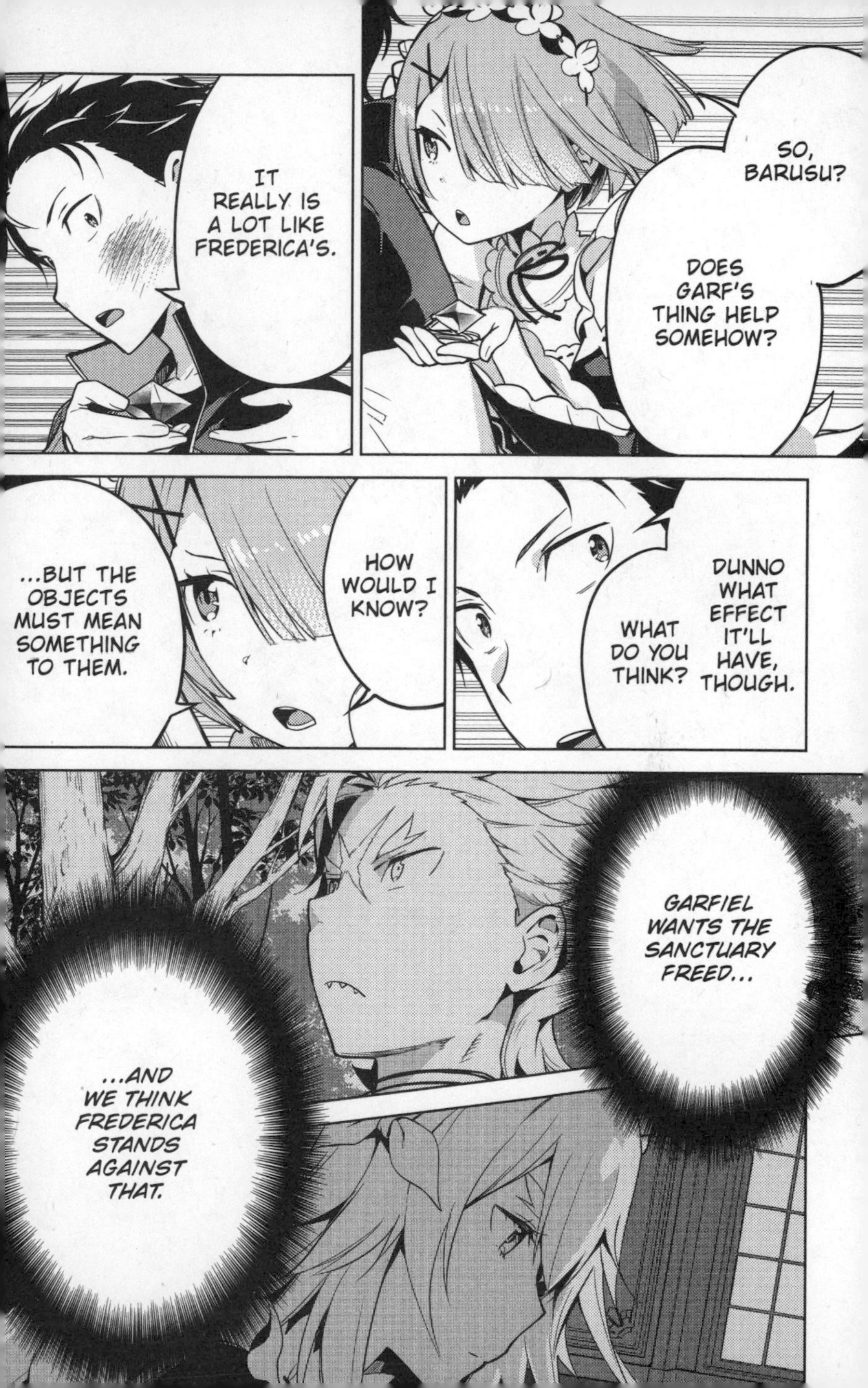
SO, BARUSU?
DOES GARF'S THING HELP SOMEHOW?
IT REALLY IS A LOT LIKE FREDERICA'S.
DUNNO WHAT EFFECT IT'LL HAVE, THOUGH.
WHAT DO YOU THINK?
HOW WOULD I KNOW?
...BUT THE OBJECTS MUST MEAN SOMETHING TO THEM.
GARFIEL WANTS THE SANCTUARY FREED...
...AND WE THINK FREDERICA STANDS AGAINST THAT.

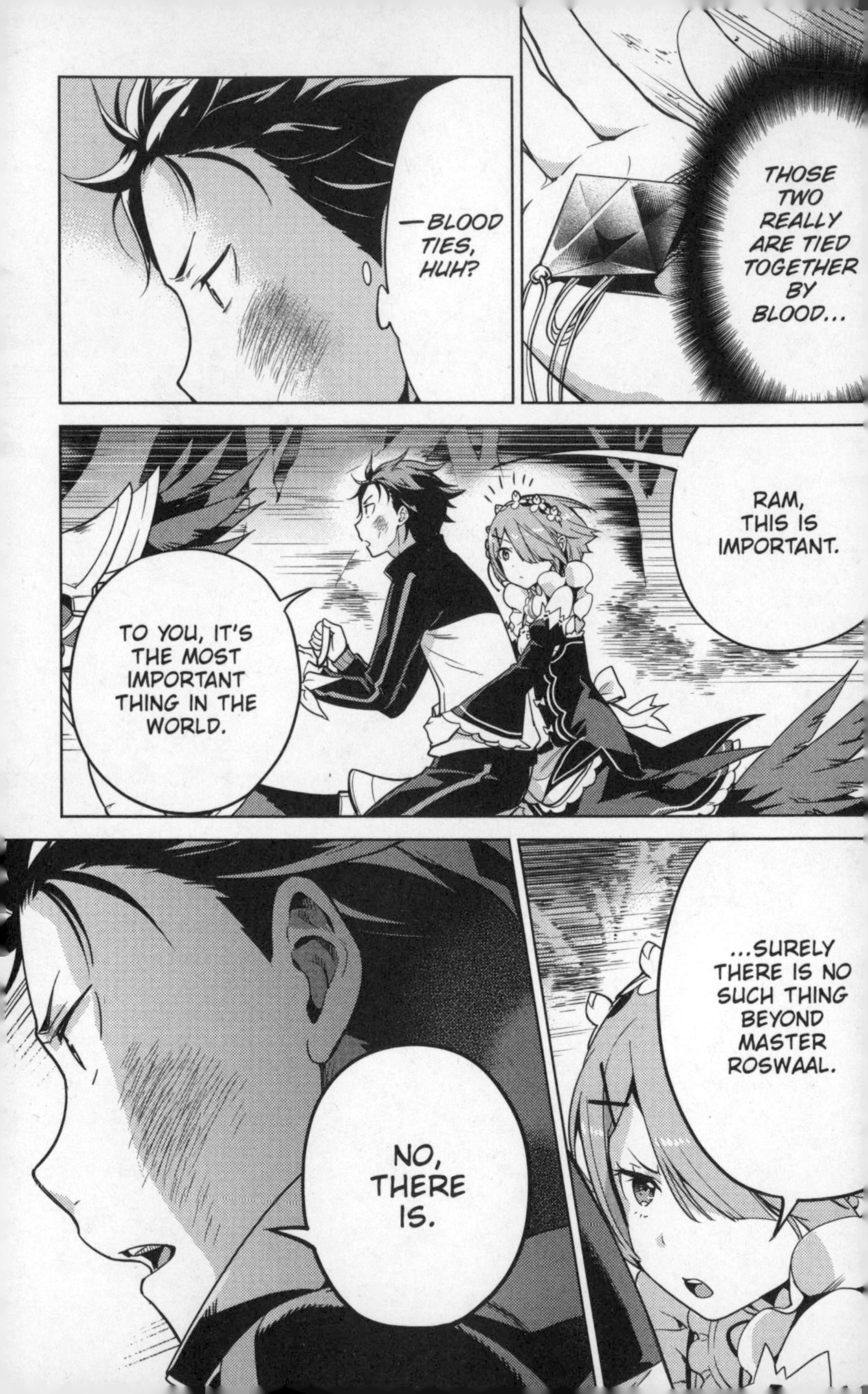
THOSE TWO REALLY ARE TIED TOGETHER BY BLOOD...
—BLOOD TIES, HUH?
RAM, THIS IS IMPORTANT.
TO YOU, IT'S THE MOST IMPORTANT THING IN THE WORLD.
...SURELY THERE IS NO SUCH THING BEYOND MASTER ROSWAAL.
NO, THERE IS.

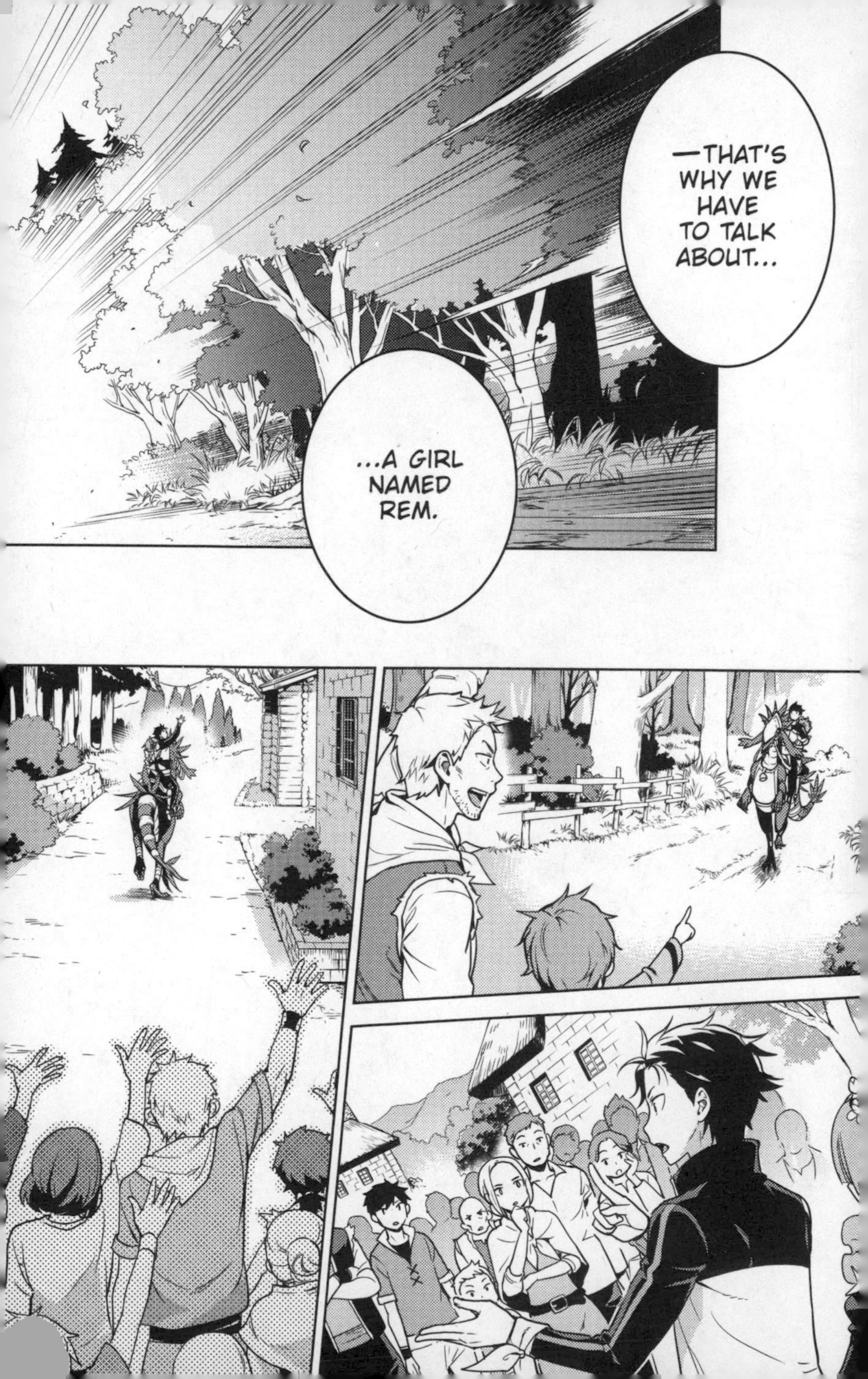
—THAT'S WHY WE HAVE TO TALK ABOUT...
...A GIRL NAMED REM.

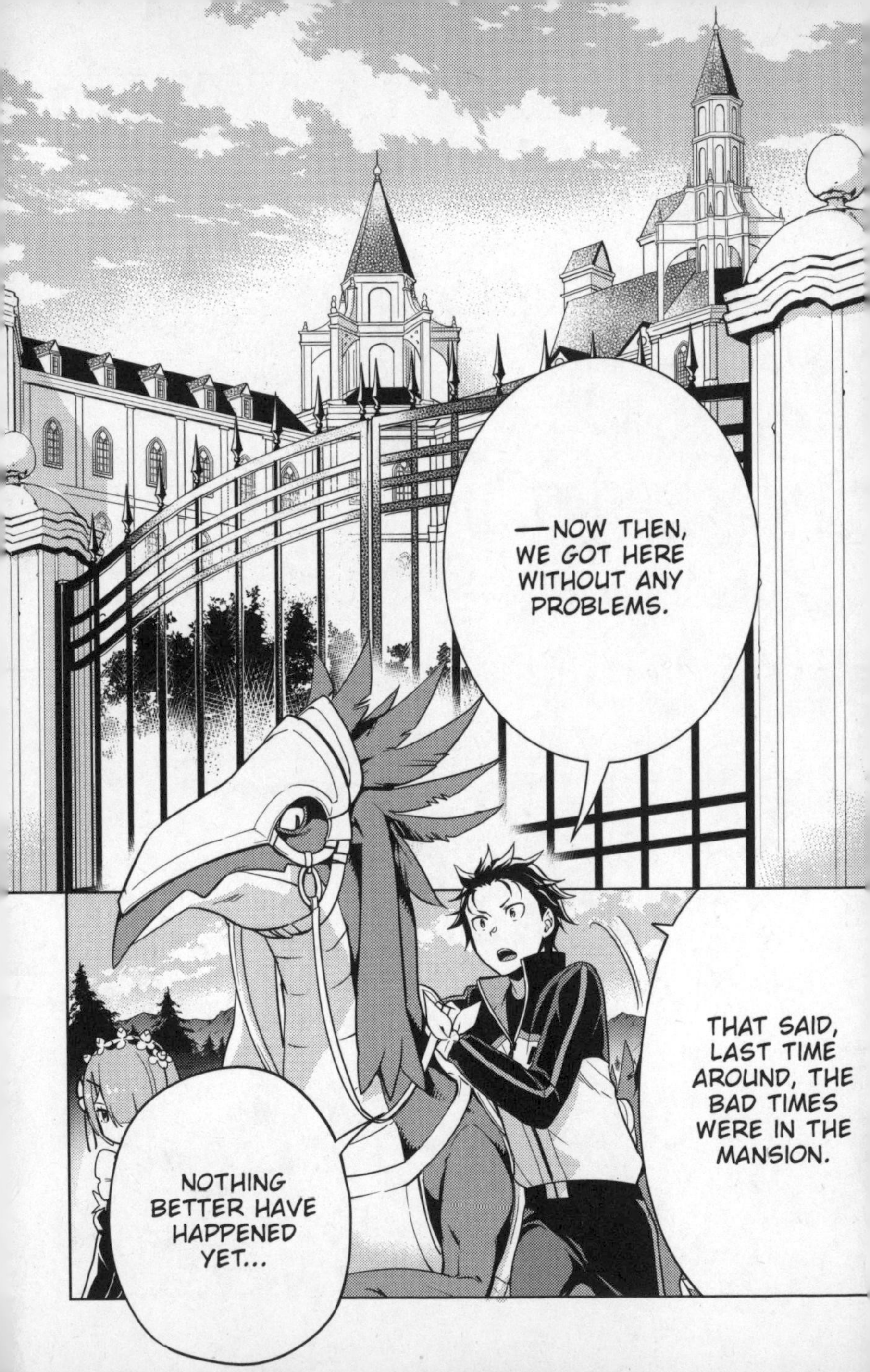
—NOW THEN, WE GOT HERE WITHOUT ANY PROBLEMS.
THAT SAID, LAST TIME AROUND, THE BAD TIMES WERE IN THE MANSION.
NOTHING BETTER HAVE HAPPENED YET...

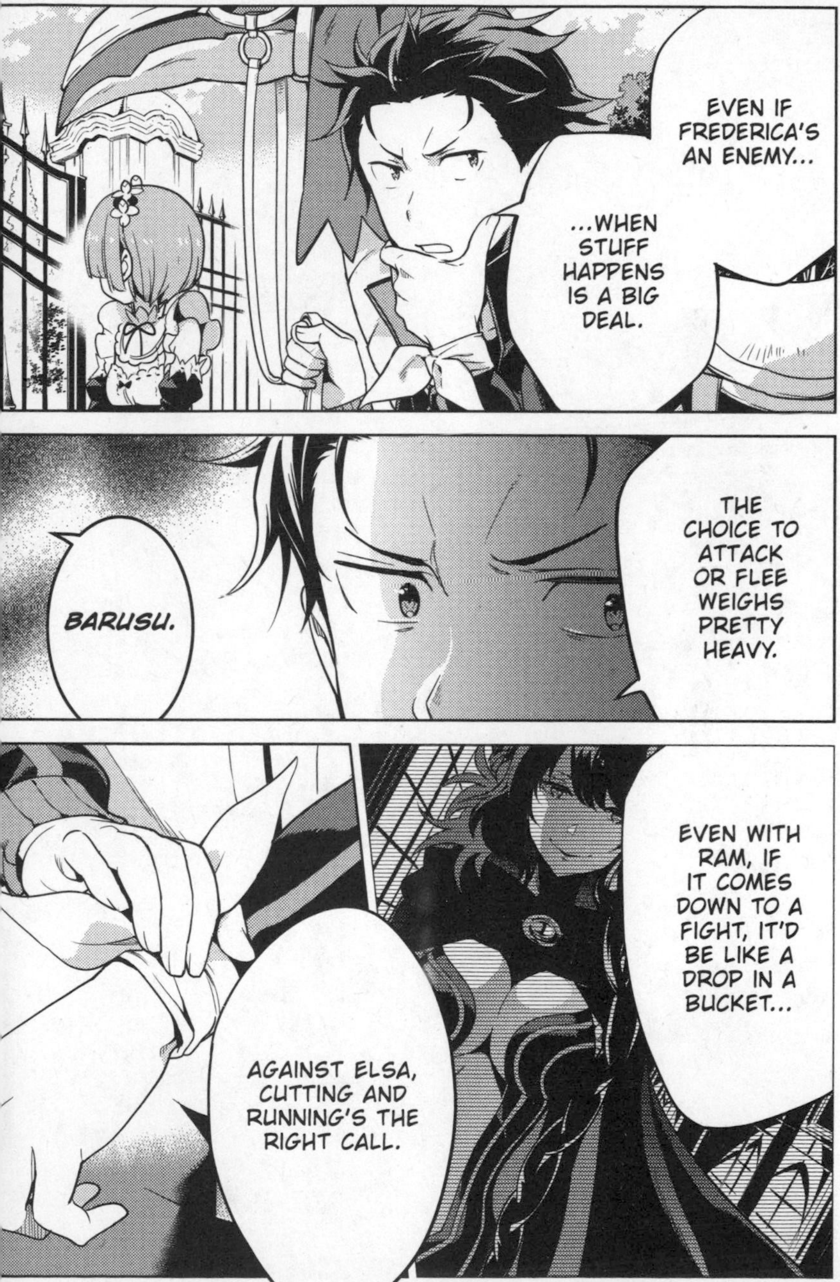
EVEN IF FREDERICA'S AN ENEMY...
...WHEN STUFF HAPPENS IS A BIG DEAL.
THE CHOICE TO ATTACK OR FLEE WEIGHS PRETTY HEAVY.
BARUSU.
EVEN WITH RAM, IF IT COMES DOWN TO A FIGHT, IT'D BE LIKE A DROP IN A BUCKET...
AGAINST ELSA, CUTTING AND RUNNING'S THE RIGHT CALL.

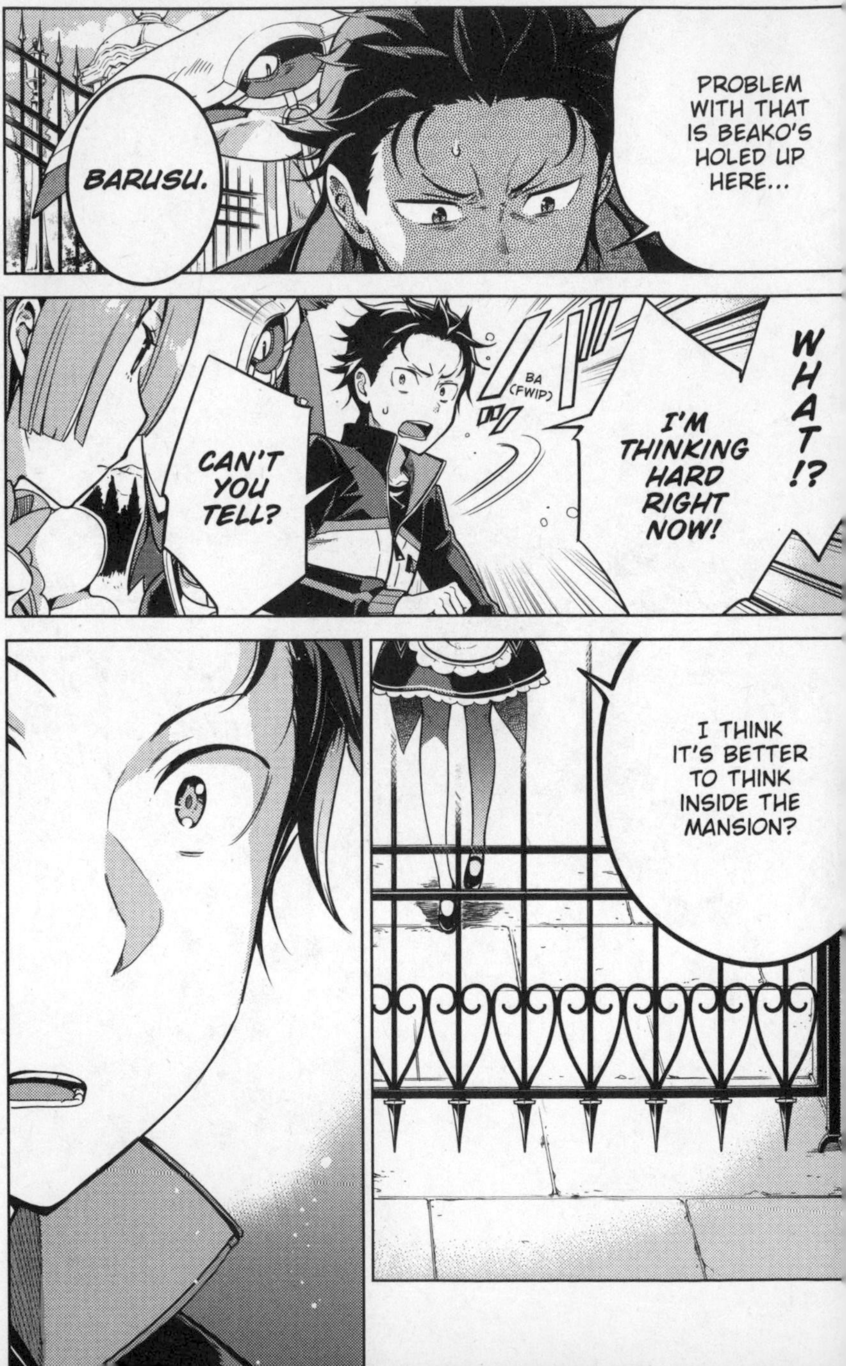
PROBLEM WITH THAT IS BEAKO'S HOLED UP HERE...
BARUSU.
WHAT!?
I'M THINKING HARD RIGHT NOW!
BA (FWIP)
CAN'T YOU TELL?
I THINK IT'S BETTER TO THINK INSIDE THE MANSION?

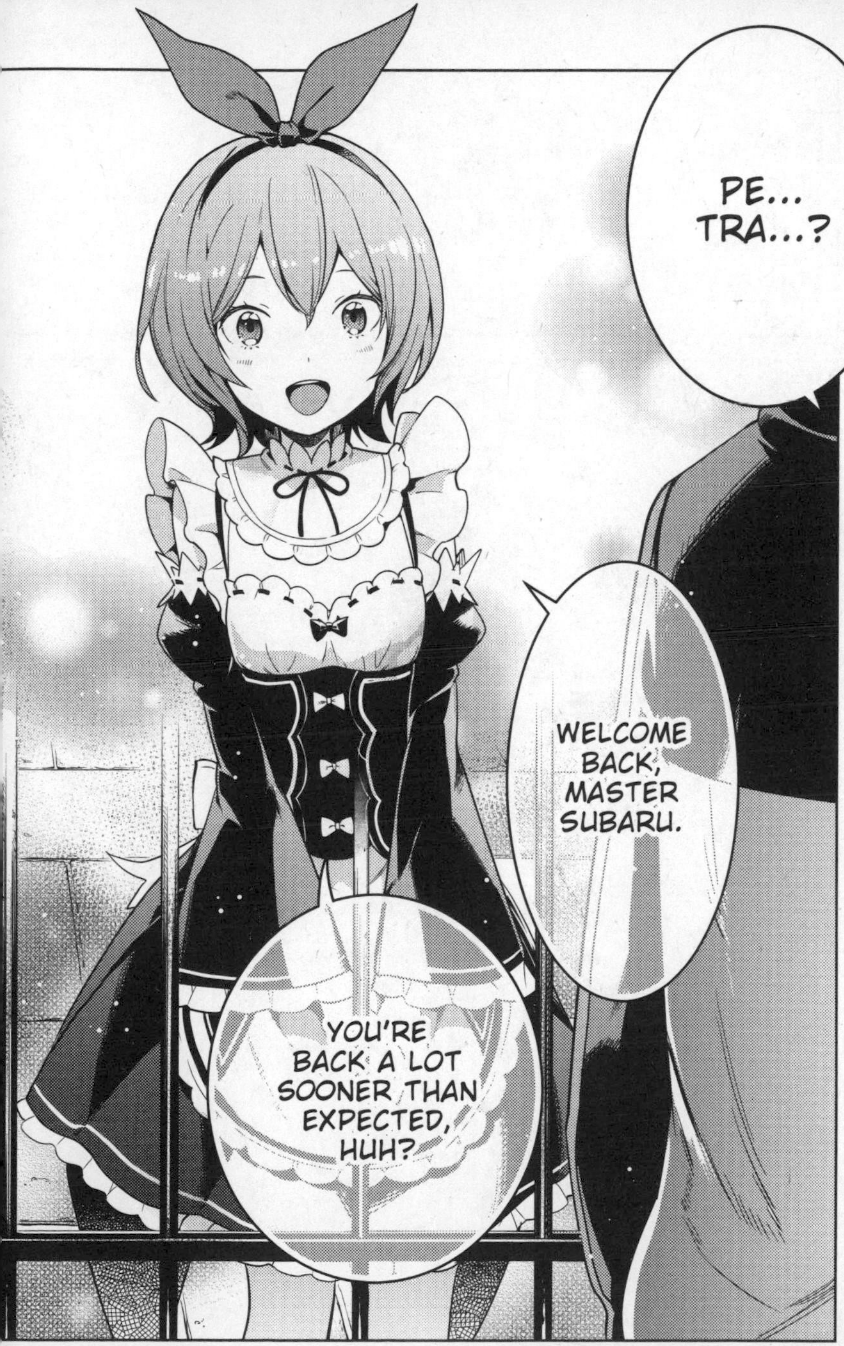
PE... TRA...?
WELCOME BACK, MASTER SUBARU.
YOU'RE BACK A LOT SOONER THAN EXPECTED, HUH?

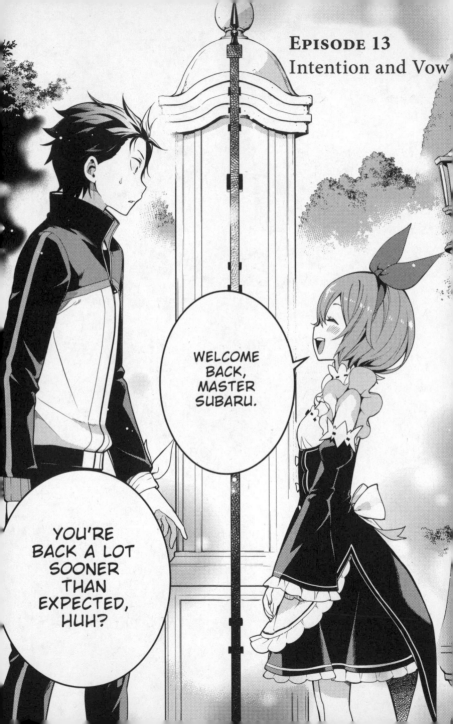

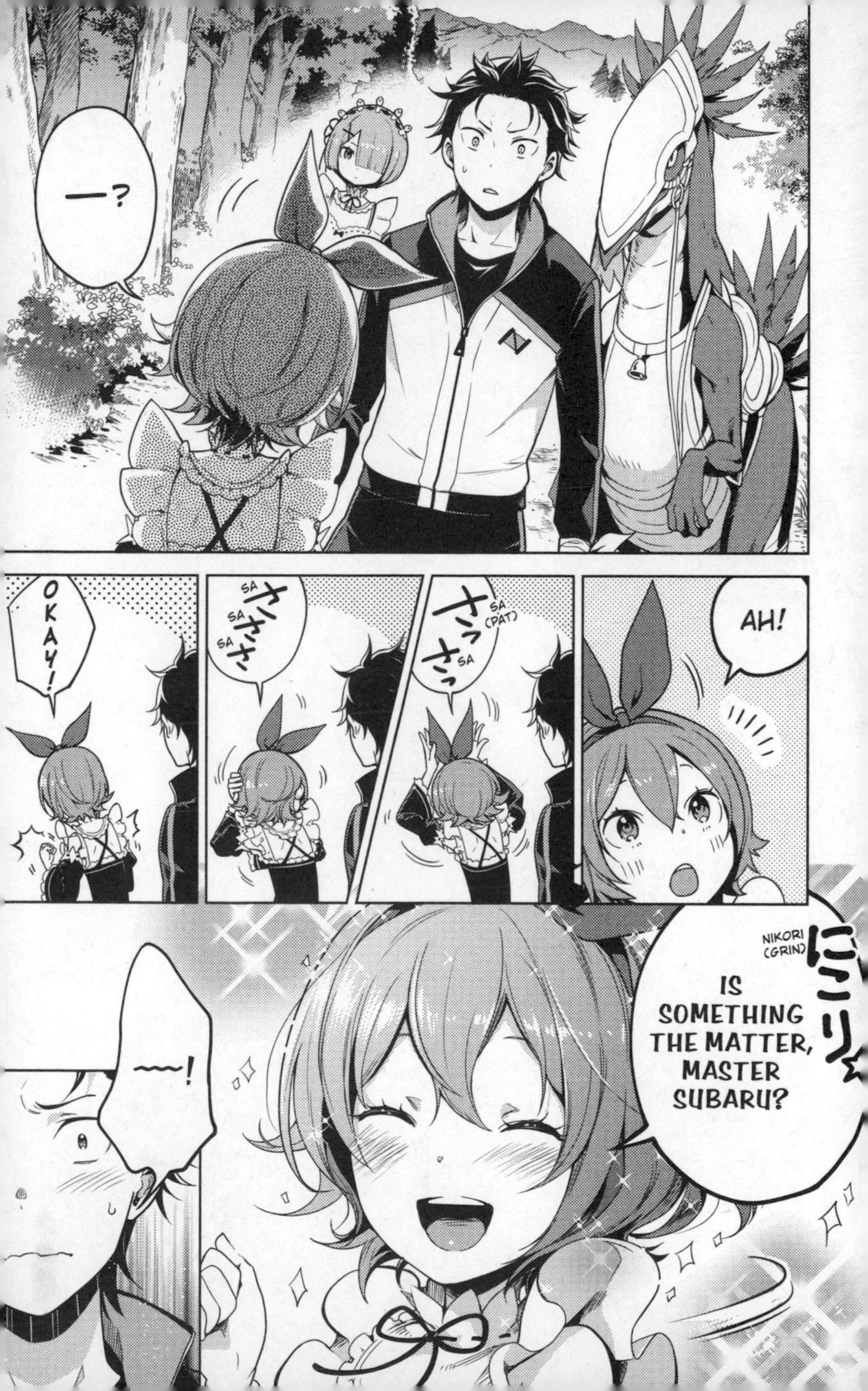

—?
AH!
SA (PAT) SA
さっさっ
SA SA SA
さささ
OKAY!
NIKORI (GRIN)
にっこり
IS SOMETHING THE MATTER, MASTER SUBARU?
——!

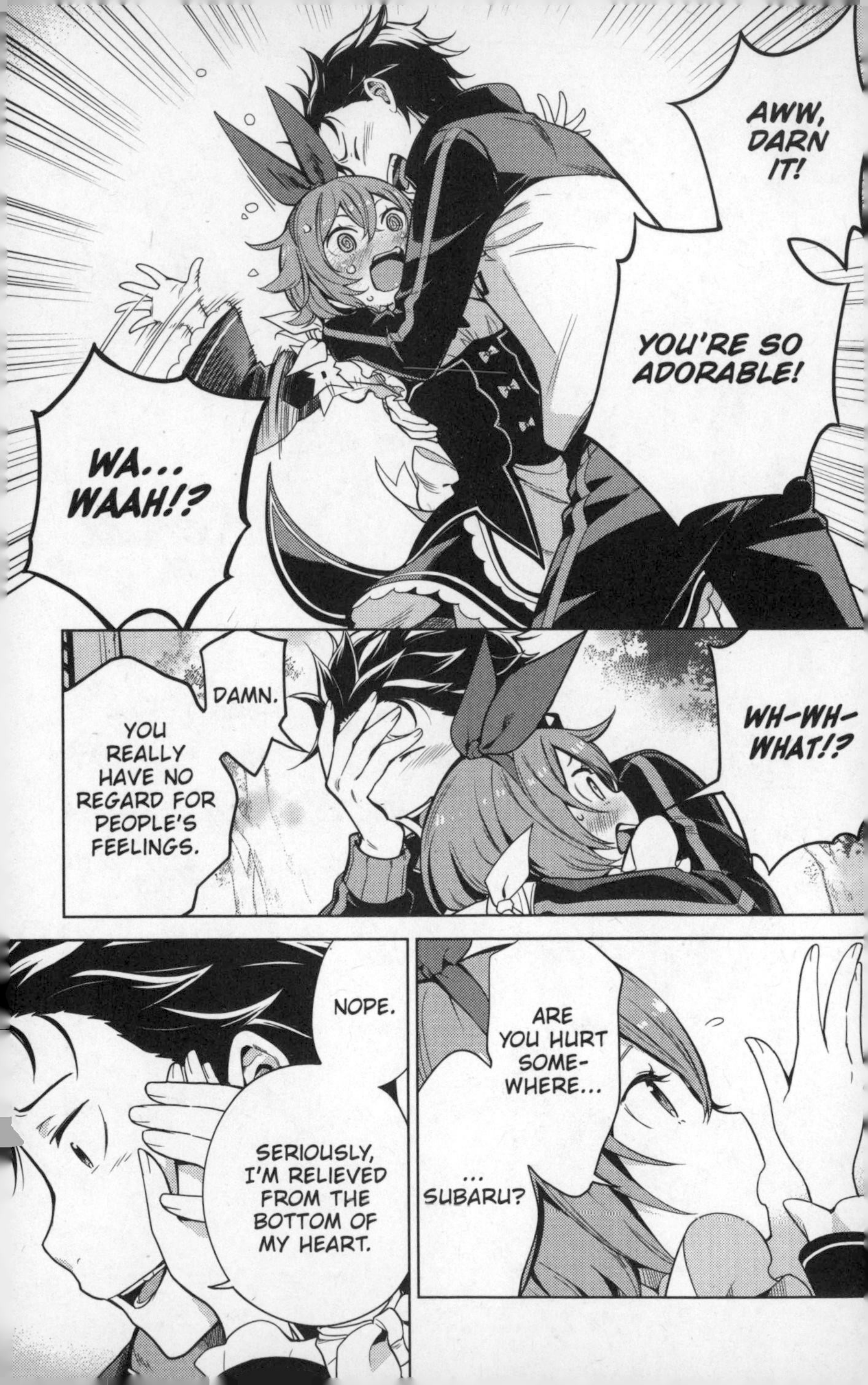
AWW, DARN IT!
YOU'RE SO ADORABLE!
WA... WAAH!?
WH-WH-WHAT!?
DAMN.
YOU REALLY HAVE NO REGARD FOR PEOPLE'S FEELINGS.
ARE YOU HURT SOME-WHERE...
... SUBARU?
NOPE.
SERIOUSLY, I'M RELIEVED FROM THE BOTTOM OF MY HEART.

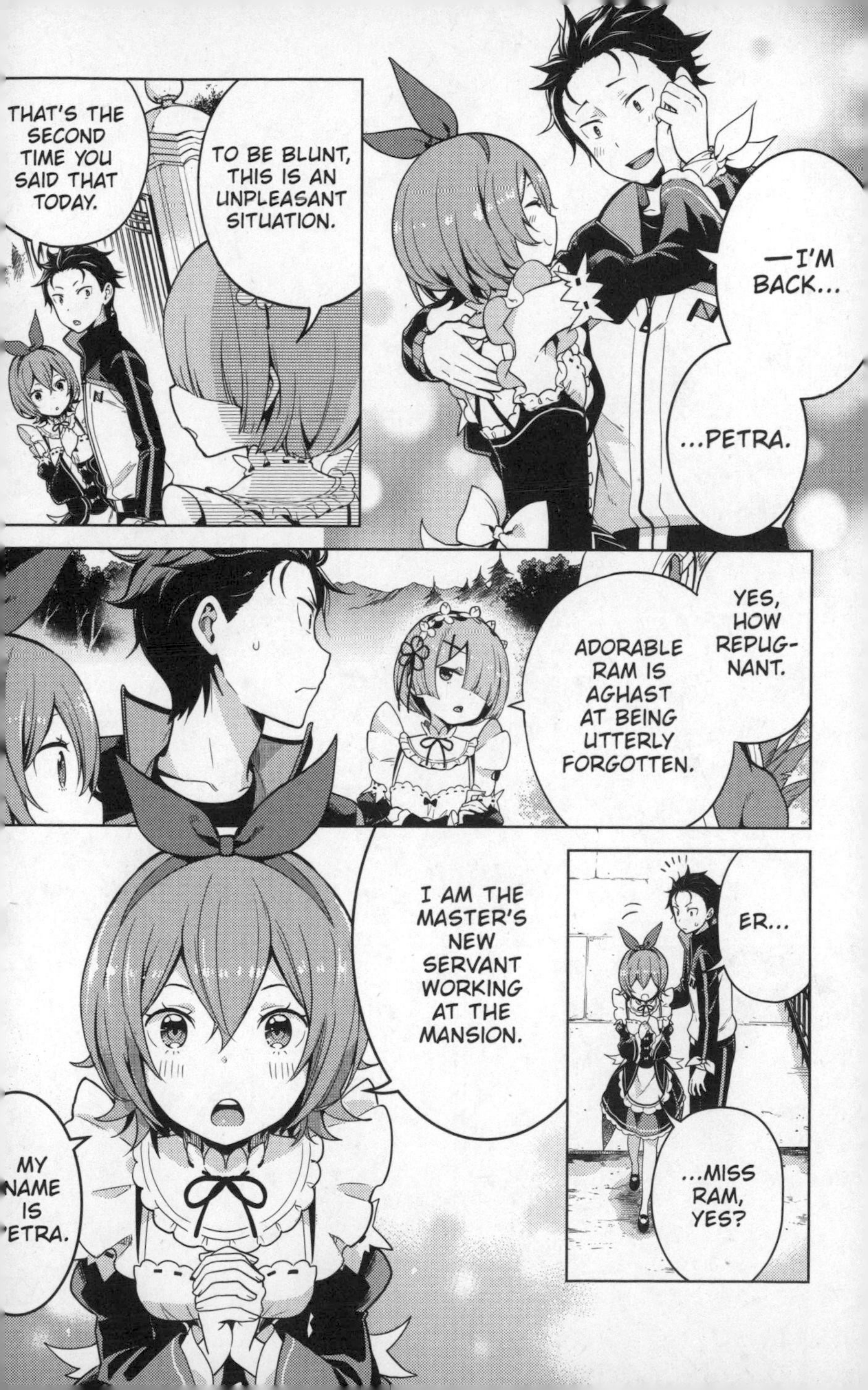
—I'M BACK...
...PETRA.
TO BE BLUNT, THIS IS AN UNPLEASANT SITUATION.
THAT'S THE SECOND TIME YOU SAID THAT TODAY.
YES, HOW REPUGNANT.
ADORABLE RAM IS AGHAST AT BEING UTTERLY FORGOTTEN.
ER...
...MISS RAM, YES?
I AM THE MASTER'S NEW SERVANT WORKING AT THE MANSION.
MY NAME IS ETRA.

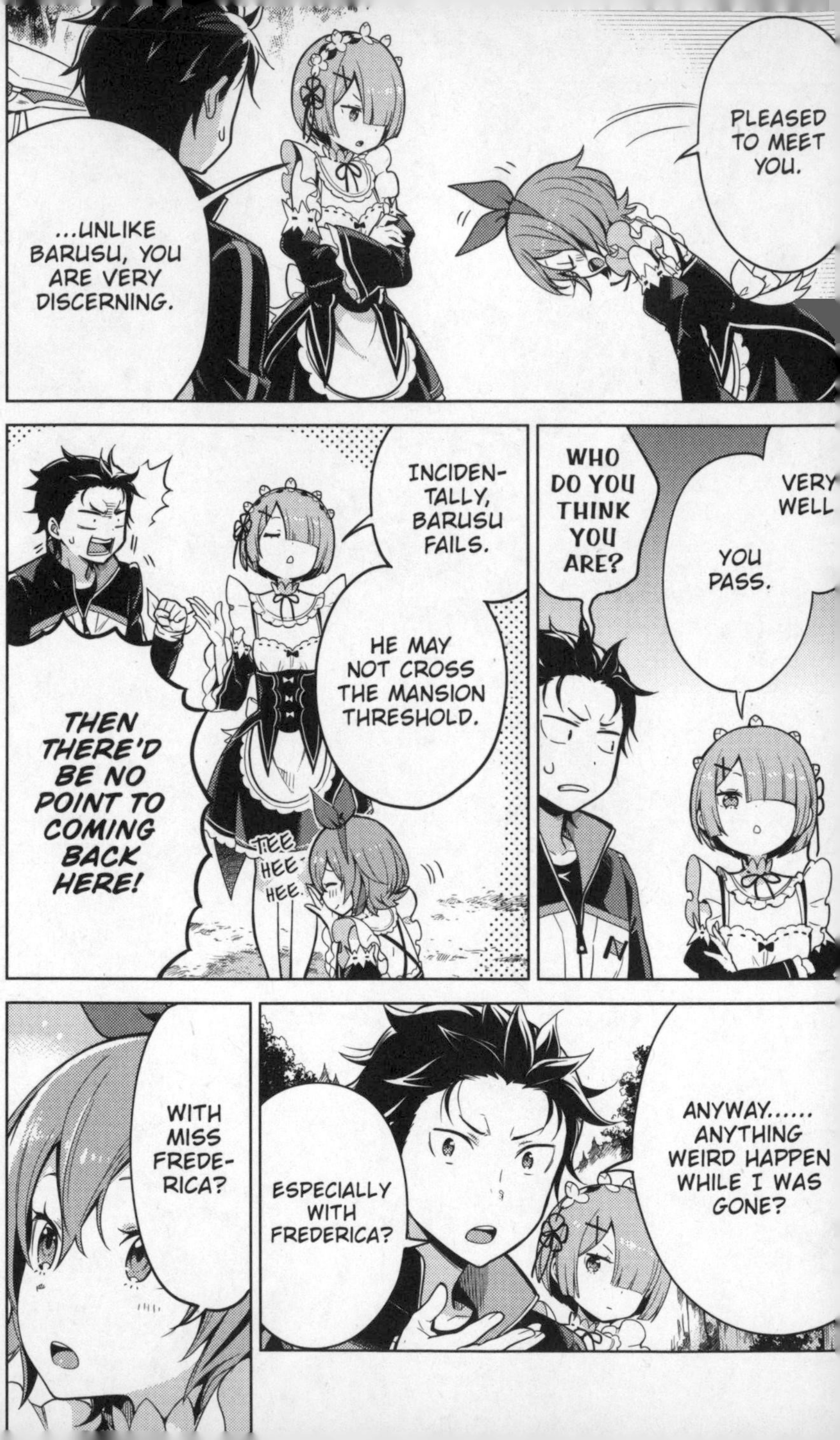
PLEASED TO MEET YOU.
...UNLIKE BARUSU, YOU ARE VERY DISCERNING.
VERY WELL
YOU PASS.
WHO DO YOU THINK YOU ARE?
INCIDEN-TALLY, BARUSU FAILS.
HE MAY NOT CROSS THE MANSION THRESHOLD.
TEE HEE HEE.
THEN THERE'D BE NO POINT TO COMING BACK HERE!
ANYWAY...... ANYTHING WEIRD HAPPEN WHILE I WAS GONE?
ESPECIALLY WITH FREDERICA?
WITH MISS FREDE-RICA?

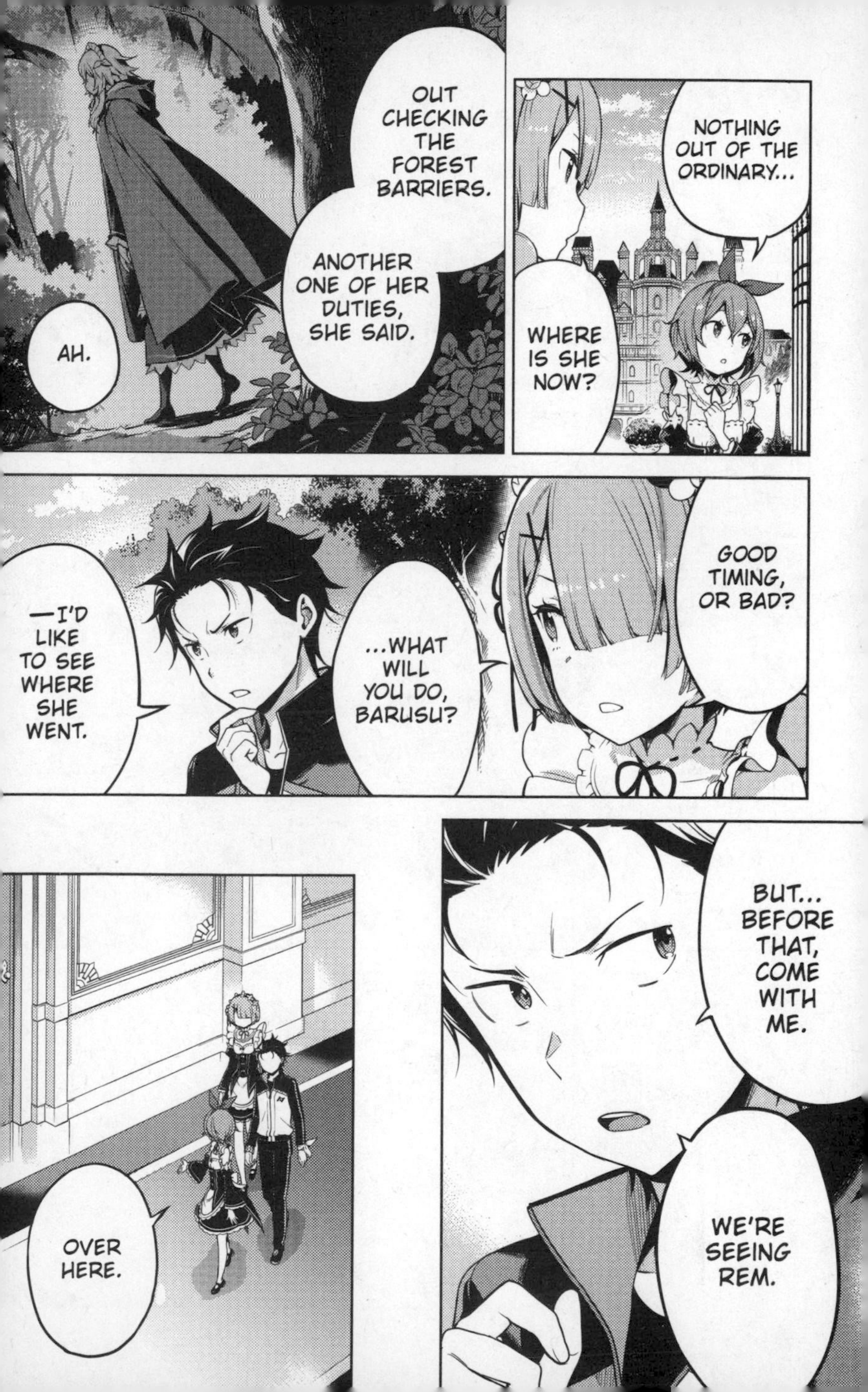
NOTHING OUT OF THE ORDINARY...
WHERE IS SHE NOW?
OUT CHECKING THE FOREST BARRIERS.
ANOTHER ONE OF HER DUTIES, SHE SAID.
AH.
GOOD TIMING, OR BAD?
...WHAT WILL YOU DO, BARUSU?
—I'D LIKE TO SEE WHERE SHE WENT.
BUT... BEFORE THAT, COME WITH ME.
WE'RE SEEING REM.
OVER HERE.

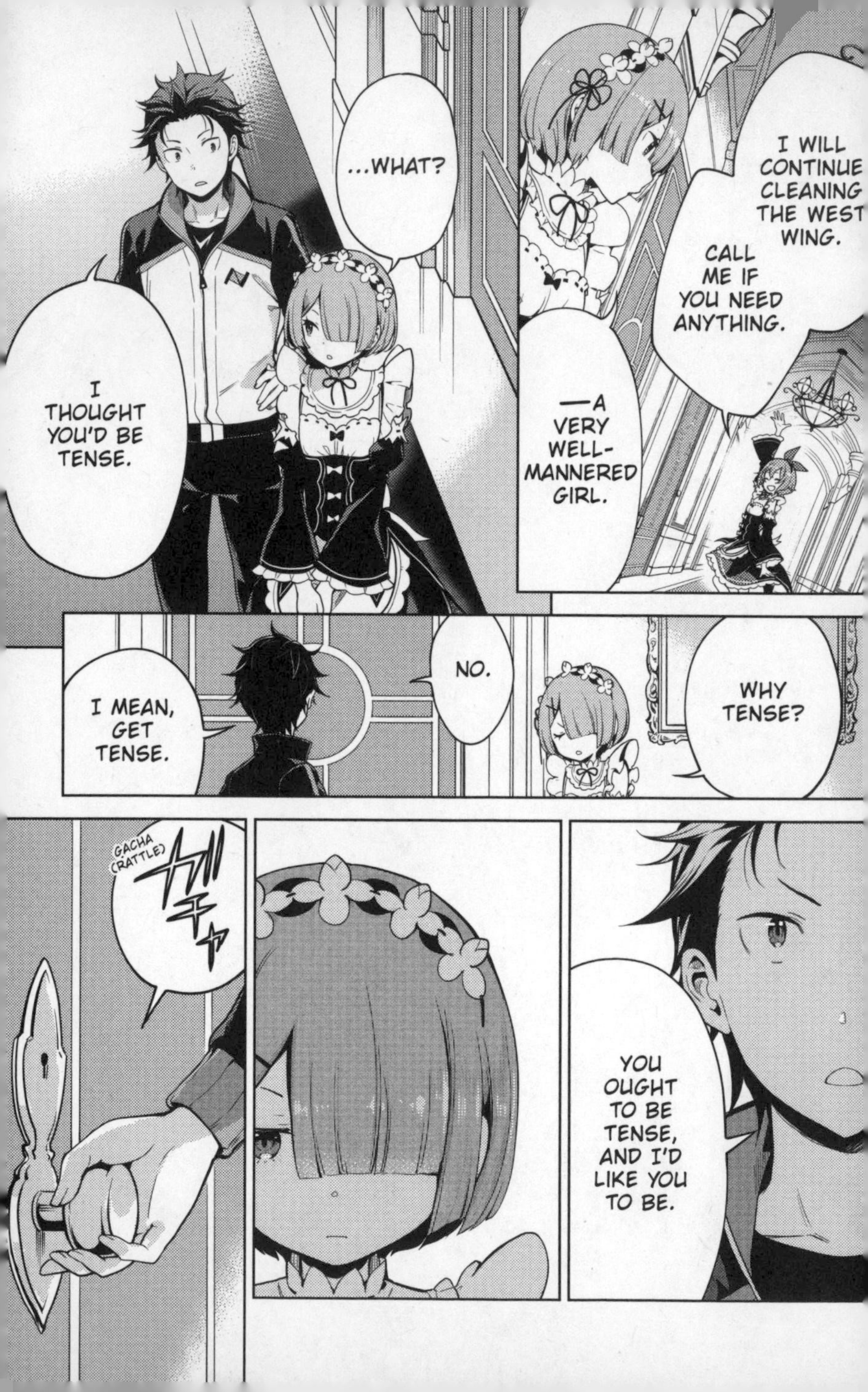

I WILL CONTINUE CLEANING THE WEST WING.
CALL ME IF YOU NEED ANYTHING.
—A VERY WELL-MANNERED GIRL.
...WHAT?
I THOUGHT YOU'D BE TENSE.
WHY TENSE?
NO.
I MEAN, GET TENSE.
YOU OUGHT TO BE TENSE, AND I'D LIKE YOU TO BE.
ガチャ
GACHA (RATTLE)

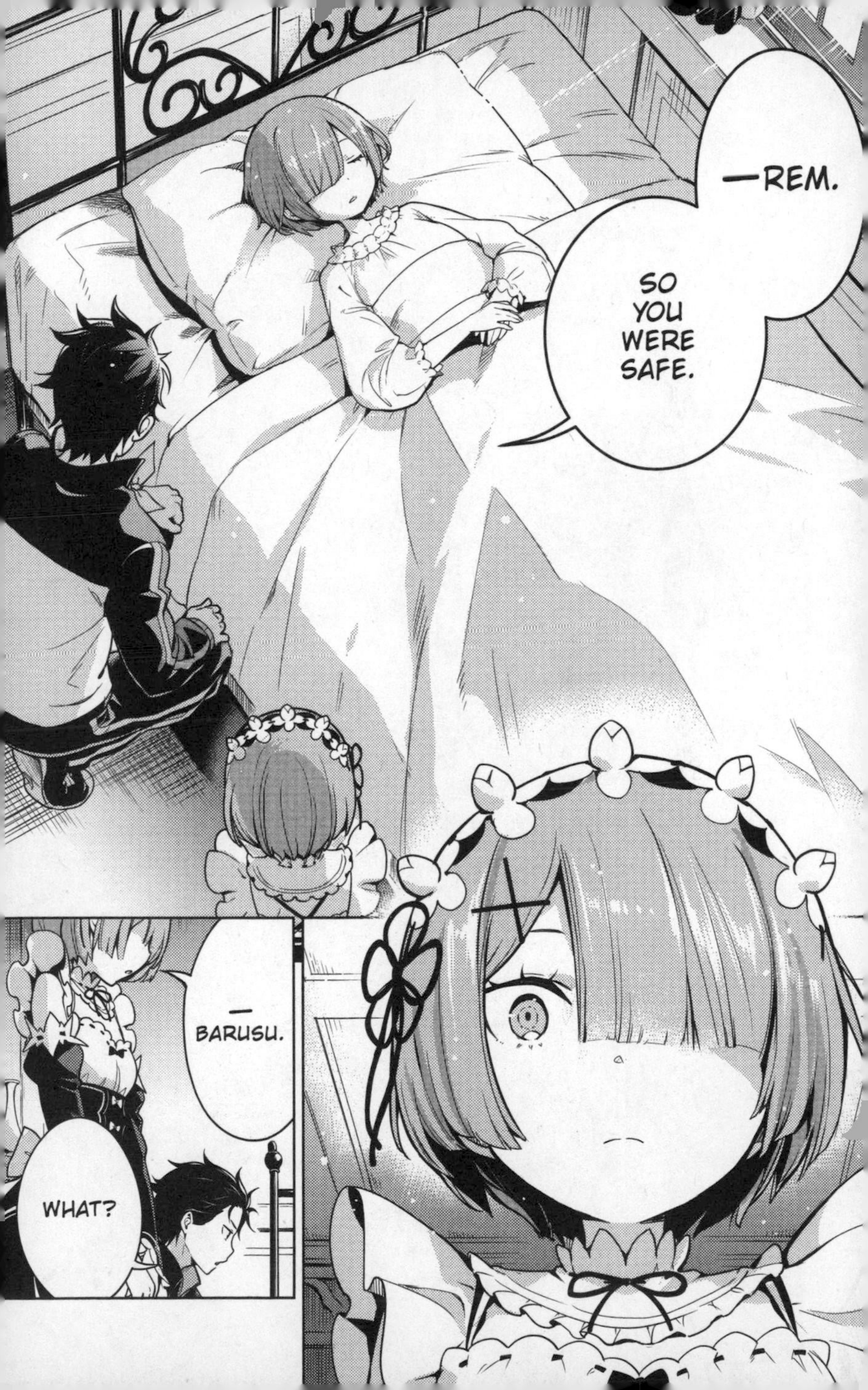
—REM.
SO YOU WERE SAFE.
—BARUSU.
WHAT?

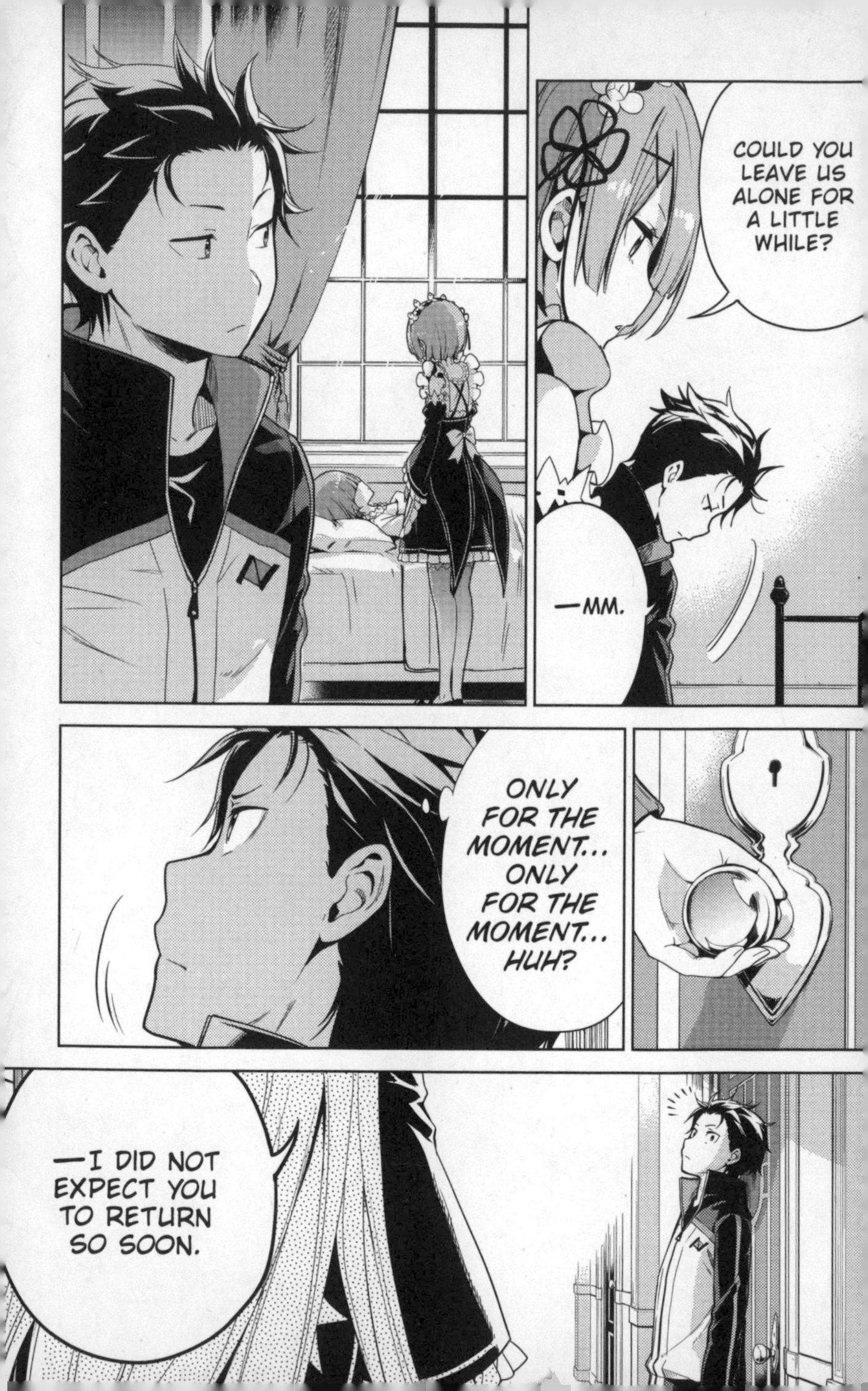
COULD YOU LEAVE US ALONE FOR A LITTLE WHILE?
—MM.
ONLY FOR THE MOMENT... ONLY FOR THE MOMENT... HUH?
—I DID NOT EXPECT YOU TO RETURN SO SOON.

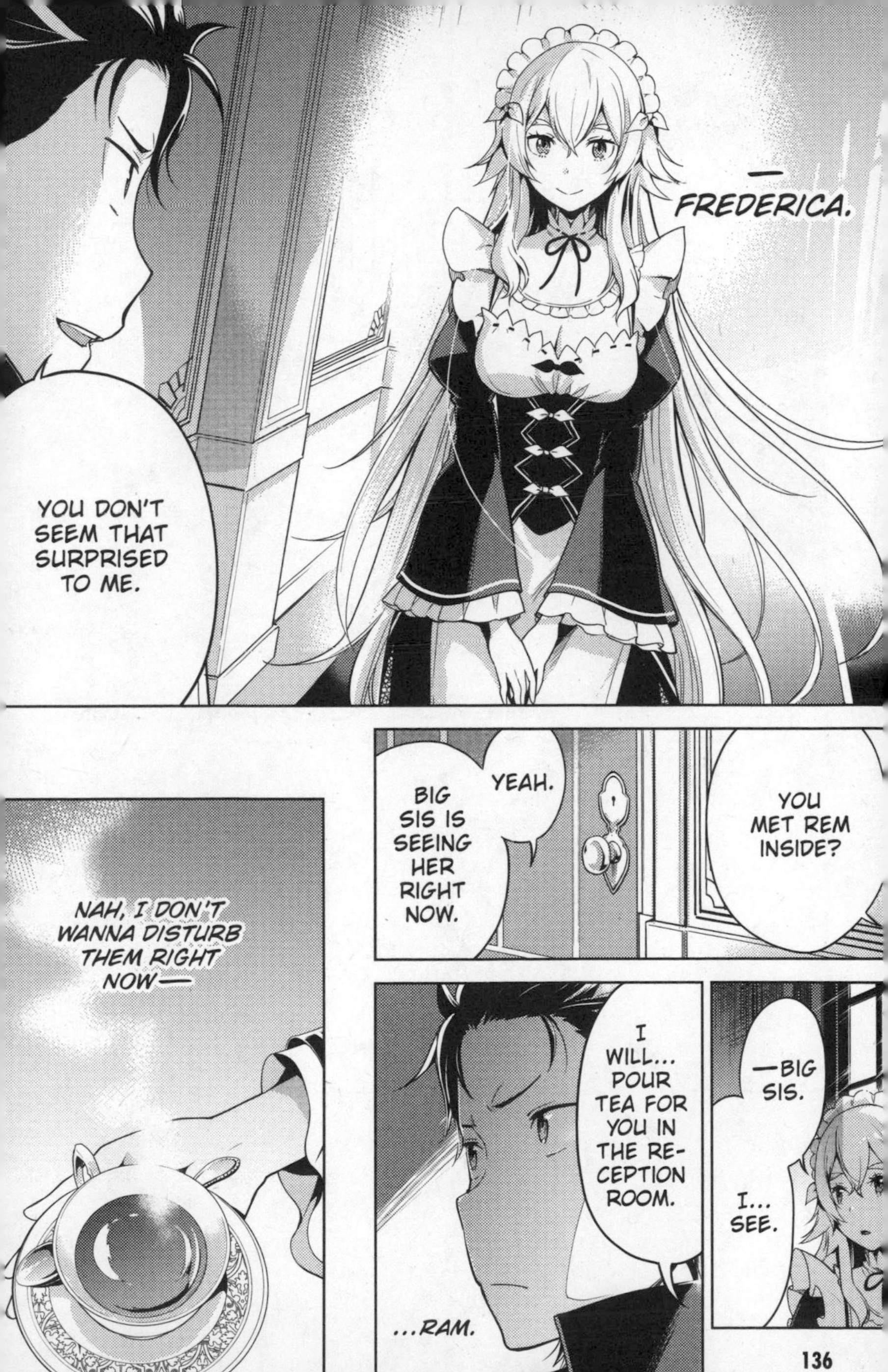
—FREDERICA.
YOU DON'T SEEM THAT SURPRISED TO ME.
YOU MET REM INSIDE?
YEAH.
BIG SIS IS SEEING HER RIGHT NOW.
—BIG SIS.
I... SEE.
I WILL... POUR TEA FOR YOU IN THE RE-CEPTION ROOM.
...RAM.
NAH, I DON'T WANNA DISTURB THEM RIGHT NOW—

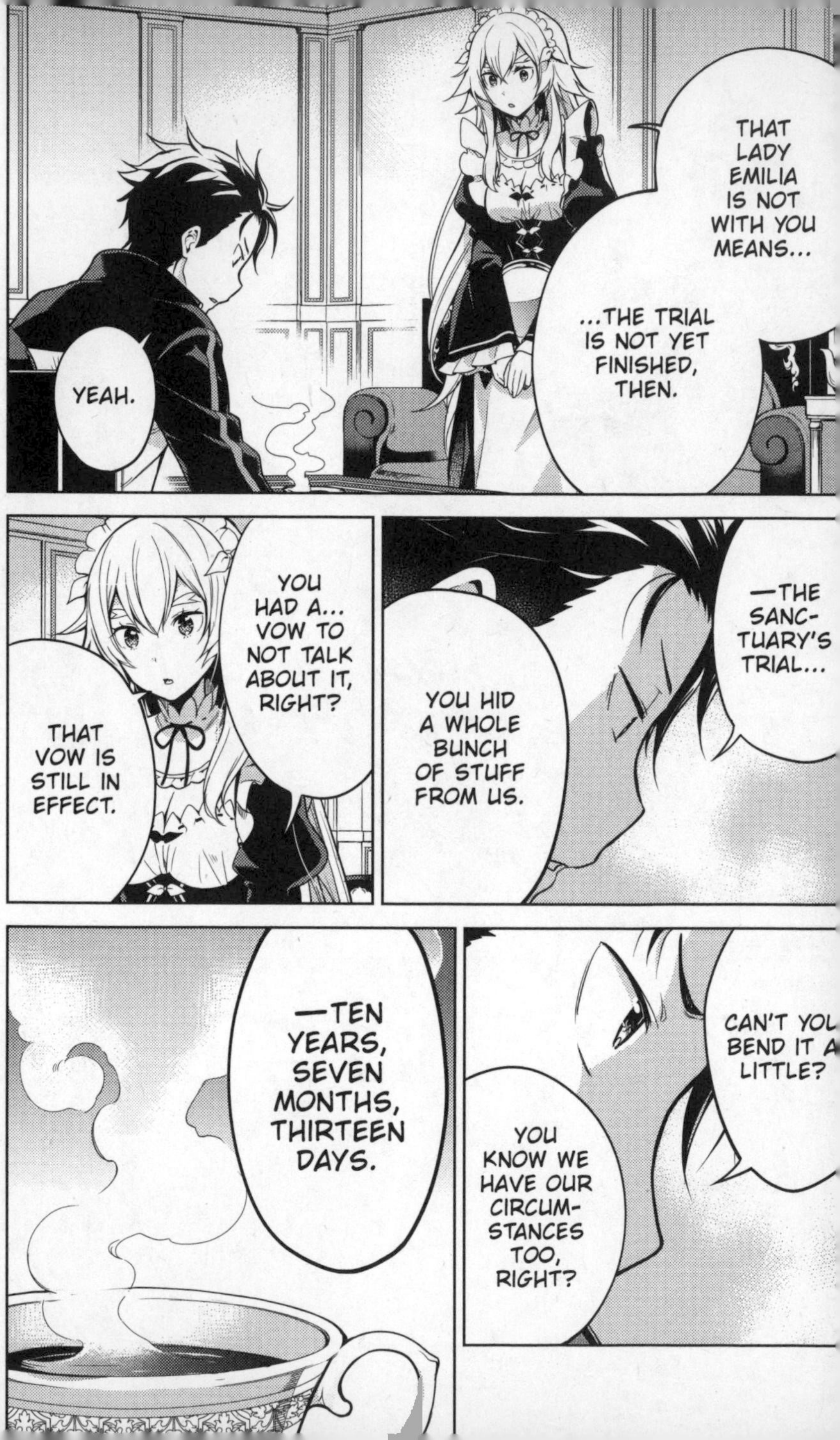
THAT LADY EMILIA IS NOT WITH YOU MEANS...
...THE TRIAL IS NOT YET FINISHED, THEN.
YEAH.
—THE SANCTUARY'S TRIAL...
YOU HID A WHOLE BUNCH OF STUFF FROM US.
YOU HAD A... VOW TO NOT TALK ABOUT IT, RIGHT?
THAT VOW IS STILL IN EFFECT.
CAN'T YOU BEND IT A LITTLE?
YOU KNOW WE HAVE OUR CIRCUM-STANCES TOO, RIGHT?
—TEN YEARS, SEVEN MONTHS, THIRTEEN DAYS.

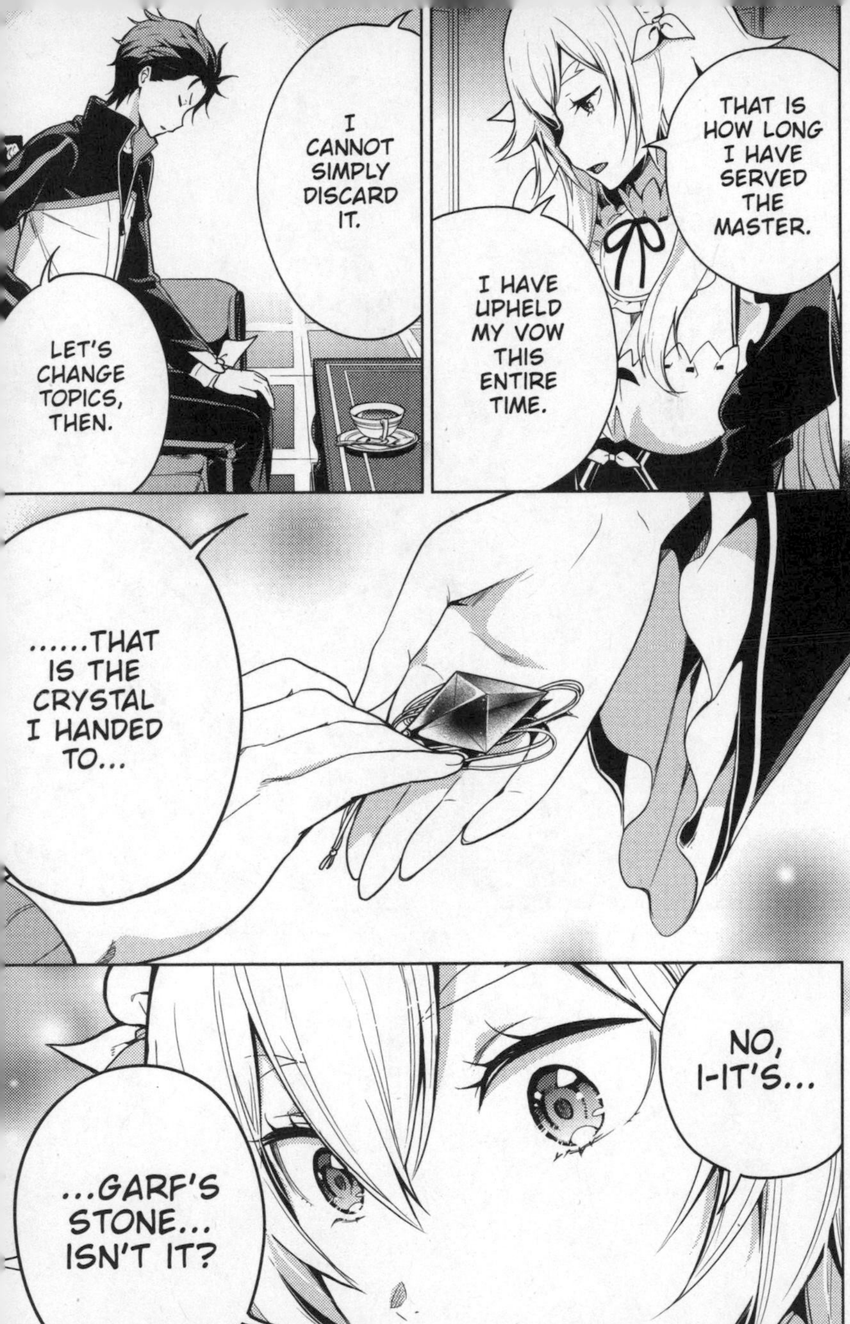
THAT IS HOW LONG I HAVE SERVED THE MASTER.
I HAVE UPHELD MY VOW THIS ENTIRE TIME.
I CANNOT SIMPLY DISCARD IT.
LET'S CHANGE TOPICS, THEN.
......THAT IS THE CRYSTAL I HANDED TO...
NO, I-IT'S...
...GARF'S STONE... ISN'T IT?

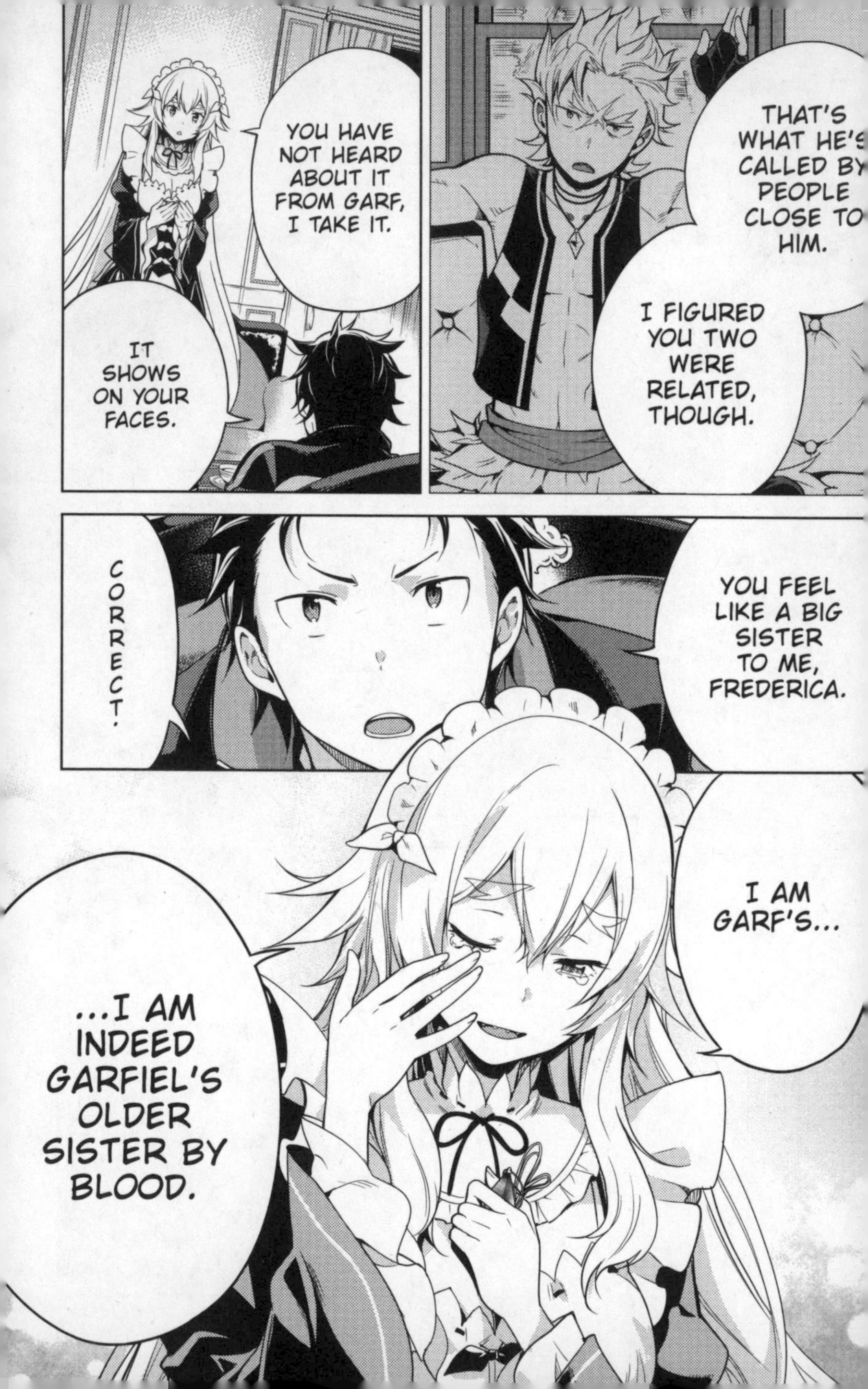
THAT'S WHAT HE'S CALLED BY PEOPLE CLOSE TO HIM.
I FIGURED YOU TWO WERE RELATED, THOUGH.
YOU HAVE NOT HEARD ABOUT IT FROM GARF, I TAKE IT.
IT SHOWS ON YOUR FACES.
YOU FEEL LIKE A BIG SISTER TO ME, FREDERICA.
CORRECT.
I AM GARF'S...
...I AM INDEED GARFIEL'S OLDER SISTER BY BLOOD.

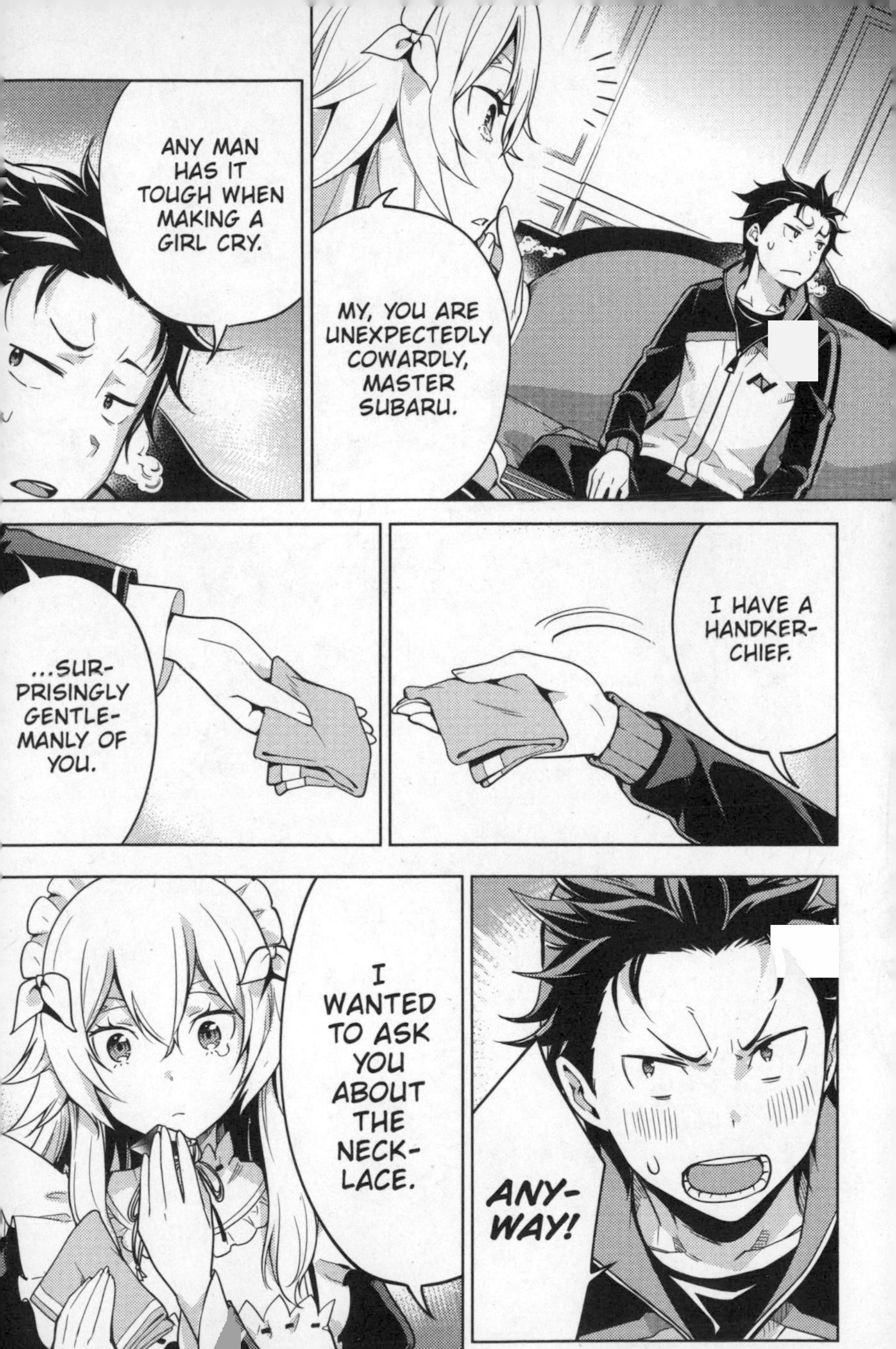
MY, YOU ARE UNEXPECTEDLY COWARDLY, MASTER SUBARU.
ANY MAN HAS IT TOUGH WHEN MAKING A GIRL CRY.
I HAVE A HANDKER-CHIEF.
...SUR-PRISINGLY GENTLE-MANLY OF YOU.
ANY-WAY!
I WANTED TO ASK YOU ABOUT THE NECK-LACE.

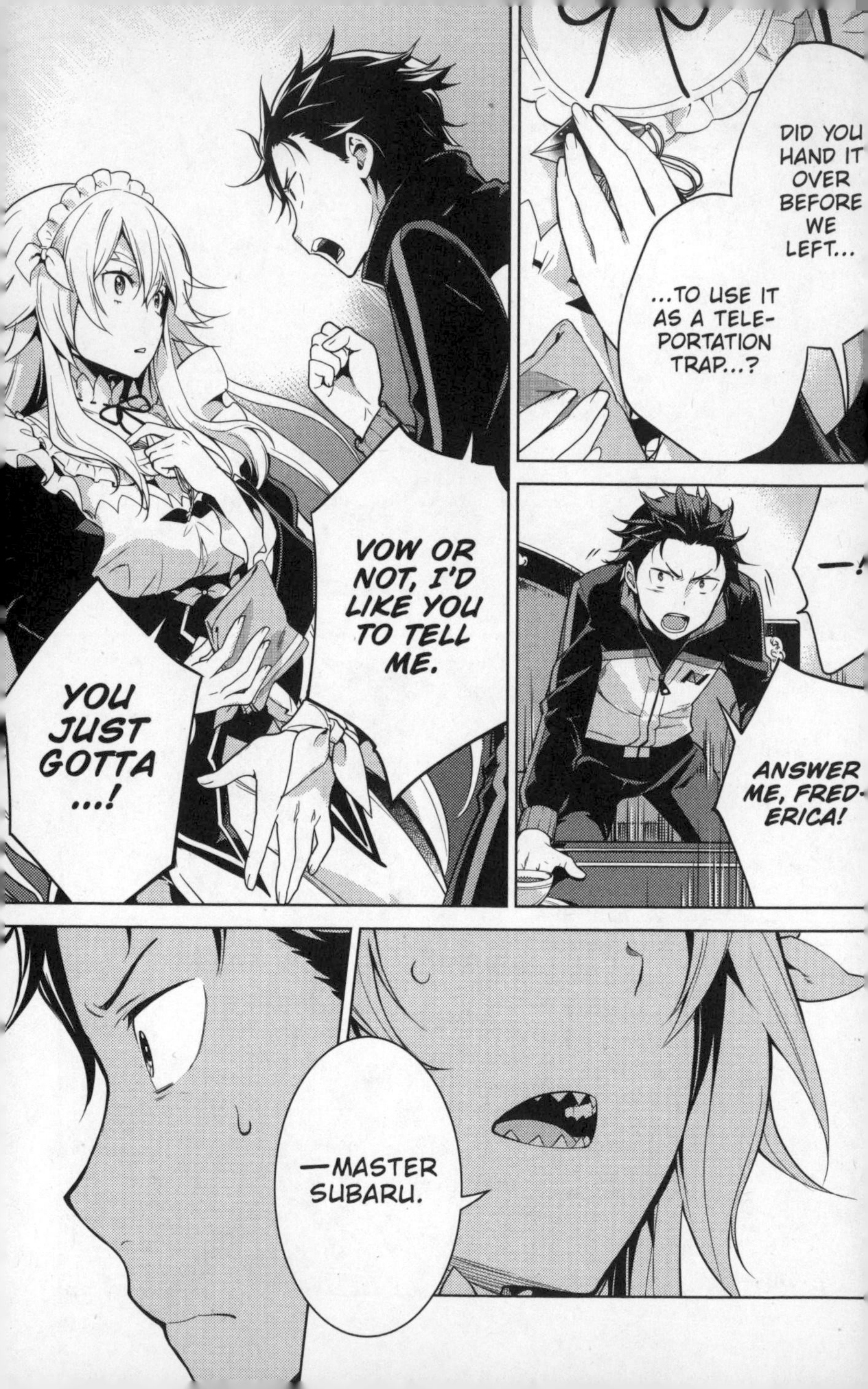

DID YOU HAND IT OVER BEFORE WE LEFT...
...TO USE IT AS A TELE-PORTATION TRAP...?
—!
ANSWER ME, FRED-ERICA!
VOW OR NOT, I'D LIKE YOU TO TELL ME.
YOU JUST GOTTA ...!
—MASTER SUBARU.

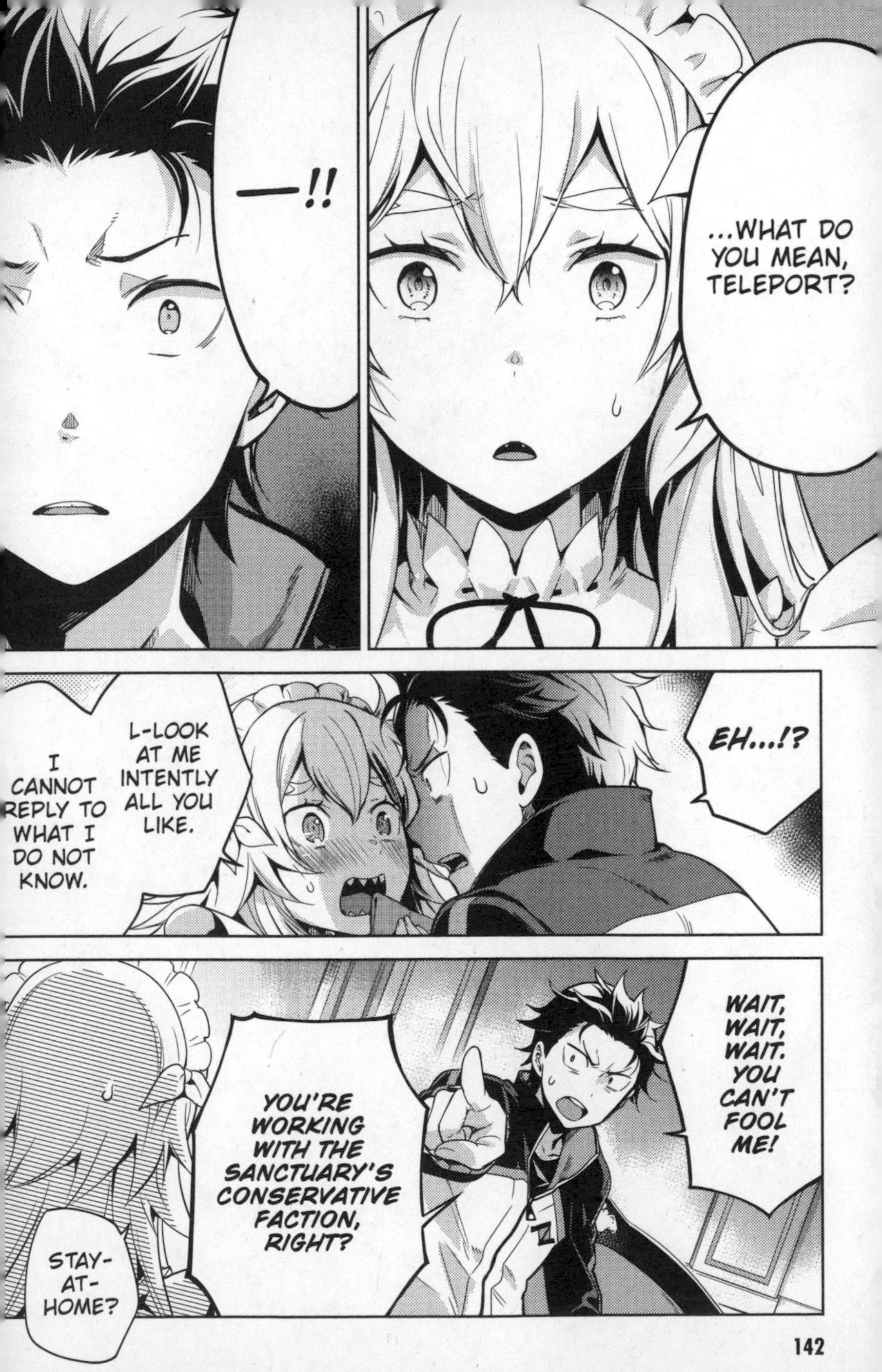
...WHAT DO YOU MEAN, TELEPORT?
—!!
EH...!?
L-LOOK AT ME INTENTLY ALL YOU LIKE.
I CANNOT REPLY TO WHAT I DO NOT KNOW.
WAIT, WAIT, WAIT. YOU CAN'T FOOL ME!
YOU'RE WORKING WITH THE SANCTUARY'S CONSERVATIVE FACTION, RIGHT?
STAY-AT-HOME?

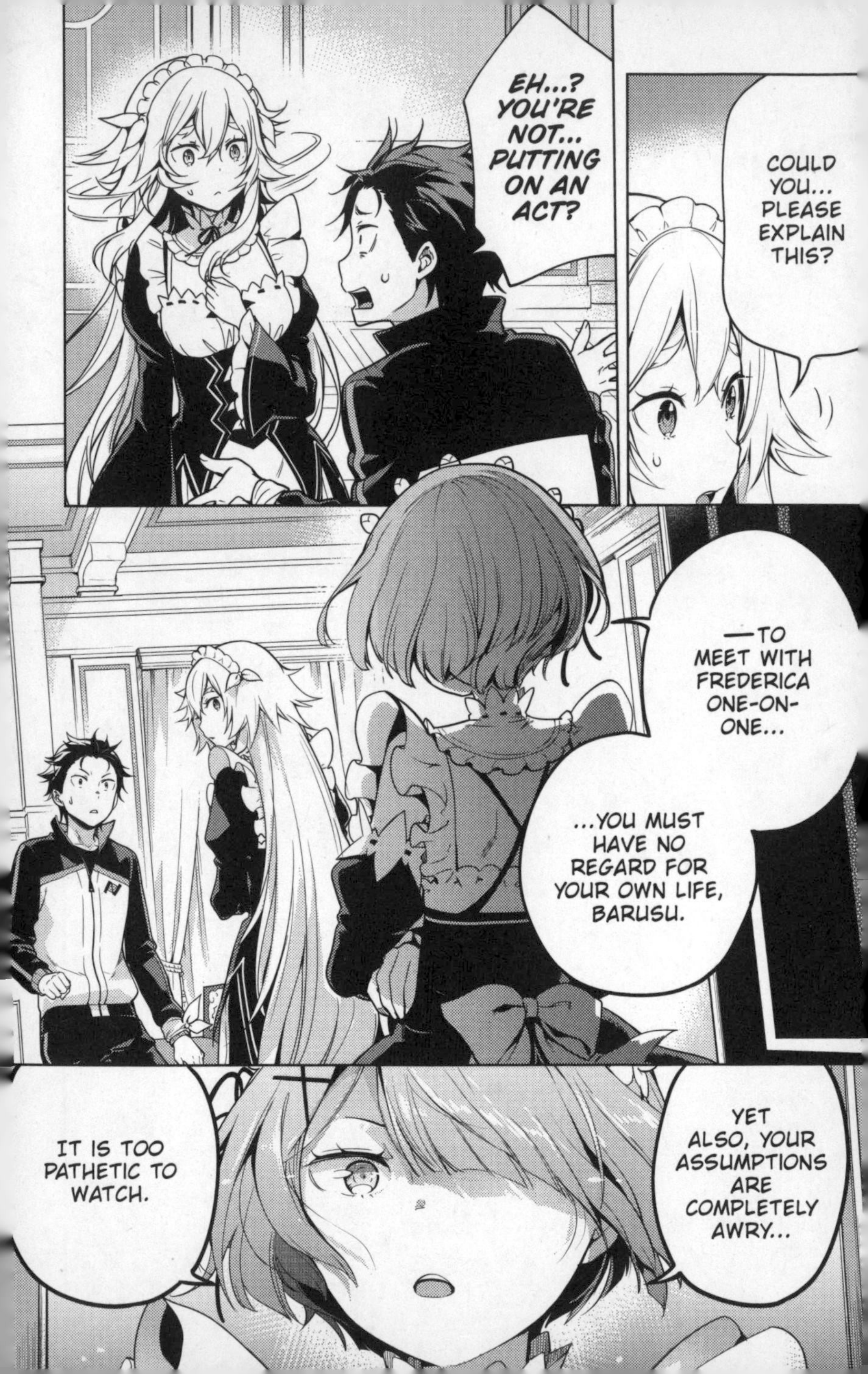
COULD YOU... PLEASE EXPLAIN THIS?
EH...? YOU'RE NOT... PUTTING ON AN ACT?
—TO MEET WITH FREDERICA ONE-ON-ONE...
...YOU MUST HAVE NO REGARD FOR YOUR OWN LIFE, BARUSU.
YET ALSO, YOUR ASSUMPTIONS ARE COMPLETELY AWRY...
IT IS TOO PATHETIC TO WATCH.

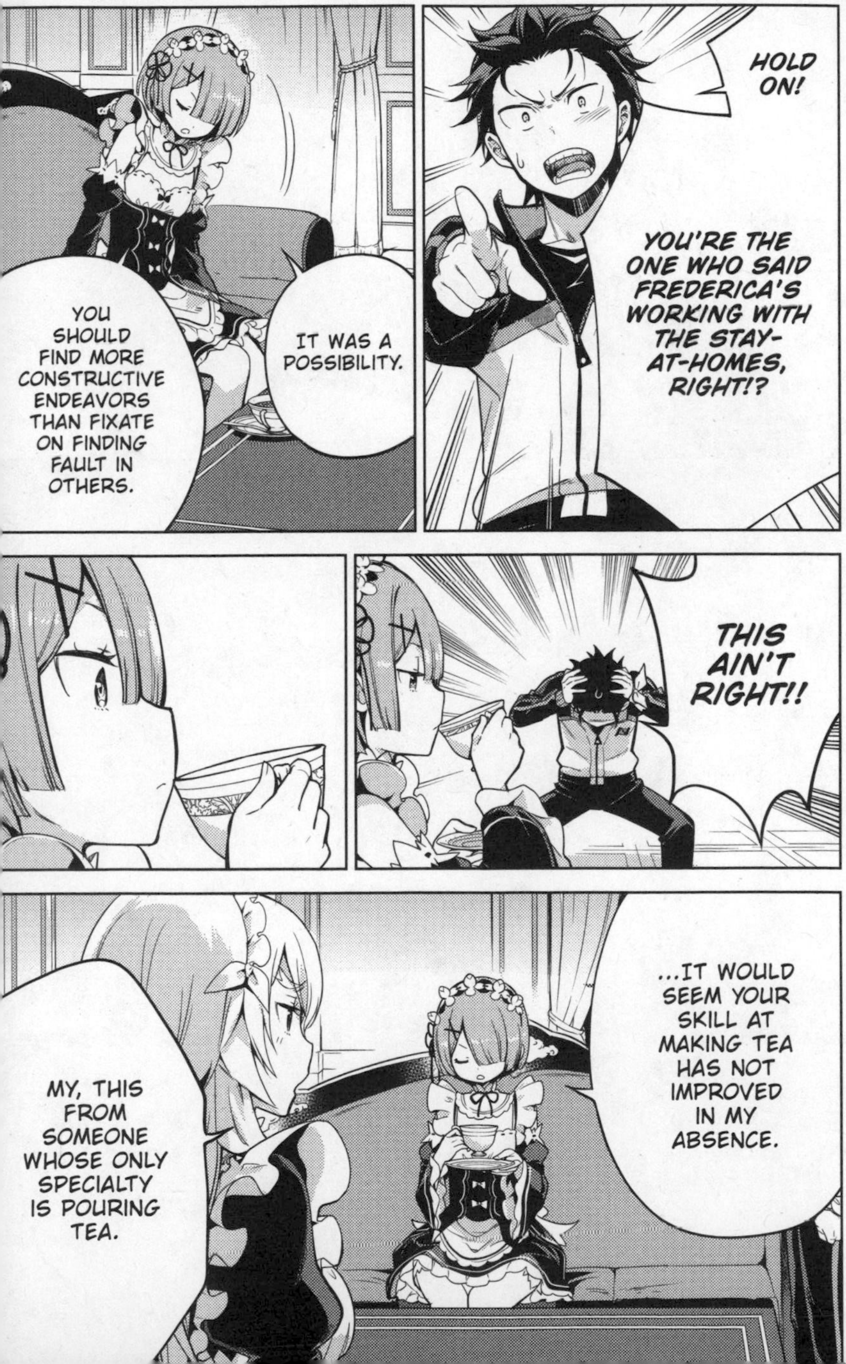
HOLD ON!
YOU'RE THE ONE WHO SAID FREDERICA'S WORKING WITH THE STAY-AT-HOMES, RIGHT!?
IT WAS A POSSIBILITY.
YOU SHOULD FIND MORE CONSTRUCTIVE ENDEAVORS THAN FIXATE ON FINDING FAULT IN OTHERS.
THIS AIN'T RIGHT!!
...IT WOULD SEEM YOUR SKILL AT MAKING TEA HAS NOT IMPROVED IN MY ABSENCE.
MY, THIS FROM SOMEONE WHOSE ONLY SPECIALTY IS POURING TEA.

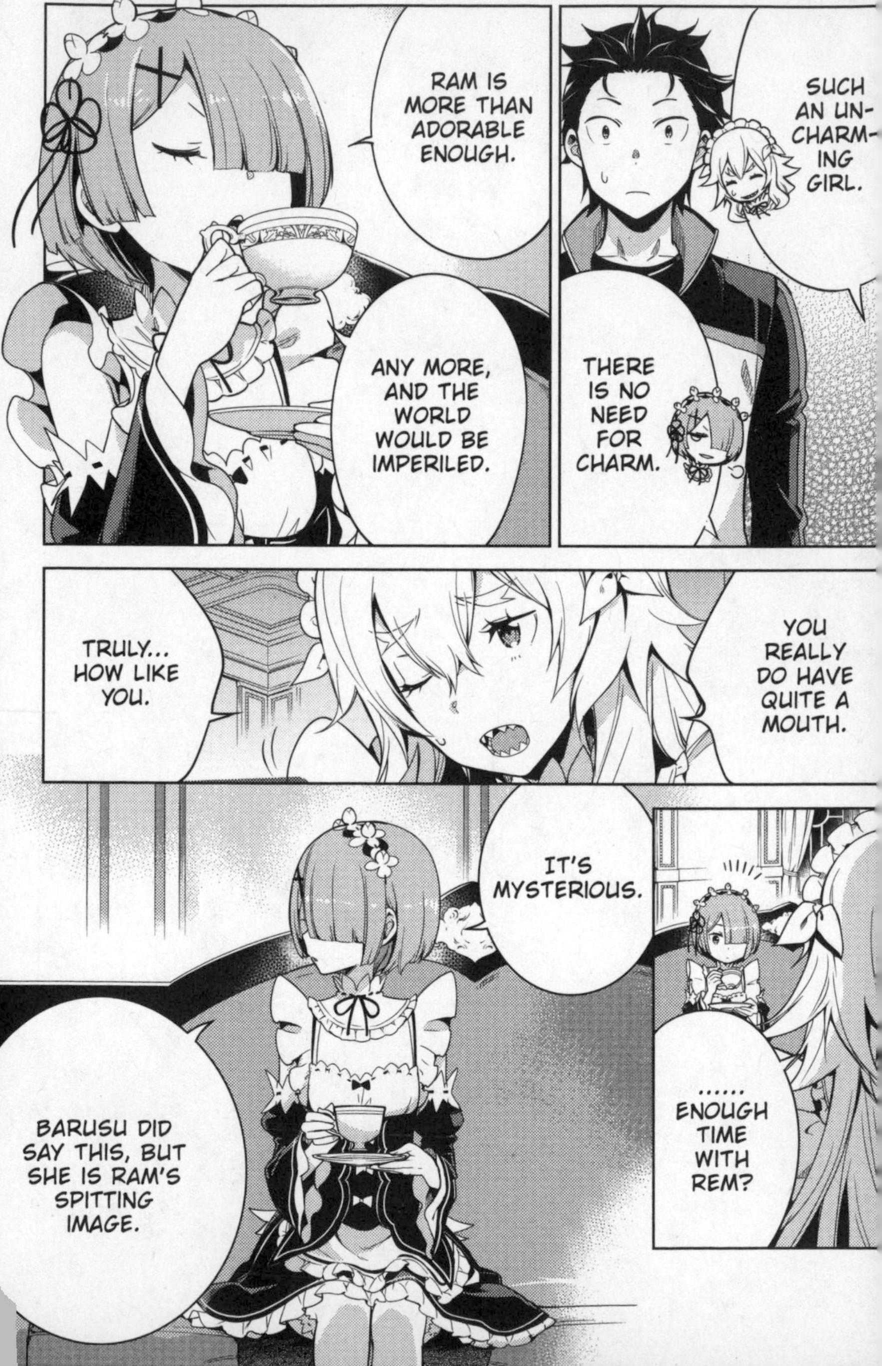
SUCH AN UN-CHARM-ING GIRL.
THERE IS NO NEED FOR CHARM.
RAM IS MORE THAN ADORABLE ENOUGH.
ANY MORE, AND THE WORLD WOULD BE IMPERILED.
YOU REALLY DO HAVE QUITE A MOUTH.
TRULY... HOW LIKE YOU.
...... ENOUGH TIME WITH REM?
IT'S MYSTERIOUS.
BARUSU DID SAY THIS, BUT SHE IS RAM'S SPITTING IMAGE.

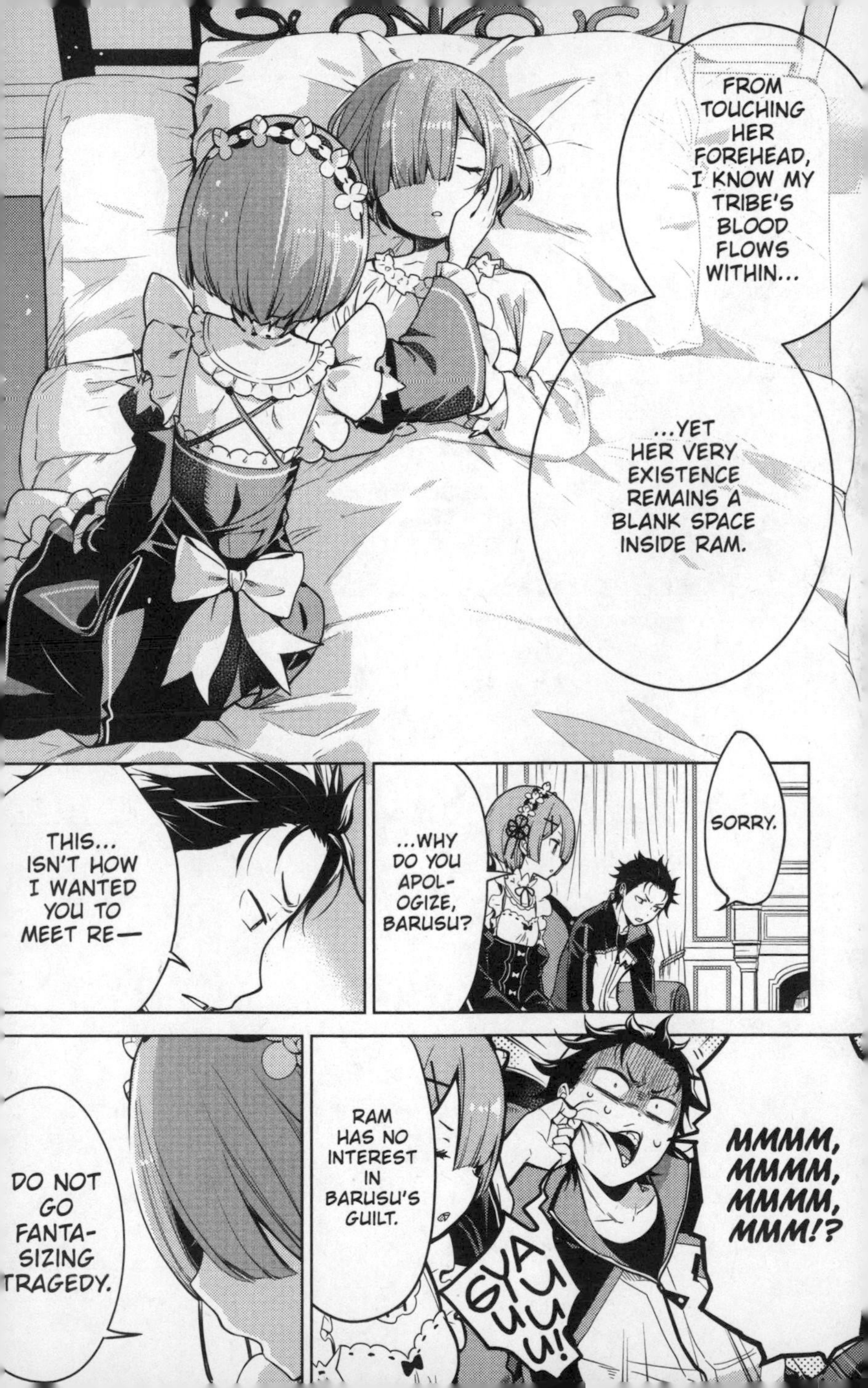
FROM TOUCHING HER FOREHEAD, I KNOW MY TRIBE'S BLOOD FLOWS WITHIN...
...YET HER VERY EXISTENCE REMAINS A BLANK SPACE INSIDE RAM.
SORRY.
...WHY DO YOU APOLOGIZE, BARUSU?
THIS... ISN'T HOW I WANTED YOU TO MEET RE—
RAM HAS NO INTEREST IN BARUSU'S GUILT.
MMMM, MMMM, MMMM, MMM!?
GYAUUUU!
DO NOT GO FANTASIZING TRAGEDY.

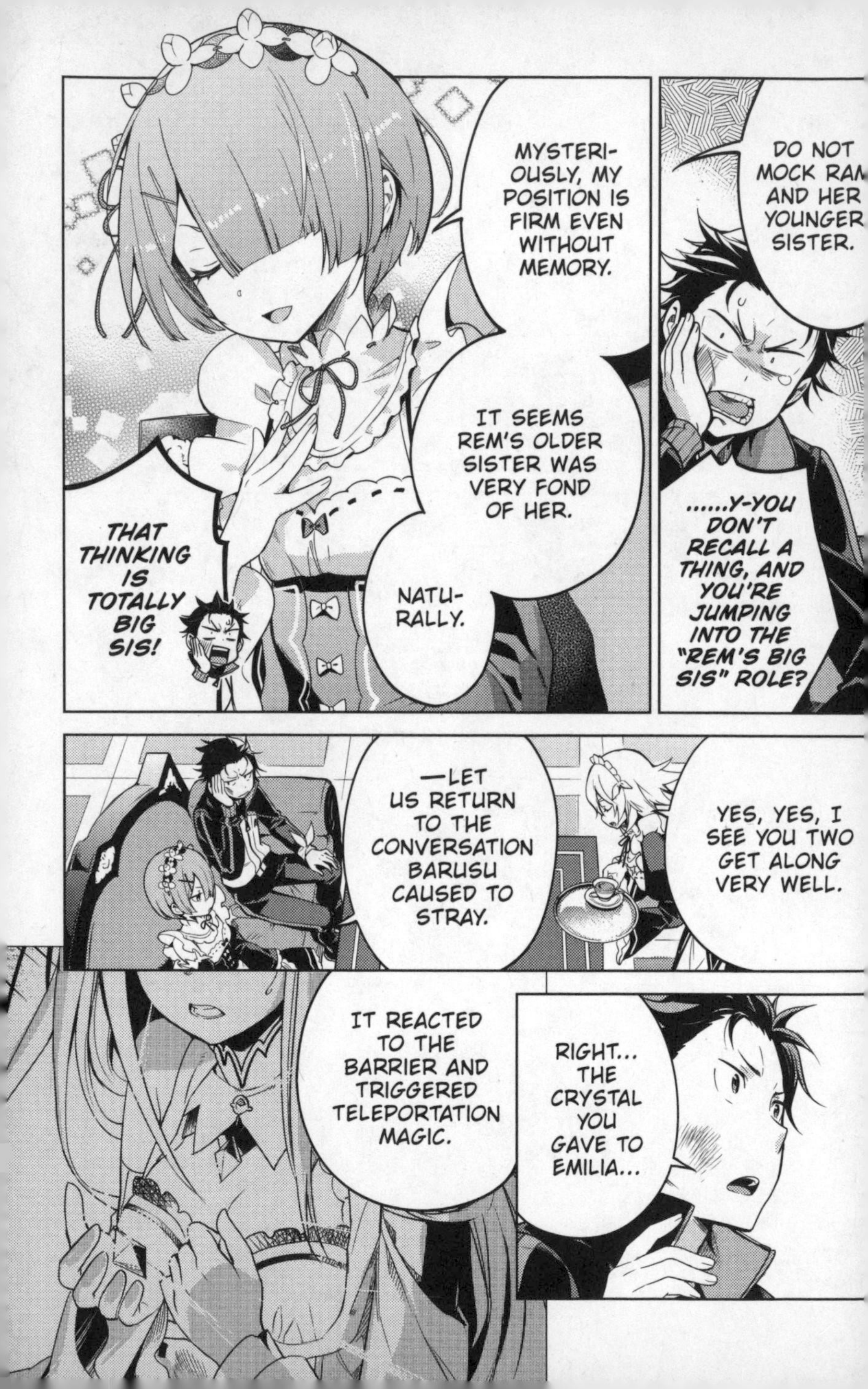
DO NOT MOCK RAM AND HER YOUNGER SISTER.
......Y-YOU DON'T RECALL A THING, AND YOU'RE JUMPING INTO THE "REM'S BIG SIS" ROLE?
MYSTERI-OUSLY, MY POSITION IS FIRM EVEN WITHOUT MEMORY.
IT SEEMS REM'S OLDER SISTER WAS VERY FOND OF HER.
NATU-RALLY.
THAT THINKING IS TOTALLY BIG SIS!
YES, YES, I SEE YOU TWO GET ALONG VERY WELL.
—LET US RETURN TO THE CONVERSATION BARUSU CAUSED TO STRAY.
RIGHT... THE CRYSTAL YOU GAVE TO EMILIA...
IT REACTED TO THE BARRIER AND TRIGGERED TELEPORTATION MAGIC.

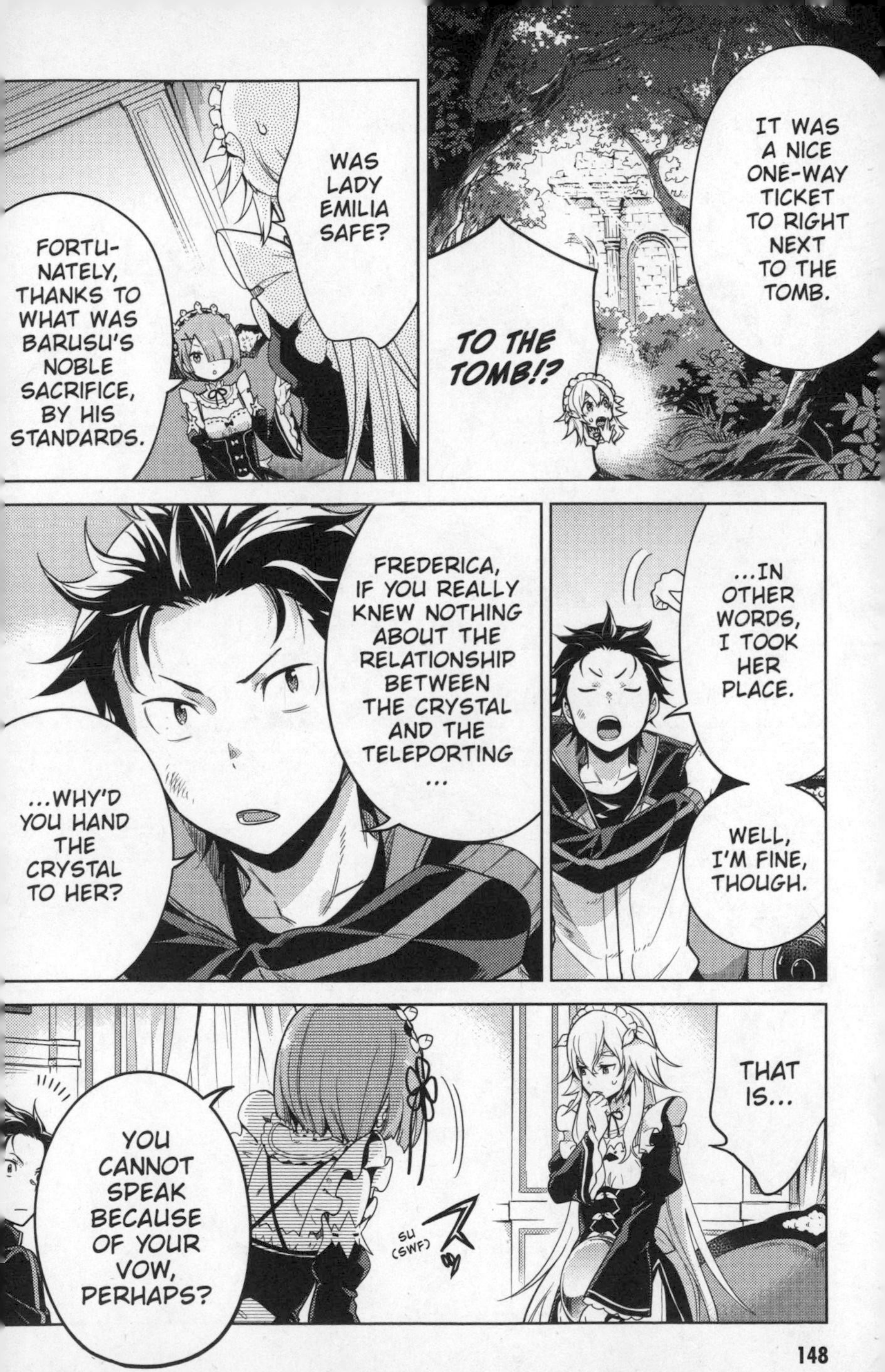
IT WAS A NICE ONE-WAY TICKET TO RIGHT NEXT TO THE TOMB.
TO THE TOMB!?
WAS LADY EMILIA SAFE?
FORTU-NATELY, THANKS TO WHAT WAS BARUSU'S NOBLE SACRIFICE, BY HIS STANDARDS.
...IN OTHER WORDS, I TOOK HER PLACE.
WELL, I'M FINE, THOUGH.
FREDERICA, IF YOU REALLY KNEW NOTHING ABOUT THE RELATIONSHIP BETWEEN THE CRYSTAL AND THE TELEPORTING ...
...WHY'D YOU HAND THE CRYSTAL TO HER?
THAT IS...
SU (SWF)
YOU CANNOT SPEAK BECAUSE OF YOUR VOW, PERHAPS?

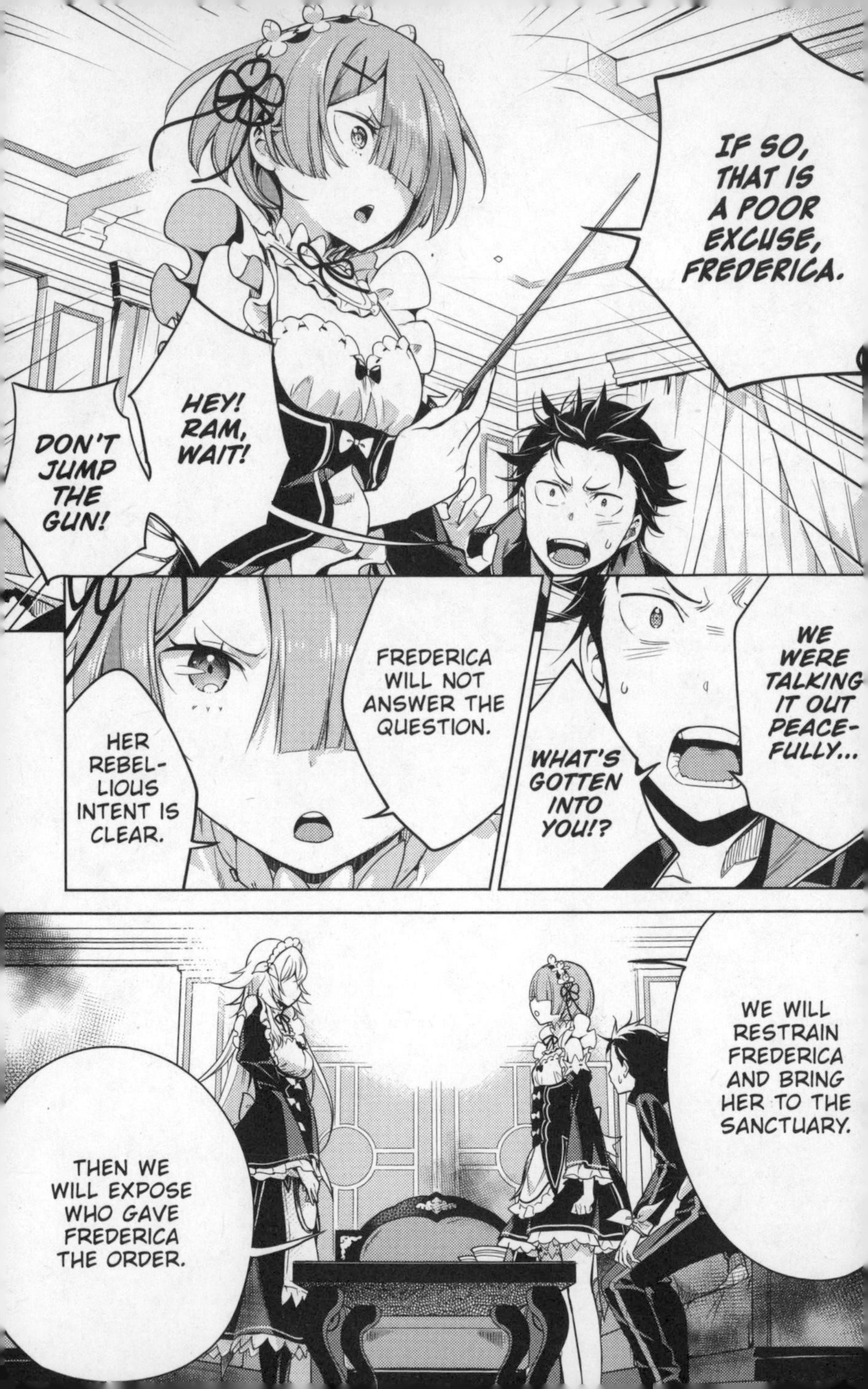
IF SO, THAT IS A POOR EXCUSE, FREDERICA.
HEY! RAM, WAIT!
DON'T JUMP THE GUN!
WE WERE TALKING IT OUT PEACE-FULLY...
WHAT'S GOTTEN INTO YOU!?
FREDERICA WILL NOT ANSWER THE QUESTION.
HER REBEL-LIOUS INTENT IS CLEAR.
WE WILL RESTRAIN FREDERICA AND BRING HER TO THE SANCTUARY.
THEN WE WILL EXPOSE WHO GAVE FREDERICA THE ORDER.

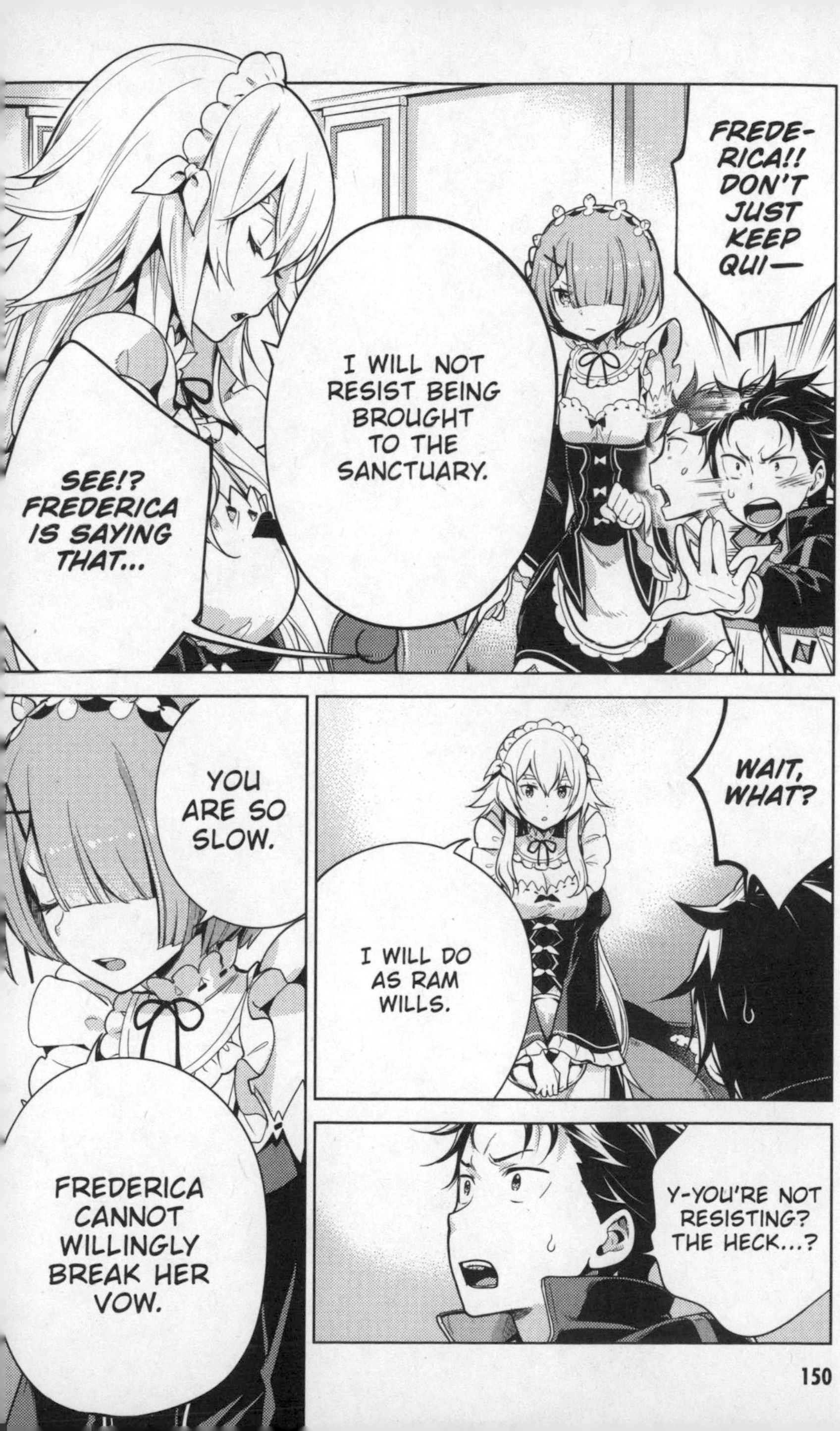
FREDE-RICA!! DON'T JUST KEEP QUI—
I WILL NOT RESIST BEING BROUGHT TO THE SANCTUARY.
SEE!? FREDERICA IS SAYING THAT...
WAIT, WHAT?
I WILL DO AS RAM WILLS.
Y-YOU'RE NOT RESISTING? THE HECK...?
YOU ARE SO SLOW.
FREDERICA CANNOT WILLINGLY BREAK HER VOW.

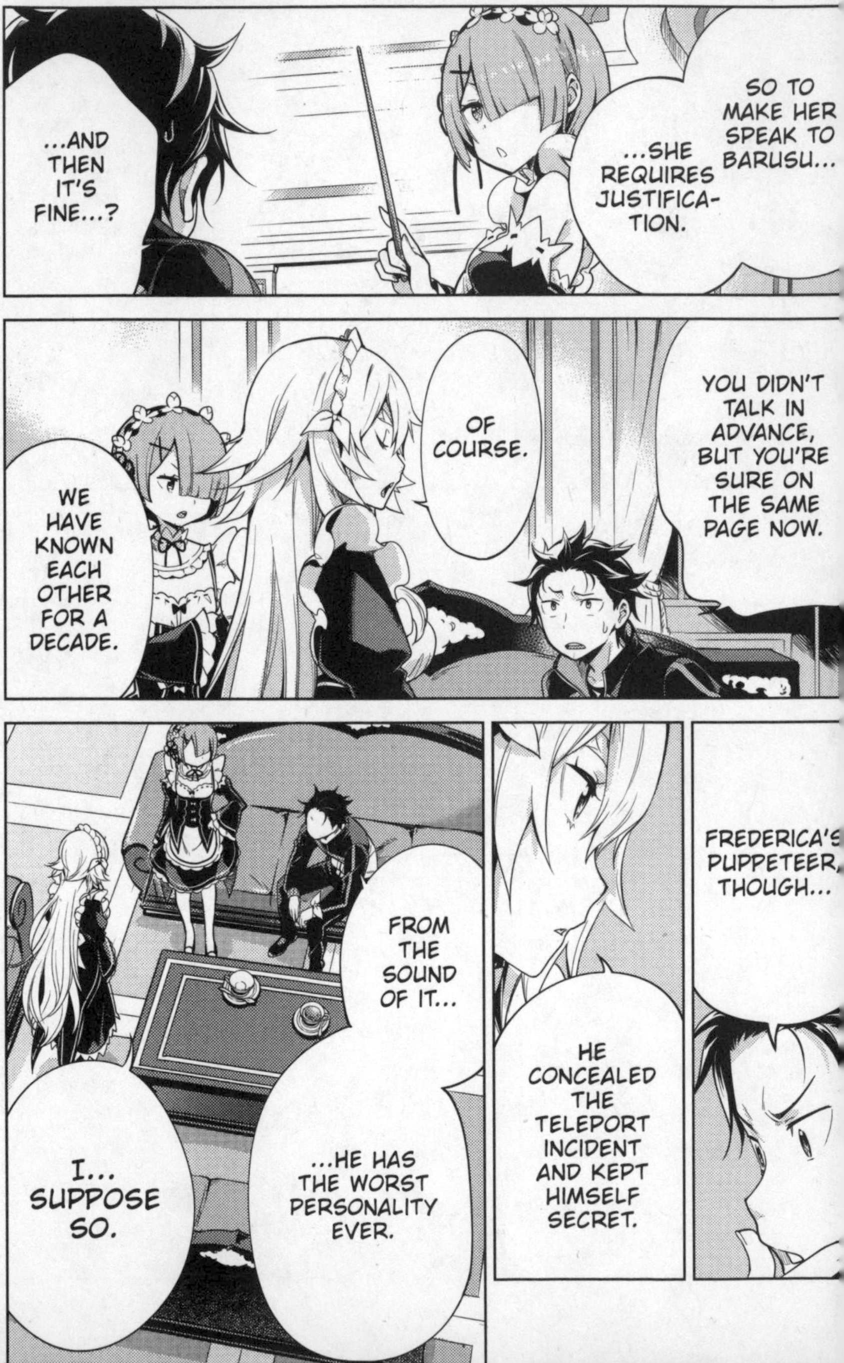
SO TO MAKE HER SPEAK TO BARUSU...
...SHE REQUIRES JUSTIFICA-TION.
...AND THEN IT'S FINE...?
YOU DIDN'T TALK IN ADVANCE, BUT YOU'RE SURE ON THE SAME PAGE NOW.
OF COURSE.
WE HAVE KNOWN EACH OTHER FOR A DECADE.
FREDERICA'S PUPPETEER, THOUGH...
HE CONCEALED THE TELEPORT INCIDENT AND KEPT HIMSELF SECRET.
FROM THE SOUND OF IT...
...HE HAS THE WORST PERSONALITY EVER.
I... SUPPOSE SO.

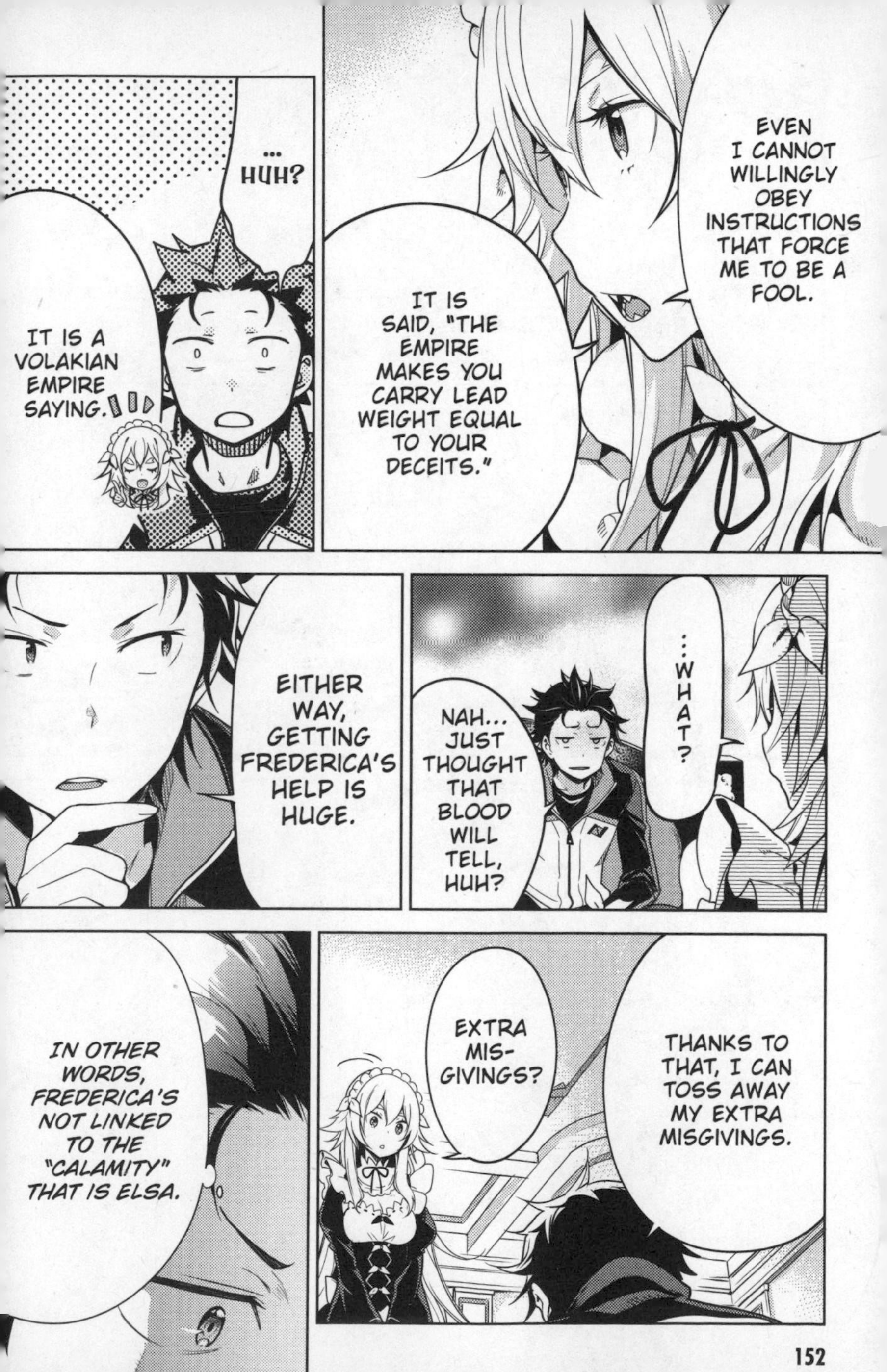
EVEN I CANNOT WILLINGLY OBEY INSTRUCTIONS THAT FORCE ME TO BE A FOOL.
IT IS SAID, "THE EMPIRE MAKES YOU CARRY LEAD WEIGHT EQUAL TO YOUR DECEITS."
... HUH?
IT IS A VOLAKIAN EMPIRE SAYING.
...WHAT?
NAH... JUST THOUGHT THAT BLOOD WILL TELL, HUH?
EITHER WAY, GETTING FREDERICA'S HELP IS HUGE.
THANKS TO THAT, I CAN TOSS AWAY MY EXTRA MISGIVINGS.
EXTRA MIS-GIVINGS?
IN OTHER WORDS, FREDERICA'S NOT LINKED TO THE "CALAMITY" THAT IS ELSA.

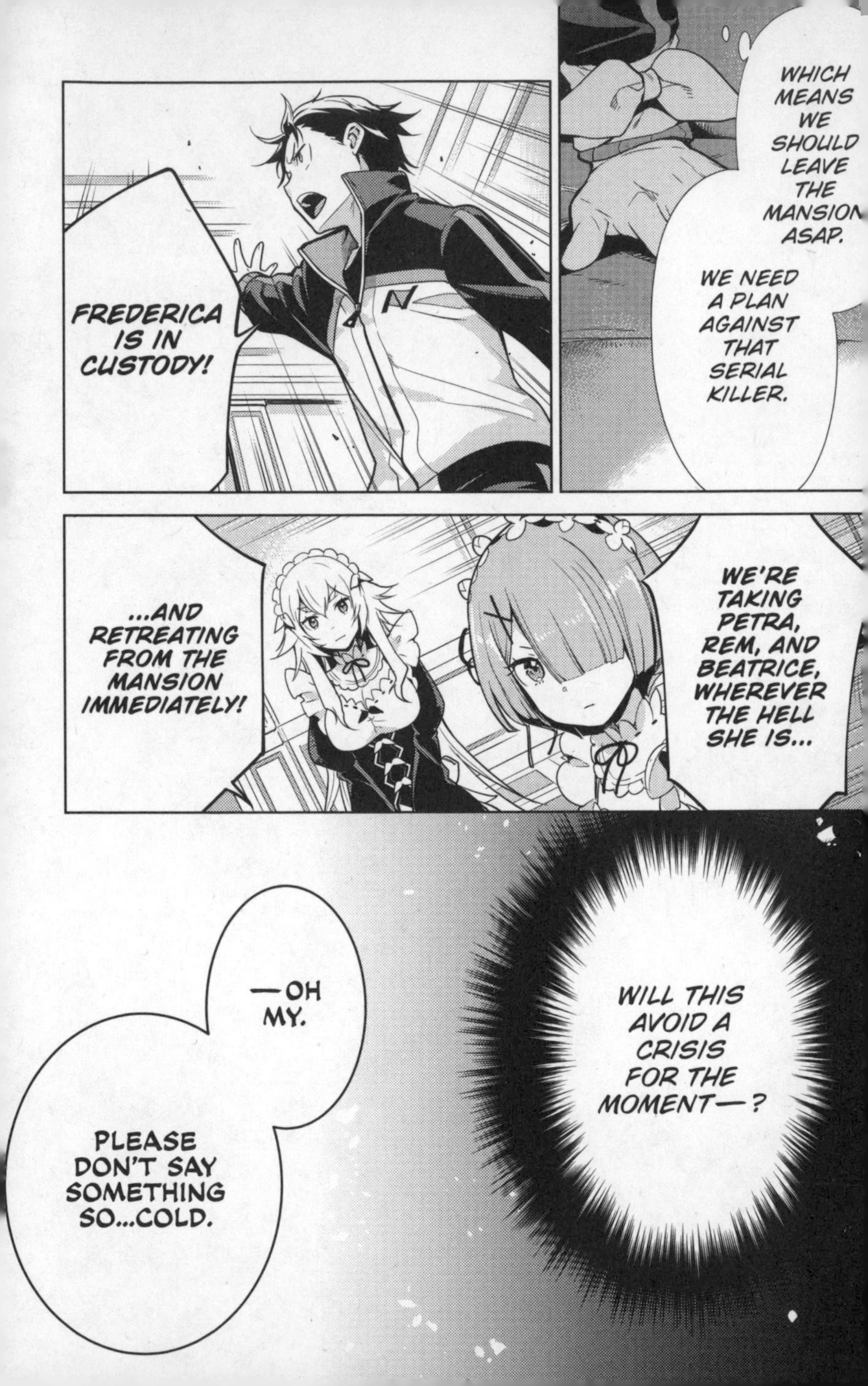
WHICH MEANS WE SHOULD LEAVE THE MANSION ASAP.
WE NEED A PLAN AGAINST THAT SERIAL KILLER.
FREDERICA IS IN CUSTODY!
WE'RE TAKING PETRA, REM, AND BEATRICE, WHEREVER THE HELL SHE IS...
...AND RETREATING FROM THE MANSION IMMEDIATELY!
WILL THIS AVOID A CRISIS FOR THE MOMENT—?
—OH MY.
PLEASE DON'T SAY SOMETHING SO...COLD.

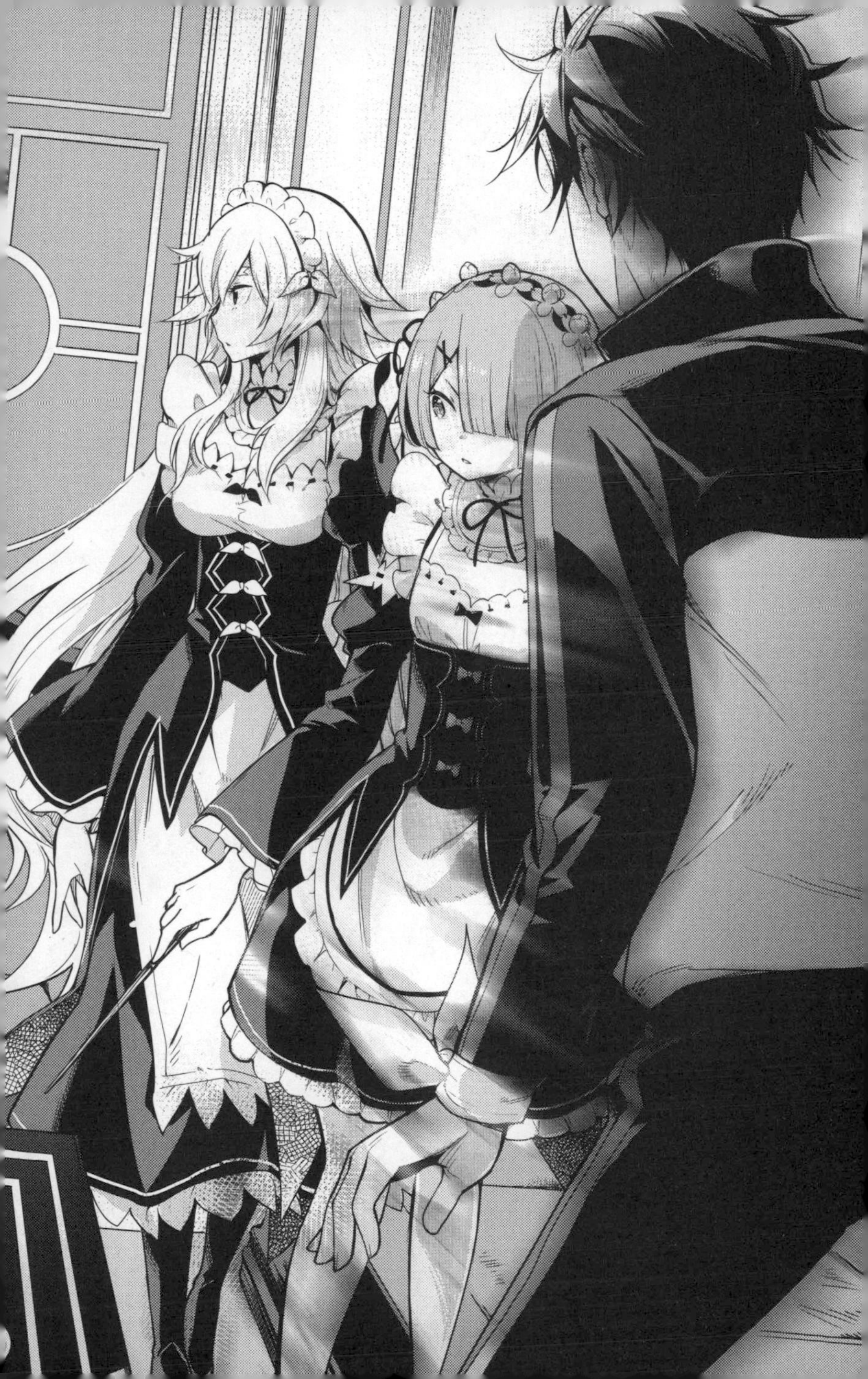

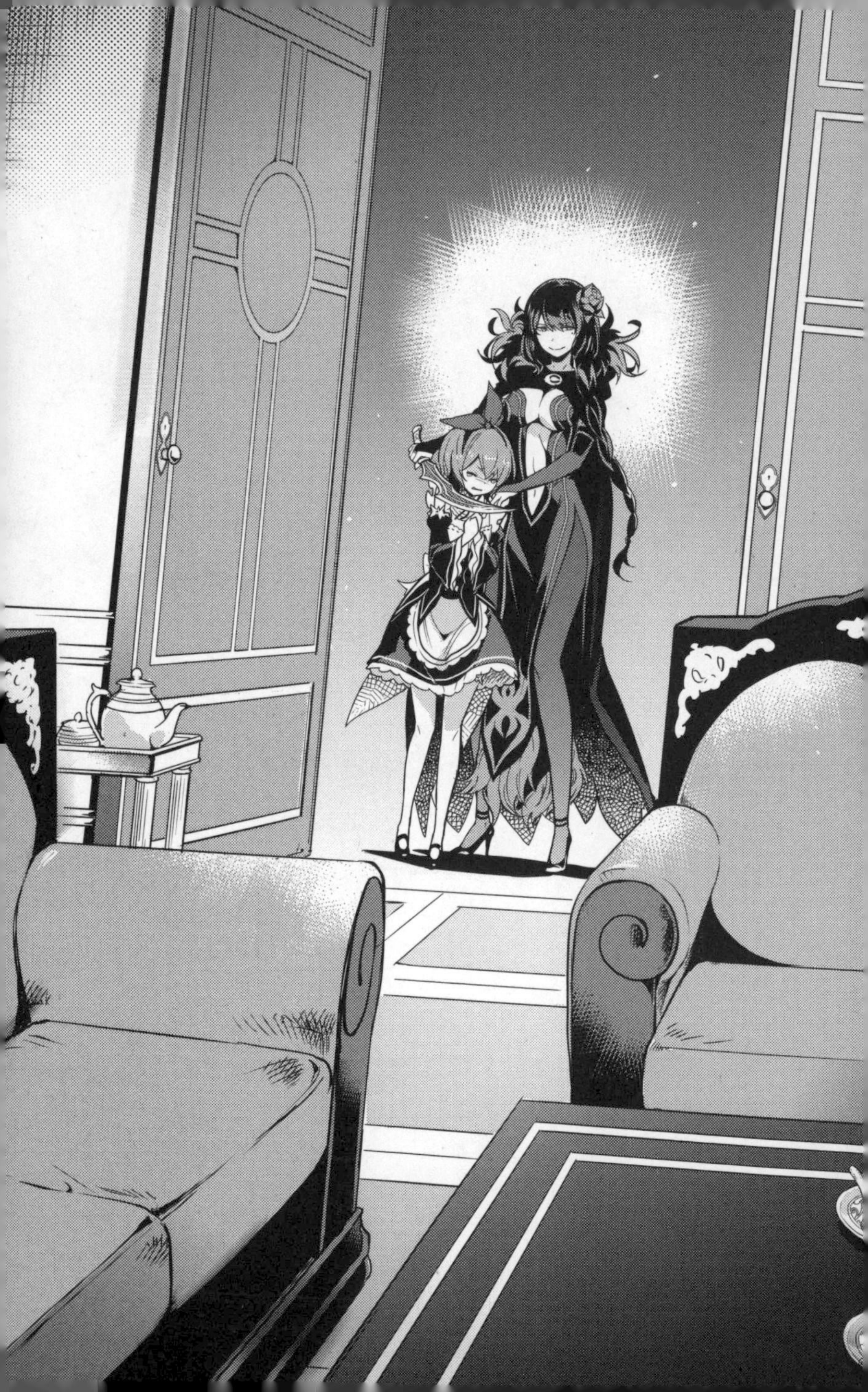

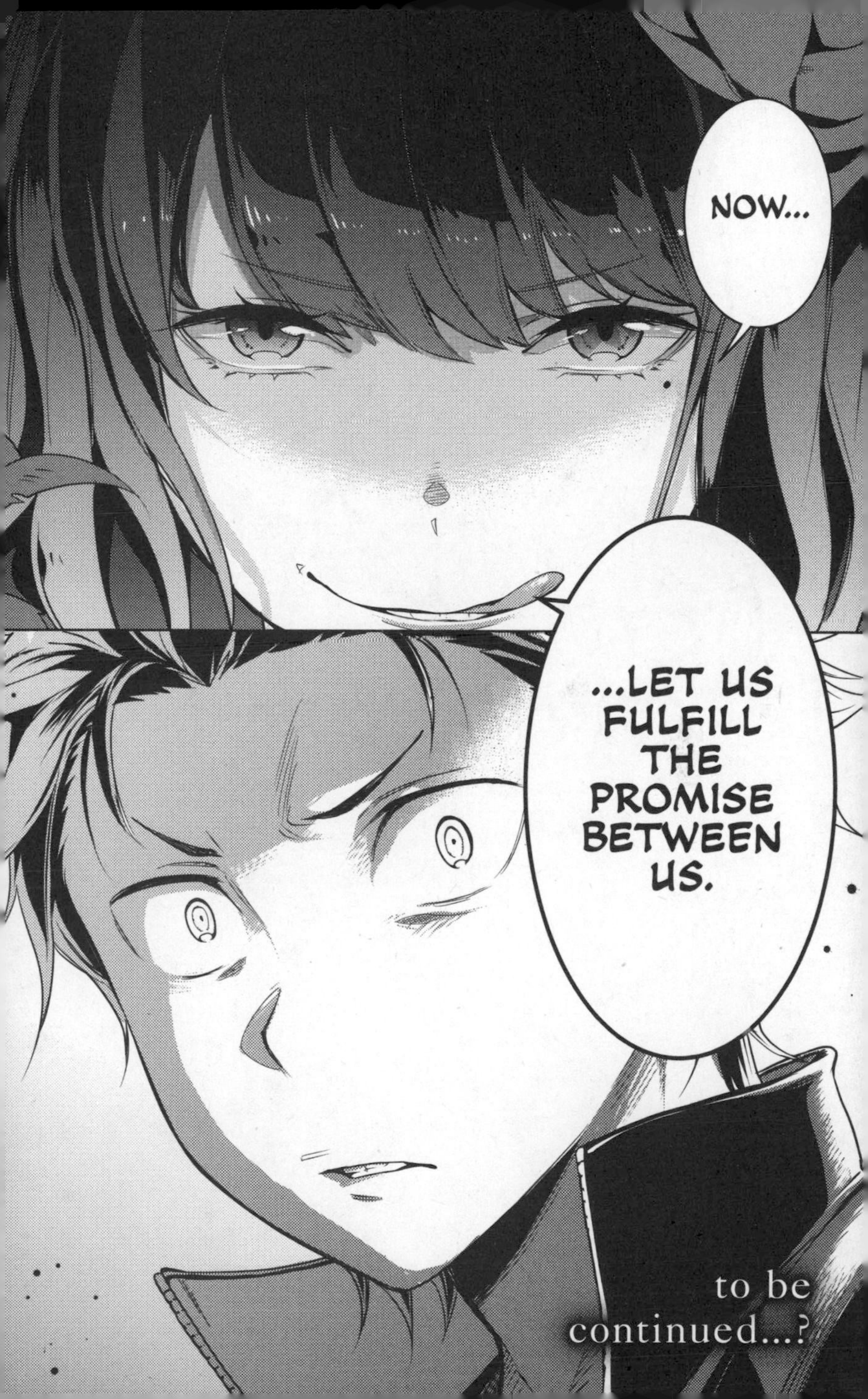
NOW...
...LET US FULFILL THE PROMISE BETWEEN US.
to be continued...?

Re:ZERO

-Starting Life in Another World-

Re:ZERO -Starting Life in Another World-

Chapter 4: The Sanctuary and the Witch of Greed

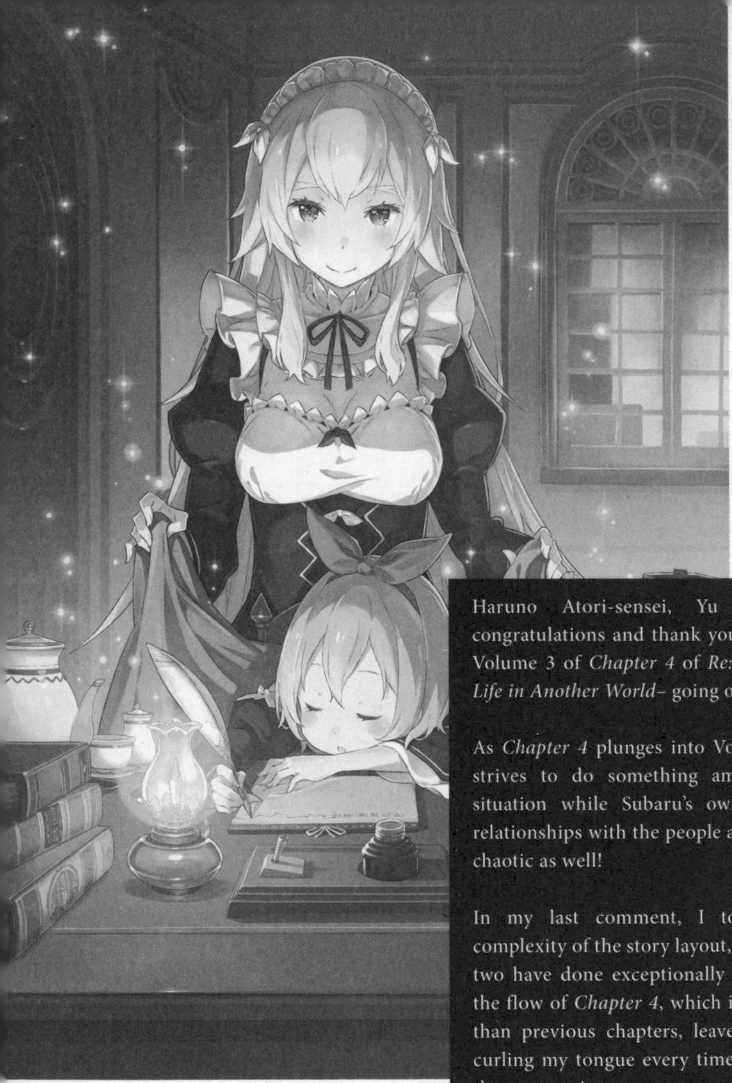

Haruno Atori-sensei, Yu Aikawa-sensei, congratulations and thank you very much for Volume 3 of *Chapter 4* of *Re:ZERO -Starting Life in Another World-* going on sale!

As *Chapter 4* plunges into Volume 3, Subaru strives to do something amid the chaotic situation while Subaru's own interpersonal relationships with the people around him turn chaotic as well!

In my last comment, I touched on the complexity of the story layout, but the way you two have done exceptionally well controlling the flow of *Chapter 4*, which is more complex than previous chapters, leaves me anxiously curling my tongue every time I double-check the manuscripts.

Going forward, as an author and as a fan, I think all of the readers will enjoy reading how you adapt into comic form portions untold in the anime and not portrayed in the light novels!

So, I eagerly await the next volume!
Subaru Will Die!

Re:ZERO -Starting Life in Another World-
Chapter 4:
The Sanctuary and the Witch of Greed

From the Author of the Original Work,
Tappei Nagatsuki

Illustration by Shinichirou Otsuka

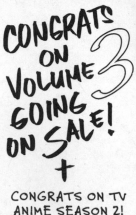

CONGRATS ON VOLUME 3 GOING ON SALE!
+
CONGRATS ON TV ANIME SEASON 2!

Re:ZERO –Starting Life in Another World– Chapter 4: The Sanctuary and the Witch of Greed

Adaptation Afterword
(Yu Aikawa)

I know it's completely different but when I look at the preexisting comic adaptations, I get so tense! (Incidentally, I watch the pre-existing anime parts with normal enjoyment.)

...But! Since the manga combines the fascinating original work with Atori-san's energy as a creator in a very "manga" sort of way, please give us your best regards going forward!

Y. AIKAWA

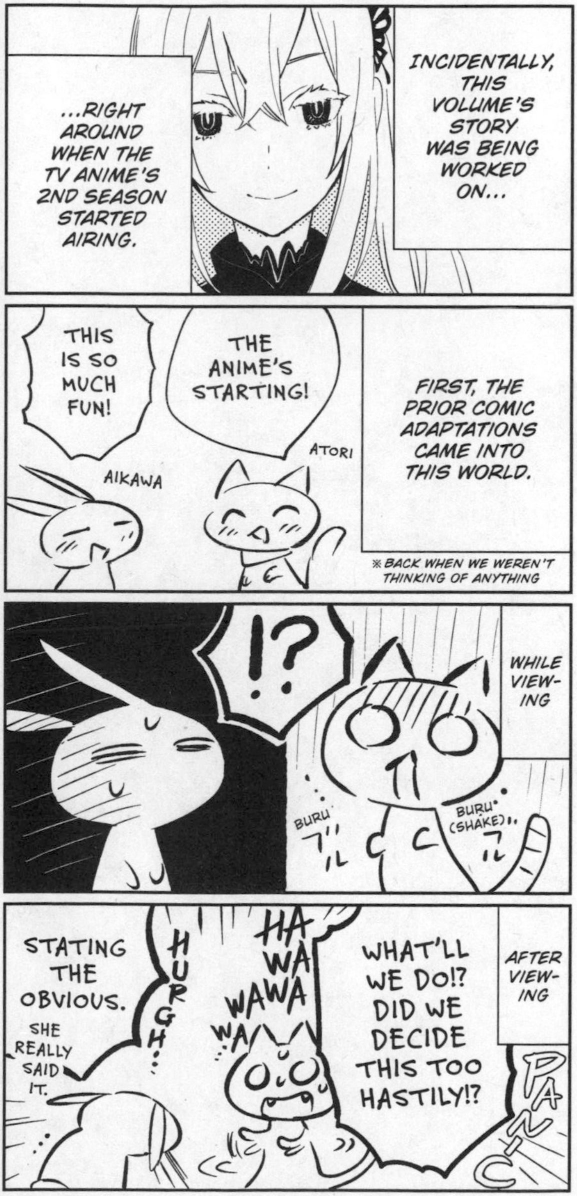
INCIDENTALLY, THIS VOLUME'S STORY WAS BEING WORKED ON...
...RIGHT AROUND WHEN THE TV ANIME'S 2ND SEASON STARTED AIRING.
FIRST, THE PRIOR COMIC ADAPTATIONS CAME INTO THIS WORLD.
※BACK WHEN WE WEREN'T THINKING OF ANYTHING
ATORI
THE ANIME'S STARTING!
THIS IS SO MUCH FUN!
AIKAWA
WHILE VIEWING
!?
BURU (SHAKE)
BURU
AFTER VIEWING
PANIC
WHAT'LL WE DO!? DID WE DECIDE THIS TOO HASTILY!?
HA WA WA WAWA WA
HURGH...
STATING THE OBVIOUS.
SHE REALLY SAID IT.

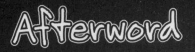

Afterword

Thank you very much for having read this book.
This is Haruno Atori in charge of the manga.
The TV anime's 2nd season of *Re:ZERO* began airing during work on Volume 3. Since the comic version was decided beforehand, the anime caught up precisely timed with the publication of this volume.
After seeing the 1st season of the animation, I was happy to watch the next, and as a manga creator, I was like, "Oh, I see!" a lot of the time.
I'm looking forward to more!
While making Volume 3, working on Episode 10 of this manga has left a particularly strong impression. But I also wish I could have watched the anime broadcast without having already known what happens thanks to Episode 10...Anyway, that's how Volume 3 went. If all of you enjoyed reading this, I'd be happy.

Adaptation: Yu Aikawa-sensei
Editors: Arimura-san, Kuro-san
Original Author: Tappei Nagatsuki-sensei
To everyone else involved in this book, thank you very much as always!

-2020, Haruno Atori

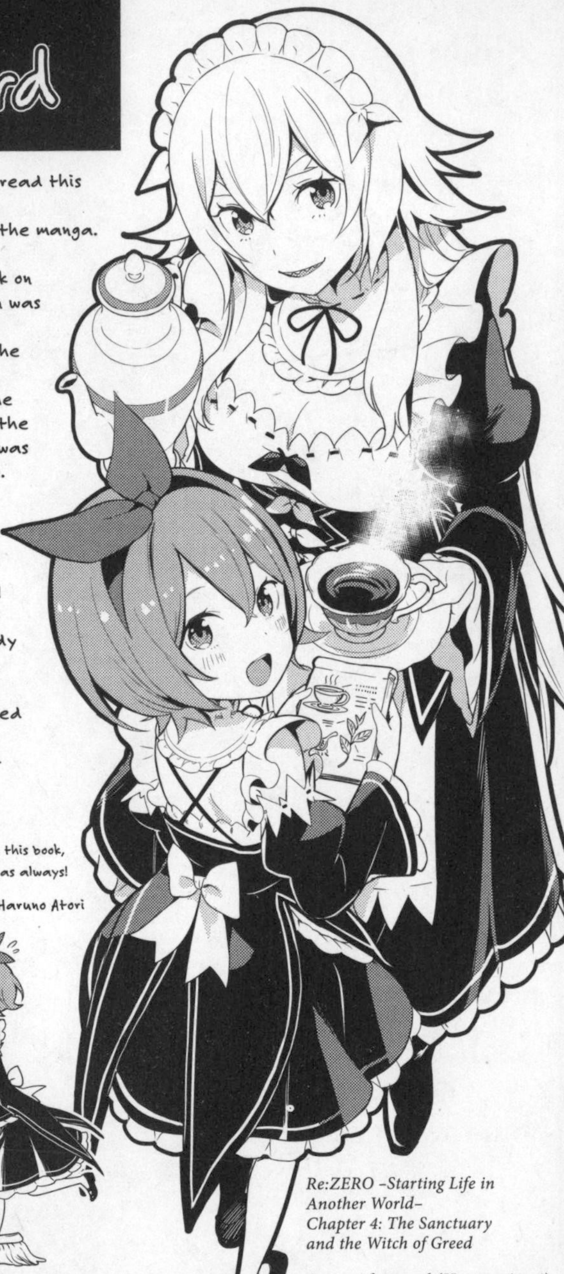

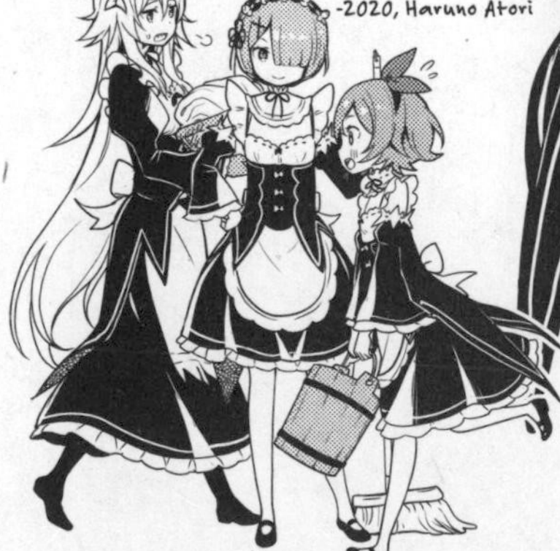

Re:ZERO -Starting Life in Another World- Chapter 4: The Sanctuary and the Witch of Greed

Artist Afterword (Haruno Atori)

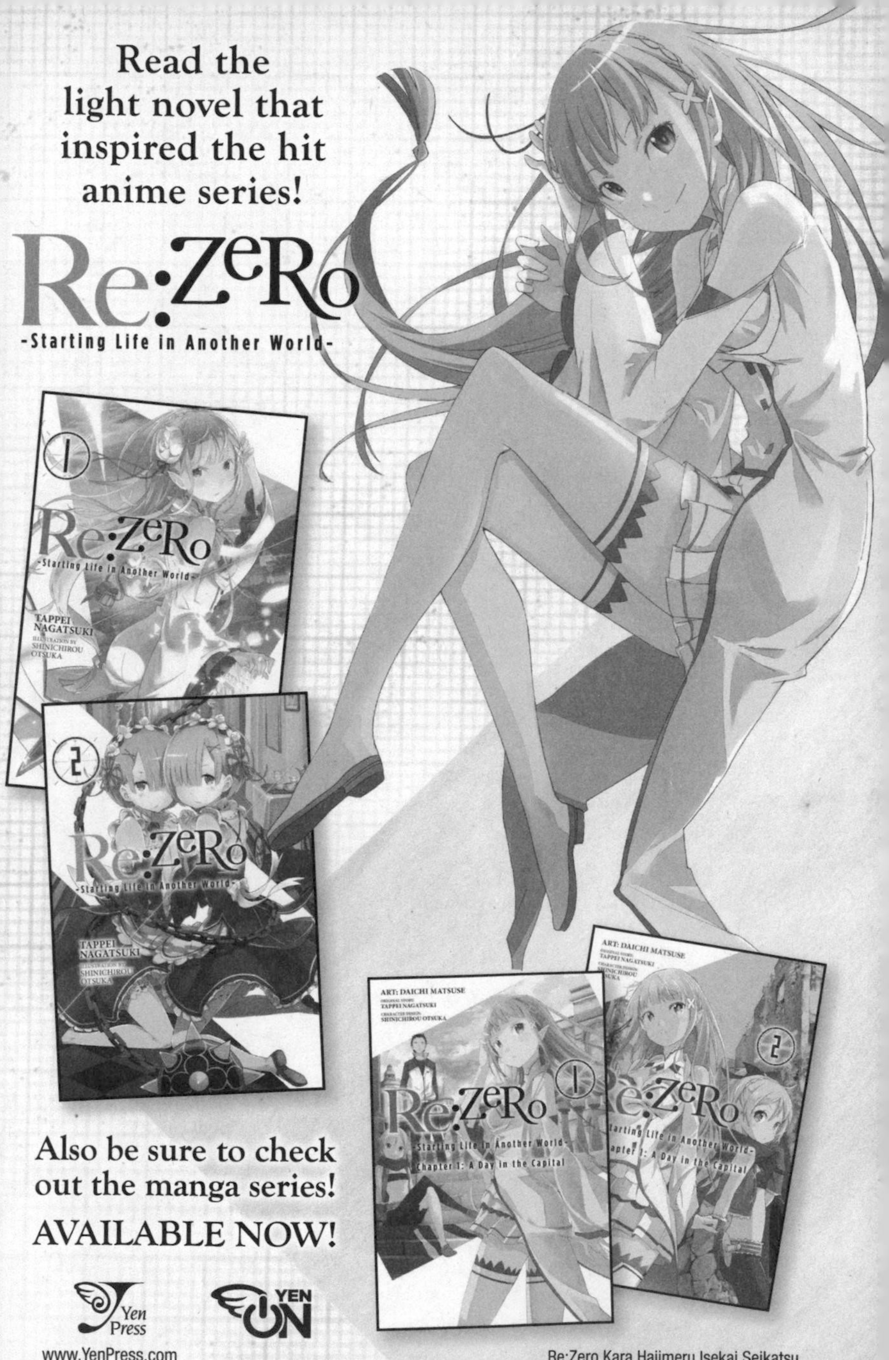
Read the light novel that inspired the hit anime series!
Re:ZeRo
-Starting Life in Another World-
Also be sure to check out the manga series!
AVAILABLE NOW!
Yen Press
YEN ON
www.YenPress.com
Re:Zero Kara Hajimeru Isekai Seikatsu
© Tappei Nagatsuki, Daichi Matsuse / KADOKAWA CORPORATION
© Tappei Nagatsuki Illustration: Shinichirou Otsuka/ KADOKAWA CORPORATION

Re:ZERO

-Starting Life in Another World-

RE:ZERO -STARTING LIFE IN ANOTHER WORLD- ③

Chapter 4: The Sanctuary and the Witch of Greed

Art: **Haruno Atori**
Adaptation: **Yu Aikawa**
Original Story: **Tappei Nagatsuki**
Character Design: **Shinichirou Otsuka**

Translation: **Jeremiah Bourque**
Lettering: **Rochelle Gancio**

RE:ZERO KARA HAJIMERU ISEKAI SEIKATSU DAIYONSHO
Seiiki to Goyoku no Majo Vol. 3
© Haruno Atori 2020
© Yu Aikawa 2020
© Tappei Nagatsuki 2020
First published in Japan in 2020 by KADOKAWA CORPORATION, Tokyo. English translation rights arranged with KADOKAWA CORPORATION, Tokyo through TUTTLE-MORI AGENCY, Inc.

English translation © 2022 by Yen Press, LLC

Yen Press
150 West 30th Street, 19th Floor
New York, NY 10001

Visit us at yenpress.com
facebook.com/yenpress
twitter.com/yenpress
yenpress.tumblr.com
instagram.com/yenpress

First Yen Press Edition: February 2022

Yen Press is an imprint of Yen Press, LLC.
The Yen Press name and logo are trademarks of Yen Press, LLC.

The publisher is not responsible for websites (or their content) that are not owned by the publisher.

Library of Congress Control Number: 2016936537

ISBNs: 978-1-9753-3993-7 (paperback)
978-1-9753-3994-4 (ebook)

10 9 8 7 6 5 4 3 2

WOR

Printed in the United States of America

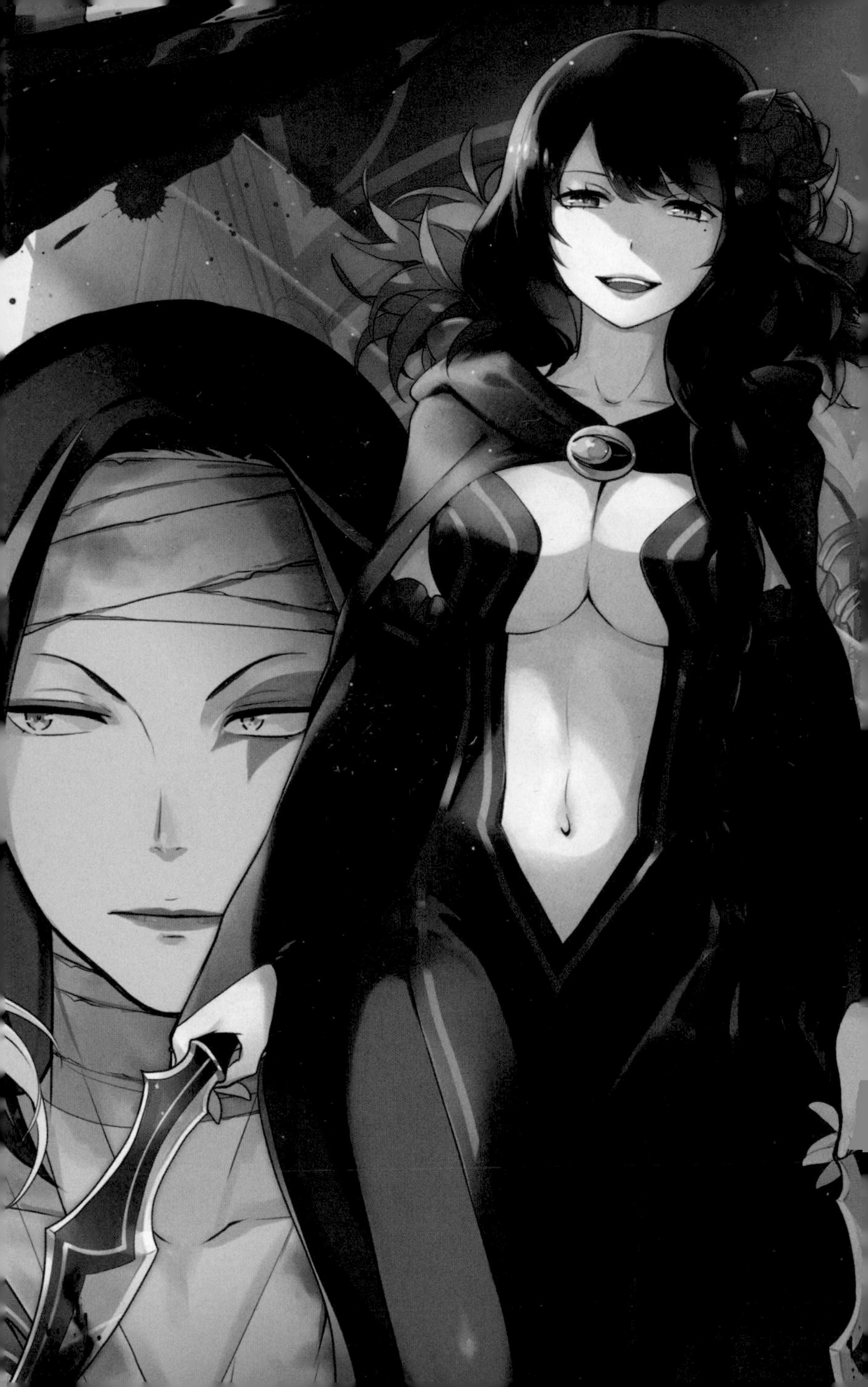

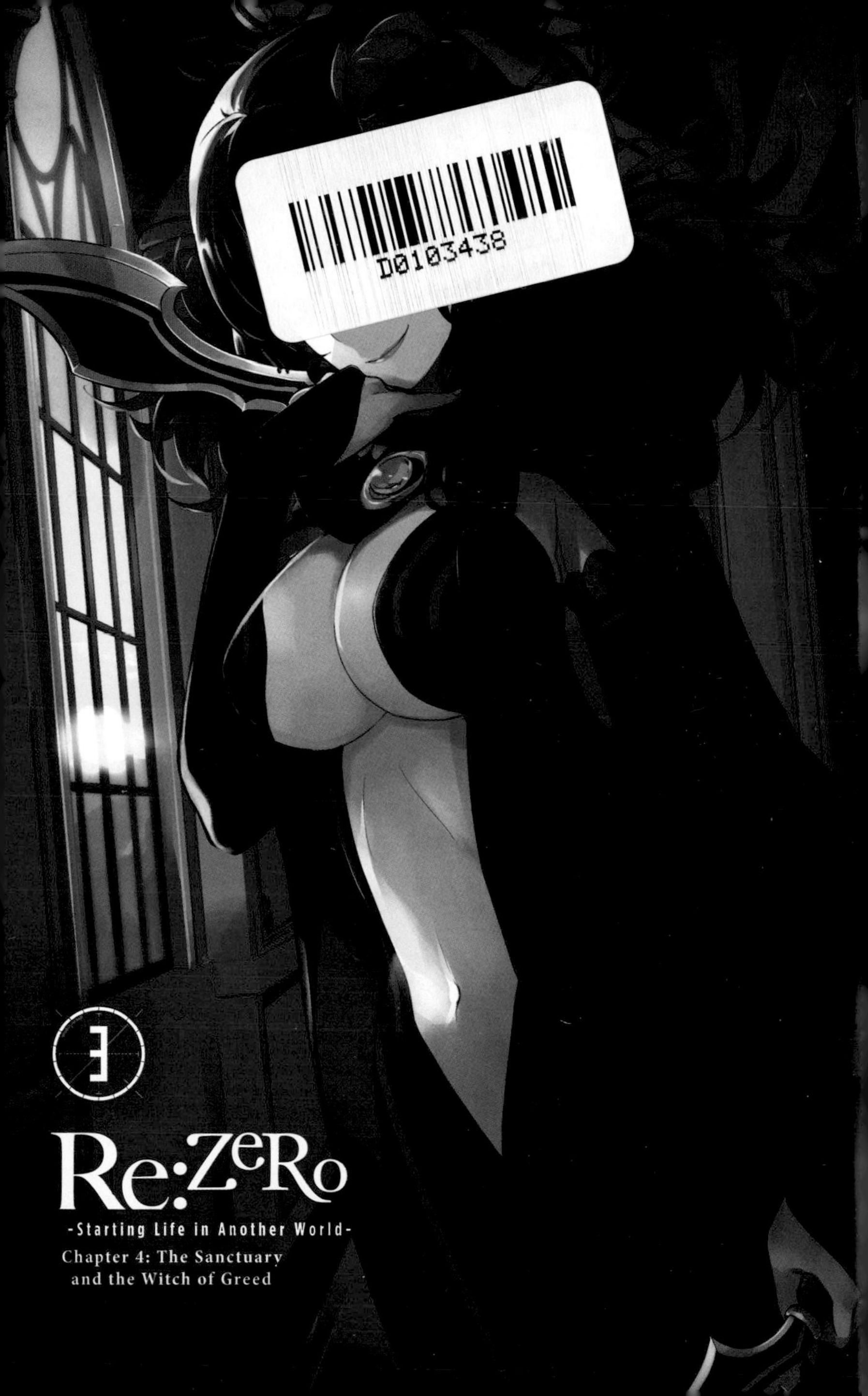

3

Re:ZeRo

-Starting Life in Another World-

Chapter 4: The Sanctuary and the Witch of Greed